"This book reveals findings about specific, age-based changes in the emotional domain of human development that are based on extensive research. The author presents interesting theoretical approaches and empirical data regarding development of emotional maturity of adolescents in general and young adults in particular. Given the centrality of Ukraine in the recent world events and, especially, effects of war on Ukrainian youth, this book has tremendous potential to be of interest to many researchers, psychologists, educators and other professionals".

— **Alexander W. Chizhik**, *Ph.D., Professor of Educational Psychology*

"Oleksiy Chebykin details extensive research into this important topic, considering how rapidly changing and challenging living conditions impact upon emotional development and in turn on personality development through childhood and beyond. Presenting theoretical and empirical data, this book will also inform the design of interventions to support young people growing up in adverse conditions. Topics examined include positive and negative tendencies in the development of emotional traits; individual characteristics of children's development; the functions of emotions in personality formation; analysis of gender differences in emotional development; factors that determine emotional maturity; and the prevention of and interventions for negative emotional manifestations".

— **Alexander M. Yemelyanov**, *Ph.D., D.Sc., Professor of Computer Science, MSCS Director, College of Business and Computing*

"This is an important book that contains a huge amount of empirical data characterizing the emotional sphere of children, adolescents and young men. It reveals trends reflecting the specifics of the development of the emotional sphere of young people, highlighting the dominant factors and personal determinants. Approaches to the psychological support of the emotional sphere of children in difficult socio-psychological conditions of life is outlined. The book will be of great interest to psychologists, teachers, educators and those who deal with this problem".

— **Nataliia Chepeleva**, *Doctor of Psychology, Professor, Academician of the NAPS of Ukraine, Deputy Director of the G.S. Kostyuk Institute of Psychology*

"In my opinion this book would be a valuable contribution to the study of this topic and it's very timely considering that Ukrainian children and adolescents are under enormous emotional stress due to the political instability facing the country. It would find readers in all the countries dealing with the flow of Ukrainian refugees and in the science community in general".

— **Inna Bedny**, *Ph.D., Experimental Psychology*

EXPERIMENTAL STUDY OF THE EMOTIONAL SPHERE OF CHILDREN, ADOLESCENTS AND EARLY ADULTHOOD IN UKRAINE

Experimental Study of the Emotional Sphere of Children, Adolescents and Early Adulthood in Ukraine examines the factors that influence emotional development of young people between 4 and 17 years old. It explores the impact on development of the social and psychological conditions of a child's upbringing, outlines the dynamic changes in emotional sphere characteristics during childhood, adolescence and young adulthood, and considers interventions to support emotional maturity.

Oleksiy Chebykin details extensive research into this important topic, considering how rapidly changing and challenging living conditions impact on emotional development and in turn on personality development through childhood and beyond. Presenting theoretical and empirical data, this book will also inform the design of interventions to support young people growing up in adverse conditions. Topics examined include positive and negative tendencies in the development of emotional traits; individual characteristics of children's development; the functions of emotions in personality formation; analysis of gender differences in emotional development; factors that determine emotional maturity; and the prevention of and interventions for negative emotional manifestations.

Experimental Study of the Emotional Sphere of Children, Adolescents and Early Adulthood in Ukraine will be valuable reading for scholars and students of child and adolescent psychology, clinical psychology, social psychology, psychotherapy and counseling, and education.

Oleksiy Chebykin, Doctor of Psychological Sciences, Academician of the NAPS of Ukraine, Professor of the Department of the Theory and Methods of Practical Psychology at the Ushinsky University (Odessa), has over 700 scientific publications and has authored texts on psychological concepts with emotional stability problems, emotional maturity, emotional regulation of cognitive activity and others.

EXPERIMENTAL STUDY OF THE EMOTIONAL SPHERE OF CHILDREN, ADOLESCENTS AND EARLY ADULTHOOD IN UKRAINE

Oleksiy Chebykin

Routledge
Taylor & Francis Group
LONDON AND NEW YORK

Cover image: Getty Images/fotosipsak

First published 2023
by Routledge
4 Park Square, Milton Park, Abingdon, Oxon OX14 4RN

and by Routledge
605 Third Avenue, New York, NY 10158

Routledge is an imprint of the Taylor & Francis Group, an informa business

British Library Cataloguing-in-Publication Data
A catalogue record for this book is available from the British Library

Library of Congress Cataloging-in-Publication Data
Names: Chebykin, Oleksiy, author.
Title: Experimental study of the emotional sphere of children, adolescents and early adulthood in Ukraine / Oleksiy Chebykin.
Description: Milton Park, Abingdon, Oxon; New York, NY: Routledge, 2023. | Includes bibliographical references and index. |
Summary: "Experimental Study of the Emotional Sphere of Children, Adolescents and Early Adulthood in Ukraine examines the factors that influence emotional development of young people between 4 and 17 years old. It explores the impact on development of the social and psychological conditions of a child's upbringing, outlines the dynamic changes in emotional sphere characteristics during childhood, adolescence and young adulthood, and considers interventions to support emotional maturity. Oleksiy Chebykin details extensive research into this important topic, considering how rapidly changing and challenging living conditions impact upon emotional development and in turn on personality development through childhood and beyond. Presenting theoretical and empirical data, it will also inform the design of interventions to support young people growing up in adverse conditions. Topics examined include positive and negative tendencies in the development of emotional traits; individual characteristics of children's development; the functions of emotions in personality formation; analysis of gender differences in emotional development; factors that determine emotional maturity; and the prevention of and interventions for negative emotional manifestations. Experimental Study of the Emotional Sphere of Children, Adolescents and Early Adulthood in Ukraine will be valuable reading for scholars and students of child and adolescent psychology, clinical psychology, social psychology, psychotherapy and counselling, and education"— Provided by publisher.
Identifiers: LCCN 2022046562 (print) | LCCN 2022046563 (ebook) | ISBN 9781032362458 (paperback) | ISBN 9781032362441 (hardback) | ISBN 9781003330943 (ebook)
Subjects: LCSH: Emotions in children. | Children—Ukraine—Social conditions. | Child psychology—Ukraine. | Emotions in adolescence. | Teenagers—Ukraine—Social conditions. | Adolescent psychology—Ukraine.
Classification: LCC BF723.E6 C54 2023 (print) | LCC BF723.E6 (ebook) | DDC 155.4/12409477—dc23/eng/20221007
LC record available at https://lccn.loc.gov/2022046562
LC ebook record available at https://lccn.loc.gov/2022046563

ISBN: 9781032362441 (hbk)
ISBN: 9781032362458 (pbk)
ISBN: 9781003330943 (ebk)

DOI: 10.4324/9781003330943

Typeset in Bembo
by codeMantra

CONTENTS

PREFACE

The knowledge of the features of the emotional sphere of a developing personality has a long history, which is reflected in psychological scientific schools of many countries. The relevance of studying the characteristics of emotions, their emergence, development, manifestation, recognition and changes attracts the attention of not only scientists, psychologists and practitioners but also other specialists. This is due to the fact that emotions are integrated with almost all functions of the psyche and influence in different ways many human activities.

In this aspect, the problem of studying emotions of a developing person for modern psychology is of particular relevance both theoretically and empirically. Despite the number of proposed theoretical approaches which are focused on understanding the patterns of development of the emotional sphere, all of them, as a rule, offer us only a relative idea of the mechanisms and its specificities that characterize this process. As for the applied data concerning development of the emotional sphere of children and young men, they also do not always allow us to reveal the adequate conditions for its formation, and changes based on the specifics of its intensity, regarding age and gender specifics.

This book presents relatively holistically supplemented generalized results of the long-term research of various aspects of the emotional development of children and young men (from 4 to 23 years of age of different sexes). In general, they reveal both theoretical and empirical data characterizing certain tendencies of differences in the characteristics of the emotional sphere in these age groups.

The basic studies were mainly conducted on children, adolescents and young men in various Odessa preschools, schools and universities.

Thus, in the first chapter "The development of emotional characteristics of 4–6 years old children depending on the conditions of life", when studying the specifics of the emotional development of children, the emphasis is made on the conditions of their life, that is, upbringing in complete and single-parent families, as well as in various preschool, school and higher educational institutions. The research results obtained in this aspect allow us to highlight both positive and negative trends in the emotional development between the groups of examinees, taking into account the conditions listed above.

It is noted that in each age period, considering worsening conditions of raising children, they display an undesirable manifestation of indicators of aggressiveness, self-regulation, ambivalence of emotions, emotional stability, frustration, etc. in different proportions. It is shown that in the structure of the mechanisms of emotional development of children, regardless of age and gender and the conditions of upbringing, emotionality is of great importance. That is why it is so crucial to take into account various factors in the development of adequate approaches in order to prevent and reduce adverse emotional manifestations in children.

Consideration of these and other data made it possible to present and test a system of prevention, as well as psychological therapy aimed at reducing negative emotional manifestations in children. This system is focused on helping child psychologists within their educational and professional training when working in practice with children, teachers and parents.

The second chapter "Research on the emotional development of children and young people 7–17 years old", as if in continuation of the previous data, illustrates complex results of studying the features of the development of the emotional sphere in schoolers aged 7–17. Here we reveal dynamic changes in the emotional sphere characteristics, taking into account the age, stage of schooling and gender of the tested.

The identified main factors in the content of the emotional sphere not only supplement the information available in this respect but also allow to optimize diagnostic approaches, and, if necessary, psychotherapy and the formation of certain manifestations in the emotional sphere. Data on personal tendencies in the genesis of the emotional sphere in describing its characteristics, with the consideration of age and gender features, are also presented.

The third chapter "Diagnostics of the development of emotional maturity in adolescence and early adulthood" is devoted to the actual problem of knowing the specifics of changes in emotional maturity in adolescents and young adults. Contemporary age psychology has rather ambiguous information regarding the content of emotional maturity, which is often confused with other phenomena.

The book proposes a conceptual model of emotional maturity, where the main components are: expression, self-regulation and empathy. Based on this model, a special technique for studying emotional maturity has been developed. Of particular interest in this aspect are the obtained results, connected with the discovery of the stages of formation of emotional maturity in adolescence and youth (ages 11–13, 14–15, 16–17 and 18–23 years), each of which has its own characteristic features of this process dynamics. The typological model of personality's emotional maturity is proposed, which contains 7 types (expressive, self-regulating, empathic, harmonious, self-regulating-empathic, expressive-empathic and expressive-self-regulating).

We express our deep gratitude to the graduate students who worked under our supervision for their participation in the research (chapters: 1 – Soprun Irina; 2 – Melnichuk Irina; 3 – Pavlova Irina), as well as to teachers, researchers, specialists and laboratory assistants of the Institute of Psychology of the South Ukrainian National Pedagogical University named after K.D. Ushinsky for their valuable advice and assistance in preparing this book.

We hope that the materials presented in the book will be useful to psychologists, researchers and practical child psychologists in the selection of an adequate system of psychotherapy for stress, anxiety and other negative emotions in many children, including those who find themselves in the adverse conditions of hostilities in Ukraine, as well as teachers, social workers, students and anyone interested in the emotional development of children.

1

THE DEVELOPMENT OF EMOTIONAL CHARACTERISTICS OF 4–6-YEAR-OLD CHILDREN IN THE DEPENDENT CONDITIONS OF LIFE

The problem of peculiarities of children's emotional sphere development is relevant both from theoretical and purely applied aspects (e.g. Bekh, 1988; Zaporozhets et al., 1986). The disclosure of psychological mechanisms that determine the development of the emotional sphere is complicated by many factors. Among them is the lack of theoretical clarity of general ideas about the nature of emotions (Vilyunas, 1984; Izard, 1980), their integrative nature (Abolin, 1987; Wund, 1984), the dynamics of their course (Vilyunas, 1990; Sannikova, 1988), ambivalence (Vasiliev, 1998), etc. At the same time, a comparative analysis of various studies allows us to acknowledge the undesirable tendencies observed in the development of the emotional sphere of contemporary children. This is a gradual growth in the number of children who show an increase in frustration, emotional tension, depression and disorder in the adequacy of emotional regulation. Among the factors that negatively affect the development of the emotional sphere, according to scientists (Kulchitskaya, 1981; Mukhina, 1989), we can mention environmental, technogenic and socio-psychological conditions of the child's life. At the same time, there is also insufficient determination of the influence of various socio-psychological factors of raising children on the development of their emotional sphere, which significantly complicates the process of finding ways to prevent and psychotherapy of adverse manifestations.

The presented results of the research show the peculiarities of the development of the emotional sphere of children 4–6 years old, who grow up in full or single-parent families, orphanages and kindergartens. There are certainly both positive and negative trends in various manifestations of the emotional sphere, taking into account age and educational conditions. At the same time, no significant differences between children of different sexes were found. It was shown that with the deterioration of educational conditions in each age group among

DOI: 10.4324/9781003330943-1

children, there are undesirable manifestations of anxiety, aggression, emotional stability, frustration and other characteristics.

At the same time, there are statistically proven differences in such indicators between children who were brought up in conditions within and outside family. It has been established that the leading factor in the structure of mechanisms of emotional growth is general emotionality. The nature of the development of the emotional sphere has its own specifics with changes in both age and conditions of upbringing. Such indicators of peculiarities in the development of the emotional sphere of children as emotional and cognitive orientation, self-regulation, emotional ambivalence, aggressiveness, emotional sensitivity and others are also important. A purpose-oriented system of prevention and reduction of emotionally negative manifestations in preschool children for future psychologists has been developed and tested. The testing of the latter showed positive results in changes of children's emotional characteristics.

These studies will be of interest to psychologists, scientists, social pedagogues, teachers, and graduate and undergraduate students.

1.1 Analysis of the conditions for the development of children's emotional sphere

The problem of analyzing conditions that influence the development of the emotional sphere of a child is a subject of study in many special (Bozhovich, 1995; Zaporozhets et al. 1986; Pashina, Ryazanova, 1993; Repin, 1962; Slivina, 1966; Tikhomirov, Klochko, 1980; Jacobson, 1964; etc.) and indirect research (Davydov et al., 1978; Lomov, 1984; Mukhina, 1986; Rubinstein, 1999; Spivakovskaya, 1988; Tatenko, 1988; Chebykin, Soprun, 2003; etc.).

The analysis of these and other works of scientists has shown that the development of a child's emotional sphere is carried out under the influence of various factors that can be divided into a number of subgroups. Conditionally, they can be categorized as psychophysiological, which characterize the biological basis of the functional blocks of the psyche and are responsible for the peculiarities of emotional processes.

According to the scheme proposed by Cannon-Bart, the emotional state is explained by the specific activity of the central nervous system and is directly related to the activity of the thalamus. D. Lindsley's so-called "anti-revolutionary theory of emotions" (1960), which is based on electroencephalographic studies of functional relations between the cortex of the large hemispheres, hypothalamus and reticular formation, considers emotions as a result of active influence on the lower cortex.

At the same time, the functions of emotions are of homeostatic regulation of visceral processes. Emotions are not only a mental phenomenon, but they also play an important role in self-regulation of the state of the organism with an environment characterized by changes in body's autonomic functions, such as the frequency of heart rate, changes in blood pressure, and narrowing and dilation of blood vessels.

All these mechanisms are regulated by the sympathetic and parasympathetic nervous systems, which ensures the functioning of subcortical structures.

It is known that any human relationship is recognized by other people through facial expressions. The latter is the center of transmission and reception of social signals, which are crucial for the development of the personality. As a channel of non-verbal communication and the leading tool in social interaction, in this case, the face transmits the emotional and meaningful connotations of language messages and acts as a certain regulator.

If, in Darwin's words, "expression is the language of emotions" (1953), then the movement of facial muscles can be considered the alphabet of this language. In this context, V.M. Bekhterev noted that in contrast to pantomime movements and gestures, facial expressions are always emotional in nature and, first of all, are a reflection of feelings of the one who speaks. Many scholars believe that the complex play of facial muscles reflects the mental state of the subject more eloquently than words.

It is known that facial expressions and gestures as elements of expressive behavior are the first non-verbal visual systems, which is learned in childhood. Appearance of understandable gestures and facial expressions in a child without special training indicates that the way of expressing emotions is obviously inherent in a person genetically.

Various experts have noted that all facial muscles used to express different emotions are formed in the period of 15–18 weeks of embryonic genesis, and changes in "facial expression" start from the 20th week of embryonic development. Hence, it can be stated that both mechanisms by means of which faces are recognized as important categories of stimuli and express certain emotions are already sufficiently formed at the time of human birth. It can be considered reasonable to say that the expression of emotions on the face is an important system of communication which functions at the time of birth.

Expressive manifestations are partly natural and partly developed socially – by imitation. It is known that a smile is a genetically programmed facial expression. So a newborn child has a semblance of a smile, and a child aged 2 or 3 months smiles at everyone he/she sees. Even infants, who have almost no cerebral cortex yet, show a resemblance of a smile.

According to various studies, the development of emotions in all infants goes through the same phases, indicating that their behavior is determined more biologically than psychologically. The first emotional reaction of a newborn is crying. Then there is a smile-like expression, reflexive, unrelated to environmental events. After a few weeks, the smile becomes more definite and the child smiles in response to various stimuli. At about two and a half months of age, a social smile appears, directed toward another person. Forms of behavior related to smiling and crying, and their development are universal, reflecting the maturation of the nervous system.

Thus, gaining from early childhood a certain experience of communicating with people, each child can more or less accurately determine the emotional state of others by their expressive movements (pantomime) and especially by facial expressions (mimics). The child can control his/her expressive movements. Therefore, the manifestations of emotions are used in the process of communication to assess the circumstances.

At the same time, one cannot ignore the development of various cognitive processes at this level, within which emotions are not only reflected but also developed together. This problem is extremely topical. Nowadays, according to the analysis conducted, only a few works consider the conditions of dependence of the emotional sphere on the development of mental processes (Rubinstein, 1999; Lomov, 1984; Leontiev, 1971; etc.).

It should be noted that the biological approach (Anokhin, 1964, 1953; Simonov, 1966; etc.) to the development of the emotional sphere has been studied widely enough. Particularly noteworthy are the works that show a reverse dependence on the activity of various functions of the vegetative system and the development of the emotional sphere.

At the same time, according to Vallon (1967), Zaporozhets (1986a,b), Makarova (1968), Shingarov (1971), etc., emotions as physiological phenomena are subject to education and training. Such training should begin at an early age when the "foundation" of the future personality is formed. In order to develop and nurture emotions that contribute to the harmonious development of human personality, it is necessary for this purpose to have a good knowledge of the complexity and regularities of emotion's life, starting from the earliest stages of childhood development (Bozhovich, 1995).

The child's emotional sphere changes as he/she grows. It can become an indirect indicator of the development of a child's personality. Feelings that appear in a person at a certain stage of his or her development, being burdened by experience, are the continuation of his or her emotions from the previous stage. Psychology has accumulated data (Volosova, 1979; Leontiev, 1983; Luk, 1982; etc.), that allows one to examine the development of the emotional sphere in the process of personality formation. From previous discoveries to modern studies (Breslav, 1986; Zaporozhets, 1986; Mukhina, 1985; Elkonin, 1971; etc.), we can trace the connection between manifestation of personal neoplasms and features of the emotional sphere. Experimental studies of ontogenesis of the emotional sphere allow us to see the sequence of complications and transformations of the functions and mechanisms of this sphere.

In infants, at first, we can distinguish only a state of calmness and emotional excitement. In further development, a certain excitement gradually begins to acquire differentiated forms of response. American researcher K. Bridges notes that emotions of sadness and joy appear at first, and then anger, disgust and fear. Older children are able to experience such emotions as jealousy, admiration, tenderness, etc.

As studies (Vallon, 1967; Kistyakovskaya, 1965; Menchinskaya, 1996; Olshannikova, 1979; Slutsky, 1996; and others) show, in the first months of life, emotional reactions have a primitive character. They develop turbulently, covering different parts of the body, and have certain stable forms of reaction. But with the growth of the child, diffuse reactions gradually change into reactions of more concrete nature, and emotions of different kinds and different attitudes appear.

A. Vallon (1967) considers emotions and reactions as the first reflexes to the presence of other people, which establish genetic roots of formation of a person. Such reactions for a child are the initial and main form of interaction with adults, the attitude of the child to the world of objects. In the process of such communication, ways of expressing different emotions are formed.

The studies of Z.V. Denisova (1978), K. Rogers (1984), A.A. Royak (1977) and others have shown that the first feeling of sympathy for the closest adult arises on the basis of the accumulation of satisfaction to a child (and therefore pleasant) acts of situational and personal communication. This feeling may arise in relation to a person who has a sufficiently regular interaction with the child. The very interaction, and not just the satisfaction of the child's vital needs, is the best condition for the emergence of positive emotions.

With the development of primary symptoms, in the period from 6 months to 3 years, the child develops syntony, i.e. somewhere in the middle of the second year of life – as the ability to respond to the emotional state of another person, especially "close" one, or as "contamination" by the appropriate emotional state in the presence of contact interaction with the advancing activity of the adult (Lisina, 1983; Galiguzova et al., 1990).

It has been noted that in early childhood, the external activity of the child emotionally imprinted is not so much the presence but the participation of an adult. Then, on the basis of external-practical activity, the child develops a special internal activity – the activity of affective-figurative imagination, which is, according to L.S. Vygotsky, the expression of other human emotions, in the process of which they not only manifest themselves but also evolve.

A person's attitude to the surrounding reality and to himself and other people is formed at a preschool age. The leading psychologists (Bozhovich, 1995; Leontiev, 1983; Elkonin, 1971; etc.) believe that the initial formation of personality during the preschool period is characterized by the child's attitude toward the world, which always has a pronounced emotional color.

As the analysis of O.V. Zaporozhets and Ya. Z. Neverovich (1974) has shown, during the transition from early preschool age, in the process of originating the simplest kinds of activity, changes in the flow of emotions that regulate productive activity take place. During the same period, there is also a change in the content of affects (emotions), which are expressed primarily in special forms of empathy and compassion.

According to Sh. Lisina (1983), the basis of empathy and the ability to "appropriate" the basic properties of another person's emotional state and to feel his or her living situation is syntony.

As it has already been, the ability to empathize (or sympathize) becomes the basis of prosocial motivation at the preschool age. Studies by O.V. Zaporozhets (1974) and his colleagues have consistently shown that this ability can arise only under the condition of emotional anticipation, i.e. ability of a child to relive the consequences of his/her future actions for significant persons.

At the same time, syntony in preschool loses its meaning, because the child is already sufficiently independent of the direct impact of the situation and the emotional state of the person close no longer "infects" him/her. The other person's condition affects the child only when the activity of his/her inclusion in the situation becomes a product of this situation and he/she is directly aware of the causes.

It is about the ability that is already appearing in preschoolers to feel the other person and to experience his/her successes and failures as their own. A good standard of such education can be models of experiments that analyze the role of co-experiencing in the formation of prosocial motives and feelings.

Thus, researches have allowed A.V. Zaporozhets (1986) to note that "the ability to empathize, experience the joys and sorrows of others as their own, which is formed in children under the influence of experience of interaction and activity in the team, leads to affective decentralization". Emotional decentralization is an indirect product of preschoolers' communication with adults. Gradually, feelings become more rational and correspond to thinking, and the child learns moral norms and correlates his or her actions with them.

The analysis carried out by L.I. Bozhovich (1995), A. Vallon (1967), D.B. Elkonin (1971) and other scientists on the development of the emotional sphere of 6–7-year-old children showed that the formation of cognitive motive and corresponding emotions runs parallel. At the same time, social emotions (attitudes toward other people, fixed by social norms) are formed more slowly than their corresponding motives.

Psychological literature lacks data on the analysis of peculiarities of children's emotional development in closed children's care institutions. Some psychological studies were made by L.I. Bozhovich (1995), P.G. Ruzskaya, L.N. Abramova (1990), E. Lisina (1983) and others.

Summarizing these and other works, it can be noted that those who have been in children's institutions since early childhood differ in their psychological characteristics of the expression of emotions from children raised in a family.

V.S. Mukhina (1989) considers the main reasons for the deviant behavior of children in orphanages to be that they do not meet their needs for love and recognition, which are crucial in shaping a child's personality. She notes that depriving a child of a constant expression of love and recognition leads to deformations in the child's personality and alienation.

Having analyzed the conditions of upbringing in boarding schools, the researcher has found a number of peculiarities in such children, regardless of age. Children do not learn the skills of productive communication. When there was a clearly expressed need for love and attention, they build their communication with peers inadequately. Due to the wrongly formed experience of interaction, they take an aggressive and negative position toward other people. Based on recent similar studies, we can say that the emotionally unstable state of a child who has been deprived of parental care, leads to a violation of affective-personal relations.

According to M.I. Lisina (1983), children in the first year of life who grow up in orphanages, differ from their peers who grow up in a family: they are languid, apathetic, lacking vitality, have reduced cognitive activity, simplified emotional manifestations, etc. These personal formations or internal structures that occur in children of this age and form the basis of a child's personality are deformed in the orphanage. Such children do not have an attachment to an adult, they are distrustful, withdrawn, sad and passive.

The analysis of studies of passivity (Galiguzova et al., 1990; and others) has shown that children of the second and third years of life who were brought up in orphanages also exhibit the above features, underdevelopment of the emotional and volitional sphere, which manifests itself in reduced emotionality.

In older age, the specific living conditions of children in closed child care institutions lead to the forced manifestation of superficial feelings and the emotional deficiency (Mukhina, 1989).

Important data concerning the peculiarities of emotional development of preschoolers who were brought up outside the family are illustrated in the research of I.A. Zalysina and E.O. Smirnov (1985). They point to noticeable differences in personal interaction, which is based on the not fully realized need for mutual understanding and empathy. Also, children raised outside the family are characterized by low emotionality and stinginess in expressing their feelings.

In this aspect, L.M. Tsaregorodtseva (1990) draws attention to the fact that other children of those orphans are nothing but a monotonous background in their lives, and in case they left this background, they are recognized rather as opponents, not as friends.

Based on these and other data, we can say that the emotional reactions of preschoolers of boarding schools, compared with children raised in families, are characterized by higher stress, emotional breakdowns, general frustration and aggression.

These data illustrate the important role of socio-psychological conditions associated with life activities and upbringing of children.

An analysis of the research (Bozhovich, 1995; Galiguzova et al., 1990; Zaporozhets, 1986; Lisina, 1983; Mukhina, 1986; Smirnova, Lagutina, 1991) shows that such conditions can be divided into two subgroups.

First, the external conditions under which the child is influenced;
Second, the inner-personal conditions related to social-motivational experience.

In the latter case, we are talking about the socially assigned emotional and personality properties of the child.

Considering the first conditions in this aspect, it can be noted that in most studies (Burmenskaya et al., 1990; Denisova, 1978; Zaporozhets, Neverovich, 1974; Kovalev, 1971; etc.), preference is given to the development of the child's personality, including child's emotional sphere, the very way child "exists", depending on social interactions. The social environment is not just an external environment, but a real source of a child's development, because it contains all the material and spiritual values that an individual can acquire in the process of his or her development. In order for a child to become a full-fledged person, he/she must be brought up among people and receive human education. However, not everything that surrounds a child and makes him grow up has the same effect on the development of his psyche. Living conditions, especially the "street", offer each child completely different circumstances for development. In addition, each well-to-do family has its own living conditions, and each disadvantaged family has its own.

An analysis of the literature available to us shows that among the social conditions that influence the development of the child's emotional sphere in the first years of life, the forms and ways of interaction with relatives are extremely relevant. Thus, many studies show that the emotional sphere of a child and his/her attitude to the environment begins to form in the family, which has different ways of influencing the emotional sphere. Love, care and attention from family members are a necessary, vital factor for a child, which gives him/her a sense of security and ensures emotional equilibrium, increases the child's self-esteem.

On the other hand, it is noted that the deficit of emotional communication and lack of attention from relatives contributes to the emergence of the child's neuroticism and anxiety (Repina, 1962). Separation from the mother or, in general, the absence of relatives also affects the development of children's cognitive functions. Particularly in relation to the language or pre-language development of infants. In a number of his works, Freud developed the idea that separation from the mother causes the infant to acutely experience his helplessness, causing in him repeatedly the emotion of fear, as a result of which the experience is fixed, coming into contact with some external object may turn into a phobia.

There have been some attempts to relieve children of pathologically fixed states in which phobias and obsessions have arisen due to their early experience of separation from their mothers. It is believed that children who grew up without a family are not capable of rich emotional experiences. A child's ability to love others is closely related to how much love he or she has received and in what form it was expressed. It is also known that the delay in the development of a child, resulting from the conditions of his/her upbringing in the first months of life, is preserved until the end of preschool age and even after the child enters a new family. The optimal age is limited to the first six months of the child's life and the first nine months of the child's life to smooth out the phenomena that were caused by the separation from the mother.

The problem of the child's deficit of communication with parents is exacerbated by the growing number of separations, and the increasing number of unhappy, conflicting families, which is an important factor in the emergence of various emotional disorders in a child. It is known that a child needs at least two years to fully overcome such a situation as a family breakdown (Burmenskaya et al., 1990; etc.).

But even full families also have psychological problems. In families where there is a mother and a father, but the atmosphere is unfavorable, the child's development is accompanied by certain psychological problems. In general, if family members do not follow a culture of communication, then certainly problems with psychological well-being occur in children.

Undoubtedly, a harmonious (happy) family has a positive effect on the child. However, the criteria for dividing families into prosperous and disadvantaged ones remain still vague. For example, a family can be complete, outwardly strong and united, and in essence, torn by contradictions that oppress the child. On the other hand, a single-parent family may be more child-friendly. For example, if a father terrorizes the whole family and leaves it, then all of its members, especially the children, sigh with relief.

A troubled family could be defined as that primarily from the point of view of parenting defects. There can also be conflicting upbringing in families when each member is raising a child "in their own way." Such education often results in neurosis and other disorders of the child's mental and emotional development (Zakharov, 1986; Elfimova, 1987; Langmeier, Matejček, 1984; Moskalenko, 1991; Mukhina, 1989; Olshannikova, 1983; etc.).

Many studies (Kistyakovskaya, 1965; Lisina, 1983; Spivakovskaya, 1988; etc.) have tried to describe the stages of emotional upbringing on the basis of parental attitudes. It has been revealed that the negative emotional nature of the mother-child relationship, mother's confrontation, her nervousness, inability to control her own state, rejection of the child, and misunderstanding of its peculiarities generates deviations not only in the development of the emotional sphere but also harm mental development of the child.

A mother's attitude and position from the first days of the child's life form the peculiarities of the child's psyche. Thus, S.Brody distinguishes several types of maternal attitudes toward the child. He points out that mothers of the first type adapt easily and are emotionally comfortable adjusting to the needs of the child. Mothers who are classified by the author as the second type do not always successfully adapt to the needs of their child. Their communication is emotionally tense and lacks independence. Some mothers, belonging to the third type, do not show interest in their child. There is no emotional warmth in their relationship, or, on the contrary, there is tight control. According to these studies, the most sensitive and traumatic consequences in the development of a child's emotional sphere are of the fourth type. Inadequacy in the mother's emotional reactions deprives the child of a sense of stability and creates anxiety.

Summarizing these and other research data, we can say that for further development the type of attitude toward her child by the mother is more important than the characteristics of her temperament. When comparing the type of care and attention of a mother to a child, taking into account the peculiarities of her development, the author shows that in an atmosphere of tenderness and love children develop without deviations. On the contrary, the absence of these deviations is a prerequisite for high risk in the emotional development of the child.

Exploring the causes of neurosis in children and emotional disorders, some researchers (Zakharov, 1986 and others) noted that the psychological type of a mother and her attitude toward a child provokes the emergence of emotional disorders such as increased emotionality and imbalance.

According to these and other studies, children from the orphanage from the moment of birth are frustrated by the lack of fulfillment of personal need for love and recognition, security and self-actualization, for normal fulfillment of physiological needs. Such children are significantly more susceptible to neuroticism than their family counterparts. The child is significantly more influenced by the atmosphere and the general living conditions of the environment. Unattended children often experience defeat throughout their lives due to life and family circumstances, which is the cause of their fears, which they cannot cope with.

Practitioners have noted that children who live in child care centers develop emotional stiffness within 3–4 years, which hinders the establishment of positive relationships with other people. In the conditions of the child's home, the child learns to influence his or her social environment, adapting it to himself, and in doing so, he or she becomes vulnerable.

Among the serious depriving conditions that cause psychological tension in children deprived of parental care, scientists (Zalysina, Smirnova, 1985; Mukhina, 1986, 1989) and others, include deformations in children's joint activity with adults.

These and other scholars also analyzed the interaction of young children with adults in the orphanage and at home, and found that at an early age the children in the children's home lacked emotional differentiation of objects into "theirs", "mine" and "others". They also did not show the manifestation of the pronoun "we" even at the age of 3.5 years.

A. Pashin and E. Ryazanov's (1993) results of the research that studied peculiarities of the emotional sphere of the children and co-workers in the orphanage can be considered very interesting. The generalization of these studies indicates that the adults involved in the upbringing of this category of children should not be characterized by a high level of anxiety, as the latter indicates alertness, a tendency to accumulate negatively colored emotions. The study conducted by the authors made it possible to note that "*teachers, educators, staff of the orphanage find it difficult to enter into social contacts, are restrained in communication*" (1993, pp. 44–52). Summarizing these and other studies gives grounds to assert that one of the reasons that form the negative emotional tension in children is barriers to communication with adults.

This position is confirmed by the studies of I. Langmeier and Z. Matejček (1984), who noted that children in social isolation show distrust and aggression toward all people, except for members of their microgroup. They show a manifestation of group dependence. The authors point out that older children are the ones who are more emotionally motivated as a result of social deprivation, which is manifested in their behavior.

Typical manifestations of deprivation situations that form negative emotional tension in children deprived of parental care, according to the opinion of M. Lisina (1983) and others, are lassitude, apathy, lack of cheerfulness, emotional attachment to adults, and self-confidence, and conflict in relationships with peers.

The results of the works of other scientists, such as G. Breslav (1986), E. Lisina (1983), T. Repina (1962) and others confirmed that for the development of the emotional sphere of children, in addition to family relationships, the conditions of interaction with other people and peers are also important. At home, the child develops typical family-specific emotional experiences such as value orientations and praise for the people around him or her. Ways of enhancing interrelations, the beginning of the child's visit to kindergarten is a powerful stimulus for the development and manifestation of social emotions. The main criteria in their formation are the reactions of the children's team, and various types of joint activities with peers. The emotional and psychological climate of the group in which the child is placed is also important. In the conditions of kindergarten, the formation of positive and negative emotional attitudes is carried out with the help of adults and peers, who give the child the opportunity to evaluate personal qualities.

These studies show that children who are prone to positive emotions are characterized by the perception of reality, self-confidence and high adaptation to the environment. They are emotionally stable, quickly come into contact with others and feel confident. Children with a tendency to negative emotions (fear, sadness and anxiety) do not have a sense of inner harmony, merging with the world. This is due to the feeling of inner tension and negative emotions caused by failures in communication. Then, in contact with others, children feel an urgent need to talk, to find support and approval.

In the above-mentioned and other studies, where adults negatively influenced children, their interaction was aggressive and demoralizing. After a positive impact, children usually tried to get in touch with their peers and showed activity and optimism. So, this evidence shows that it is possible to correct certain emotional complexes in children in socio-psychological conditions.

Confirmation of these data is found in the studies of I. Zalysina and E. Smirnov (1985). The authors drew attention to the remarkable differences in the personal interaction of children, which is based on the need for mutual understanding and compassion. Children raised outside the family were distinguished by their lower emotionality and less activity in real communicative situations with peers. Researchers concluded that these children do not have the necessary development of meaningful and emotional aspects of interpersonal interaction. In communication with both peers and adults, they have a weak need for empathy and almost no desire to coordinate their assessment with a partner.

In this aspect, it is necessary to cite other data, which states that preschool children in the children's home are characterized by the affective disruptions, the general tension of emotional frustration, which is expressed in aggression. Conditions of raising a child in an orphanage, limited emotional and identification relations with a child are not favorable for the development of compassion and realization of a child's need for recognition from the side of adults and peers.

To understand the emergence of deforming causes for the development of the emotional sphere in orphans, it is not enough to indicate only the narrowness, limitation of their contacts with adults. It is also important to take into account the intensity of contact with peers as simple qualitative characteristics. It is known that in an orphanage, a child communicates with the same rather narrow group of peers. Attribution to a certain group of peers happens to be unconditional. This leads to the fact that relationships between peers are formed not as friendly, but by the type of relatives, as between brothers and sisters. Such unconditionality in communication, on the one hand, can be considered as a positive factor that contributes to emotional stability and protection, when a group of peers becomes a certain analog of a family; on the other hand, such contacts do not contribute to the development of emotional features that would also ensure a relationship with peers, the ability to establish equal relationships with strangers, and to adequately assess their strengths and emotional states that are necessary for friendly communication (Bozhovich, 1995; Mukhina, 1989).

As mentioned above, the child's relationship with other children outside the family plays a significant role in the formation of behavioral disorders, as well as negative character traits. By interacting with peers in the children's team, the child learns acceptable and unacceptable forms of behavior.

These and other data indicate that a child's regular attendance at a preschool (kindergarten) institution may contribute to the development of aggression. It can be assumed that children who communicate with peers have more opportunities to "practice" aggressive behavior than those children who attend kindergarten irregularly. Of course, through communication, children pass on to each other their knowledge of both negative and positive nature.

Summarizing the socio-psychological conditions, we can state that the personal formation of a child's emotional sphere depends to a great extent on their influence. At the same time, the nature of this development can be both positive and negative. This is especially evident in the frequency and depth of their manifestation in the child's conscience.

It has been proved that a significant part of a child's emotional experience (i.e. dynamics of expressive actions, adequacy of emotional response, development of empathy, self-regulation and expressiveness of personal characteristics of general emotionality, anxiety, sensitivity, frustration, etc.) is formed under the influence of social conditions in the preschool period.

The more complete is the social status of these conditions, the more favorable is the development of the emotional status of a child.

The degree of favorability is quite wide. The key is the presence or absence of parents in this process, the complexity or one-sidedness in the organization of child rearing. Based on the analysis and real observations of the conditions of raising children for further research, we distinguish the following groups:

- preschool children, who are brought up only in families;
- children who stay in families and preschool institutions;
- children from single-parent families (brought up by one parent or close relatives);
- children from the orphanage.

The chosen division is certainly conditional, but it provides an opportunity to analyze the most typical circumstances of the conditions that influence the development of the emotional sphere of children.

By revealing the peculiarities of the development of the emotional sphere of children in mentioned conditions, we can not only comprehend their scientific significance in terms of prognostic potential, but also, if necessary, to develop specific recommendations for targeted prevention and psychotherapy of its undesirable manifestations in preschool children.

1.2 Distinctions in the development of the emotional sphere of children

Having summarized the available literary data on methods, and also having taken into account the basic requirements for them, we based our work on the following when developing and selecting them for the study of children's emotional sphere:

Firstly, that the methods chosen were accessible for their implementation with children of the selected age group;
Secondly, they must be sufficiently tested and valid in the practice of psychological testing;
Thirdly, that they can be used for examining the emotional sphere of children in the limited conditions of educational institutions;
Fourthly, that the obtained results of the selected methods make it possible to record certain indicators of the characteristics of the emotional sphere of children in qualitative characteristics and quantitative units;
Fifthly, that the chosen methods in a certain way allow us to approach the diagnostics of the same indicators of the emotional sphere in an integrated manner.

According to these principles and as a result of performed preliminary work the adapted basic methods for examining children's emotional sphere, were adapted as well:

- The test "House. Tree. Man", for the assessment of emotional insecurity (P1)*, anxiety (P2), self-doubt (P3), feelings of inferiority (P4), hostility (P5), frustration (P), communication difficulties (P7), depressiveness (P8);

- "Kinetic family drawing" Barnes – family comfort (P9), anxiety (P10), confrontation (P11), feelings of inferiority (P12), hostility (P13);
- "Anxiety test" Temple R., Dorki M., Amen A. – anxiety (P14);
- Adapted method "Teping test" of Chernikova's for the assessment of emotional stability (P15).
- The diagnostics of joy (P16), anger (P17), shyness (P18), interest, curiosity (P19), offense (P20), fear (P21), emotionality (P22) was performed according to our modified method of Dembo scale, based on expert assessment.
- To diagnose the domination of emotionality (P23) we used the test of Delgado "The ratio of the emotional and rational in behavior".
- The study of emotional stability (P24), self-regulation (P25), emotional arousal (P26), aggressiveness (P27), confrontation (P28), anxiety (P29), frustration (P30) was conducted using the "Color Test" of Luscher.

Proposed self-assessment and expert assessment technique may help to identify the necessity of prevention and psychotherapy of disorders in children's emotional sphere (P31), the adequacy and use of diagnostic tools for studying children's emotional sphere (P32), the effectiveness of counseling teachers and parents on prevention and leveling negative emotional manifestations in children (P33), and also the efficiency of using preventive and psychotherapeutic techniques for children's negative emotional manifestations (P34).

**Note: Hereinafter, the names of indicators will be presented in abbreviated form.*

These techniques allowed to identify and record the appropriate level of each indicator (Appendix 1). Selected methods are presented in detail (Soprun, Chebykin, 2020).

To specify the results obtained by the above methods, we also used a sampling observation and testing.

A total of 268 preschool children were examined: 61 children under the age of 4 years, 58 children under the age of 5 years, and 149 children under the age of 6 years. Following the purpose of the study on the base of this specified sample, we have singled out the following relevant groups and subgroups:

- children of 4–5 years old brought up only in the family – "b", 6 years old – "a";
- children brought up in the family and in a kindergarten: 4 years – "e", 5 years – "d", 6 years – "c";
- children raised in a single-parent family: 4 years old – "f", 5 years old – "g", 6 years old- "h";
- children from the children's home: 4 years old – "k", 5 years old – "j", 6 years old – "i".

Referring to the obtained results of an experimental study of individual data on the emotional sphere in 4-year-olds raised only in the family environment among them was found a certain number of those who showed sufficient variability in most indicators from minimum to maximum values.

Thus, the greatest variability was observed in the parameter of hostility (P5), anxiety (P10) and others. The individual value of indicators, which characterize manifestations of different modalities of emotions, is worth attention. Here the variance between individual values ranges from high to rather low. Moderate variability was observed in the indicator of emotional stability (P22), self-regulation (P25), anxiety (P29) and frustration (P30).

The average value of the parameters diagnosed indicates that children in this subgroup have a good social welfare (x = 5.2 points), moderate anxiety (x = 4.0 points) and self-confidence (x = 1.8 points). The average values of family comfort indicators (x = 7.6 points) and the social anxiety indicator (x = 6.0 points) are of some concern. In other cases, the average value indicates a sufficient level of manifestation of the diagnosed features of the development of the emotional sphere.

Examining the data obtained in the study of 4-year-old children who were brought up both in the family and in kindergarten, we found that such indicators as anxiety (P2), communication difficulties (P7) have a significant variance in individual values. According to the data on family comfort (P9), general emotionality (P22), joy (P16) and curiosity (P19), most of these children's indicators are above their average values.

As for the indicators of self-regulation (P25), most of the children have a sufficiently good level. The same can be said for the anxiety indicator (P29).

The average value in this subgroup shows that 4-year-olds raised in a family and kindergarten are quite confident. They have a low depressiveness (P8), anxiety (P2), feelings of inferiority (P4) and hostility (P5). At the same time, they exhibit a lower level of social anxiety (P10).

Of importance for us were the individual values of the primary data of children from the orphanage. Paradoxically enough, according to initial data, the largest variance in this sample was observed in indicators of anxiety (P10), communication difficulties (P7), hostility (P5), conflict (P11) and emotional stability (P15). In this group there are children who, in comparison with others, have a significantly higher value of the indicators being diagnosed. The variation in the indices of anger from 1.3 to 5.8 conventional units is worth mentioning. The average values obtained from these children compared to the previous groups show a slight increase in parameters of depressiveness (P8), anxiety (P14), average emotional stability (P15), optimism (P16), above the average level of shyness (P18), sadness (P20) and general emotionality (P22).

Indicators of individual peculiarities of the emotional sphere of 5-year-old children are characterized by a certain specificity. Some of the data obtained in children of this age group who stayed in the family and kindergarten, show fairly pronounced variance in the values of such indicators as anxiety (P2) and hostility (P5). Although some variability is observed in a number of cases, it is not significant enough to be taken into account. Of a special attention for us is the indicator of anxiety (P2) with its the range in values from 1 to 16 points.

A very low variability was registered for the indicators of optimism (P16), shyness (P18) and others.

The average values in this sample allow us to conclude that children raised in a family and kindergarten have sufficient social security (P1), insignificant level of hostility (P5) and communication difficulties (P7). Anxiety is to some extent pronounced (P2).

The individual values of indicators that describe peculiarities of the development of the emotional sphere in 5-year-old children from single-parent families show that they have a similar tendency as the previous group. However, they manifested most clearly in the indicator of anxiety (P2). In other cases, the difference between the values is quite moderate. The average values of the indicators show that children from single-parent families have some difficulties in communication (P7), they have a fairly moderate level of emotional stability (P15), average level of optimism (P16) and average expression of anger (P17), as well as increased frustration (P30).

Primary indicators that characterize features of the development of the emotional sphere in 6-year-old children raised in a full family reveal the greatest variability in hostility (P15), communication difficulties (P7) and also in family comfort (P9). Values in some of these indicators are within the range of 1 point and in others 10 points. Individual differences in insecurity (P1) and anxiety (P2) are less pronounced. Here the difference among children is 2–3 points.

Variation in the indicators (P11), (PI2), which accordingly characterize confrontation and feelings of inferiority, is insignificant. Here we obtained the minimal values of these indicators. Sufficient variability appeared for indicators (P16)–(P22), which characterizes the expressiveness of the modality of different emotions. The largest variance is observed in the indicator of optimism (P16) and curiosity (P19). In the latter case, the maximum value of their expression in children was found. As for the indicators (P23)–(P30), there are also some differences between the individual values of the emotional sphere: from "−1" and more.

There is a certain number of children in this group who have a sufficiently pronounced discrepancy in all of the diagnosed indicators.

Summarizing the primary data, we can note that the identified individual differences in the values of the indicators are, obviously, a natural phenomenon. And as shown, in the majority of children the average indicator in this group is mostly at a low level of manifestation, or above the average. We would like to remind that in our investigations rather complex emotional manifestations were diagnosed, and this complexity may explain the tendency in the development of children's emotional sphere. We see that the majority of children had a high level of optimism.

At the same time, according to primary data obtained from children raised in families and kindergartens, the greatest variability is recorded in the indicators of anxiety (P2), anger (P17) and emotional stability (P15). In other cases, the variability of indicators is presented, but at a moderate level. This group consists of children with the majority of diagnosed indicators at a low level. The average group value of the diagnosed indicators in the group of 6-year-old children raised in a family and kindergarten shows a fairly pronounced manifestation of modesty (P18) and high values of curiosity (P19). At the same time, the tendency to heightened anxiety is noticeable.

The data obtained in children aged six from the orphanage indicate that the tendency of variability, observed in previous groups, preserved here. In this group, there are children in whom the diagnosed indicator is at a low level, in others it is represented within the range of average value.

This analysis shows that the primary data characterizing the development of the emotional sphere of children brought up in different conditions have the greatest variability in indicators of anxiety, aggressiveness, emotional stability and frustration.

This is evidenced by the fact that in each group there is a certain number of children in whom the level of diagnosed indicators in some cases approaches to low values, and in others – to medium and high.

1.3 Differences in the development of children's emotional sphere

Primary data analysis revealed a rather high variability in the expression for all the indicators. This may testify that every of the surveyed group includes children with different levels of development of the emotional sphere. These tendencies in determining the diapason of variability may indirectly indicate that selected subgroups differ in the specificity of the development of individual indicators that characterize peculiarities of the emotional sphere. This is also confirmed by the average values of the diagnosed parameters that have different characteristics of their representation. Such results give us reason to conclude that there are certain disparities in certain features of the emotional sphere of children in the examined subgroups. However, in order to confirm the presence or absence of such differences, it is necessary to conduct an in-depth analysis for their reliability.

The results of the research conducted according to the methodology "House. Tree. Man" show that data on the peculiarities of the development of the emotional sphere of 4-year-old children raised in different conditions in some cases have statistically reliable differences. Thus, it was found that children raised only in a family environment statistically reliably differ from children raised in the family and in kindergarten by indicators of self-doubt ($t = 2.6$; $P < 0.05$), frustration ($t = 3.5$; $P < 0.05$), communication difficulties ($t = 3.2$; $P < 0.05$) and depressiveness ($t = 2.1$; $P < 0.05$). There are quite clear differences between this group and children raised in an orphanage in terms of self-doubt ($t = 2.1$; $P < 0.05$) and frustration ($t = 3.4$; $P < 0.05$).

At the same time, the data characterizing the emotional sphere of children raised in the family and kindergarten statistically reliable differs from the data of those raised in orphanage. There are differences in such indicators as anxiety (t = 2.0; P <0.05) and communication difficulties (t = 2.5; P <0.05).

There are also significant differences in the index of depressivity between children who were raised only in a family and single-parent children (Table 1.3.1).

As we can see, concerning indicator of anxiety (P2) there are no differences between the groups b – e, b – f, b – k, they are manifested only among children in the group k – e. Values of self-doubt indicator (P3) show clear difference between the groups b – e and b – k. Similar differences are observed in the indicator of frustration (P6) and difficulties in communication indicator (P7). There are valid differences between groups b – e and b – k, and by indicator (P8) of depression between groups b – e and b – f. Remarkably, but no statistically valid differences found in the hostility index (P5) in any case.

TABLE 1.3.1 Statistically reliable differences in the indicators describing the peculiarities of the development of 4-year-old children brought up in different conditions, according to the "House. Tree. Man" method

Statistical values	*Indicators*				
	P_2	P_3	P_6	P_7	P_8
	b e	b e	b e	b e	b e
x	4.0 4.7	1.8 0.0	2.3 4.3	5.8. 8.1	2.7 2.1
x^2	2.0 2.4	0.7 1.5	1.5 1.4	2.0 1.8	0.9 0.38
m	2.0 3.0	2.0 2.0	1.0 3.0	3.0 10.0	3.0 2.0
n	4.0 4.0	2.0 2.0	2.0 4.0	6.0 9.0	3.0 2.0
t	= NS	=2.6*	=3.5*	=3.2*	=2.1*
	b f	b f	b f	b f	b f
x	4.0 3.7	1.8 2.3	0.3 3.7	5.7 6.0	2.7 2.0
x^2	2.0 0.58	0.7 0.58	1.5 2.0	2.0 1.7	0.9 0.0
m	2.0 4.0	2.0 2.0	1.0 0.0	3.0 7.0	3.0 2.0
n	4.0 4.0	2.0 2.0	2.0 3.0	6.0 7.0	3.0 2.0
t	= NS	= NS	= NS	= NS	=2.8*
	b k	b k	b k	b k	b k
x	4.0 3.0	1.8 2.5	2.3 3.9	5.7 6.1	2.7 2.4
x^2	2.0 1.5	0.7 1.2	1.5 0.9	2.0 2.3	0.9 1.0
m	2.0 2.0	2.0 2.0	1.0 4.0	3.0 3.0	3.0 2.0
n	4.0 3.0	2.0 2.5	2.0 4.0	6.0 6.5	3.0 2.0
t	= NS	=2.1*	=3.4*	= NS	= NS
	k e	k e	k e	k e	k e
x	3.2 4.7	2.5 0.0	3.9 4.3	6.1.8.1	2.4 2.1
x^2	1.5 2.4	1.2 1.5	0.9 1.4	2.3 1.8	1.0 0.38
m	2.0 3.0	2.0 2.0	4.0 3.0	3.0 10.0	2.0 2.0
n	3.0 4.0	2.5 2.0	4.0 4.0	6.5. 9.0	2.0 2.0
t	=2.0*	= NS	= NS	= 2.5*	= NS

**Significance level at P <0.05.*

It can be noted that the identified differences in some way indicate that children from orphanages are more distrustful and less anxious. While children raised only in the family are less frustrated, but more cooperative.

Examining the results obtained by the methods of "Kinetic family drawing", "Anxiety test" and "Tapping test" in children of four years old, we have found a number of statistically reliable differences in diagnostic indicators of emotional development. The analysis showed that the greatest number of reliable differences were found between children who were raised in a family and those who stayed in a family and kindergarten. In particular, this is seen in indicators of family comfort ($t = 5.2$; $P < 0.05$), confrontation ($t = 2.2$; $P < 0.05$) and emotional comfort ($t = 2.4$; $P < 0.05$).

Statistically reliable differences (Table 1.3.2) also show a certain difference between children from single-parent families and those raised in orphanages or in a complete families.

As seen from the table, between groups b – e for the indicators of (P9) family comfort (P9), confrontation (P11), feelings of inferiority (P12) and emotional stability (P15), there are reliable differences; in the groups b – k, they are found in indicators (P9), (P11) and (P15); and between groups b – f in indicators (P11)

TABLE 1.3.2 Statistically valid difference in the indicators characterizing peculiarities of the development of 4-year-old children brought up in different conditions, according to the "Kinetic family drawing" and "Tapping test" techniques

Statistical values	*Indicators*			
	P_9	P_{11}	P_{12}	P_{15}
	b e	b e	b e	b e
x	7.6. 3.5	0.8 3.2	0.8 1.8	1.1 0.65
x^2	1.9 2.1	1.0 1.5	1.1 1.5	0.4 0.23
m	7.0 3.0	0.0 4.0	0.0 2.0	1.2 0.9
n	7.5 3.0	0.0 4.0	0.5 2.0	1.2 0.6
t	= 5.2*	=4.8*	=2.0*	=3.9*
	b f	b f	b f	b f
x	7.6 2.7	0.8 3.0	0.8 3.3	1.1 0.77
x^2	1.9 2.9	1.0 1.0	1.1 2.1	0.4 0.21
m	7.0 1.0	0.0 0.0	0.0 0.0	1.2 0.0
n	7.5 1.0	0.0 3.0	0.5 4.0	1.2 0.7
t	= NS	= 2.2*	= NS	= 2.0*
	b k	b k	b k	b k
x	7.6 2.7	0.8 3.0	0.8 1.0	1.1 0.8
x^2	1.9 1.1	1.0 2.5	1.1 1.3	0.4 0.3
m	7.0 3.0	0.0 0.0	0.0 0.0	1.2 1.0
n	7.5 3.0	0.0 3.5	0.5 0.0	1.2 0.9
t	= 5.0*	=3.1*	= NS	= 2.4*

**Significance level at* $P < 0.05$.

and (P15). Regarding other indicators – anxiety (P10, P14) and hostility (P13), no significant differences were found.

The results can be explained by the fact that children raised strictly in the family feel the greatest family comfort and emotional stability, the absence of conflict, less feelings of inferiority compared to other children.

Analyzing the results of the study to determine statistically reliable differences in indicators obtained with the help of the methods of "Expert assessment of the expression of various emotional modality" and "Ratio of emotional and rational behavior" between different subgroups of 4-year-olds, we also found out a number of differences. In particular, between groups of children raised only in the family and those who stayed in the family and kindergarten. The largest number of differences were observed by indicators of optimism, shyness and curiosity ($t = 3.0$ $P < 0.05$), anger and anxiety ($t = 2.5$; $P < 0.05$) and resentment ($t = 2.3$ $P < 0.05$).

This group also differs from children raised in kindergarten by indicators of curiosity ($t = 5.4$; $P < 0.05$), resentment ($t = 3.6$; $P < 0.05$) and anxiety ($t = 2.9$; $P < 0.05$).

Differences are also recorded between children from orphanages and children raised in family and kindergarten (Table 1.3.3).

As seen from the results of given research, a significant difference is observed between groups b – e in indicators of (P16), (P17), (P18), (P19), (P20) and (P21). Slightly less significant it was found at the level of reliable differences between children in groups b – k by curiosity (P19), sadness (P20) and anxiety (P21) indicators. As for the differences between children of groups b – f, here it is traced by indicators of joy (P16) and shyness (P18), and between groups k – e by indicators of optimism (P16) and anger (P17).

The results obtained can be explained by the fact that children who were raised solely in the family environment, compared to children from other groups, have the least anxiety, they are less shy and touchy. Children from orphanages, compared to children raised in other settings, are more anxious, easily offended and less inquisitive.

Considering the features of statistically reliable differences between all groups of 4-year-old children who were diagnosed by the Luscher test, we found only a few such differences (Table 1.3.4).

There are significantly reliable differences in the indicators of emotional stability (P24), self-regulation (P25) and frustration (P30) between groups b – k, and groups b – e by parameter of self-regulation (P25). In other cases, no statistically reliable differences were detected.

The results of data obtained by the method "House. Tree. Man" showed that the greatest number of reliable differences by the importance of the development of the emotional sphere in 5-year-olds was found among those from the orphanage compared to children from single-parent families. Specifically for the indicator of anxiety ($t = 2.3$; $P < 0.05$) and frustration ($t = 2.4$; $P < 0.05$). They also have differences with children being brought up in a family and kindergarten,

TABLE 1.3.3 Statistically reliable differences in indicators that characterize the development of the emotional sphere of 4-year-olds brought up in different conditions, according to the "Expert assessment of the expression of various emotional modality" technique

Statistical values	*Indicators*					
	P_{16}	P_{17}	P_{18}	P_{19}	P_{20}	P_{21}
	b e	b e	b e	b e	b e	b e
x	2.6 5.9	2.6 5.0	2.6 6.3	2.6 5.9	2.6 5.0	2.6 5.6
x^2	2.6 2.0	2.6 2.5	2.6 2.6	2.6 2.7	2.6 1.9	2.4 1.9
m	2.6 0.0	2.6 3.0	2.6 5.7	2.6 7.7	2.6 5.1	1.5 6.0
n	2.6 5.7	2.6 3.8	2.6 6.8	2.6 7.1	2.6 5.1	2.6 6.0
t	= 3.0*	= 2.5*	= 3.0*	= 3.0*	= 2.3*	= 2.5*
	b f	b f	b f	b f	b f	b f
x	8.0 6.1	3.0 6.7	3.6 6.0	8.4 4.9	3.6 3.9	3.5 3.8
x^2	1.6 0.75	1.5 3.2	2.0 1.2	1.2 3.8	1.2 3.2	2.4 3.5
m	8.2 5.7	3.4 0.0	4.4 0.0	7.9 0.0	2.8 0.0	1.5 0.0
n	8.2 5.7	3.4 8.1	3.9 6.1	7.9 3.1	3.6 2.5	2.6 1.9
t	= 2.6	= NS	= 2.3	= NS	= NS	= NS
	b k	b k	b k	b k	b k	b k
x	8.0 7.2	3.0 2.3	3.6 5.1	8.4 5.1	3.6 5.0	3.5 5.8
x^2	1.6 1.4	1.5 1.2	2.0 2.7	1.2 2.0	1.2 0.7	2.4 2.0
m	8.2 7.6	3.4 1.4	4.4 4.3	7.9 2.4	2.8 5.2	1.5 6.7
n	8.2 7.6	3.4 1.9	3.9 5.0	7.9 5.2	3.6 5.1	2.6 6.7
t	= NS	= NS	= NS	= 5.4*	= 3.6*	= 2.9*
	k e	k e	k e	k e	k e	k e
x	7.2 5.9	2.3 5.0	5.1 6.3	5.1 5.9	5.0 5.0	5.8 5.6
x^2	1.4 2.0	1.2 2.5	2.7 2.6	2.0 2.7	0.7 1.9	2.0 1.9
m	7.6 0.0	1.4 3.0	4.3 5.7	2.4 7.7	5.2 5.1	6.7 6.0
n	7.6 5.7	1.9 3.8	5.0 6.8	5.2 7.1	5.1 5.1	6.7 6.0
t	= 2.0*	= 3.4*	= NS	= NS	= NS	= NS

**Significance level at P <0.05.*

by indicator of self-doubt (t = 3.1; P <0.05) and children who stayed solely in the family by indicator of frustration (t = 3.6; P <0.05).

It should be noted that this technique revealed differences in children who were brought up only in the family, and those who stayed in the family and kindergarten, in particular by indicators of insecurity (t = 2.2; P < 0.05), self-doubt (t = 3.7; P <0.05) and frustration (t = 2.0; P <0.05). In turn, reliable differences in the indicator of anxiety were found between children from complete families and those from single-parent families (Table 1.3.5).

As we can see, the indicators of emotional insecurity (P1), self-doubt (P3) and frustration (P6) revealed statistically reliable differences between children in groups b – d, and groups g – j in the indicator of anxiety (P2) and frustration (P6).

TABLE 1.3.4 Statistically reliable differences in indicators that characterize the features of the development of the emotional sphere in 4-year-olds brought up in different conditions, according to the Luscher test

Statistical values	*Indicators*		
	P_{24}	P_{25}	P_{30}
	b e	b e	b e
x	0.8 0.31	0.9 0.38	−0.4 −0.85
x2	0.9 0.63	0.7 0.51	0.5 −0.8
m	0.0 0.0	1.0 0.0	0.0 0.0
n	0.5 0.0	1.0 0.0	0.0 −1.0
t	= NS	= 2.1*	= NS
	b k	b k	b k
x	0.8 0.2	0.9 0.3	−0.4 −0.9
x2	0.9 0.8	0.7 0.5	0.5 0.8
m	0.0 0.0	1.0 0.0	0.0 −0.1
n	0.5 0.0	1.0 0.0	0.0 −0.1
t	= 2.0*	= 2.5*	= 2.5*

**Level of significance at P <0.05.*

There are statistically reliable differences in (P2) parameter between children in group b – g, in (P6) between children in groups b – j and in (P3) between d – j.

These differences may indicate that:

First, children from orphanages are less anxious, more frustrated, distrustful than other children;

Second, children raised only in the family environment feel more protected, but they are less confident and frustrated.

Considering the results obtained in children aged five years using the methods of “Kinetic family drawing”, “Anxiety test” and “Tapping test”, we also found a number of statistically reliable discrepancies between indicators that characterize different features of the development of the emotional sphere. According to the analysis, the largest number of reliable differences was found between children who were brought up only in the family and children who stayed in the family and kindergarten; in particular, by parameters of family comfort ($t = 5.6$; $P < 0.05$), anxiety ($t = 2.8$; $P < 0.05$), confrontation ($t = 4.3$; $P < 0.05$), emotional stability ($t = 3.1$; $P < 0.05$) and others (Table 1.3.6).

On the whole, the indicators revealed significant differences between groups b – d in terms of family comfort (P9), anxiety (P10), confrontation (P11), feelings of inferiority (P12) and emotional stability (P15). Similar differences are observed between children of groups b – g, except for the indicator (P12). Also, as can be seen from Table 1.3.6, the differences were also found between children of groups b – j by indicators (P9), (P11) and (P15) and between children of groups

TABLE 1.3.5 Statistically reliable differences in the indicators that characterize specific features of the development of the emotional sphere of 5-year-olds brought up in different conditions, according to the "House. Tree. Man" method

Statistical values	*Indicators*			
	P_1	P_2	P_3	P_6
	b d	b d	b d	b d
x	2.0 4.0	2.0 5.4	2.0 3.1	2.0 3.4
x^2	2.0 1.7	2.0 3.8	2.0 1.2	2.0 1.6
m	2.0 4.0	2.0 3.0	2.0 2.0	2.0 3.0
n	2.0 4.0	2.0 4.5	2.0 3.0	2.0 3.0
t	= 2.2*	= NS	= 3.7*	= 2.0*
	b g	b g	b g	b g
x	5.2 4.6	4.0. 6.4	1.8 2.3	2.3 2.8
x^2	1.5 2.8	2.0 2.4	0.7 0.71	1.5 1.3
m	4.0 1.0	2.0 7.0	2.0 2.0	1.0 3.0
n	5.5 5.0	4.0 6.0	2.0 2.0	2.0 3.0
t	= NS	= 2.5*	NS	NS
	b j	b j	b j	b j
x	5.2 4.5	4.0 4.1	1.8 1.9	2.3 4.0
x^2	1.5 1.4	2.0 2.3	0.7 1.1	1.5 0.89
m	4.0 4.0	2.0 6.0	2.0 1.0	1.0 5.0
n	5.5 4.0	4.0 4.0	2.0 2.0	2.0 4.0
t	NS	NS	NS	= 3.6*
	d j	d j	d j	d j
x	4.0 4.5	5.4 4.1	3.1 1.9	3.4 4.0
x^2	1.7 1.4	3.8 2.3	1.2 1.0	1.6 0.89
m	4.0 4.0	3.0 6.0	2.0 1.0	3.0 5.0
n	4.0 4.0	4.5 4.0	3.0 2.0	3.0 4.0
t	NS	NS	= 3.1*	NS
	g j	g j	g j	g j
x	4.6 4.5	6.4 4.1	2.3 1.9	2.8 4.0
x2	2.8 1.4	2.4 2.3	0.71 1.0	1.3 0.89
m	1.0 4.0	7.0 6.0	2.0 1.0	3.0 5.0
n	5.0 4.0	6.0 4.0	2.0 2.0	3.0 4.0
t	NS	= 2.3*	NS	= 2.4*

**Significance level at* $P < 0.05$.

d – j by indicators (P10) and (P12), and by indicator (P10) statistically reliable differences for the groups g – j.

It should be noted that there are still reliable differences in some indicators between groups of children from orphanages and other children's institutions.

For example, it was found that children raised in an orphanage, in terms of family comfort differ significantly from children who stayed only in the family environment ($t = 5.6$, $P < 0.05$). Similar differences were found in this respect in

TABLE 1.3.6 Statistically proven differences in indicators that characterize the specifics of the development of the emotional sphere of children at the age of five raised under different conditions, according to the "Kinetic family drawing" and "Tapping test" methods

Statistical values	*Indicators*				
	P_9	P_{10}	P_{11}	P_{12}	P_{15}
	b d	b d	b d	b d	b d
x	1.2 3.8	1.2 2.7	1.2 2.8	1.2 1.8	1.2 0.75
x^2	1.2 1.6	1.2 2.0	1.2 1.6	1.2 1.4	1.2 0.25
m	1.2 3.0	1.2 4.0	1.2 3.0	1.2 0.0	1.2 0.9
n	1.2 3.0	1.2 3.0	1.2 3.0	1.2 2.0	1.2 0.8
t	= 5.6*	= 2.8*	= 4.3*	= 2.4*	= 3.1*
	b g	b g	b g	b g	b g
x	7.6 3.8	1.2 2.4	0.8 2.4	0.8 1.2	1.1 0.7
x^2	1.9 2.3	0.7 1.3	1.0 1.3	1.1 1.3	0.4 0.17
m	7.0 3.0	1.0 3.0	0.0 3.0	0.0 0.0	1.2 0.9
n	7.5 4.0	1.0 3.0	0.0 3.0	0.5 1.0	1.2 0.7
t	= 3.9*	= 2.4*	= 3.0*	= NS	= 3.5*
	b j	b j	b j	b j	b j
x	7.6 3.7	1.2 1.3	0.8 3.3	0.8 0.8	1.1 0.73
x^2	1.9 2.0	0.7 1.4	1.0 2.4	1.1 1.0	0.4 0.31
m	7.0 3.0	1.0 1.0	0.0 4.0	0.0 0.0	1.2 0.6
n	7.5 3.0	1.0 1.0	0.0 3.5	0.5 0.0	1.2 0.6
t	= 5.6*	= NS	= 4.1*	= NS	= 3.1*
	d j	d j	d j	d j	d j
x	3.8 3.7	2.67 1.3	2.8 3.3	1.8 0.85	0.75 0.73
x^2	1.6 2.0	2.0 1.4	1.6 2.4	1.4 1.0	0.25 0.31
m	3.0 3.0	4.0 1.0	3.0 4.0	0.0 0.0	0.9 0.6
n	3.0 3.0	3.0 1.0	3.0 3.5	2.0 0.0	0.8 0.6
t	= NS	= 2.4*	= NS	= 2.4*	= NS
	g j	g j	g j	g j	g j
x	3.8 3.7	2.4 1.3	2.4 3.3	1.2 0.85	0.7 0.73
x^2	2.3 2.0	1.3 1.4	1.3 2.4	1.3 1.0	0.17 0.31
m	3.0 3.0	3.0 1.0	3.0 4.0	0.0 0.0	0.9 0.6
n	4.0 3.0	3.0 1.0	3.0 3.5	1.0 0.0	0.7 0.6
t	= NS	= 2.0*	= NS	= NS	= NS

**Level of significance at P <0.05.*

parameters of conflict (t = 4.1; P <0.05) and emotional stability (t = 3.1; P <0.05). These children also differ from children raised in a family and kindergarten in terms of anxiety and inferiority (t = 2.4; P <0.05).

These results may indicate that children raised only in the family environment experience greater family comfort, less anxiety, confrontation, less inferiority and greater emotional resilience than other children.

Children from orphanages, compared to children raised in other conditions, have situational anxiety, as well as increased confrontation.

According to the "Expert assessment of the expression of the different emotional modalities" technique and the test "The ratio of emotional and rational behavior" there are statistically reliable differences between children raised in families and kindergartens, and children from orphanage by parameters of shyness ($t = 4.1$; $P < 0.05$), curiosity ($t = 2.3$; $P < 0.05$), anxiety ($t = 4.9$; $P < 0.05$) and general emotionality ($t = 2.8$; $P < 0.05$).

For their part, children from orphanages statistically differ in a number of indicators from children raised only in a family. The latter is evident in the parameters of anger ($t = 3.2$; $P < 0.05$), curiosity ($t = 4.5$; $P < 0.05$) and offense ($t = 2.8$; $P < 0.05$).

However, the greatest number of reliable differences was found between children who stayed only in the family and those raised in the family and kindergarten. In particular, for all indicators of the "Expert assessment of the expression of the different emotional modalities" technique (Table 1.3.7).

According to the indicators obtained, quite significant differences were revealed between children in groups "b – d" on (P16), (P17), (P18), (P19), (P20) and (P21), (P22), between groups b – g on indicators (P16), (P17), (P18), (P19) and (P20), and groups "d – j" on indicators (P18), (P19), (P20), (P21) and (P22). The smallest difference is revealed in groups "b – j" on indicators (P17), (P19), (P20) and groups "d – g" on indicators (P18) and (P21).

These results may indicate that children raised solely in the family environment, unlike others, experience lesser anger, resentment and anxiety. They are also moderately emotional.

Children who stayed in the family and day care center are more shy, anxious and emotional, while those raised in the orphanage are more aggressive and less shy.

Examining the peculiarities of **statistically verifiable differences** in indicators tested by the Luscher test, we also found some differences in the subgroups of 5-year-old children with different upbringing conditions (Table 1.3.8).

As we can see, the indicator of emotional stability (P24) show differences between groups "b – d", "d – j" and "g – j", the indicator of self-regulation (P25) – between groups "b – d" and "g – j", while the confrontation parameter (P28) – only between groups "d – j". True, there are no statistically reliable differences in emotional arousal (P26) and aggressiveness (P27).

The results of the study obtained with the help of the "House. Tree. Man" method show that the peculiarities of the development of the emotional sphere of 6-year-old children brought up in different conditions in a number of cases have reliable differences. For example, it was found that children who were raised only in a family environment statistically significantly differ from children who stayed in the family and kindergarten by indicator of anxiety ($t = 2.5$; $P < 0.05$), from those raised by only one parent – by indicators of frustration ($t = 2.3$; $P < 0.05$) and depressiveness ($t = 3.1$; $P < 0.05$), and from children in the children's home, by indicator of insecurity ($t = 3.2$; $P < 0.05$) and self-doubt ($t = 3.7$; $P < 0.05$) (see Table 1.3.9).

As seen from Table 1.3.9, we have found statistically reliable differences between groups "a – i" on indicators (P1), (P2), (P3), (P6) and (P7), in groups

TABLE 1.3.7 Statistically proven differences in indicators that characterize specific features of the development of emotional sphere of 5-year-old children brought up in different conditions, according to the "Expert assessment of the expression of the different emotional modalities" technique

Statistical values	*Indicators*						
	P_{16}	P_{17}	P_{18}	P_{19}	P_{20}	P_{21}	P_{22}
	b d	b d	b d	b d	b d	b d	b d
x	4.9 6.4	4.9 4.6	4.9 6.6	4.9 6.5	4.9 5.5	4.9 6.0	4.9 5.9
x^2	4.9 1.3	4.9 2.2	4.9 2.3	4.9 1.9	4.9 1.6	4.9 1.1	4.9 0.9
m	4.9 6.4	4.9 2.3	4.9 5.8	4.9 6.1	4.9 5.1	4.9 6.2	4.9 6.2
n	4.9 6.4	4.9 4.4	4.9 6.7	4.9 7.1	4.9 5.5	4.9 6.0	4.9 6.1
t	= 3.0*	= 2.4*	= 4.0*	= 3.4*	= 3.8*	= 3.4*	= 2.8*
	b g	b g	b g	b g	b g	b g	b g
x	4.9 5.9	4.9 5.4	4.9 4.1	4.9 5.8	4.9 5.1	4.9 4.7	4.9 5.2
x^2	4.9 1.9	4.9 1.8	4.9 1.6	4.9 2.4	4.9 1.7	4.9 1.4	4.9 1.6
m	4.9 6.8	4.9 0.0	4.9 5.6	4.9 6.2	4.9 6.3	4.9 6.0	4.9 6.5
n	4.9 6.4	4.9 5.8	4.9 4.4	4.9 6.2	4.9 6.2	4.9 4.9	4.9 6.0
t	= 2.6*	= 3.2*	= NS	= 2.7*	= 2.3*	= NS	= NS
	b j	b j	b j	b j	b j	b j	b j
x	8.0 7.1	3.0 5.4	3.6 3.8	8.4 4.5	3.6 5.2	3.5 4.1	5.0 5.0
x^2	1.6 1.6	1.5 2.9	2.0 1.9	1.2 3.5	1.2 2.1	2.4 1.3	0.9 1.2
m	8.2 8.7	3.4 8.1	4.4 5.6	7.9 8.8	2.8 4.2	1.5 4.8	4.1 5.5
n	8.2 7.5	3.4 6.2	3.9 3.0	7.9 4.9	3.6 5.2	2.6 4.2	4.9 6.
t	= NS	= 3.2.*	= NS	= 4.5*	= 2.8*	= NS	= NS
	d g	d g	d g	d g	d g	d g	d g
x	6.4 5.9	4.6 5.4	6.6 4.1	6.5 5.8	5.5 5.1	6.0 4.7	5.9 5.2
x^2	1.4 1.9	2.2 1.8	2.3 1.6	1.9 2.4	1.6 1.7	1.1 1.5	0.9 1.6
m	6.4 6.8	2.3 0.0	5.8 5.6	6.1 6.2	5.1 6.3	6.2 6.0	6.2 6.5
n	6.4 6.4	4.4 5.8	6.7 4.4	7.1 6.2	5.5 6.2	6.0 4.9	6.1 6.0
t	= NS	= NS	= 3.3.*	= NS	= NS	= 2.3*	= NS
	d j	d j	d j	d j	d j	d j	d j
x	6.4 7.1	4.6 5.4	6.7 3.8	6.5 4.5	5.5 5.2	6.0 4.1	5.9 5.0
x^2	1.3 1.6	2.2 2.9	2.3 1.9	1.9 3.5	1.6 2.1	1.1 1.3	0.9 1.2
m	6.4 8.7	2.3 8.1	5.8 5.6	6.1 8.8	5.1 4.2	6.2 4.8	6.2 5.5
n	6.4 7.5	4.4 6.1	6.7 3.0	7.1 4.9	5.6 5.2	6.0 4.2	6.1 5.3
t	= NS	= NS	= 4.1*	= 2.3*	= NS	= 4.9*	= 2.8*

**Significance level at P <0.05.*

"c – i" on indicators (P1), (P4), (P5), (P6) and (P7), between groups "a – h" – by indexes of frustration (P6) and depressiveness (P8). Groups "a – c" has differences in anxiety parameter (P2), and groups "i – h" in parameter (P8).

For their part, the indicators that characterize the emotional sphere of children who stayed in the family and kindergarten, statistically differ significantly from similar indicators of children from orphanages. There are statistically reliable differences in the indicators of insecurity ($t=3.1; P<0.05$), inferiority ($t=2.6; P>0.05$),

TABLE 1.3.8 Statistically reliable differences in indicators that characterize the development of the emotional sphere in 5-year-old children brought up in different conditions, according to the "Luscher test"

Statistical values	*Indicators*		
	P_{24}	P_{25}	P_{28}
	b d	b d	b d
x	0.57 0.22	0.57 0.67	−0.3 −0.72
x^2	0.57 0.55	0.57 0.69	0.57 0.57
m	0.57 0.0	0.57 0.0	−1.0 −1.0
n	0.57 0.0	0.57 1.0	0.57 −0.1
t	= 2.0★	= NS	= NS
	b g	b g	b g
x	0.57 0.11	0.57 0.0	−0.3 −0.44
x^2	0.57 0.78	0.57 0.87	0.57 0.73
m	0.57 0.0	0.57 0.0	−1.0 0.0
n	0.57 0.0	0.57 0.0	0.57 0.0
t	= NS	= 2.4★	= NS
	d j	d j	d j
x	0.57 1.0	0.57 1.1	−0.72 −0.2
x^2	0.57 0.86	0.57 0.72	0.57 0.83
m	0.57 1.0	0.57 1.0	−1.0 0.0
n	0.57 1.0	0.57 1.0	−1.0 0.0
t	= 3.3★	= NS	=2.3★
	g j	g j	g j
x	0.11 1.0	0.0 1.1	−0.44 −0.2
x^2	0.78 0.86	0.87 0.72	0.73 0.83
m	0.0 1.0	0.0 1.0	0.0 0.0
n	0.0 1.0	0.0 1.0	0.0 0.0
t	= 2.6★	= 3.0★	= NS

★*Significance level at P <0.05.*

frustration (t = 4.6; P < 0.05), hostility (t = 2.0; P <0.05), and the indicator of difficulties in communication (t = 5.0; P <0.05). There are still some statically proved differences and some tendencies toward differences in other indicators.

The obtained results give us reason to note that the greatest difference in the subgroups of 6-year-old children who were raised in different conditions appeared to be between those who, first, were brought up only in a family home or orphanage, and those who were brought up in families and in a day care center from children in orphanage.

As we can see, the children from the orphanage, based on the received data, differ in almost all indicators of the emotional sphere from the children who were brought up only in the family and kindergarten.

Analyzing the results of a study related to the value of statistically reliable differences in indicators obtained using other methods ("Kinetic picture of the

TABLE 1.3.9 Statistically proven differences in the indicators that characterize features of the development of the emotional sphere of 6-year-old children brought up in different conditions, according to the "House. Tree. Man" method

Statistical values	*Indicators*							
	P_1	P_2	P_3	P_4	P_5	P_6	P_7	P_8
	a c	a c	a c	a c	a c	a c	a c	a c
x	4.7 3.8	3.8 5.3	1.9 2.3	2.6 2.1	5.7 4.7	2.7 3.1	4.9 4.0	2.8 2.8
x^2	1.5 2.3	1.7 2.2	0.8 1.2	1.1 1.3	2.4 1.9	1.5 1.1	2.3 1.9	1.2 1.4
m	4.0 1.0	3.0 5.0	2.0 1.0	3.0 1.0	4.0 5.0	1.0 3.0	3.0 3.0	2.0 2.0
n	4.5 3.0	3.0 5.0	2.0 1.0	3.0 2.0	5.5 5.0	2.5 3.0	4.0 4.0	2.0 2.0
t	= NS	= 2.5*	= NS	= NS	= NS	= NS	= NS	= NS
	a h	a h	a h	a h	a h	a h	a h	a h
x	4.7 6.0	3.8 4.5	1.9 2.0	2.6 2.5	5.7 7.0	2.7 5.5	4.9 6.0	2.8 2.0
x^2	5.1 1.4	1.7 2.1	0.8 1.4	1.1 0.7	2.4 2.8	1.5 0.7	2.3 1.4	1.2 0.0
m	4.0 0.0	3.0 0.0	2.0 0.0	3.0 0.0	4.0 0.0	1.0 0.0	3.0 0.0	2.0 2.0
n	4.5 0.0	3.0 4.5	2.0 2.0	3.0 2.5	5.5 7.0	2.5 5.5	4.0 6.0	2.0 2.0
t	= NS	= NS	= NS	= NS	= NS	= 2.3*	= NS	= 3.1*
	a i	a i	a i	a i	a i	a i	a i	a i
x	4.7 5.5	3.8 5.5	1.9 2.6	2.6 3.1	5.7 5.7	2.7 4.9	4.9 7.5	2.8 2.9
x^2	1.5 1.6	1.7 2.1	0.8 1.1	1.1 1.3	2.4 2.1	1.5 1.9	2.3 2.3	1.2 1.4
m	4.0 6.0	3.0 6.0	2.0 2.0	3.0 3.0	4.0 7.0	1.0 6.0	3.0 7.0	2.0 2.0
n	4.5 6.0	3.0 6.0	2.0 2.0	3.0 3.0	5.5 6.0	2.5 5.0	4.0 8.0	2.0 2.0
t	= 2.0*	= 3.2*	= 2.8*	= NS	= NS	= 4.7*	= 3.7*	= NS
	c i	c i	c i	c i	c i	c i	c i	c i
x	3.8 5.6	5.3 5.5	2.3 2.6	2.1 3.1	4.7 5.7	3.1 4.9	4.0 7.4	2.8 2.9
x^2	2.3 1.6	2.2 2.1	1.2 1.1	1.3 1.3	1.9 2.1	1.1 1.9	1.9 2.3	1.4 1.4
m	1.0 6.0	5.0 6.0	1.0 2.0	1.0 3.0	5.0 7.0	3.0 6.0	3.0 7.0	2.0 2.0
n	3.0 6.0	5.0 6.0	2.0 2.0	2.0 3.0	5.0 6.0	3.0 5.0	4.0 8.0	2.0 2.0
t	= 3.1*	= NS	= NS	= 2.6 *	= 2.1*	= 4.6*	= 5.0*	= NS
	i h	i h	i h	i h	i h	i h	i h	i h
x	5.6 6.0	5.3 5.6	2.6 2.0	3.1 2.5	5.7 7.0	4.9 5.5	7.5 6.0	2.9 2.0
x^2	1.5 1.4	2.2 2.1	1.1 1.4	1.4 0.7	2.1 2.8	1.9 0.7	2.3 1.4	1.5 0.0
m	4.0 0.0	5.0 6.0	2.0 0.0	3.0 0.0	7.0 0.0	6.0 0.0	7.0 0.0	2.0 2.0
n	4.5 0.0	5.0 6.0	2.0 2.0	3.0 2.5	6.0 7.0	5.0 5.5	8.0 6.0	2.0 2.0
t	= NS	= NS	= NS	= NS	= NS	= NS	= NS	= 3.5*

**Significance level at* $P < 0.05$.

family", "Tapping test", "Anxiety test"), between different subgroups of 6-year-olds, a number of similar trends were identified.

The greatest number of statistically reliable differences was also found between children who were brought up only in a family solely and children from an orphanage; in particular, in the indicator of anxiety ($t = 5.7$; $P < 0.05$), confrontation ($t = 3.9$; $P < 0.05$), and the indicator of inferiority ($t = 2.0$; $P < 0.05$). Children from orphanages also differ from children who stayed in kindergarten and family in terms of family comfort (t = 2.1; $P < 0.05$) and aggressiveness (t = 4.9; $P < 0.05$).

The statistically reliable differences presented (Table 1.3.10) show that there is a certain difference between children who were raised in a family only and children who were in a family and kindergarten.

As we can see, in this case a significant difference is observed between group "a – i" in terms of anxiety (P10), confrontation (P11) and feelings of inferiority (P12), and between group "a – c" in indicators (P10) and (P11), group "c – i" according to the indicator of family comfort (P9) and hostility (P13), and by indicator (P11) between groups "a – h".

We can say that these results to some extent confirm the previous analysis.

Continuing the review of the results related to the identification of statistically reliable differences in the diagnosed indicators of the emotional sphere in 6-year-old children raised under different conditions, we can see that they are most clearly recorded among children of the above subgroups by joy (t = 3.4; $P < 0.05$), sorrow (t = 2.8; $P < 0.05$) and general emotionality (t = 2.3; $P < 0.05$) parameters.

Also, according to the method of "Expert assessment of the expression of the modality of different emotions" and the test "The ratio of emotional and rational behavior", statistically reliable differences are clearly recorded in children raised in family and kindergarten, and children from orphanage in terms of shyness (t = 3.0; $P < 0.05$), anxiety (t = 4.0, $P < 0.05$) and general emotionality (t = 2.8; $P < 0.05$).

Children who stayed in a children's home also differ statistically significantly from children from single-parent families. This is observed in the indicator of shyness (t = 4.9; $P < 0.05$) and general emotionality (t = 2.2; $P < 0.05$). Other, less significant, differences in the indicators obtained by these methods also were recorded (Table 1.3.11).

There are statistically reliable differences between groups "a – c" on indicators (P16), (P18), (P19), (P20) and (P21), between group "c – i" by indicator (P18), (P20), (P21) and (P22), and between groups "a – h" on indicator of anger (P17), shyness (P18) and interest (P19). Also for the indicator of joy (P16), (P19) and emotionality (P22) between groups "a – i", and group "i – h" by indicators (P18) and (P22).

These results may indicate that children from orphanages are less shy and less abusive, but more anxious than children who have been in a family settings. They are also less emotional than them, that is, show lesser optimism and curiosity.

Examining the features of statistically reliable differences in indicators diagnosed by the Luscher test, we found only these differences in the subgroups of 6 year old children (Table 1.3.12).

From the above, we see that reliable differences are found in the indicators of self-regulation (P25) and frustration (P30) between groups "a – c", and between "c – i" by the indicator (P30). According to other indicators (P26), (P27), (P28) and (P29), no significant differences were recorded.

Summarizing the results of the latest analysis, aimed at establishing differences in the indicators of the emotional sphere between different subgroups of

TABLE 1.3.10 Statistically proven differences in the indicators characterizing peculiarities of the development of the emotional sphere of 6-year-old children brought up in different conditions, according to the "Kinetic drawing of the family" method

Statistical values	*Indicators*				
	P_9	P_{10}	P_{11}	P_{12}	P_{13}
3	a c	a c	a c	a c	a c
x	1.0 5.0	1.0 3.3	1.0 2.5	1.0 1.7	1.0 0.5
x^2	1.0 2.3	1.0 1.6	1.0 1.7	1.0 1.2	1.0 0.7
m	1.0 3.0	1.0 4.0	1.0 3.0	1.0 2.0	1.0 0.0
n	1.0 5.0	1.0 3.0	1.0 2.5	1.0 2.0	1.0 0.0
t	= NS	= 4.8★	= 3.5★	= NS	= NS
	a h	a h	a h	a h	a h
x	5.1 1.5	1.4 1.0	0.9 4.5	1.4 3.5	1.2 1.5
x^2	2.8 2.1	1.0 1.4	1.3 0.7	1.3 2.1	1.4 0.7
m	5.0 0.0	1.0 0.0	0.0 0.0	0.0 0.0	0.0 0.0
n	5.0 2.0	1.0 1.0	0.0 4.5	1.5 3.5	1.0 1.5
t	= NS	= NS	= 2.3★	= NS	= NS
	a i	a I	a i	a i	a i
x	5.1 3.8	1.4 3.5	0.9 2.6	1.4 2.2	1.2 1.7
x^2	2.8 1.9	1.0 1.7	1.3 1.8	1.3 1.7	1.4 1.0
m	5.0 5.0	1.0 4.0	0.0 2.0	0.0 0.0	0.0 2.0
n	5.0 4.0	1.0 4.0	0.0 2.0	1.5 2.0	1.0 2.0
t	= NS	= 5.7★	= 3.9★	= 2.0★	= NS
	c i	c I	c i	c i	c i
x	5.0 3.8	3.3 3.5	2.5 2.6	1.8 2.2	0.54 1.7
x^2	2.3 1.9	1.6 1.7	1.7 1.8	1.4 1.7	0.7 1.0
m	3.0 5.0	4.0 4.0	3.0 2.0	2.0 0.0	0.0 2.0
n	5.0 4.0	3.0 4.0	2.5 2.0	2.0 2.0	0.0 2.0
t	= 2.1★	= NS	= NS	= NS	= 4.9★

★*Significance level at* $P < 0.05$.

6-year-olds, we can state that with the change in social status the peculiarities of child's emotional sphere development change also.

This is most evident between the subgroups of children from the orphanage and those raised in different family settings. There are also differences between children who stayed solely in family environment and children who were raised in a family home and a day care center.

Thus, the analysis of statistically reliable differences in indicators characterizing the peculiarities of development in the emotional sphere of children who were raised in different conditions, allows us to note the following:

Four-year-olds from an orphanage differ significantly from children raised in other settings by a number of indicators. In particular, statistically reliable

TABLE 1.3.11 Statistically verified differences in indicators that characterize the peculiarities of the emotional sphere of children of six years old brought up in different conditions, according to the "Expert assessment of the expression of the modality of different emotions" method

Statistical values	*Indicators*						
	P_{16}	P_{17}	P_{18}	P_{19}	P_{20}	P_{21}	P_{22}
	a c	a c	a c	a c	a c	a c	a c
x	7.8 6.0	3.6 4.4	3.7 6.2	8.6 6.3	3.7 5.2	3.7 5.4	5.2 5.6
x^2	1.7 1.9	2.5 2.2	2.1 2.3	1.1 3.1	1.7 1.8	2.3 2.3	1.2 1.8
m	8.6 5.5	3.9 1.5	3.9 8.2	10.0 9.4	2.9 3.4	1.0 6.7	4.1 5.7
n	8.2 6.4	3.6 3.9	4.0 6.8	8.6 7.8	3.9 5.3	3.3 6.1	4.9 5.8
t	= 3.3*	= NS	= 3.6*	= 3.4*	= 2.8*	= 2.3*	= NS
	a h	a h	a h	a h	a h	a h	a h
x	7.8 6.0	3.6 3.6	3.7 6.7	8.6 6.9	3.7 4.5	3.7 4.5	5.2 5.6
x^2	1.7 1.9	2.5 0.3	2.1 0.1	1.1 1.2	1.7 1.4	1.7 1.4	1.2 0.42
m	8.6 5.5	3.9 0.0	3.9 0.0	10.0 0.0	2.9 0.0	2.9 0.0	4.1 0.0
n	8.2 6.4	3.6 3.6	4.0 6.7	8.6 6.9	3.9 4.5	3.9 4.5	4.9 5.6
t	= NS	= 2.2*	= 5.9*	= 2.8*	= NS	= NS	= NS
	a i	a i	a i	a i	a i	a i	a i
x	7.8 5.9	3.6 3.4	3.7 4.1	8.6 5.4	3.7 3.8	3.7 2.6	5.2 4.2
x^2	1.7 2.6	2.5 3.0	2.1 3.0	1.1 3.1	1.7 2.7	2.3 3.0	1.2 1.8
m	8.6 9.1	3.9 0.7	3.9 0.4	10.0 0.4	2.9 0.4	1.0 0.8	4.1 4.6
n	8.2 6.6	3.6 3.2	4.0 3.4	8.6 4.6	3.9 3.8	3.3 0.9	4.9 4.4
t	= 3.2*	= NS	= NS	= 5.2*	= NS	= NS	= 2.2*
	c i	c i	c i	c i	c i	c I	c I
x	6.0 5.9	4.4 3.4	6.2 4.1	6.3 5.4	5.2 3.8	5.4 2.6	5.6 4.2
x^2	2.0 2.6	2.3 3.0	2.4 3.0	3.1 3.2	1.8 2.6	2.4 3.0	1.8 1.8
m	5.5 9.1	1.5 0.7	8.2 0.4	9.4 0.4	3.4 0.4	6.7 0.8	5.7 4.6
n	6.4 6.6	3.9 3.2	6.7 3.4	7.6 4.6	5.3 3.8	6.1 0.9	5.8 4.4
t	= NS	= NS	= 3.0*	= NS	= 2.3*	= 4.0*	= 2.8*
	i h	i h	i h	i h	i h	i h	i h
x	5.9 6.6	3.4 3.6	4.1 6.7	5.4 6.9	3.9 4.5	2.6 4.8	4.2 5.6
x^2	2.7 2.0	3.0 0.3	3.0 0.14	3.2 1.2	2.6 1.4	3.0 1.2	1.8 0.4
m	9.1 5.5	0.7 0.0	0.4 0.0	0.4 0.0	0.4 0.0	0.8 0.0	4.6 0.0
n	6.6 6.4	3.2 3.6	3.4 6.7	4.6 6.9	3.8 4.5	0.9 4.8	4.4 5.6
t	= NS	= NS	= 4.9*	= NS	= NS	= NS	= 2.2*

**Significance level at* $P < 0.05$.

differences were found in parameters of self-doubt, frustration, family comfort, resentment and anxiety;

Five-year-olds from an orphanage differ significantly by parameters of anxiety and frustration from children raised in a single-parent family, and by self-doubt, curiosity, anxiety and emotionality from children who stayed in the family and kindergarten. There is also a statistically reliable difference in terms of frustration, family comfort, confrontation, emotional resilience,

TABLE 1.3.12 Statistically valid differences in indicators that characterize the development of the emotional sphere of 6-year-old children brought up in different conditions, according to the "Luscher Test".

Statistical values	*Indicators*	
	P_{25}	P_{30}
	a c	a c
x	1.0 0.62	−0.1 −0.88
x^2	0.50 0.50	1.0 0.86
m	1.0 1.0	0.0 −1.0
n	1.0 1.0	0.0 −1.0
t	= 2.5*	= 2.6*
	c I	c i
x	0.62 0.67	−0.83 −0.06
x^2	0.50 0.74	0.86 1.12
m	1.0 1.0	−1.0 0.0
n	1.0 1.0	−1.0 0.0
t	= NS	= 3.2*

**Significance level at P <0.05.*

anger, curiosity and resentment compared to the group of children who were raised only in the family;

Six-year-olds from an orphanage have statistically reliable difference with children raised in a family home and a day care center in terms of insecurity, inferiority, frustration, hostility, communication difficulties and also differences in indicators of insecurity, self-doubt, frustration and difficulties in communication with children raised only in the family.

Based on the above results, which characterize statistically reliable differences, we can also state that children raised in orphanages differ from other children in more pronounced frustration and aggressiveness, anxiety, confrontation and lesser shyness. They also have some difficulties in communication.

1.4 Relationship of indicators of the emotional sphere in children brought up in various conditions

As a previous research has shown, the differences in the emotional sphere of children of different ages, who were brought up in unequal social conditions, have their own specifics. However, for a more complete analysis of the described differences, it is important to identify and investigate those internal structural mechanisms that determine their specificity. With this in mind, we carried out a correlation and factor analysis of the relationships between the diagnosed indicators in each selected group of subjects.

At the same time, we assumed that if the previously detected indicators, which recorded reliable differences in the selected samples, confirm their dependence on the links with other parameters, they may be considered as the leading ones in the structure of factors determining the development of the emotional sphere in one or another group of children. In turn, this greatly facilitated the selection and development of conditions and methods aimed at the formation, prevention and treatment of the emotional sphere of children who were brought up in different conditions.

The previous results of the study showed that in 4-year-old children raised in a complete family the indicator of general emotionality (P22) positively correlates with shyness (P18), (r = 0.7); anxiety parameters (P21), (r = 0.65); anxiety (P2), (r = 0.6); resentment (P20), (r = 0.8); anger (P17), (r = 0.54); and negatively with a feeling of inferiority (P12), (r = −0.52). There is also a negative correlation between aggressiveness (P27), anxiety (P29), and confrontation (P28).

The obtained interrelations can be explained by the fact that the general emotionality is the leading parameter in this structure. The fact that anxiety, resentment and anger have the greatest connections with it indicates, on the one hand, their natural basis and domination, along with other emotional manifestations at this age. The detected negative interrelationships with the feeling of inferiority, as well as with indicators of frustration and confrontation, indicate that with the change of these features, there is a change in aggressiveness and general emotionality.

Studying the features of the factor structure of indicators that characterize the development of the emotional sphere of children aged four to five, who were brought up only in the family, we can identify three main factors (Table 1.4.1).

The first factor we call "a factor of emotionality", the second – "aggressiveness" and the third one – "cognitive activity". These are the main features in the structure of emotional development of children 4–5 years old, who were brought up only in the family. The dominant features here are general emotionality, cognitive activity and aggressiveness, as evidenced by the data of factor weight of indicators from (P5) to (P15).

Children of the same age who stayed in the family and kindergarten have a more complex structure of the interrelations. Here are five major sets of correlations around curiosity indicator (P19). The latter at a sufficiently high level correlates with joy (P16), (r = 0.7); anxiety (P21), (r = 0.7); general emotionality (P22), (r = 0.9); and self-regulation (P25), (r = 0.5). As in the previous group, a significant number of correlations were found in the indicator of general emotionality (P22). It seems to develop a whole new structure of correlations of the above-mentioned correlator with the latter at a sufficiently high level (r = 0.9). In addition, the indicator of general emotionality (P22) also correlates with joy (P16), (r = 0.7), anxiety (P21), (r = 0.8) and self-regulation (P25), (r = 0.5).

This subgroup also has a number of negatively correlated interrelations of aggressiveness parameter (P27) and with indicators of self-doubt (P3), (r = −0.6), feelings of inferiority (P4), (r = −0.5) and frustration (P6), (r = −0.6).

TABLE 1.4.1 Factor structure of indicators characterizing featuresof the emotional sphere of children four to five years old raised only in the family

Indicators	*Values*
Factor 1	
P22 emotionality	0.798
P17 anger	0.786
P20 offense, sadness	0.74
P2 anxiety	0.684
P16 joy	0.63
P5 hostility	0.627
P25 self-regulation	0.613
% of total variance	15.013
Factor 2	
P27 aggressiveness	−0.839
P29 anxiety	0.812
P28 confrontation	0.677
P18 shyness	0.556
P7 communication difficulties	0.511
% of total variance	13.687
Factor 3	
P19 curiosity, interest	−0.91
P14 anxiety	0.798
P26 emotional excitement	−0.679
P15 emotional resilience	0.592
% of total variance	12.76

In turn, the indicator of self-doubt (P3) negatively correlates with anxiety (P10), ($r = -0.7$), anger (P17), ($r = -0.6$) and aggressiveness (P27), $r = -0.6$).

Based on the above, we can say that these children feel more confident due to the change in aggressiveness and confrontation

An in-depth analysis shows that the identified relationships are to some extent reflected in the factor structure.

Based on the presented results, the first factor can be designated as "emotionally-cognitive". It includes situational anxiety and resentment, general emotionality, and also curiosity and balance of emotional and rational features of personality regulation.

The second factor can be described as "confidence". It is formed on such features as self-doubt, feelings of inferiority, insecurity and personal anxiety.

The third factor can be described as "emotional stability", the fourth – "self-regulation" and the fifth – the factor of "family comfort" (Table 1.4.2).

At the same time, the share of selected factors in the amount is 57%, while the value of the percentage contribution of each factor is insignificant.

Analyzing the previous correlation results of the given relations of indicators that characterize the peculiarities of the development of the emotional sphere in

TABLE 1.4.2 Factor structure of indicators characterizing peculiarities of the emotional sphere of 4-year-old children raised in a family and kindergarten

Indicators		*Values*
	Factor 1	
P21 anxiety		0.976
P20 offense		0.868
P22 emotionality		0.849
P19 curiosity, interest		0.786
P23 the emotional-the rational		0.641
% of total variance		15.36
	Factor 2	
P3 self-doubt		−0.94
P4 inferiority feeling		−0.823
P1 insecurity		0.655
P10 anxiety		0.615
% of total variance		12.517
	Factor 3	
P24 emotional resilience		−0.934
P16 joy		0.707
P18 shyness		0.582
% of total variance		10.342
	Factor 4	
P25 self-regulation		−0.889
P17 anger		0.666
% of total variance		9.608
	Factor 5	
P11 confrontation		−0.927
P9 family comfort		0.914
% of total variance		9.236

children four years old from orphanage, we have revealed several sets of relationships. The first of them is formed on the basis of the shyness parameter (P18), which at a rather high level correlates with general emotionality (P22), ($r = 0.8$), anxiety (P21), ($r = 0.7$), frustration (P30), ($r = 0.6$) and others.

The other complex is connected with the manifestation of optimism, i.e. with an indicator of joy (P16).

The results of the research give us grounds to assume that in the structure of emotional features of personal development of children raised in an orphanage, shyness and curiosity are quite pronounced against the background of increased emotionality. It should also be noted that in these children, the relationship between anxiety and frustration indicates their possible resilience.

An in-depth investigation at the level of factor analysis in some way confirms the assumption made above. In the structure of diagnosed indicators, the first place is taken by the factor categorized as "emotional ambivalence", in which the general emotionality and fear, curiosity and shyness, and pleasure and frustration are interrelated. The share of this factor is about 18% (Table 1.4.3).

The other factor here may be described as "internal aggressiveness", which is formed on self-doubt, hostility, self-regulation and confrontation. Its share is about 10%. The third factor in this structure is insignificant in its contribution and is mainly related to communication problems.

As shown in the structure of the factor interrelation of this group of subjects, though the tendency to similarity with the previous group is noted, but the dominant function is associated with a set of indicators that characterize both the general emotionality and its unfavorable background. Thus, summarizing these data, we can note that children raised in orphanages by the development of emotional sphere have approximately the same structure of mechanisms of

TABLE 1.4.3 Factor structure of indicators characterizing specifics of the emotional sphere of children four years old brought up in an orphanage

Indicators		*Values*
	Factor 1	
P22 emotionality		0.99
P21 fear		0.908
P19 curiosity, interest		0.881
P18 shyness		0.87
P16 joy		0.755
P30 frustration		0.633
% of total variance		17.72
	Factor 2	
P3 self-doubt		0.777
P5 hostility		0.751
P25 self-regulation		−0.682
P6 confrontation		−0.681
% of total variance		10.367
	Factor 3	
P7 communication difficulties		0.878
P27 aggressiveness		0.792
P2 anxiety		−0.489
% of total variance		8.65
	Factor 4	
P20 offense, sadness		0.911
P11 confrontation		0.703
P13 hostility		−0.628
% of total variance		8.122
	Factor 5	
P8 depressiveness		0.946
P29 anxiety		−0.55
% of total variance		6.941

interaction of diagnosed indicators, but its orientation is mainly connected with the most clearly traced problems at the level of development of external aggressiveness and communication problems.

Passing to the next age group – **children of five years old, being raised in a family and kindergarten**, we see that in the structure of the correlation between the diagnosed indicators, the leading position is occupied by general emotionality (P22). This is quite evident in the group raised in a family and kindergarten. Here, this indicator correlates with resentment (P20), ($r = 0.8$), curiosity (P19), ($r = 0.7$) and anger (P17), ($r = 0.6$) and has a negative interconnection with confrontation (P11), ($r = -0.5$). In this structure, there are a number of correlations: the indicator of anger with anxiety and confrontation at the level of negative values.

All this gives us reason to say that children raised in kindergarten and family have a significant link between emotionality and curiosity, which can change in the situation of anxiety and confrontation.

The further results of factor analysis show that the first position in the structure of diagnosed indicators here is taken by the factor described as "general emotionality". It can change in case of confrontation situation. Another factor – "family comfort" – indicates that a favorable family situation may be determined by changes in anxiety.

The third factor, described as "passive aggression", forms on the basis of negative value of shyness and positively correlated value of the feeling of inferiority. The remaining factors in this structure are less than 10% (Table 1.4.4).

Examining the previous results of the correlations between data obtained in children from single-parent families, we found that indicators such as emotionality, anxiety, sadness and communication difficulties have the highest number of correlations.

The generalization allows us to consider that an essential component in the structure of the mechanisms of emotional development of children of the given group is, firstly, the features of interrelation of pleasure, anger, shyness and anxiety. Secondly, the interaction of anxiety, feeling of inferiority, hostility and self-doubt. It has also been shown that anxiety, diagnosed by various methods, correlates quite widely with other manifestations of the emotional sphere.

We can explain this by the in-depth fact that at this age the child is already beginning to show his attitude to the conditions of his upbringing in the form of worry, anxiety. This is evidenced by the results of factor analysis (Table 1.4.5), where the first position is taken by the emotionality factor, the share of which is about 25%. The other factor defined as "internal anxiety", and the third – a factor of "emotional self-regulation".

Summarizing the results of correlation and factor study, it can be noted that children raised in a single-parent family, in the structure of emotional development have a rather complicated processes associated with unstable manifestations of general emotionality, the development of anxiety and also with inadequate emotional response to different situations.

TABLE 1.4.4 Factor structure of indicators that characterize the specifics of the emotional sphere of children at the age of five, being raised in a family and kindergarten

Indicators		*Values*
	Factor 1	
P22 emotionality		0.899
P20 offense, sadness		0.895
P21 anxiety		0.799
P17 anger		0.713
P19 curiosity, interest		0.602
P11 confrontation		−0.498
% of total variance		15.171
	Factor 2	
P9 family comfort		0.807
P5 hostility		−0.717
P2 anxiety		−0.656
P25 self-regulation		0.349
P8 depressiveness		0.349
% of total variance		12.316
	Factor 3	
P1 emotional insecurity		0.819
P12 inferiority feeling		−0.721
P16 joy		0.651
% of total variance		9.874
	Factor 4	
P6 confrontation, frustration		0.832
P30 frustration		0.78
P7 communication difficulties		0.439
P23 emotional – rational		−0.376
% of total variance		8.653

The previous results of the correlation analysis of the diagnosed indicators of the emotional sphere, which were obtained in 5-year-old children who were raised in an orphanage, showed that there is a significant amount of sets. Just like in the previous group, there are connections of the indicator of the general emotionality with other parameters. However, a number of complex relationships have been revealed also. In particular, the indicator of family comfort with curiosity, general emotionality and self-regulation at the level of negative values. This may indicate that family comfort in children of this age is associated with inadequate communication.

In the same subgroup, the indicator of self-doubt (P3) has positive correlation with the indicator of depressiveness (P8), (r = 0.5) anxiety (P10), (r = 0.4) and shyness (PI8), (r = 0.5) and negatively correlates with the indicator of confrontation (P11), anger (P17) and sadness (P20). These values, which characterize the general emotionality, are quite closely related to each other. There are also a number of

TABLE 1.4.5 Factor structure of indicators characterizing the specifics of the emotional sphere of 5-year-old children brought up in a single-parent family

Indicators	*Values*
Factor 1	
P22 emotionality	0.984
P21 anxiety, fear	0.95
P19 curiosity, interest	0.911
P20 offense, sadness	0.905
P16 joy	0.855
P17 anger	0.77
P1 insecurity	0.77
P18 shyness	0.734
% of total variance	24.937
Factor 2	
P29 anxiety	−0.96
P23 emotional – rational	0.828
P13 hostility	0.824
P2 anxiety	0.782
P30 frustration	0.776
P9 family comfort	−0.767
P8 depressiveness	−0.581
% of total variance	17.726
Factor 3	
P17 communication difficulties	0.977
P4 inferiority feeling	0.792
P3 self-doubt	0.778
P5 unfriendliness	0.759
P24 emotional resilience	−0.672
P27 aggressiveness	−0.631
% of total variance	16.526

close correlations between hostility parameter at the level of negative values and the indicators of joy, anger, resentment, anxiety and emotionality. The value of curiosity (P19) in this group correlates positively with indicators of content and family comfort, and negatively – with communication difficulties and confrontation.

As seen, the structure of correlational interrelations is distinguished by a greater complexity of the dependence of emotional indicators. We can interpret these relationships by the fact that the children of this group are characterized by increased emotionality. However, more complex transformations are taking place in the structure of its functioning mechanisms, which are characterized by the one hand, increased sensitivity at the level of curiosity and confrontation, as well as by the development of a certain hostility.

The result of in-depth factor analysis shows that the first position in the emotional structure of children from orphanage is taken by the factor that we also called "emotional ambivalence", just like the previous age group. The share of this factor is about 16% (Table 1.4.6). It is formed with opposite emotional features such as joy and confrontation, a favorable family situation, shyness and self-doubt. In the latter case, we can note that on the basis of children's perception of this age of the conditions of upbringing in the orphanage, they obviously form a complex of shyness and self-doubt. The other factor, which we described as "formative frustration", is also represented at the level of 15% and combines a number of opposite in direction and sign emotional features. Such as sadness, anxiety, emotionality and frustration, as well as anger, hostility and aggressiveness.

Based on the above, we can make an assumption that the lack of sufficient emotional comfort in children of this group creates conditions for the development of anxiety, frustration and aggressiveness.

Considering the results of correlation and factor analysis made on indicators obtained in 6-year-old children, it was found that in the group of those raised in a full family, three sets of correlations are clearly distinguished. First, it is a set of indicators related to general emotionality that expanded quite significantly at the level of anger. Secondly, it is a set of correlations, which is mainly formed around parameters of anxiety. Also in this subgroup a number of paired correlational interrelations are revealed.

We can explain the existence of such connections by the fact that, as in the previous group, the general level of emotionality in 6-year-old children raised in a full family is the leading factor. At the same time, there is a certain dependence

TABLE 1.4.6 Factor structure of indicators characterizing the specifics of the emotional sphere of 5-year-old children brought up in an orphanage

Indicators	*Values*
Factor 1	
P16 joy	0.798
P11 confrontation	−0.784
P19 curiosity, interest	0.761
P9 family comfort	0.725
P18 shyness	0.71
P3 self-doubt	0.687
% of total variance	15.797
Factor 2	
P20 sadness	0.899
P17 anger	0.804
P21 anxiety	0.775
P13 hostility	−0.768
P22 emotionality	0.673
P6 frustration	0.613
P27 aggressiveness	0.59
% of total variance	14.87

of changes in anxiety in the expression of optimism, general emotionality, self-regulation and confrontation.

The in-depth results of the factor analysis allowed us to determine that the first position in the structure of the studied interconnections of children raised in a full family is taken by the "emotional sensitivity" factor (15%) (Table 1.4.7). The latter is formed on the general emotionality, resentment, anger, shyness and a certain feeling of inferiority.

Another factor we categorized as the "emotional isolation". It consists of indicators of anxiety, insecurity, frustration, hostility and confrontation. To some extent, the third factor is close in content to the second one. Considering the weight of this factor, we see that the greatest influence on the formation of such a structure has the indicators of hostility and confrontation. Accordingly, we can make an assumption that the upbringing of children in the family in itself involves the emergence of selfishness, which is reflected in such structural changes.

The study of similar correlations and factor data obtained from 6-year-olds raised in a family and kindergarten shows a fairly wide range of correlations that are formed on the basis of two indicators of general emotionality and anxiety.

TABLE 1.4.7 Factor structure of indicators characterizing the specifics of the emotional sphere of six years old children who were brought up only in the family home

Indicators		*Values*
	Factor 1	
P22 emotionality		0.897
P20 offense, sadness		0.873
P17 anger		0.769
P18 shyness		0.739
P4 inferiority feeling		0.631
% of total variance		14.629
	Factor 2	
P16 joy		0.685
P29 anxiety		0.668
P1 insecurity		−0.623
P30 frustration		0.618
P13 unfriendliness		0.581
P6 confrontation		−0.515
% of total variance		12.406
	Factor 3	
P28 confrontation		0.839
P27 aggressiveness		−0.756
P26 emotional excitation		0.691
P10 anxiety		0.662
P15 emotional resilience		0.660
% of total variance		11.945

We explain this relationship by the fact that children raised in a family and kindergarten, on the one hand, have a more favorable and stable relationship between various positive manifestations in the emotional sphere, that is, their peculiarities of the development of the emotional sphere are characterized by more adequate and varied conditions of activity that lead to such a result.

On the other hand, the interaction of anxiety with other features of the emotional sphere may be a certain symptom of their lack of self-regulation in non-standard conditions.

These results are in some way confirmed by in-depth factor analysis (Table 1.4.8). The first factor, which we call "open emotionality", is formed due to curiosity, optimism, resentment and anxiety.

The second factor – "emotional and social adaptation" – indicates that anxiety and shyness, which have a negative correlation, can have a different effect on the peculiarities of a child's emotional behavior. As for the third of the following factors, its weight in the overall structure is quite limited.

The results obtained allow us to make an assumption that a number of social problems arise in children of six years of age who were brought up in the family

TABLE 1.4.8 Factor structure of indicators characterizing the specifics of the emotional sphere of 6-year-old children brought up in a family and kindergarten

Indicators	*Values*
Factor 1	
P22 emotionality	0.987
P19 curiosity, interest	0.937
P20 offense	0.9
P21 fear	0.875
P16 joy	0.838
% of total variance	17.041
Factor 2	
P4 inferiority feeling	0.879
P10 anxiety	−0.726
P18 shyness	−0.568
P17 communication difficulties	0.566
P17 anger	0.488
% of total variance	10.46
Factor 3	
P8 depressivity	0.878
P29 anxiety	−0.703
P3 self-doubt	0.654
P30 frustration	−0.503
% of total variance	8.928
Factor 4	
P28 confrontation	0.898
P25 self-regulation	0.478
% of total variance	5.221

and kindergarten. Obviously, they are related to the inconsistency of the emotional reflection of the conditions of kindergarten, as well as home conditions. The latter circumstance may have a possible influence on the structure of peculiarities of interrelation of diagnosed indicators, which determine the specifics of the development of the emotional sphere.

Examining the previous results of correlations of diagnosed indicators in 6-year-old children from the orphanage, we found a fairly large set of correlations, which are formed at the level of indicators of interest and hostility. Moreover, in the latter case, its values are mostly negative, as hostility (P13) negatively correlates with the indicators of family comfort, optimism, shyness, curiosity, anxiety, general emotionality and emotional resilience. This gives us reason to say that a symptom of hostility in children of this age group may be invoked by a variety of emotional attitudes, and any change in them may cause aggression. As for the indicator of curiosity, which has become the leading indicator in terms of general emotionality, it can be explained by increased emotional activity in the process of realizing their cognitive needs.

Further in-depth factor analysis on this sample showed that the negative tendency in the structure of the development of emotional features in these subjects somewhat prevails over the positive ones. Thus, the first factor (Table 1.4.9), which we refer to in this structure as "ambivalent emotional", is formed due to resentment and curiosity, satisfaction and shyness, fear and self-doubt.

TABLE 1.4.9 Factor structure of indicators characterizing the specifics of the emotional sphere of 6-year-old children brought up in an orphanage

Indicators		*Values*
	Factor 1	
P22 emotionality		0.976
P20 offense		0.827
P19 curiosity		0.827
P16 joy		0.816
P18 shyness		0.796
P21 fear		0.783
P3 self-doubt		0.562
% of total variance		18.354
	Factor 2	
P9 family comfor		−0.87
P5 hostility		0.673
P11 confrontation		0.638
% of total variance		7.96
	Factor 3	
P12 inferiority feeling		0.906
P25 self-regulation		0.639
% of total variance		7.377

The second factor – "aggressiveness" – is formed on the basis of indicators of family comfort, as well as hostility and confrontation. The third and subsequent factors in this structure can only indicate certain tendencies in the unfavorable development of the emotional sphere of children in this group. Here, for children from the orphanage the feeling of inferiority, confrontation, hostility, communicative difficulties and depression occupy priority positions in the structure of diagnosed indicators of emotional sphere.

Summarizing the results of the study in this part, we can note that the specifics of the correlation between the diagnosed indicators of the emotional sphere in children 4–6 years old, brought up in different conditions, has a number of distinctive features that manifest themselves at the level of the tendency to increase the number and the density of connections with changes in educational conditions. Also, the fact that in all structures of diagnosed indicators, regardless of age and upbringing, the overall emotionality is dominant for the number of links detected by other parameters. At the same time, we can also say that the factor structure to some extent confirms, and in some cases supplements, the identified correlations. This is clearly demonstrated by the presence of indicators with opposite values in the structure of factors for children of different ages, who were not raised in the same conditions. This is most clearly expressed in all groups of children raised in an orphanage.

Thus, the results of detailed and in-depth analysis of primary data, between group and correlative differences and factor structures, allow us to identify not only the specifics of the characteristics of changes in the emotional sphere, but also the main features and mechanisms between them. That facilitates to a more adequate approach to the system of prophylaxis and psychotherapy of undesirable manifestations in the emotional sphere in children brought up in different conditions.

1.5 The system of prevention and reduction of negative emotional manifestations in children and its approbation in educational and professional training of psychologists

Based on our own experimental data and other works (Zakharov, 1986; Zaporozhets et al., 1986; Elfimova, 1987; Kulchitskaya, 1981; etc.), aimed to prevent and reduce negative emotional manifestations in children, and considering implementations of the theory of emotional regulation of cognitive activity, we have developed a system of targeted psychological training for students who specialize in the field of child psychology (Tikhomirov, Klochko, 1980).

When selecting such a tool for implementation of the results of the study, we relied primarily on the fact that the reduction of deviations in the development of the emotional sphere of preschool children can not be realized without sufficient professional psychological training of relevant specialists. Secondly, preparing psychologists for practical activities, we also hoped for a large-scale use and implementation of the obtained results in practice.

When creating the content of the psychotherapeutic system of diagnosis and correction of negative emotional manifestations in preschool children, we took into account the previous training of students in age and educational psychology, as well as psychodiagnostics and psychotherapy.

The developed system "Fundamentals of prevention and reduction of negative emotional manifestations in preschool children" is a set of interrelated theoretical and training sessions, built on the basis of adaptation of the working methods and principles presented in the scientific manual "The theory and methodology of emotional regulation of educational activities" (Chebykin, 1999; Chebykin, Maksymenko, 2007).

In constructing this system, we first of all took into account the experimental data obtained in the observational experiment. Namely: undesirable peculiarities of increased manifestation, anxiety, aggressiveness and frustration, in fact, in all children of 4–6 years old, regardless of the conditions of upbringing. Also, this tendency is most evident in children raised in orphanages. The developed system of such specialized psychological training in the field of diagnostics and psychotherapy of negative emotional manifestations in preschool children is designed for its implementation in the training of psychologists.

The theoretical part of this system was designed to update the students' basic understanding of emotions and their functions in the structure of the developing personality. Clarification of the psychological characteristics of the features of the emotional sphere of today's preschool children who are brought up in different social conditions, and in-depth disclosure of the content of the most complicated negative manifestations in the development of the emotional sphere of children.

The practical training part is focused on:

- In the aspect of the last provision, it was envisaged to improve the psychological – exercising skills related to diagnostics of peculiarities of emotional development of preschool children;
- mastering various techniques and methods aimed at prevention and psychotherapy of negative emotional manifestations in preschool children; as well as the forming the basics of their self-regulation.
- preparation of psychology students to conduct consultative work with educators and parents in order to create the necessary conditions for raising children who have a deficit in the development of the emotional sphere.

The proposed system is based on the conceptual understanding of the theory of educational and professional activity aimed primarily at improving the professional competence of students in the field of diagnostics, prevention and psychotherapy of undesirable emotional manifestations in preschool children before the beginning of their psychological practice.

That is, in this case, the process of educational and professional training is conditioned by both internal psychological mechanisms and external psychological and pedagogical conditions of emotion regulation. The combination of the latter makes it possible to provide adequate internal motivation of students and to form the basis of a creative and professional approach to solving problems of prevention and leveling of undesirable emotional manifestations in children.

In designing the program classes, we regarded the psychological mechanisms as certain stages in the development of cognitive activity (orientational-emotional, executive and reflexive-evaluative).

On the first stage, when selecting didactic material, as well as the conditions of its presentation, it was taken into account that the students' minds are dominated by external signs of productive motives for attaining a specific goal. To ensure this stage, the important external psychological conditions were modeling of the novelty effect.

Later, the main content of knowledge and skills related to diagnostics and psychotherapy of children's emotional deviations was considered, the necessity to simulate in the classroom such external psychological and pedagogical conditions that contributed to compassion through dramatization was taken into account. This enabled us to intensify the inner resultant motives for the formation of a general goal aimed at the facts and regularities of both the emergence and changes of undesirable features in the development of the emotional sphere of children. In this case, such conditions contributed to the manifestation of "activating functions of emotions" in mastering of professionally important activities of psychology students.

At the reflective and evaluative stage, in the process of consolidation of knowledge and skills in the students, it is important simulate in the classroom a situation of tension and relaxation, that allowed to form their inner motivation and emotional stability when using the acquired knowledge and skills directly in practical activities.

Generally speaking, the developed system consisted of a programmatic material designed for 24 hours, which includes 8 theoretical and 16 practical training sessions.

In theoretical sessions, the novelty effect was achieved by creating problematic situations. For example, stating the ambivalence of the emotion function. That is, when the same emotion in the same situation is demonstrated with positive and negative consequences for the child's development. Further on, the effect of dramatization was achieved through the selection of appropriate material, which illustrated the difficulties of integrating emotions. At the final stage, we modeled problematic situations, in which students were asked to identify the functions of emotions on the basis of their knowledge. For example, they were offered photographs of children with an incorrect assessment of emotional expression. The students' task was to find arguments that could confirm or give an adequate assessment of emotional expression.

When considering the psychological characteristics of the age specifics of the emotional sphere of preschool children, the novelty effect was achieved by identifying neoplasms in the emotional development of children 4–6 years old through demonstrating certain of their features. The effect of dramatization was created by revealing the contradictions of the influence of external and internal factors on the development of children's emotional sphere. During the consolidation of knowledge, students were given different characteristics of children's emotional development, with deliberately wrong features. The students' task was to find and correct those incorrect features.

When considering the topic "Psychological analysis of negative emotional features in the development of the emotional sphere of children", the novelty effect was achieved through the presentation of difficulties in identifying negative manifestations in the emotional sphere, which occur on the verge of health and pathology. This was achieved by illustrating various external features of children's faces and the characteristics of certain modalities of emotions.

Further on, the effect of dramatization was achieved through the modeling of emotional manifestations at the level of state and properties. For example, anxiety was considered as a state and a property. In order to consolidate the acquired knowledge, students were offered facial expressions with various negative emotional manifestations. Students had to group emotions according to their likeness. For example, all those that have a symptom of aggression or anxiety.

Practical training sessions directly combined theoretical and practical parts.

Thus, when considering the aspects of preschool children's emotional development diagnostics, the novelty effect was achieved by citing examples that demonstrated insufficient effectiveness to assess the development of emotional characteristics of children by using only one technique. The results of different methods, which evaluated one property of the emotional sphere and had both differences and common characteristics were demonstrated. For example, anxiety according to the Taylor method, and according to the Luscher Color Test. At the further stage, when mastering a comprehensive approach to the diagnosis of the emotional sphere, the dramatization effect was achieved due to the complexity of the combination of different theoretical and methodological concepts laid both in the basis for understanding emotions themselves and methodological foundations in constructing of the strategy. During the consolidation and use of the methods, the effect of the tension was achieved by various methodological remarks of the opponents, when the students defended the obtained own results of the diagnostics.

When reviewing and mastering the approaches of techniques in "Prevention and psychotherapy of negative emotional manifestations in preschool children", the novelty effect was achieved by modeling the complexity of differentiation, such peculiarities of the emotional sphere as frustration, fear and others. This was achieved by selection and illustration of didactic materials, both external and internal manifestations of these features.

The complexity of identifying situational and static moments in these features and choosing adequate methods of their correction was emphasized. Subsequently, in modeling the situation of dramatization, a comparative analysis of different techniques and methods aimed at correcting the deviations in the emotional sphere was carried out. At the same time, attention was drawn to the fact that violation of the sequence in their implementation may lead to insufficient influence on the peculiarities of the emotional sphere of children. Also in this aspect, it was shown that combining different methodologies in psychocorrection can also be positive in some cases and negative in others. During the consolidation of mastered techniques and methods of psychocorrection, the students were offered certain methods and techniques which were focused on the elimination of deviations in emotional features that were inadequate in their target orientation. For example, some techniques that were not adequate for use at this age were illustrated.

When reviewing the topic "Psychological counseling of educators and parents in dealing with children with deviations in the emotional sphere", the novelty effect was achieved by modeling examples of limited understanding and incompetent attitude of adults to negative manifestations in the emotional sphere of children. In other words, the urgent appeal to the prevention of undesirable manifestations in the emotional sphere of children was emphasized. Later on, when implementing specific activities for teachers and parents, for effective dramatization were given examples of plans and scenarios for such activities, which drew attention to the active involvement of parents in both understanding the peculiarities of children's emotional development and creating adequate conditions for emotional education. In conclusion, in order to consolidate the skills associated with counseling of parents and teachers, were given specific examples of improper tactics in the organization of this process. The students' task was to identify this and suggest the right approaches and methods for consultation of teachers and parents.

In approbation of the proposed system of psychological and pedagogical experiment were involved 25 students, divided into two subgroups: experimental, which included 12 people who underwent special training, and a control group, which included 13 people who took a special course "Children's Anxiety".

After the experiment on the educational and training part, the traditional attestation of students was carried out, after which they were sent to practice. In the process and at the end of the internship the students of the control and experimental groups studied the effectiveness of acquired knowledge and skills based on self-assessment and expert assessment (the latter was completed by practical psychologists). As mentioned above, the following competencies were assessed:

- Identification of the necessity of prevention and psychotherapy of deviations in the emotional sphere of children (P31);
- adequacy of identification and use of diagnostic tools for studying peculiarities of the emotional sphere of children (P32);
- effectiveness of counseling teachers and parents on the prevention and leveling of unwanted emotional manifestations in children (P33);
- effectiveness of using techniques, prevention and psychotherapy of negative emotional manifestations in children and self-regulation (P34).

As the results of approbation and implementation of the suggested system show, students who have passed the training on the indicator of the necessity of assessment of the deviations in the emotional sphere of children have only a tendency to differ, but statistically they do not differ significantly. So, we can assert that all students in fact equally define the problem as urgent. The only difference is that the students of the experimental group better differentiate the problems in emotional development.

Regarding the indicator of diagnostics of the development of peculiarities of the emotional sphere by the average signs, there is a significant difference. As the further statistical analysis shows, the students of the experimental group are statistically significantly reliable differ from the students of the control group ($t = 4.6$; $P < 0.01$).

Based on this, we can say that students who have undergone special training are more effective in using diagnostic tools of peculiarities of the emotional sphere in preschool children. That is, they are more competent. This is evidenced by the qualitative analysis of the obtained results, when students of the control group only listed the possible methods, and those from experimental group actually used them in their work in practice.

Considering the importance of the indicator of psychological counseling of teachers and parents, we also see a very significant difference between the data of the control and experimental groups. In the latter group, this difference is statistically reliable ($t = 4.9$; $P < 0.01$).

That is, we can say that in practice, students who mastered the proposed system were more competent to conduct psychological counseling of educators and parents on problems that arise in the field of emotional education. The data of those consultative conversations, both individual and group, which were conducted by the students of the experimental group in practice, have proved to be very qualitative. These included discussions such as "Development of the emotional sphere in preschool children", "Overcoming fear and aggression" and so on. The control group gave only fragmentary instructions on how to organize such work.

Considering the obtained data, after the practical course on the indicator of psychotherapy of negative emotional manifestations and the development of self-regulation, we noticed a very significant difference between the parameters of competence in experimental and control groups. An in-depth analysis revealed a reliable difference between them (Table 1.5.1).

Thus, we can say that the students of the experimental group implement in practice various technologies and approaches aimed at prevention and reduction of negative emotional manifestations in children. This is evidenced by a qualitative analysis of methods and techniques they used when working with children, educators and parents. Most of all, it was achieved by modulating different social and psychological conditions of interaction, communication, role-playing and competitive games, positive incentives and more. Summarizing the results of testing of the proposed system, it should be noted that its implementation in the

TABLE 1.5.1 Specific features of statistically verifiable differences in the indicators that characterize the competence of psychological training of the students of the control and experimental groups in determining the diagnosis and prevention of manifestations in the emotional sphere of children

Statistical values	*Indicators*			
	P_{31} E C	P_{32} E C	P_{33} E C	P_{34} E C
x	3.23 3.08	2.58 0.58	3.0 2.31	3.3 2.15
x2	0.83 0.67	0.67 0.48	0.59 0.51	0.46 0.31
t	= 0.49	=4.6*	= 4.9*	= 5.0*

**Significant differences at P <0.01; E – experimental group; C – control group.*

educational and professional training of students was positively reflected in the direct practical work on the prevention and psychotherapy of negative emotional manifestations during the student's internship.

Thus, as a result of scientific and methodological research, the system of purposeful training of students of psychology in the diagnostics and psychotherapy of negative emotional manifestations in preschool children has been developed and tested. Its grounding on conceptual understanding of the theory of emotion regulation of educational and professional activity and the regularity of combining theoretical knowledge and practical skills proved to be effective.

It was found that students who underwent a specialized system of training in the period of psychological practice, more effectively used the skills of diagnosing features of the emotional sphere and means of prevention and psychocorrection of negative emotional manifestations in children compared to students who did not pass this training. This is evidenced by statistically significant differences between the control and experimental groups, on such indicators as: competence in the psychotherapy of disorders in the emotional sphere of children; diagnostics of the development of the emotional sphere; counseling of teachers and parents; correction of negative emotional manifestations and the development of self-regulation.

****

In general, the obtained both theoretical and imperial data allow us to note that the system of conditions that influence the development of the emotional sphere of the child is a rather complex formation. It can be divided into biological and socio-psychological partitions. Both of them are closely intertwined in the real development. At the same time, the ratio of both biological and social factors changes at different stages of child's development. The influence of social and psychological conditions essentially determines the development of the child's emotional sphere. At the same time, the nature of its formation can have both positive and negative sides.

It is shown that a significant part of the child's emotional experience (i.e. dynamics of expressive actions, adequacy of emotional response, development of empathy, self-regulation, as well as expressiveness of emotional features, anxiety, sensitivity, frustration, etc.) is formed under the influence of social conditions in the preschool period. Given the latter provision, it can be argued that the peculiarities of the development of the emotional sphere of the child are determined by the specific conditions of his or her upbringing.

The more complete the social status of these conditions, the more favorable the development of the emotional status of the child. Based on the performed analysis and real observations of the conditions of upbringing, we distinguish the following groups of children. These are those who are brought up: only in families; in families and preschools; in single-parent families (one of the parents or close relatives); and in children's homes.

Based on the analysis of primary indicators characterizing the peculiarities of the development of the emotional sphere in 4-year-old children who were brought up only in the family, it was found that the greatest variability is in the indicators of hostility, anxiety and others. The individual value of indicators, which characterize manifestations of various modalities of emotions, is noteworthy. Here the variance between individual values ranges from high levels to rather low. Moderate variability here is the manifestation of emotional stability, self-regulation, anxiety and frustration.

Considering the data obtained in the study of 4-year-old children who were raised both in the family and in kindergarten, we have managed to find that such indicators as anxiety and communication difficulties have a significant variance in individual values. Of great importance for us are the individual values of children's primary data from the orphanage. Paradoxically, they were the most discordant in this sample in terms of anxiety, communication difficulties, hostility, confrontation and emotional resilience.

Certain specifics have the data that characterize the individual peculiarities of the emotional sphere of children at the age of five. Referring to these data, children who grew up in a family and kindergarten, have a sufficiently pronounced variance in the values of such indicators as anxiety and hostility. The individual values of indicators that characterize the peculiarities of the development of the emotional sphere in children of five years of age, who were brought up in a single-parent family, show that they have a similar tendency to the previous group. However, they are most clearly manifested by the indicator of anxiety. Five-year-olds from an orphanage have slightly different primary data. The greatest variability in this group was in the indicators of hostility, communication difficulties, confrontation, anxiety and frustration.

Looking at the results of the primary indicators characterizing the emotional sphere of 6-year-old children who were raised in a family home, we found that the greatest variability is observed in the rate of hostility and communication difficulties, as well as family comfort. The data obtained in 6-year-old children from orphanages indicate that the tendency of variability observed in previous groups is still present here. The analysis of primary data from the examined groups showed that there are children with different levels of manifestations of diagnosed indicators that characterize the peculiarities of the emotional sphere development.

Summarizing the results of the analysis of all primary data reflecting the peculiarities of the development of the emotional sphere of children, we can state that in all groups there was variability in the range from minimum to maximum values of the indicators. It is most clearly seen in manifestations of anxiety, aggression, emotional stability and frustration. These tendencies in variability may indicate that selected subgroups differ in the specificity of the manifestation of the values of individual indicators that characterize the peculiarities of the development of the emotional sphere of children. This is also confirmed by the average values of the diagnosed manifestations of parameters that have different features of their representation. This gives grounds to assert that there are certain differences in certain features of the emotional sphere of children in the examined subgroups. However, in order to confirm the presence or absence of such differences, it was not necessary to conduct an in-depth analysis for their validity.

The results of a study carried out according to the "House. Tree. Man" method show that children raised only in the family statistically and reliably differ from children raised in the family and kindergarten by parameters of self-doubt, frustration, communication difficulties and depressiveness. There are clear differences between this group and children from the orphanage by parameters of self-doubt and frustration. At the same time, the data characterizing the emotional sphere of children raised in families and kindergartens are statistically reliable and different from the data of children from orphanages. Differences were found in such indicators as anxiety and difficulties in communication.

It should be noted that the differences identified by this methodology in some way indicate that children who stayed in the orphanage are more distrustful and less anxious, while children raised solely in a family are less frustrated and more cooperative.

Analyzing the results of the research related to the identification of statistically reliable differences in the indicators obtained with the help of selected techniques between subgroups of 4-year-old children, we also found a number of differences. In particular, between groups of children who stayed only in the family and children who were raised in the family and kindergarten. The greatest number of differences was found in the parameters of optimism, shyness and curiosity, anger, anxiety and resentment. This group of children differs from children from the orphanage by indicators of curiosity, resentment and anxiety. The results obtained can be explained by the fact that children raised only in the family, compared to children in other groups have the least anxiety, are less shy and abusive. Children from orphanage, compared to children who were raised in different environments, were more anxious, more easily offended and less inquisitive.

The following results were obtained using the "House. Tree. Man." technique. It was found that the greatest number of reliable differences in the importance of the development of the emotional sphere in children at the age of five was found between children from orphanages compared to those from single-parent families, in particular, by the indicator of anxiety and frustration. There are also differences between children raised in a family and a kindergarten by the parameter of self-doubt, and children who were raised only in the family by the parameter of frustration.

The differences found to some extent indicate that the children who were brought up: a) in the orphanage – are less anxious, more frustrated and untrustworthy compared to other children; and b) in the family only – feel more protected, but less confident and frustrated.

The data obtained with the help of the "Kinetic picture of the family", "Anxiety test" and "Tapping test" methods from 5-year-old children show that the greatest number of significant differences was found between children who were brought up only in the family and those who stayed in a family home and a day care center, in particular, for the indicator of family comfort, anxiety, confrontation, emotional stability and others. It has been established that children from orphanages differ significantly in terms of family comfort from children who were raised only in the family. Similar differences were found in this regard for the indicator of confrontation and emotional stability. These children also differ from children raised in a family and kindergarten in terms of anxiety and inferiority. The results can be explained by the fact that children who were raised only in a family environment, compared to other children, feel greater family comfort, less anxiety and confrontation, feeling of inferiority and greater emotional stability. Children from orphanages compared to children raised under other conditions have situationally pronounced anxiety, as well as heightened confrontation.

The results of the research obtained with the help of the "House. Tree. Man" method showed that data on the peculiarities of the emotional sphere development in 6-year-old children, who were brought up in different conditions, in some cases have significant differences. It was found that children who were brought up only in the family, statistically and reliably differ from children who stayed in the family and kindergarten by the parameter of anxiety; and from children with only one parent – by parameters of frustration and depression; and from children from the orphanage – by insecurity and self-doubt. The obtained results give us grounds to note that the greatest difference in the subgroups of 6-year-olds who were brought up under different conditions was found between those who, first, were brought up only in the family and orphanage, and those raised in a family and kindergarten, with children from an orphanage. As seen, children from orphanages differ in almost all of their emotional areas from children who were raised only in a family and kindergarten.

Analysis of research results related to the identification of statistically reliable differences in indicators obtained using other techniques ("Kinetic picture of the family", "Tapping test", "Anxiety test"), between different subgroups of 6-year-olds, revealed a number of similar trends. The greatest number of statistically reliable differences was also found between children raised only in the family and children from orphanages. In particular, by parameters of anxiety, confrontation and feeling of inferiority. Children from orphanages differ from children raised in kindergarten and family in terms of family comfort and aggressiveness.

According to the "Expert assessment of different emotions modality manifestations" method and the "The ratio of emotional and rational behavior" test, statistically valid differences are clearly recorded between children raised in families and kindergartens, and children from orphanages by such parameters as timidity, anxiety and general emotionality. The children who stayed in the orphanage also differ statistically significantly from the children raised in a single-parent family. The same is true for the parameters of shyness and general emotionality. These results may indicate that children raised in an orphanage are less shy and less touchy, but are more anxious than children raised in a family setting. They are also less emotional, that is, they show less optimism and curiosity.

The analysis of the data obtained in the subgroups of 6-year-old children indicates that with the changes in the social status of education, the peculiarities of the development of their emotional sphere also change. It is most clearly seen between the groups of children in the orphanage and others raised in different family settings.

This analysis allows us to note: first, the children from orphanage by a number of indicators differ statistically and reliably from the others by the parameters of anxiety, resentment, anger and feeling of inferiority. There is also a negative interrelations correlation between aggressiveness, anxiety and confrontation.

These interrelations can be explained by the fact that general emotionality is the leading factor in this structure. Children of the same age, who were brought up both in the family and in kindergarten, have a more complex structure of the interrelations. Here were revealed five major sets of correlations that are formed around the curiosity indicator. The latter at a sufficiently high level correlates with joy, anxiety, general emotionality and self-regulation. Also, as in the previous group, a significant number of correlations were found in the indicator of general emotionality. It seems to develop a whole new set of relations of the above-mentioned correlator with the latter at a fairly high level. Besides, the indicator of general emotionality also correlates with joy, anxiety and self-regulation. In this subgroup, a number of negatively correlated relationships between aggressiveness and self-doubt, feelings of inferiority and frustration were found. An in-depth factor analysis shows that the revealed interrelations find their reflection in the factor structure in some way. Based on the presented results, the first factor can be described as "emotional-cognitive", and it includes situational anxiety and resentment, general emotionality, as well as curiosity and balance of emotional and rational peculiarities of the personality regulation. The second factor – "confidence" – is formed on such parameters as self-doubt, feelings of inferiority, insecurity and personal anxiety.

The developed system of diagnostics and reduction of negative emotional manifestations in preschool children is a complex of interrelated theoretical and training sessions, based on the concept of emotional regulation of educational and professional activities, and designed for students of psychology. The theoretical part of this system includes: expanding the basic notions of students about emotions and their functions in the structure of the developing personality; clarification of the psychological characteristics of the features of the emotional sphere development in today's preschool children who are brought up in different conditions, as well as in-depth disclosure of the nature of the most complex negative manifestations in the development of children's emotional sphere.

The practical part of this system is aimed at forming the basis for the diagnostics of prevention and psychotherapy of negative features in the emotional sphere of preschool children. As a result of this experiment, we observed significant changes in the value of prevention indicator at the level of psychological counseling of teachers and parents between the control and experimental groups ($t = 4.9$; $P < 0.01$).

It was found that data of features of psychotherapy of negative emotional manifestations and the development of self-regulation after the formative experiment increased more in the experimental group compared to the control group ($t = 5.0$; $P < 0.01$).

The results of the formative experiment allow us to conclude that the students who underwent special training (experimental group) are better prepared in diagnosing the peculiarities of the emotional sphere, by using psychocorrection methods while dealing with adverse events, and in counseling parents and educators, compared to students who have not undergone such training (control group).

1.6 Conclusions

1. It has been shown that the development of the emotional sphere of preschool children is influenced by both internal factors of biological and psychophysiological nature as well as external socio-psychological conditions of the specifics of family upbringing, informality of mutual relations between children and the conditions of educational process in different institutions. The most widespread are four types of upbringing conditions, namely: only in the family; in single-parent families and kindergartens; in single-parent families; and in orphanages.
2. It was found that the greatest variability in the examined children, from the minimum to the maximum values, is observed in the indicators of anxiety, aggressiveness, emotional stability and frustration. At the same time, no significant difference was observed between children of different genders. In each age group, there are children where the level of evaluated indicators has a complex structure, that is, different indicators have ambiguous representations.

3 It is proved that the data on anxiety, aggressiveness, depressiveness, emotional stability and frustration in the context of difficulties in communication on its average values tended to differ in each age group among children educated in different socio-psychological conditions.

4 It has been revealed that children:

- Four-year-olds brought up in an orphanage differ statistically and reliably from children raised in a family and kindergarten by a number of indicators, namely indicators of self-doubt, frustration, family comfort and resentment;
- Five-year-olds from the orphanage are also statistically and reliably different in terms of anxiety and frustration from children raised in a single-parent family, and in terms of self-doubt, curiosity and general emotionality from children who stayed in the family and kindergarten. There is also a significant difference in indicators of frustration, family comfort, confrontation, emotional resilience, anger, curiosity and resentment between them and a subgroup of children who had been raised only in the family;
- Six-year-olds from the orphanage have a statistically significant difference with children raised in the family and kindergarten on the following indicators: insecurity, feelings of inferiority, frustration, hostility and communication difficulties. They also differ in indicators of insecurity, self-doubt, frustration and difficulties in communication with children who were brought up only in the family. There were some statistically reliable differences in individual indicators between children raised in the family and those who stayed in the family and kindergarten. Quantitatively, they are more represented in children of four years old by indicators of anxiety and communication difficulties. This gives us grounds to state that children from orphanages differ from other children by more pronounced frustration and aggressiveness, confrontation and a lower degree of shyness. They also have some communication difficulties.

5 It has been experimentally proved that in the structure of children's emotional development mechanisms (regardless of age, sex and conditions of upbringing), the main factor is the general emotionality or its separate components. This is evidenced by the data of correlation and factor analysis. The latter shows that an important factor in the development of the emotional sphere of children **aged four**, who were brought up only in the family, is general emotionality (15%), aggressiveness and cognitive activity (12%); for children raised in the family and kindergarten – emotional and cognitive orientation (15%) and self-regulation (12%); for children from the orphanage – emotional ambivalence (-18%) and internal aggressiveness (17%). In children **aged five**, who were brought up: in the family and kindergarten – general emotionality (-15%); family comfort and aggressiveness (-12%); in children from single-parent families – emotional instability

and self-regulation (-25%); and in those from the orphanage – emotional ambivalence (-15%) and frustration (-14%). **Six-year-old** children that were raised: only in the family – emotional sensitivity (-15%) and emotional isolation (-12%); for those who stayed in the family and kindergarten – open emotionality (-17%); and for children from the orphanage – ambivalent emotionality (-18%) and aggressiveness (-7%).

6 A targeted system for the prevention and reduction of emotionally negative manifestations in preschool children has been developed.

The testing and implementation of the proposed system in the professional training of psychology students in practice significantly increased their professional competence in diagnostics of the development of emotional features, the level of necessity to decrease negative emotional manifestations in children, their psychocorrection, and the counseling of teachers and parents in this regard.

References

Abolin, L.M. (1987). *Psychological mechanisms of human emotional stability.* Kazan: Kazan University Press.

Anokhin, P.K. (1964). *Emotions.* In: Big Medical Encyclopedia: Vol. 35. Moscow: Publishing house medicine, 339357.

Bekh, I.D. (1988) *Features of the psychological mechanism of volitional awakening.* In: Emotional regulation of educational activities. Materials of the conference of the Academy of Pedagogical Sciences, Moscow, 8–10.

Bozhovich, L.I. (1995). *Problems of personality formation.* Moscow. Voronezh: Publishing House Academy of Pedagogical Sciences, 135–302.

Breslav, G.M. (1986). *Upbringing of moral norms of the child in the family.* Voprosy Psychologii, 1, 41–47.

Burmenskaya, G.V., Karabanov, O.A., Leaders, A.G. (1990). *Age-psychological counseling.* Moscow: Publishing house Moscow State University.

Chebykin, O.Y. (1999). *Theory and methods of emotional regulation of educational activities.* Handbook. Odessa: AstroPrint.

Chebykin, O.Y., Maksymenko (2007). *Emotional regulation of the learning process, ergonomics and psychology developments in theory and practice.* London: CRC Press, Taylor and Francis, Boca Raton, London, New York, 325–339.

Chebykin, O.Y., Soprun, I.P. (2003). *Emotional sphere of children and features of its development.* Odessa: The Academy of Pedagogical Sciences of Ukraine.

Darwin, C. (1953). *Expression of emotions in animals and men.* Collected works, Vol. 5. Moscow.

Davydov, V.V., Elkonin, D.B., Markova, A.K. (1978). *The main issues of modern psychology of primary school children.* In: Problems of general, age and pedagogical psychology. Moscow: Academy of Pedagogical Sciences, 180–205.

Denisova, Z.V. (1978). *Mechanisms of emotional behavior of the child.* Leningrad: Nauka.

Elfimova, N.V. (1987). *Functions of emotions in creating a motivational component of activity.* In: Emotional regulation of educational activity. Moscow: Publishing house materials of the conference of emotional regulation of educational activity, 24–31.

Elkonin, D.B. (1971). *To the problem of periodization of mental development in childhood.* Voprosy Psychologii, 4, 6–20.
Galiguzova, L.N., Mishcheryakova, S.Y., Tsaregordtseva, L.M. (1990). *Psychological aspects of the education of children in orphanages and children's homes.* Voprosy Psychologii, 6, 17–25.
Izard, K.E. (1980). *Human emotions.* Moscow: Publishing House of Moscow State University.
Kistyakovskaya, M.Y. (1965). *About stimuli causing positive emotions at the child of the first months of life.* Voprosy Psychologii, 2, 137–138.
Kovalev, A.G. (1971). *Education of feelings.* Moscow: Pedagogika.
Kulchitskaya, E.I. (1981). *Education of feelings in a child.* Kiev: Institute of Psychology Kyiv.
Langmeier, I., Matejczek, Z. (1984). *Mental deprivation in childhood.* Prague: Progress Publishing.
Leontiev, A.N. (1971). *Needs, motives, emotions.* Lecture notes. Moscow: Publishing House of Moscow State University.
Leontiev, A.N. (1983). *Selected psychological works:* In 2 volumes. Moscow: Pedagogika.
Lindsley, D.B. (1960). *Emotions.* In: Experimental psychology. Moscow: Inostrannaya Literatura Publishing, 629–684.
Lisina, M.I. (1983). *Education of young children in the family.* Kiev: Znanie, 1983.
Lisina, M.I. 1983. (not Sh.) *Upbringing of younger children in the family.* Moscow: Znanie
Lomov, B.F. (1984). *Methodological and theoretical problems of psychology.* Moscow: Nauka.
Luk, A.N. (1982). *Emotions and personality.* Moscow: Znanie.
Makarova, E.I. (1968). *The development of emotion in children of early age.* In: Physiology of higher nervous activity. Moscow: Academy of pedagogical sciences publishing house.
Menchinskaya, N.A. (1996). *Psychological development of a child from birth to ten years.* Moscow: IPP.
Moskalenko, V.D. (1991). *A child in an "alcoholic" family: psychological portrait.* Voprosy Psychologii, 4, 65–73.
Mukhina, V.S. (1985). *Child psychology.* Moscow: Prosveshcheniye.
Mukhina, V.S. (1986). *Psychology of a preschool child.* Alma-Ata: Mektep.
Mukhina, V.S. (1985) *Psychological assistance to children brought up in boarding schools.* Voprosy Psychologii, 32–39.
Olshannikova, A.E. (1979). *From three to twelve (on the emotional upbringing of preschoolers and primary school children).* Semja i Schkola, 9, 26–28.
Olshannikova, A.E. (1983). *Emotions and education.* – Moscow: Znanie.
Pashina, A.K., Ryazanova, E.P. (1993). *Features of the emotional sphere of inmates and staff of orphanages.* Journal of Psychology, 14, 1, 44–52.
Repina, T.A. (1962). *Senses of the child.* Doshkolnoe Vospitanije, 1, 26–35.
Rogers, K. (1984). *Empathy.* In: Psychology of emotions. Texts. Moscow: Moscow State Uni Publishing house of Moscow State University.
Royak, A.A. (1977). *Emotional well-being of a child in a kindergarten group.* Doshkolnoe Vospitanije, 2, 12.
Rubinstein, S.L. (1999). *Fundamentals of general psychology.* Moscow: UchPedGiz, 1946 (Re-edition. St. Petersburg: Peter, 1999).
Ruzskaya, P.G., Abramova, L.N. (1990). *How to treat complaints of preschool children in kindergarten.* Voprosy Psychologii, 4, 96–103.
Sannikova, O.P. (1988). *Emotionality as a factor in the regulation of difficulties in communication.* In: Emotional regulation of educational activities. Moscow: USSR Academy of Pedagogical Sciences Publishing, 233–238.

Shingarov, G.K. (1971). *Emotions and feelings as a form of reality reflection*. Moscow: Nauka.
Simonov, P.V. (1966). *What is an emotion?* Moscow: Nauka.
Slivina, L.S. (1966). *Children with affective behavior*. Moscow: Prosveshchenie.
Slutsky, V.M. (1996). *Social isolation and mental development in older preschoolers: An analysis of the cognitive, emotional and personal development*. Journal of psychology, 1, 86–96.
Smirnova, E.O., Lagutina, A.E. (1991). *Awareness of experience of children in the family and in kindergarten*. Voprosy Psychologii, 6, 30–37.
Soprun I., Chebykin, A. (2020). *On methods for studying the emotional characteristics of children 4–6 years old (scientific and methodological recommendations)*. Odessa: Ushinsky University.
Spivakovskaya, A.S. (1988). *The prevention of children's neuroses. Complex psychological correction*. Moscow: Publishing House of Moscow University.
Tatenko N.A. (1988). *Psychological features of readiness for school of six-years-old children with deviations in the emotional and volitional sphere*: Dissertation abstract. Kiev.
Tikhomirov, O.K., Klochko, V.E. (1980). *Emotional regulation of mental activity*. Voprosy Psychologii, 5, 23–31.
Tsaregorodtseva, L.M. (1990). *Psychological aspects of raising children in orphanages and children's homes*. Voprosy Psychologii, 6, 17–25.
Vallon, A. (1967). *Mental development of a child*. Moscow: Prosveschenije.
Vasiliev, I.A. (1998). *The role of intellectual emotions in regulation of mental activity*. Journal of Psychology, 4, 49–60.
Vilyunas, V.K. (1984). *The main problems of the psychological theory of emotion*. In: Psychology of emotions. Texts. Moscow: Moscow State Uni Publishing House of Moscow State University, 3–28.
Vilyunas, V.K. (1990). *Psychological mechanisms of human motivation*. Moscow: Publishing House of Moscow State University.
Volosova, E. (1979). *Development of emotions in children*. Preschool #ducation, 11, 57–59.
Zakharov, A.I. (1986). *How to identify fears in children*. Moscow: Pedagogika.
Zalysina, I.A., Smirnova, E.O. (1985). *Some features of the psychological development of preschoolers brought up outside the family*. Voprosy Psyhologii, 4, 31–38.
Zaporozhets, A.V., Neverovich, Y.Z. (1974). *About genesis, function and structure of emotional processes in a child*. Voprosy Psychologii, 6, 59–73.
Zaporozhets, A.V., Neverovich, Y.Z., Kosheleva, A.D. et al. (1986). *Development of social emotions in preschool children*. Moscow: Moscow State University publishing house 258–284.
Zaporozhets, A.V. (1986a). Selected psychological works. (in 2 vol.). Moscow: Pedagogy Publishing House.
Zaporozhets, A.V. (1986b). *Psychological development of the child*. Moscow, 1, 2, 258–284.
Zaporozhets, O.V., Neverovich, Y.Z. (1974). *About genesis, function and structure of emotional processes in a child*. Voprosy Psychologii, 6, 59–73.

2

A STUDY OF THE EMOTIONAL DEVELOPMENT OF CHILDREN AND ADOLESCENTS 7–17 YEARS OLD

The study of the emotional sphere of children is the subject of numerous studies (Zaporozhets, Neverovich, 1974; Kulchitskaya, 1981; Chebykin, Melnichuk, 2004; etc.). The relevance of understanding the process of emergence, genesis and influence of emotions in the life of a child is due to their integrative approaches and close interweaving with various functions of the psyche (Vilyunas, 1984; Dodonov, 1987; Sannikova, 1984; Rubinstein, 1976; Tikhomirov, 1980; etc.).

Summarizing various studies (Grote, 1880; Izard, 1980; Lindsley, 1960; Nosenko, Egorova, 1996; Reikovsky, 1979; etc.), we may note that emotions, as integral components of mental activity, change the process of human life. The influence of emotions on the course of many mental processes intensifies the need to understand the mechanisms of their emergence, development and their possible correction in the educational process.

Available data regarding the development of emotional characteristics in children of different ages and genders (Avdeeva, Meshcheryanova, 1991; Bauer, 1985; Kon, 1978; Lichko, 1983; Mukhina, 1985; Elkonin, 1960; etc.) demonstrate insufficient study of this problem. At the same time, some researches (Viskovatova, 1976; Isaev, 2000; Kulchitskaya, 1981; etc.) acknowledge numerous complications in the development of the emotional sphere of children.

On the basis of theoretical and experimental studies performed, this work shows that such features as multidirectional anxiety, family aggressiveness and emotional lability are informative indicators in the dynamics of the emotional sphere of children, depending on their age and gender. The methodological system for studying the emotional sphere of children at the level of assessing emotional maturity has been further developed. The characterization of the genesis of the emotional sphere of children has been clarified according to the data on the intensity of anxiety manifestation in children, adolescents, boys and girls aged 8, 11, 14 and 17; self-regulation and empathy in boys and girls

DOI: 10.4324/9781003330943-2

aged 16; aggression – in children, adolescents, boys and girls aged 9, 11 and 16; depression – in adolescents of 12 and 13 years old; emotional lability in adolescents, boys and girls aged 11, 13 and 17.

We hope that the presented results of the research will be useful both for specialists studying the problem of the development of emotions and for practical psychologists working in the system of education.

2.1 Functions of emotions in the development of personality

The problem of the functions of emotions is one of the central ones both in purely methodological studies and in theoretical and experimental studies (Vasilishina, 2000; Kulchitskaya, 1981; Olshannikova, 1983; etc.). Works of Abolin (1987), Kalin (1983), Chebykin, Melnichuk (2004) and other researchers show that more than twenty functions of emotions are recorded in modern psychology. At the same time, the question of their systematic description remains open. In fact, all researchers in their studies directly or indirectly analyze the functions of emotions. In psychology, the idea of the positive and negative influence of emotions on human behavior and activity is most clearly stated. There are works in which attempts are made to classify emotions on the basis of their functions (Woodworth, 1950; Wundt, 1984; Grote, 1880; Simonov, 1966).

Other authors reduce the number of emotion functions to specific activation mechanisms. In particular, these are such functions as incentive (Leeper, 1984), mobilizing (Vilyunas, 1984; Lindsley, 1960) and activating (Vilyunas, 1984; Lindsley, 1960). Thus, E. Gellhorn believes that the acceleration and enhancement of reactions that support the individual's and species' existence of living systems is one of the most striking features of emotional response. When emotions arise, the activation of nerve centers occurs, carried out by non-specific structures of the brain stem that transmits excitation in non-specific ways (Ilyin, 2001). Some authors consider "incentive" and "motivating" functions as manifestations of one (Leeper, 1984; Petrazhitsky, 1993; etc.). Other authors (Vilyunas, 1984; Lindsley, 1960; etc.) define activating or mobilization-activating (Kulchitskaya, 1981) function of emotions as one of the leading ones. According to the "activation" theory, emotions provide an optimal level of excitation of the central nervous system and its specific substructures. Activation of the nervous system and, first of all, its vegetative structure results in changes in both internal organs and the whole organism, thereby causing the mobilization (or demobilization) of energy resources.

The other group of researchers (Kulchitskaya, 1981) believes that the activation of the nerve centers and the whole organism, which occurs during emotional arousal, implies this function. It (the function) depends on the individual characteristics of a person, therefore it cannot be considered generally valid. It is known that changes in the activity of internal organs – the mobilization of the body's forces – depend on the level of excitation, the sign and the substance of the emotion. Emotions that increase the level of arousal cause mobilization changes: they prepare the body for an attack, a quick achievement of a goal, or for a flight. So, in the works of Wundt (1984), Kennon (1927), Simonov (1966) and others there is a clear correlation between the functions of emotions with certain levels of agitation.

W. Wundt considered emotional process on the basis of three components: pleasure-unpleasure, excitation-calming and tension-resolution. The author, analyzing the emotional space-time continuum, called its relation to the space of images – the mechanism of associations. This position is also confirmed in the works of James (1984). According to Wundt (1984), the dynamics of the manifestation of emotions or the form of their flow is different: from short-term reactions in the form of a special, affected experience to a long-term stable general experience.

In recent years, a number of theoretical and experimental works focused on finding a certain unified universal function of emotions have appeared. In particular, these are studies conducted by Vilyunas (1984), Dodonov (1987), Leontiev (1983), Shingarov (1971) and other researchers. Thus, B.I. Dodonov and a number of other authors (Vilyunas, 1976; Dodonov; 1987; Klapared, 1984; etc.) single out the evaluation function of emotions as the main one. Even Charles Darwin noted that emotions emerged in the process of evolution as a means by which living beings establish the significance of certain conditions for satisfying their needs (Darwin, 1953). This function is based upon a subjective component of emotional response (experience) at the first stage of voluntary control (when a need arises with further deployment of a motivational process on its basis) and at the last stage (evaluation of the result achieved).

Other authors (such as Leontiev, 1983; Simonov, 1966) expand this function to a cognitive-evaluative one, pointing to its link with cognition. Along with the evaluation function, the most common one is the motivation function. Thus, according to S.L. Rubinshtein, "... an emotion in itself contains an attraction, a desire, an aspiration directed toward the object or away from it, just as an attraction, a desire, an aspiration is always more or less emotional" (Rubinstein, 1999: 489). According to a number of modern concepts, this function is the most frequently analyzed (Vilyunas, 1984; Izard, 2000; Chebykin, 1992; etc.). Even Aristotle (1927) singled out its various manifestations: desire as a pleasure anticipated in the future; intention to bind together elementary experiences of pleasure-displeasure, emotions of fear, anger, etc.

Some prerequisites for considering this function are presented by Descartes (1950), Spinoza (1984) and a number of other philosophers. V.K. Vilyunas singled out the function of evaluation and motivation on the grounds that "they are carried out by emotional experience in relation to their own subject, i.e. 'inside' of an emotional phenomenon" (Descartes, 1950: 56). Further on, regarding the function of motivation, the author emphasizes that motivation is an 'internal' function of an emotional phenomenon only insofar as it is expressed in the perception of some object as impulsive, desirable, to the extent that motivation leads to real activity, i.e. causes "processes external to the emotional phenomenon itself; – it is a function of a holistic emotional manifestation" (Descartes, 1950: 56).

In foreign literature, this function is also considered a motivational one. Thus, M. Arnold emphasizes that

> the relationship between emotions and motivation depicted in theoretical literature remains completely unclear. Although it has been argued over and over again that emotions motivate, however no one is able to come forward and unequivocally explain exactly how this happens.
>
> *(Arnold, 1969: 1041)*

Significant attention should be focused on the expressive function of emotions (Izard, 1980; Yakovleva, 1997; etc.), represented in sound reactions, facial expressions, pantomime, and in other reactions fixed in the course of evolutionary and social development. This function allows a person or animal, through the expressive component of emotions, to inform the other one about its own state, which, in turn, facilitates communication, prevents aggression from another person or animal, and also helps to recognize the needs and conditions that another subject has at the moment. This function is the main one in non-verbal communication.

The regulatory function deserves special attention, which lies in the fact that emotions, having the function of consolidation-inhibition, reinforcement and trace formation, affect the accumulation and actualization of individual experience, i.e. this function allows to regulate the processes of cognition on the substantive content. In the process of communication, the regulatory function is to coordinate the order of statements. In this case, a combination of various functions is observed (for example, the signaling function is combined with the protective one).

Thus, based on this understanding of the regulatory function, it is possible to identify such components as consolidation-inhibition (Anokhin, 1964), reinforcement (Simonov, 1966) and trace formation (Leontiev, 1983). P.V. Simonov emphasizes that "the phenomenon of reinforcement occupies a central position in the system of concepts of science dealing with higher nervous activity, since the formation, existence, extinction and specific features of any reflex depend on the fact of reinforcement" (Psychology of emotions, 1984: 182). I.P. Pavlov considered reinforcement as "the action of a biologically significant stimulus (food, harmful stimulus, etc.) which transmits a signal value to other biologically insignificant stimulus combined" (Psychology of emotions, 1984: 182).

In some research, anticipatory and heuristic functions are equated (Vasiliev I. A., Popluzhny V. L., Tikhomirov O. K., 1980), deriving from the ability to trace and actualize a fixed emotional image. Emotions inform the body about the significance of a particular stimulus (when emotions are incorporated into sensory processes), and the information function of emotions is thus distinguished (Kulchitskaya, 1981; Simonov, 1966; etc.).

There are studies highlighting the so-called communicative function of emotions (Ilyin, 2001; Schopenhauer, 2000). Their essence is in the fact that emotions are used to manipulate other people. Emotions help a person achieve the satisfaction of his needs through a change of the behavior of other people in a needed direction.

Thus, the analysis of modern literature has shown that such basic functions of emotions as evaluative or cognitive-evaluative (Vilyunas, 1976; Grote, 1879–1880; Klapared, 1984; Leontiev, 1983; Simonov, 1984), the function of experiencing (Vilyunas, 1984; Izard, 2000; Chebykin, 1992), regulatory function (Weiner, 1997; Dodonov, B.I. 1980; Kolot, 1999; Lomov, 1984; Reinvald, 1987; Rubinstein, 1959; Tikhomirov, Klochko, 1980), activating (Wundt, 1984; Simonov, 1966), disorganizing (Klapared, 1984; Leeper, 1984; Psychological Dictionary, 1997), expressive (Grote, 1879–1880; Yakovleva, 1997), anticipating (Vasiliev, 1998; Zaporozhets, Neverovich, 1974; Tikhomirov, Klochko, 1980; Chebykin, 1992), inciting or motivating (Weiner, 1997; Vilyunas, 1990; Gromova, 1980; Leeper, 1984; Morozova, 1979; Petrazhitsky, 1993), integrative (Wundt, 1912), informational (Kulchitskaya, 1981; Simonov, 1966) and others can be defined.

The generalization of theoretical and experimental studies facilitates to conditionally grouping functions of emotions into several classes. First, there are functions associated with the indicative basis of mental activity. These include such functions as evaluative or cognitive-evaluative, expressive, heuristic and others. Second, those associated with the process of development of psychophysiological systems of human activity. These are such functions as regulatory, activating, inciting and others.

2.2 External and internal factors that determine the development of the emotional sphere

The problem of the development of emotions depends on many conditions and factors. Summarizing data in the literature available (Bozhovich, 1972; Vilyunas, 1976; Dodonov, 1978; Izard, 2000; Reikovsky, 1979; Reinvald, 1987; and others), it can be noted that the disclosure of both factors and regularities of development of person's emotional sphere largely depends on those theoretical and conceptual ideas that researchers use in their search. Analysis and systematization of factors influencing the development of the emotional sphere of a child are difficult due to the variety of sources that generate them (Vygotsky, 1970; Galperin, 1976; Leontiev, 1983; Olshannikova, 1983; Rubinstein, 1976; etc.).

Based on these and other studies, it is conditionally possible to single out several groups of factors that determine the genesis of the emotional sphere.

Thus, in some works, such factors are considered to be purely biological ones (Anokhin, 1964; Wundt, 1984; James, 1984; Kennon, 1927; Lobzin, Polyakova, 1984; Simonov, 1966 and others), in others – social factors (Vygotsky, 1970; Galperin, 1976: 39; Zaporozhets, Neverovich, 1974; Leontiev, 1983;

Olshannikova, 1983) and other factors. At the same time, some experts refer to the latter ones as external factors, while the former – to internal ones.

As it is known, "the biological significance of emotions is determined by their evaluative function, due to which the body seeks to respond to environmental changes in advance and quickly, to mobilize energy resources necessary for actions aimed at meeting immediate needs" (Anokhin, 1964: 341). A number of researchers (Anokhin, 1964; Gelgorn, Lufborrow, 1966; Kennon, 1927; Lindsley, 1960; Naem, 1984; Simonov, 1966 and others) see the development and functioning of certain brain structures, primarily limbic formations (hippocampus, hypothalamus, thalamus, etc.); the activity of endocrine glands (reticular formation, pituitary gland, neocortex, etc. – are among the most significant here); and also changes in the somatic sphere; manifestation of the biological need necessary for vital functions – as sheer biological factors.

Of particular note are the studies (Wundt, 1912; Woodworth, 1950; Izard, 2000; Reikovsky, 1979; Chebykin, Melnichuk, 2004), related to the description of the specifics of the genesis of emotions. In the latter case researchers (Gelgorn, Lufborrow, 1966; Darwin, 1953; Dembo, 1948; Lindsley, 1960; Reikovsky, 1979) propose a theoretical model, which comes down to the fact that a person has a number of emotions that manifest themselves and slightly change in the process of evolution. They are usually genetically inherited and have a biological basis of origin.

If internal factors are being observed, then those biological ones that associate with the satisfaction of basic needs will obviously dominate at the first stages of a child's mental development. Yet emerging and developing emotions in some studies (Abolin, 1987; Galunov, 1978; Izard, 2000; Olshannikova, 1978; Plutchik, 1962 and others) are called primary ones, while others (Izard, 1980) call it basic. Some authors (Woodworth, 1950; Wundt, 1912; Gelgorn, Lufborrow, 1966; Darwin, 1953; Dembo, 1948; Kennon, 1927; Lindsley, 1960; Reikovsky, 1979) call it basal. With the expansion of social factors influencing a child's psyche, according to a number of studies (Grote, 1879–1880; Izard, 2000; Chebykin, 1992), these emotions give rise to their derivatives. Moreover, the list of these derivatives or, as other authors point out, secondary emotions, formed on the basis of the primary one (joy, for example) forms a complex of other positive emotions.

Such phenomena may successfully be illustrated in the expression and development of both – main (primary) and derived (secondary) emotions in the works of Izard (2000) and Chebykin, Melenchuk (2004). In the studies of Chebykin, considering cognitive activity as an example, it was experimentally proved that irritation and anger are emerging in the process of development of aggression. While boredom gives rise to such emotions as indifference, resentment and disappointment (Chebykin, 1992: 62). Moreover, in the latest experiments with students, the author has shown that in emotions of surprise and bewilderment – the leading component is surprise; in boredom, indifference and disappointment prevail; in interest, inquisitiveness and curiosity – interest; in doubt and uncertainty – doubt; in anger and irritation – anger; joy, pleasure – joy; fear, worry and anxiety – fear; shame and embarrassment – shame; resentment and disappointment – resentment (Chebykin, 1992: 64).

Internal factors that have an influence on genesis of the emotional sphere are also associated with the specifics of the development of views (Chomskaya, Batova, 1992), mental processes (Vasiliev et al., 1980; Vygotsky, 1991; Dodonov, 1987; Zinchenko, 1995; Klapared, 1984; Kopina, 1982; Tikhomirov, Klyuchko, 1980; Chomskaya, Batova, 1972) and memory processes (Gromova, 1980; Ilyuchenyuk, 1988; Leontiev, 1983; Nosenko, Egorova, 1996; Rubinstein, 1976). This dependence is clearly traced in the works by O.K. Tikhomirov, who considered the process of thinking as one of the key factors in the development of the emotional sphere (Vasiliev, 1974, 1998; Vasiliev et al., 1980; Kopina, 1982; Tikhomirov, 1969; Vasiliev, 1974, 1998; Kopina, 1982). The results of such research emphasize the interdependence and interdetermination of the development of the emotional sphere with mental processes.

It should be especially noted that the development of the emotional sphere is also influenced by personal experiences that arise and are fixed in the features of character, his or her moral and ethical qualities. Further on they serve as the basis for the development of a person's emotional sphere and his/her spiritual culture (Bukin, 1976; Vygotsky, 1970; Kovalev, 1971; Yakobson, 1966; etc.).

Other specialists (Bozhovich, 1972; Zaporozhets, Neverovich, 1974; Lisina, 1983; Mukhina, 1985; Simonov, 1966; Smirnova, Lagutina, 1991; Yakobson, 1966: 185; etc.) do not deny the role of biological factors in the development of emotions, however, give priority to the social factors of human life. On the other hand, P.K. Anokhin points out that

> human emotions are mostly determined socially. They, as well as human actions, are determined by the norms of morality and law inherent to every socio-economic formation. Therefore, the highest forms of emotions are generated on the basis of social (moral) needs and spiritual (aesthetic, intellectual) needs.
>
> *(Ananiev, 1980: 340)*

A number of authors (Breslav, 1984; Zemskaya, 1986; Kovalev, 1971; Cohn, 1989; Krutetsky, 1977; Lisina, 1983; Romanova, 1983; Sermyagina, 1991) relate specifics of the relationship in which a child is brought up, circumstances of informal communication with adults and peers (Cohn, 1989; Leontiev, 1983; Morgun, 1981) and conditions of upbringing in educational institutions (Shepel, 1987) to the social factors, as they significantly affect the development and formation of human emotions.

According to A.G. Kovalev, it is "the moral and psychological atmosphere of a child's life in the family that is of great importance in the formation of his moral feelings" (Kovalev, 1971: 31). In this regard, we can agree with the statement that "a person with mother's milk perceives the psychology of a particular social group to which he belongs" (Kovalev, 1971: 31).

Additionally, the means of art and literature, rituals, traditions and much more (Bukin, 1976; Semenov, 1988; Shlyakhova, 1981) may also be attributed to the social factors as they directly affect the emotional sphere within the framework of cognitive activity of the educational process. Thus, "... in the upbringing of moral feelings, all types of art are of a great importance... Art (music, painting, cinema, theater, literature) affects by artistic images, generating empathy, awakening various emotions" (Kovalev, 1971: 44).

Summarizing the results of various scientific studies (Bogomolova, 1991; Bukin, 1976; Semenov, 1988; Flegontova, 1975; and others), it can be stated that under current conditions the formation of the emotional sphere of a child is significantly influenced by the achievements of scientific and technological progress, media and various cultures as well. As for the latter, the culture as an instrument of expressing emotional states among different peoples, has different forms of representation in content and action. "In various life situations, depending on age, gender, culture and most importantly, depending on motives and attitudes, the expressive movements of facial muscles can be strengthened or weakened, suppressed or masked, and even reflect the opposite state the subject is actually experiencing (for example, smile at fear)" (Kovalev, 1971: 10).

The studies of Chinese literature conducted by Kleinberg (Nagaev, Bendas, 1982: 56) are very illustrative. The examples show certain differences in the development of a culture of expressing emotions among peoples of China and Europe. In particular, there are characteristics that coincide and those that do not coincide with the generally accepted manifestations of emotions in Europe. So, to describe fear, the Chinese, for example, use the following expressions: "Everyone was trembling, their faces were the color of clay"; "The hair stood on end, and goosebumps ran through the body"; "Cold sweat covered his body, he was trembling incessantly"; etc. These expressions are similar to expressions of fear in European cultures. In order to describe anger, such expressions were used: "He gnashed his teeth, grinding them to powder"; "His eyes opened wide and became round (for us, this means rather surprise or fear)"; "He was so angry that he fainted several times" (we Europeans would rather faint from fear); etc. (Nagaev, Bendas, 1982: 57).

As for laughter and tears, here we also observe the manifestation of different emotions depending on the country, people and traditions. Similar differences can be traced in other emotional relationships. For instance, tears are an almost universal expression of sadness, however, "cultural norms determine manner and the duration of crying" (Nagaev, Bendas, 1982: 57). For example, in Montenegro, at the funeral ceremony, women and men have to cry at different times, and Mexican Indians cry during religious ceremonies, after which they return to a joyful mood. The emotional connotation of laughter in China is opposite to the accepted perception. Their laughter may mean anger. In the old days, misfortune was reported with a smile – to reduce it. In Japan, the person being reprimanded had to smile, but not reveal the back teeth.

A generalization of these and other research results shows a rather strong influence of external social factors that determine the development of not only a culture of manifesting emotions in expression and actions but also deeper emotional relationships that characterize the specifics of the emotional behavior of a particular nation or nationality.

In addition, as the analysis of scientific, scientific-methodical and fiction literature shows (Avdeeva, Meshcheryanov, 1991; Bauer, 1985; Bozhovich, 1972; Vygotsky, 1991; Davydov, 1986; Zaporozhets, Neverovich, 1974; Cohn, 1989; Lichko, 1983; Marshak, 1961; Morgun, 1981; Shlyakhova, 1981; Elkonin, 1960), at each age stage of development, it is possible to single out leading social factors that influence the formation of the emotional sphere of a child.

Summarizing the data of these and other studies, we may state that for a newborn, the most important factor influencing the development of emotions is the immediate contact with mother, and those conditions that satisfy his basic needs.

In infancy, besides the above-mentioned factors, the conditions of non-verbal communication manifested by parents and the surroundings of a child, play an important role. Specific influences are also exerted by inanimate objects in the form of various toys and general emotional comfort in the family.

For children from one to three years, the leading factors determining the development of the emotional sphere are conditions for play activity, and also the specifics of child's communicative interaction with adults.

At the age of three to seven years, along with the above factors, the key activity is a cognitive function related to the child's perception of works of art and literature. The most important condition influencing the formation of the child's emotional sphere is all types of play activity typical for a given age.

At primary school age, the range of factors influencing the genesis of the emotional sphere expands significantly. The factors of organization of the educational process and those of informal relations with peers come to the fore.

In adolescence, along with the previous period in the development of a child's feelings dominate biological changes associated with puberty. They define specificity and a direction of expression of occurrence and development of new feelings.

In young adults, those social and psychological conditions influence the personal self-assertion of young men and women, which form the basis of their life positions that can be attributed to the leading factors.

It should be noted that selected factors are not limited to the listed ones and, with the expansion of research, they might be supplemented by others. It is also important to emphasize that the selection of the leading factors at each subsequent age does not exclude the influence of factors from the previous life period.

Regarding the problem of analyzing and systematizing the factors influencing the development of a child's emotional sphere, it seems to us that the most acceptable is to subdivide them not into biological and social, but into external and internal factors.

Such an assumption may be justified by the fact that internal factors can include both biological and personal ones. In the latter case, we are talking about socially formed or acquired emotions in the process of life.

Speaking about external factors, we propose to refer to them as all external influences on the emotional sphere of a child.

The list of such conditions can also be associated with the impact on both – the subconscious and conscious entity of a child's personality. This vision allows a more differentiated approach to the description of various factors influencing the development of a person's emotional sphere.

It should be noted that over recent years we see an increase in the number of studies (Viskovatova, 1976; Isaev, 2000; Kulchitskaya, 1981) in which so-called global factors are singled out. Such factors – environmental, socio-economic, informational and technogenic – may have significant indirect and direct impacts on the development of the sphere of human feelings.

Summarizing the results of the study in this section, we can draw the following conclusion.

- It has been established that the list of factors influencing the development of a child's emotional sphere is largely associated with life conditions. In this case, conditionally, all factors that determine the genesis of the emotional sphere can be divided into internal (including biological and personally acquired) and external (including both purely socio-psychological and natural-technogenic).
- It is revealed that the leading factors for newborns are conditions of the emergence of basic needs; in infancy – conditions of non-verbal communication, and also general emotional comfort in the family; at younger preschool age – conditions for organizing gaming activities and specifics of communicative interaction; in senior preschool age – conditions for the development of cognitive activity, as well as all types of play activities; at primary school age – conditions for organizing the educational process and communication with peers; in adolescence – biological changes associated with puberty, and in young adults – conditions for personal and professional self-determination.
- It was shown how problematic is to reveal the strength of positive and negative influences on the development of a child's emotional sphere. That is, the conditions and criteria for the optimality of factors with regard to their consequences are not defined.

In general, summarizing study results in this part of the work, it should be noted that the problem of emotions' genesis in modern psychology is considered ambiguously. Summing up existing approaches and definitions of emotions in the scientific literature available to us, it can be noted that emotions are a complex mental process associated with the reflection of an attitude in the shape of a specific polymodal sensory tone, aimed at the actions of internal and external factors of human life.

The data obtained give grounds to group conditionally existing theories that explain the nature of genesis into two divisions. To the first, we refer those systemic theories that describe the specifics of the emergence of emotions and development (Vilyunas, 1976; Wundt, 1912; Izard, 1980; Simonov, 1984). The second direction includes numerous research results, which quite fragmentarily describe conceptual foundations of the emergence of emotions and development in terms of their relationship with other mental phenomena (Anokhin, 1964; Kennon, 1927; Lindsley, 1960; Leeper, 1984; etc).

Equally significant are the data that, to a certain extent, confirm the results of previous studies. First, this is due to the fact that emotions closely interact and integrate with other properties, processes and states, which significantly complicates their study. Second – as was shown – the influence of emotions on a developing personality is carried out through their functions. In today's psychology, more than 20 functions of emotions are identified, and their significance depends on the specifics of human activity. The latter include evaluative function, the function of experience, regulating, activating, disorganizing, anticipating, motivated or motivating, informational and other functions of emotions.

It is significant to stress that there are indications that emotions have a considerable impact primarily on the development of cognitive processes and the formation of children's personal qualities. Their most fundamental influence is on the formation of the cognitive interest in moral and ethical qualities of the developing behavior of the individual.

Generalization of the factors that determine the genesis of the emotional sphere also facilitates systematizing them into two large groups, which we designate as external and internal factors. Internal factors include biological issues associated with the satisfaction of basic needs, the specifics of the development of the feeling realm, cognitive processes, and also with personal experiences. External factors include the social environment of a child, the nature of informal communication with adults and peers, and conditions of education and training. Besides, external factors may include the means of art and literature, rituals, traditions, advances in technology, media and also global factors (environmental, socio-economic, technogenic, etc.) that have both a direct and indirect impact on the development of the emotional sphere of children and young men.

2.3 Analysis of individual data characterizing features of the development of the emotional sphere of children of different ages and gender

Based on the purpose of the work, for the study of the emotional sphere of a developing personality, we selected a large number of tested and common techniques. At the same time, we did not exclude the possibility of duplicating individual values of indicators to increase the validity and characterization of the diagnosed features. The final list includes:

- the technique of "Self-assessment", proposed by T.V. Dembo and S.Ya. Rudinstein, modified by T.M. Gabriel. This technique allows to diagnose personal self-esteem (P1);
- the "House-Tree-Man" method proposed by J. Buck. It allows to diagnose feelings of rejection (P2), hostility (P3) and feelings of inferiority (P4);
- the technique "Kinetic Family Drawing", proposed by V. Wolf, V. Hules, adapted by R. Burns and S. Kaufman. It made it possible to diagnose family anxiety (P5), family aggressiveness (P6) and self-doubt (P7);
- the "Non-existent animal" method proposed by M.D. Drukorevich allows to diagnose personal anxiety (P8), personal aggression (P9) and personal self-esteem (P10);
- "Personal questionnaire of G.Eysenck" makes it possible to assess neurotism (P11);
- "Anxiety scales", proposed by C. Spielberger and adapted by Yu.L. Khanin, allows to diagnose reactive anxiety (P12) and personal anxiety (P13);
- "Questionnaire of emotional maturity", developed by us, assesses its main components – expressivity (P14), self-regulation (P15) and empathy (P16);
- "Freiburg Personality Questionnaire", developed at the University of Hamburg together with the Hungarian psychologist Karody and modified at the University of St. Petersburg allows us to assess neuroticism (P17), spontaneous aggression of the "introtensive type" (P18), depressivity (P19), irritability (P20), balance (P21), reactive aggression of the "extratensive type" (P22), shyness (P23) and emotional lability (P24). The given abbreviations for the parameters will be used hereinafter. The characteristic values of the diagnosed indicators are presented in Appendix 2. Selected methods are presented in detail (Melnichuk, Chebykin, 2021).

The total number of children surveyed – 566.

Of these, aged 7 (grade 1) – 90 children,
8 y.o (grade 2) – 115
9 y.o. (grade 3) – 59
11 y.o. (grade 5) – 28
12 y.o. (grade 6) – 23
13 y.o. (grade 7) – 45
14 y.o. (grade 8) – 78
15 y.o. (grade 9) – 51
16 y.o. (grade 10) – 25
17 y.o. (grade 11) – 52

Review of individual data is of much importance for further clarification of both the specifics of diagnosed indicators' manifestation for each student and figuring out the range of individual values, i.e. their variability.

Analysis of parameter values of personal self-esteem (P1) in 7-year-old children shows that for eleven schoolchildren its level has the maximum intensity. At the same time, for three subjects this level does not exceed 20 points, i.e. is in the low range.

As for the primary data on personal self-esteem (second indicator) (P10), here we observe an insignificant spread of primary results, as the maximum values are found in four children, and the minimum – in seventeen.

Concerning the feeling of the inferiority parameter (P4), a certain variability in values was also revealed. In particular, a high level of this indicator was found in seven children, and a rather low level – in eighteen schoolchildren. Approximately the same trend remains for the parameter of self-doubt (P7). Here we see a quite large deviation in individual data, where the highest values were recorded in thirteen schoolchildren, and the lowest – was in twenty-two.

Each of the above parameters has a different quantitative representation. Thus, for example, high values are recorded in 64% of 7-year-olds, low values in 32% of school kids, and approximately 4% of children have adequate characteristics in terms of self-esteem. These data indicate that the majority of 7-year-old children rate their mental and character qualities highly, considering themselves to be quite healthy and happy. In turn, quite a lot of children of this age have low self-esteem.

If we look at the results obtained in children of 7 years old, we will see that according to the rejection parameter (P2), six children show a high level of it, while in nine children the feeling of rejection is in the zone of minimum values. Here the range is somewhat narrowed and ranges from 1 to 2 points. Approximately the same trend is maintained for the anxiety in the family parameter (P5), where the minimum values were found in eleven cases, and the maximum in ten subjects. As for the indicator characterizing personal anxiety (P8), most children of this age show its sufficient intensity. In particular, in twenty subjects its value is fixed at a low level, and in three – at a high level.

Each of the above anxiety parameters has a different quantitative representation. Thus, high individual values were recorded for 43% of children, average values – for 34% and 23% – low.

Regarding individual values of the indicator reflecting the level of hostility (P3) among 7-year-old kids, based on the data presented, a certain variability in its values is also visible. In nine cases this parameter is weakly expressed, and in six children it is quite high.

Primary data of family aggressiveness (P6) show a wide spread in parameter values. In particular, for four children this parameter is presented at a high level, and in thirty-one the level is low. Quite different picture is observed for the parameter of personal aggression (P9), namely, in twenty-eight subjects this indicator is in the zone of low values, and in nine children – in the high values zone.

Analyzing the obtained results, we may state that in approximately 80% of 7-year-old children the parameters of multidirectional aggression are within the range of low values, in 20% – in the high area range. These data demonstrate that, in general, children of this age are not aggressive, but some kids tend to show hostility in certain circumstances.

Three 8-year-old schoolchildren have quite high personal self-esteem indicators (P1). Moreover, only one subject falls in the zone of low values, i.e. his score did not exceed forty points. Analysis of the diagnosable data of personal self-esteem (P10) in examinees within this age group indicates that in eight cases this parameter level is in the zone of underestimation while one subject overestimates personal capabilities.

Individual data regarding the inferiority index (P4) in 8-year-old schoolchildren show considerable spread. For twenty-four children, this parameter falls to the area of minimum values, and only for one kid, it is at a maximum. Self-doubt index (P7) with high values recorded in seven children, and low values recorded in four.

Thus, individual data obtained from 8-year-old subjects indicate that 64% have a high level of self-esteem and approximately 36% – the low one. At the same time, most children do not experience feelings of inferiority and are quite confident in themselves.

The rejection index (P2) in 8-year-old children also has a substantial spread. Thus, its maximum values are observed in seven children and in two cases P2 is insignificant. At the same time, the family anxiety index (P5) also show spread, with five schoolchildren in the zone of maximum values and two – in the low. High values of the personal anxiety (P8) parameter are recorded in eleven children and low – in fourteen.

Considering primary data on the emotional sphere in 8-year-old students, we can note that for this age category indicators are expressed quite unevenly. Thus, high figures of anxiety are detected in 52% of subjects; 30% of children show low level of anxiety and approximately 18% – average, i.e. at the age of eight, about half of the total number of examinees tend to often experience high-intensive anxiety, and only some children can be called moderately anxious. The number of non-anxious junior schoolchildren at this age is bigger than in the previous age group.

It is important to note that the nature of variability of the hostility index (P3) in 8-year-old children is also uneven. In seven cases the studied parameter is presented minimally, while in five subjects it is expressed quite significantly. Regarding the family aggressiveness indicator (P6), in the spread of individual data, we observe almost the same trend. Seven children are in the area of low values, and not a single tested subject was identified to have any high value. Regarding the indicator of personal anxiety (P8), some variability in individual values is also recorded. Thus, according to the results of our study, eleven children have a rather high level of anxiety, while five children have low.

These outlined primary values give us reason to state that in the surveyed sample three subgroups of school kids can be singled out: a group with a high level (about 34%) of aggression indicators; a group with a low level of values (about 36%) and a group of children with a level below the average (about 30%).

Considering individual data of personal self-esteem indicator (P1) in the age group of 9, we find three subjects with maximum figures level. At the same time, this level is not sufficiently expressed in two cases and falls into a low area.

Primary results on inferiority feeling (P4) in children of this age show a considerable spread of its values. In particular, in seventeen people this parameter is minimally expressed and in three cases it is fairly high. Quite different picture is seen in the case of the self-doubt index (P7). In twenty-five children, this parameter is expressed at a high level and only five show a rather low value. On personal self-esteem (P10), we have obtained somewhat different results. Namely, in three children this parameter reaches high values, and in three, it falls low.

The above parameters, as we see, have different quantitative representations. Thus, high values are observed for 80% of the subjects, and for about 20%, they are low.

Evidently, the majority of 9-year-old children have somewhat overestimated self-esteem and they do not experience an inferiority complex. In turn, we noted an increase in self-doubt in children of this age.

Considering primary data of 9-year-old children regarding the feeling of rejection (P2), we see a high level of it in six children, and a low in five. Anxiety in the family parameter (P5) shows approximately the same trend, at least in the dispersion of primary values. At the same time in four cases, this parameter is minimally expressed, and in five, it is fairly high. It is important to note that regarding the personal anxiety indicator (P8), a range of values fluctuates from one to six points. The studied indicator is low in eleven cases, and high in nine.

Based on data analysis on indicators of various manifestations of anxiety, it can be noted that approximately 33% of all subjects have a rather high level of anxiety, approximately the same percentage of children have a low level, and 34% of children have this indicator of average values.

Index of hostility (P3) fluctuates within the limits of the minimum values in seventeen 9-year-olds, and in seven cases, it is above the average.

As for the parameter of family aggressiveness (P6), the disparity is less pronounced. In particular, in twenty-three cases it lies in the area of low values, and in six, it is in the medium.

Indicator of personal aggression (P9) shows slight variability from 1 to 3 points with a shift to low values. In twenty-four cases, it is at its lowest level, and in four, it is above the average.

Having analyzed individual data in percentage terms, we see that various manifestations of aggression in children of this age are mostly at a high level and only a small portion exceeds the medium level of values.

Analyzing primary data of self-esteem indicators in 11-year-old children on the personal self-esteem parameter (P1), we find not a single subject in the maximum values zone, while four subjects are in the zone of high values, i.e., ranging from 85 points or more. The majority of subjects stay in the range of average data. Within the limits of low values, not a single test subject was also identified.

Regarding the data obtained from children of this age, it is seen that by inferiority index (P4), nine examinees have minimal and two have high values. As for the parameter of self-doubt (P7), we observe a slight variability in the range from 1 to 2 points. At the same time, in ten subjects this parameter is minimally represented, and only one child is in the zone of maximum values. Quite different trend is observed in the spread of primary values of the personal self-esteem parameter (P10), where three children are at a low level, and four children are in the high.

In this age group, we can also note certain differences in the representation of the studied indicators. So, for example, approximately 80% of fifth graders have the level of this parameter in the zone of overestimation, and 20% underestimate his/her personal capabilities.

Considering individual data of 11-year-old children for rejection feeling (P2) parameter, we see that two children are in the zone approaching low values and four subjects are in the zone of maximum values.

Approximately the same picture is noted for the family anxiety parameter (P5). Here the range somewhat narrows and fluctuates in the range from 0 to 2 points. Thus, high values of this parameter are recorded in ten subjects and in four children below the average.

Variability in terms of personal anxiety (P8) ranges from 1 to 2 points. At the same time, one subject was found in the zone of low values, however, none of the students has high values.

These individual data permit us to single out three groups in the examined sample of children. That is, a group of children with a high level of P8–50% of all schoolchildren, and two groups with medium and low levels (25% of students in each).

The indicator of neurotism (P11) demonstrates the following: fifteen children are in the normosthenic zone, i.e. in the zone of average values on a scale of emotional instability, where H (a {9; 15}). On the scale of emotional instability in the concordant zone, i.e. in the zone of high values, where K (a{0;8}) only two schoolchildren are recorded. While in the zone of supra-discordant, i.e. in the zone of low values of emotional instability, where D (a{16;24}) eleven children of the studied age were noted.

Analysis of the data obtained indicates that 7% of the subjects are in the concordant zone (high values), 53% are in the normosthenic zone (average values), and 39% of fifth-grade students are in the supra-discordant zone (low values of emotional instability). This means that the majority of 11-year-old children are generally emotionally stable, calm and carefree. Only a small part of 11-year-old children has a tendency to be hypersensitive to reactions, tension and dissatisfaction with themselves and the world around them.

Analyzing indicators of reactive and personal anxiety (P12, P13), the following results of individual values may be noted: for reactive anxiety (P12) individual data is scattered mainly from 31 to 35 points. At the same time, in fifteen subjects this parameter is clearly insufficiently expressed, and only in one case, it reaches a high level. A slightly different trend is observed in the spread of individual data of personal anxiety (P13) in 11-year-old children, where one subject has minimal value and eleven subjects are in the zone of maximum results.

The values of expressiveness index (P14) indicate a considerable spread of individual data. Namely, for one subject of the fifth grade, this parameter is presented at a low level, and for another one, it is at its high. That is, 3% of all subjects are in the zone of low and 3% in the zone of high values, while 94% of children are within the average zone. Hence, 11-year-old schoolchildren are generally good at using facial expressions, gestures and intonation in communication.

If we look at the results characterizing the self-regulation index (P15), we can see that one test subject is at the level of low values and four show relatively high values, which in percentage terms are 3% and 14%, respectively. Approximately 83% stay in the zone of average values. These data indicate that schoolchildren of this age group are able to regulate their emotions in communication.

Based on primary data of the neuroticism parameter (P17), we can draw a conclusion that in the surveyed sample of subjects of the fifth grade, 35% (i.e. ten students) stand out with a high level and 65% have an average level.

Regarding the indicator of spontaneous aggression (P18) in children of 11 years old, we can note that ten subjects show its high level, which is 35% of students in the fifth grade; about 65% of tested are at the level of average data.

It should be noted that a rather low variability is observed in the depressiveness index (P19). Within the range of high values, seven subjects were noted, that is approximately 25% of the total number. At the same time, 75% of the examined are in the zone of average values.

As for the parameter (P20), which characterizes irritability, one can see approximately the same trend in the variability of individual data. Not a single test subject is observed in the low values zone, with twenty students staying within the high values, which is about 71%. Consequently, 29% of fifth graders found the average values.

If we look at data obtained on the equilibrium indicator (P21), it can be observed that nine children have relatively high values, which is 32% of fifth graders. Not a single subject was found within the low values, which means that 68% of the tested are in the zone of average values.

Analysis of the reactive aggression parameter (P22) shows a more pronounced spread, that has a fairly high variability ranging from 3 to 9 points. Here, low values are found in one case, which is only 4% of fifth-grade students. High values are recorded in twenty-one students, which makes 75% of children and the remaining 21% stay within the average values.

Regarding individual data on shyness indicator (P23), we also see as for the previous parameter, one subject has high values of this parameter, which makes 4% of fifth graders, and eleven subjects show low values, which is about 39% of students. The rest – about 57% of fifth graders – are in the area of average values.

Analyzing primary data obtained on the indicator of emotional lability (P24) in children of the fifth grade, we get the following: for two subjects this parameter is at a fairly low level, which makes 7%; fourteen children (50%) are in the zone of high values and, therefore, 43% of students show average data.

Thus, the majority of 11-year-old schoolchildren are characterized by unstable emotional states, manifested in frequent mood swings, increased excitability, irritability, a tendency to affective response, and an aggressive attitude toward their social environment. On the other hand, they evince moderate protection against the stress factors in typical life situations, based on self-confidence, optimism and activity.

We find it particularly important to consider values of personal self-esteem indicator (P1) in this sample for 12-year-old children. In two cases, children show very high levels above 90 points. At the same time, in one case, the indicator value went to the minimum. Regarding primary data on the parameter of inferiority feeling (P4), there is a sufficient dispersion of values. In particular, in three subjects this parameter is minimally expressed and in one it is in the high-value area. The spread of the self-doubt parameter (P7) is less pronounced; it mainly ranges from 0 to 2 points. In particular, in thirteen cases this indicator is not significant enough and in one goes into the area above the average values.

These primary data give us reason to say that 13% of sixth-grade students have a low level of self-esteem. Approximately 78% of cases are in the area of high values. Only about 9% of students have indicators characterizing adequate self-esteem.

In this age group, we can also observe certain disparities in the representation of diagnosed indicators. So, according to the parameter of rejection feeling (P2), in the complex of parameters studied, low values are recorded in five subjects, and six show figures above average. In terms of anxiety in the family (P5) the scatter of data is less pronounced. In particular, twelve schoolchildren have primary values in the low values area, and only for one subject, the value is high.

Regarding data obtained on the indicator of reactive anxiety (P12), we can note that in sixteen cases it is in the low-value area, and in four – in that of the high. The parameter of personal anxiety (P13) demonstrates a slightly different picture in the spread of individual values. In particular, in one child this parameter is minimally expressed, while in ten others it is quite high.

On the grounds of primary data of parameters describing various manifestations of anxiety, we may say that in the surveyed sample of 12-year-old children, two groups can be conventionally selected – a group with a high level of indicators (about 25%) and a group of examinees with values below the average (about 75%).

Considering values of the hostility parameter (P3) in children of the studied age group, we see that in five cases its level is minimal. At the same time, in three children this parameter is expressed quite significantly. Regarding the indicator of family aggressiveness (P6), there are ten children with a level of hostility in the area of minimal values and only one child with a value pretty high. Regarding spontaneous aggression indicator (P18) we note a sufficient scatter in individual values. In particular, in six subjects it is expressed at a rather high level and in one – at a relatively low level. A different trend in the scatter of individual data is observed for the parameter of reactive aggression (P22), where it mainly ranges from 7 to 9 points. At the same time, in nineteen subjects this indicator is clearly expressed, and only in one subject, it is in the low value area.

Considering primary data of sixth-grade school kids, we can note that in this age category, each indicator is expressed unevenly. Thus, high values are observed in approximately 60% of cases, and in approximately 28% – the values are low. This indicates that a large number of 12-year-old children express hostility and aggressive attitudes toward the social environment, and show impulsive behavior.

Analyzing individual values of the expressiveness index (P14) among sixth-grade students, we found three subjects with quite low values, which makes up 13% of all observed age groups. In four cases (17%), this parameter is in the high-value area. The rest 70% of children show average values of expressiveness.

Primary data of the self-regulation parameter (P15) indicate five subjects in the area of low values, which is 21% of all children of the sixth grade, and in three cases (13%), this parameter reaches high. Thus, 66% of sixth graders stay in the zone of average values. As for the parameter of empathy (P16), here we identify six children with values below their average, which makes 26%. At the same time, in eight cases, this parameter is in the high range.

These data indicate that, in general, 12-year-old schoolchildren have developed the ability to deal with the emotional state of others, arbitrarily express their emotions, control their manifestations in a given situation, manage their own behavior and influence at the behavior of other people.

Rather, a low variability was recorded for the neuroticism parameter (P17), where the range of values narrows to 6–8 points. At the same time, nine children on this parameter have high values, which is 30% of the studied sample. In the meantime, not a single child is found in the area of low values. Consequently, about 70% of sixth graders show average values for the studied indicator.

Individual data on the depressiveness parameter (P19) in children of 12 show approximately the same trend in the spread as in the previous case. In particular, in fourteen children P19 is expressed at a fairly high level, which makes 60% of a sample and, in turn, not a single subject has shown low value. Consequently, about 40% of the examined subjects fall into the area of average values for the specified indicator.

When looking at data obtained from 12-year-old children, we will see that there is also an insignificant variation in primary results on the irritability parameter (P20). Namely, fifteen schoolchildren (65%) show high values, and only one subject shifted to the average values, which is 4% of sixth-grade children.

Based on primary data on the equilibrium indicator (P21), it can be seen that in the surveyed sample of sixth graders, three groups of children can be conditionally singled out. That is, five children (20%) have shown high values. The second group (26% of the subjects) with low-level values, and the third (54%) – those students who have shown average values.

According to the shyness indicator (P23), the spread of primary data mainly ranges from 6 to 8 points. At the same time, five subjects (20% of sixth graders) have a high level of P23, and not a single test subject is in the area below the average values. That means that about 80% of children by this indicator are at the level of average values.

Regarding the last indicator in the complex of the studied parameters – emotional lability (P24), in the spread of individual data we see approximately the same picture as that of the previous parameter. In particular, ten children found a high level of it, which makes up 43% of students in the sixth grade, one subject (4%) shows below the average values, and the rest 53% of the subjects are in the average values area.

Thus, 12-year-old children show a moderate level of neuroticism and depression, an average degree of stability to the effects of stress factors in typical life situations, and some instability of emotional state; many experience mood swings, increased excitability and irritancy.

Analysis of indicators identified by the parameter of personal self-esteem (P1) in children of 13 years of age is very illustrative. Here we have two subjects whose level is in the high range, i.e. over 90 points. At the same time, one of the subjects is below the average values.

Primary data on inferiority feeling (P4) demonstrate certain variations. Low values of P4 are detected in eighteen subjects and values above averageare detected in four. Approximately the same trend is observed with the self-doubt parameter (P7), which shows a considerable scatter in individual data. Namely, in twelve cases the studied parameter is at the lower boundary and in two – at a high level. The parameter of personal self-esteem (P10) is at minimum values area in three test subjects, and in another three – at a high level.

Considering those initial data, we may split the surveyed sample of adolescents aged 13 into two groups. The first group includes subjects with high levels of self-esteem (70% of children), and the second – with values below average (about 30%).

Regarding the set of anxiety parameters, we observe the following values: on the parameter of feeling rejected (P2), we can state the fact that in three examinees this parameter is expressed within the limits of high values and no one has results within the limits of low values. The family anxiety index (P5) has a more pronounced scatter in individual data than the previous parameter. Namely, eight children had low values of it, while in eleven cases values are rather high.

It is important to consider the data on personal anxiety in this sample. Here, the range of values is somewhat narrower and ranges from 1 to 2 points. At the same time, one examinee is recorded within the minimum values and not a single student was observed within the limits of above-average values. For the indicator (P12), which is considered reactive anxiety, we can note six children with a high level of expression of the parameter under study and three children with a low level. If we turn to the values characterizing the index of personal anxiety (P13), we will see a slightly different picture in the scatter of individual data. Namely, in eleven students, the personal anxiety index is expressed at a high level and none is found within low values.

Each of the above-mentioned anxiety parameters has a different quantitative representation. So, for example, high values are recorded in 60% of cases, and in about 40%, the values are below average.

Considering the primary data on aggression indicators for the seventh-grade children, we can note that in them each indicator has an unequal representation of its levels. Thus, for the hostility parameter (P3), we observe nineteen children in the area of minimum values and one subject is recorded in the zone of above-average values.

As for the primary results for the family aggression parameter (P6), we see that twenty-five children have a minimal level of aggression and two subjects had a fairly high level. For the personal aggression indicator (P9), the scatter in individual data is less pronounced and mainly ranges from 0 to 2 points. At the same time, low values were recorded for three examinees, and not a single subject was recorded in the zone of above-average values. Considering the primary data of the spontaneous aggression parameter (P18), we can state a significant variability with a shift to higher values. Namely, this parameter is expressed as much as possible in five subjects and clearly insufficient in six children. For the reactive aggression parameter (P22), we observe approximately the same scatter of individual data as for the previous parameter. At the same time, eight children have a high expression of this parameter and only two have it in the zone of below-average values.

Summarizing the obtained results of the primary data on indicators of aggression indicators, we can note that approximately 20% of the seventh-grade testees are within the high values of this parameter and approximately 80% are recorded within the low values.

Analyzing individual data on neurotism index (P11), we should note that in three children this parameter is in the concordant zone, where K (a {0; 8}), i.e. in the zone of high values of emotional instability – that makes 6% of the tested 13-year-old students. In the normosthenic range, where H (a {9; 15}), eleven children are found, which, in turn, represents 24% of all seventh graders. And on the last parameter of the neuroticism indicator, supra-discordant, where D (a {16; 24}), as we see it, twenty-nine subjects are found to have data characterizing low values on the emotional instability scale, which is approximately 70% of all children of the seventh grade. Thus, the majority of 13-year-olds are calm, carefree and quite content with themselves, and they are not characterized by heightened sensitivity, tension and anxiety.

If we turn to the results obtained for the expressivity index (P14) for seventh-grade children, we can note a sufficient scatter in the individual data. Namely, seven children are found in the range of low values, which is approximately 15% of 13-year-olds, and nine children (20%) are in the area of high values. Thus, approximately 65% of students are traced in the zone of average values.

As for individual data reflecting the level of self-regulation (P15), seven examinees were recorded here in the zone of low values, i.e. within the range not exceeding 4 points, which makes up 15% of seventh graders. Only two pupils are in the zone of maximum values, which is about 4%. And about 80% of all examinees are in the zone of average values.

Regarding the empathy parameter (P16), we can record the fact that five children have low values of this parameter (about 11% of seventh graders). In turn, six children recorded high values (13%) for this age category. Thus, approximately 76% of children have average values on the empathy parameter.

These data indicate that 13-year-old children generally have developed the ability to understand the emotional state of others, to express their emotions voluntarily, to manage their own emotional state and behavior, and as well as to influence the behavior of others. However, among adolescents in this group, there are those who have poorly formed these skills.

Analyzing individual data on the neuroticism parameter (P17) in the seventh-grade test subjects, we see that its low level is found in two cases, which is about 5% of students of the studied age and nineteen (42%) are in the zone of high values, and approximately 52% of the test subjects occupy the limits of the average values of the neurotic parameter.

Summarizing individual data on the depressiveness index (P19), we see a weakly pronounced scatter, mainly ranging from 7 to 9 points. In particular, twenty-four examinees have this parameter presented at a fairly high level, which amounts to 53% of seventh-grade children. It should also be noted that not a single subject is recorded in the zone of low and below-average values. This means that about 47% of students occupy the range of average values of the depressiveness index.

It is important to note that according to the irritability parameter (P20), we can trace approximately the same data scatter as in the previous parameter. At the same time, this indicator is at a high level for twenty-four schoolchildren (about 53%). Only two test takers are low enough, which is about 4% of students in this age group. Consequently, almost 43% of children are at the average level.

Based on the primary data of the equilibrium index, we can say that three groups of children can be conventionally identified in the surveyed sample of adolescents 13 years old. The first group includes seven children with a high level of the parameter under study (16%). The second group includes examinees with low values – eleven persons (25%), and the third group includes subjects with average values (about 40% of children).

Analyzing individual data for the shyness index (P23), we see that eighteen children have a high level of shyness, which is approximately 40% of seventh graders. Three children have a low level of values and, consequently, about 7% of the tested are in the zone below-average values. About 43% of children have a medium level of shyness.

Considering the indicator of emotional lability (P24), we see a weakly pronounced scatter of individual data, where within the maximum values are found twenty-three pupils, which is about 51% of examinees; in the zone of fairly low values – three subjects (about 7% of seventh graders) and, consequently, 42% of students occupy the range of average values of this index.

Thus, children of 13 years old have a rather high level of neuroticism and depression, low immunity to stress factors of ordinary life situations, a certain stiffness, uncertainty and instability of emotional state, many are characterized by mood swings, increased excitability, irritability and tendency to affective reaction.

As for the individual values of the parameter of personal self-esteem (P1) in 14-year-old children, we can see that in two of the subjects its level is highly expressed. At the same time, in the other two children, this level does not exceed the limit of 30 points, and therefore is in the area of low values.

Summarizing the primary data on self-assessment parameters, we see that the nature of variability is also ambiguous. In particular, the feeling of inferiority (P4) revealed twenty examinees whose level is clearly insufficient and three subjects whose level is expressed as much as possible. Approximately the same trend persists for the self-doubt indicator (P7), where seventeen children are found to have a rather low level, and only one subject has it is in the area of high values for the parameter in question. The personal self-esteem indicator (P10) reveals variability with a shift to higher values. In particular, a low level of self-esteem is observed in six children. In turn, this level is quite high in the other six examinees.

These primary data described give us reason to say that three subgroups can be identified in the sample of children surveyed, that is, a group of children with a high level (about 70%), a group with a medium level (about 10%), and a group with a below medium level (19%). Consequently, most adolescents aged 14 evaluate their personal qualities highly, they are confident and have no feelings of inferiority. At the same time, some children have a rather low assessment of themselves, their abilities and their perspectives, which causes them to feel inadequate.

Examining individual values for the feeling of rejection (P2) for eighth-grade students, we see that for six children it has a minimum expression. At the same time, this level is quite high for seven students.

It is important to consider the values of the family anxiety indicator (P5) in this sample. Here we can state the fact that for eighteen examinees the parameter under study is in the zone of minimum values and for six persons in the zone of above-average values.

If we turn to the results characterizing the personal anxiety indicator (P8), we can see that in seven children it is expressed at a low level; in nine cases it is within fairly high values.

The study of the individual data of the reactive anxiety index (P12) shows that thirty-six children have a high level of this parameter, and fourteen have a rather low level.

According to the indicator (P13), which we regarded as personal anxiety, we can see that a high level is recorded in thirty-five of the subjects. At the same time, three schoolchildren are in the zone of low values.

Each of the above-mentioned anxiety parameters has a different quantitative representation. Thus, 60% of the children of the studied age have a high level of anxiety parameters, and approximately 40% have a rather low level. These data indicate that the majority of 14-year-olds often tend to experience anxiety, but the object of anxiety at this age is less often family relationships and more often relationships with peers and adults outside the family.

Examining the hostility parameter (P3) in 14-year-old children, we can note a significant scatter in the individual data, mainly ranging from 0 to 6 points. Thus, four children were noted in the zone of high values. At the same time, nine children can be observed in the zone of minimum values.

For the family aggression indicator (P6), the variability in the values is somewhat narrower. Specifically, this parameter is characterized by minimal expression in twenty-three eighth graders, and only in one subject, it is recorded in the zone of high values.

For the personal aggression indicator (P9), we can see thirteen students with a parameter expressed at a fairly low level, and fourteen students with it expressed quite highly.

Considering the individual data of students of the age under study, we can record the fact that the neurotism indicator (P11) is reflected quite ambiguously in the number of representations for 14-year-old students. Thus, high values of emotional instability are observed in ten children; i.e. in the concordant zone, where K is (a{8;0}). In the zone of normosthenics, where H is (a {9; 15}), twenty-one examinees are observed to be in the zone of average values on the emotional instability scale. And, finally, in the zone of low values of emotional instability, i.e. in the range of supra-discordant range, where D is (a{16;24}), the greatest number of examinees, namely forty-five people.

The value of the spontaneous aggression index (P18) is also important. Here you can see two examinees whose level is clearly insufficient, i.e. ranging from 0 to 1 point. Despite this, twenty-six eighth graders have a sufficiently high level of the indicator under study, i.e. within the range of 8–9 points.

Based on the primary data, we can say that in the sample of children under study for the reactive aggression index (P22), forty-five students are recorded whose level is within the above-average values, and only one subject is within the range of low values.

These primary data allow us to conclude that there are two groups of 14-year-olds in the surveyed sample of children with aggression parameters: a group with high levels (approximately 70%) and a group with lower-then-average levels (about 30%). Children in the first group can be characterized as impulsive and prone to aggressive attitudes toward the social environment. Children of the second group, as a rule, are not aggressive.

Analysis of the values of the neuroticism index shows the following data: high values of emotional instability can be seen in 13% of the examinees; average values in 28%; and low values in 59% of eighth-grade students.

Considering the expressivity indicator (P14), we see that in the range of low values, where a {0; 4}, eighteen subjects are identified, which in turn is approximately 23% of children aged 14, in the range of high values, where a {9;12}, eight subjects are recorded, which is 11% of eighth graders. And, consequently, 76% of children of this age have a medium level of expressiveness index.

For the self-regulation parameter (P15), it can be noted that seven examinees are within low values, which is approximately 8% of students of the age under study. At the same time, nineteen children are recorded within high values, i.e. 25% of eighth graders. The rest of the children are in the zone of average values for this parameter, which is about 67% of the subjects of the eighth grade.

Analyzing the individual data of the empathy parameter (P16), we can state the fact that the range of values slightly widens toward higher values. At the same time, thirteen schoolchildren, i.e. 19% of all are in the zone of low values; seventeen are in the zone of high values, which is 30% of students of this age and the remaining 51% are children with average values for the empathy parameter.

Thus, 14-year-old adolescents differ from representatives of the previous groups by high self-control and the ability to control and adjust their emotional state according to the goal set. In general, they have sufficiently developed expressive and empathic skills.

It is important to consider the values of the indicator of the neuroticism index (P17) in this sample. Here we can note that the character of its variability is also ambiguous and mainly ranges from 3 to 9 points. Thus, we see that the low level of values is traced in six children, which is 10% of eighth-grade students. Twenty-nine examinees are within high parameters, which is approximately 41% of children in this age category; and the limits of average values for the parameter under study are found in 49% of students.

As for individual values of the depressiveness index (P19) of 14-year-old children, as the presented data show, the nature of their variability is ambiguous and predominantly ranges from 4 to 9 points. At the same time, thirty-two examinees are noted in the range of high values for the studied indicator, which is approximately 41% of eighth-grade students. Ten examinees are observed in the range of low values, which is 13% of 14-year-old schoolchildren. Consequently, 46% of children have average values of the depressiveness index.

Considering the parameter of irritability (P20), we can state the fact that thirty-one students have high data on this parameter, which makes 40%; two subjects are in the zone of low values, which is 3% and 57% of the subjects are within the average parameters.

It is important to note that in terms of the equilibrium indicator (P21), twelve students are within the high level and seventeen are within the low level, which is 16% in the first case and 22% of eighth-grade children in the second. About 62% of the examinees are in the zone of average values.

The variability in the parameter of shyness (P23) is somewhat narrower for the studied parameter and ranges from 5 to 8 points. At the same time, four children with a low level of shyness were recorded, i.e. 6% of eighth graders. Twenty-two examinees were noted in the range of high values, which makes up about 29% of pupils of this age and, consequently, about 65% of eighth graders are identified within the average values.

A somewhat different picture is observed for the emotional lability indicator (P24). In particular, high values were recorded for twenty-eight examinees, i.e. about 36% of eighth graders, low values were traced for sixteen children – 21% of the examinees; and about 57% of students were recorded in the zone of average values of the emotional lability index.

Thus, among 14-year-old children, there is a fairly large number of those whose neuroticism and depressive tendencies remain at a high level. In general, most of the subjects have a moderate resistance to stress, along with some predisposition to react passively to ordinary life situations, anxiety, stiffness and uncertainty, which may hinder social interaction. At this age, the number of adolescents prone to affective reactions and mood swings decreases, and the number of children with good self-control increases.

Considering the individual data of ninth-grade students in terms of self-esteem parameters, we can see the following results: the personal self-esteem indicator (P1) revealed its high level for four subjects of examinees, i.e. from 85 points and above, and for three children, the level is below the average level. The feeling of inferiority (P4), revealed a weakly pronounced scatter, mostly ranging from 0 to 2 points (see Appendix B.8). At the same time, eleven students were recorded within the minimum values, and three students of this age group could be noted within the range of sufficiently high values.

The self-doubt parameter (P7) has a somewhat different variability, where we can trace two students within low values, and only one within sufficiently high values.

The second indicator of personal self-esteem (P10) is presented in 15-year-old schoolchildren as follows: the values below the average are found in four subjects, and above the average – in six.

Such described primary data give us grounds to say that three subgroups can be formed in the surveyed sample. That is, a group of children with high levels (51%), a group of children with values below average (24%), and a group with average self-esteem (25%). This testifies to the adequacy of most 15-year-olds' self-esteem, self-confidence and the absence of feelings of inferiority.

As for the individual values of indicators that reflect the level of anxiety in 15-year-old adolescents, the data presented in the table of primary values show that the nature of their variability is also ambiguous. For example, for the feeling of rejection parameter (P2), schoolchildren of the ninth grade have the following results: one subject is reflected in the zone of minimum values and four – within the high data range.

A somewhat different trend in the spread of primary values is observed for the family anxiety indicator (P5), where one examinee was identified within the low data range and eleven schoolchildren of the surveyed age are within the fairly high range.

For the personal anxiety index (P8), the scatter among ninth graders is less pronounced and mostly ranges from 0 to 3 points. At the same time, it is insufficiently reflected in nine of the subjects, and in five cases, it is in the range above the average values.

Regarding the reactive anxiety parameter (P12), twenty-four examinees could be noted with a level that is clearly insufficiently expressed, i.e. a < 30. However, in six subjects this parameter is found to be within the range of high values, i.e. a>46.

Analysis of individual data of the personal anxiety index (P13) indicates that two subjects were recorded within the low values and nine – within the high values.

Based on the analysis of individual values of anxiety indicators, we can note that about 45% of ninth graders have a rather high level of anxiety, and the rest 55% of them have it level within the range of low and below-average values.

Considering the primary data on the hostility parameter (P3) among students of the ninth grade, we can note that in twenty cases this parameter is expressed insignificantly. At the same time, for four of the subjects, it is presented at a fairly high level.

Analyzing individual data for the family aggression indicator (P6), we can see approximately the same tendency in the dispersion of individual values in the previous indicator. Namely, low values are recorded for nine children and high – for one subject.

It is important to examine the values of the personal aggression index (P9) in this sample. Here, as we see, fifteen children in this age category have low values and seven – above the average values.

Summarizing the data of the spontaneous aggression indicator (P18), we can note a sufficient dispersion in its values. Thus there are twenty-three children in the zone of high values, and nine – in the zone of below-average values.

As for the reactive aggression index (P22), the range is wider, ranging from 2 to 9 points. In particular, high values of the index are recorded in fourteen subjects, and below-average values in sixteen 15-year-olds.

Each of the above-mentioned parameters of aggression has a different quantitative representation. Thus, for example, 31% of ninth graders have a high enough level of aggression and about 22% have values below the average. At the same time, for 47% of the subjects, this level occupies the range of average parameters.

Continuing to consider the individual data of the emotional sphere of 15-year-old children, we can note that according to neurotism index (P11), three subjects have a high level of emotional instability, i.e. they are in the concordant zone, where K is (a{0;8}). In the normosthenic zone, where H is (a {9; 15}), i.e. in the zone of average values on the emotional instability scale, twenty subjects are identified. And in the zone of low values on the scale of emotional instability, i.e. in the zone of supra-discordant, where D is (a {16; 24}), twenty-five students are observed.

Analyzing the primary results obtained, we can state that 7% of children have a high level of emotional instability, 41% have average values, and 52% of the subjects have low values.

Looking at the individual data obtained in the study of expressivity (P14), we can note that six children have an insufficient level of expressivity, which is 12% of the ninth-grade subjects, and nine children have a fairly high level, which is 14%. Consequently, the remaining about 64% of examinees are traced in the zone of average values for this parameter.

If we turn to the results that characterize the self-regulation index (P15), in this age group we can also note certain differences in the representation of the diagnosed parameter. For example, low values are recorded for four examinees, and this, in turn, is 8% of 15-year-old children; high values are traced in twelve children, which is 24% of the subjects of the ninth grade; and about 68% of the surveyed persons have average values of the self-regulation index.

For the empathy parameter (P16), there are nine children whose level of this indicator is at rather low positions, which makes 16% of all ninth graders. At the same time, for fifteen examinees (30%), the values of the parameter under study are reflected quite strongly. Consequently, about 54% of the examinees are in the zone of average values of the empathy index.

An analysis of primary data for the parameter of neuroticism (P17) shows that eighteen children have high values for this parameter, which is about 35% of the subjects; low values are observed in ten (20%) students, and average values are traced in 45% of children.

The analysis and significance of the data revealed for the depressiveness index (P19) are important. Here the range somewhat narrows and ranges from 4 to 8. At the same time, its level is quite high for twenty subjects and amounts to 39% of ninth-grade students. Two examinees are recorded within the range of low values, i.e. about 3% of students and approximately 58% of ninth graders have average values for depression.

Considering the individual data of the irritability index (P20), we can note that five children are in the zone of low values and twenty-nine students – within high parameters.

Based on the analysis of the individual values of the irritability index, we can state the fact that approximately 9% of ninth graders have the studied index within the low range; 55% – within the high data; and about 36% – within the average value.

As we see, the range of values for the equilibrium index (P21) expands. In particular, fourteen examinees have a fairly high level of P21, which is 28% of ninth graders. Sixteen children are found to be within the low range, which is about 33% of students of the age under study. And, consequently, about 39% of ninth graders are in the zone of average values.

If we look at the data for the shyness index (P23), we can note the range of values that range mostly from 5 to 8 points (see Appendix B.8). In particular, thirteen examinees are reflected in the zone of maximum values, which is about 25% of 15-year-olds and three children (6%) are observed within the low values. The majority of children were recorded in the zone of average values, namely 69%.

According to the emotional lability index (P24), we can see approximately the same picture in the scatter of individual data as in the previous parameter. In particular, low values are observed in seven children, and high – in seventeen. Such presented primary data allow us to say that three subgroups can be distinguished in the sample of children under study, that is, a group with a high level (33% of all numbers), a low level (14% of schoolchildren), and a group with average values (about 53% of the subjects).

Thus, the majority of children at age of 15 show stabilization of the emotional state, reduction of impulsive, aggressive and neurotic reactions, and increased resistance to stressful situations, activity and optimism. However, a fairly large proportion of children have a tendency to form negative emotional states.

Examining the values of the personal self-esteem indicator (P1) in 16-year-old children, we see that four subjects have a fairly high level of it and none has it within the range of low values. In percentage terms, this represents 16% of children with an overestimation of self-esteem and 84% of students with adequate self-esteem (see Appendix 3.9).

Analyzing the individual data of the neurotism indicator (P11), we can note that within the concordant, i.e. high values of emotional instability, six examinees are observed; within the normosthenic, i.e. average data on a scale of emotional instability eight subjects were observed; and within the low values of emotional instability, i.e. in the zone of supra-discordant, ten students were identified.

Based on the primary data, we can say that in the surveyed sample of children, we can identify three groups of children according to the parameter of neuroticism, where 26% of the subjects are in the concordat zone; in the normosthenic zone, 33% of students are in the tenth grade, and 41% of students are recorded in the supra-discordant zone.

According to the reactive and personal anxiety parameters (P12), (P13), the following data can be noted in children of 16 years of age: twenty-two schoolchildren are traced within the low level of the reactive anxiety parameter (P12); for the personal anxiety parameter (P13), four students are noted within low values. A high level of reactive anxiety (P12) was not detected in any case, and average values are found in two students. Six tenth-grade students were found to be within the high level for the indicator (P13), and 14 subjects showed average values of the parameter under study.

Each of the above anxiety parameters has a different quantitative representation. So, for example, high values are recorded in 24% in terms of personal anxiety, and average values were found in 56% of the studied parameter. At the same time, high values on the reactive anxiety index are found in 88% of schoolchildren, and in 12% of children, they are within the average data.

On the expressiveness parameter (P14), we can see five examinees whose level is clearly insufficient, which amounts to 20% of tenth-grade students. In turn, three of the subjects have a high level, and this is 12% of 16-year-olds. The remainder is children with a medium level – 68% of students are on the expressiveness index.

Considering individual data on the self-regulation parameter (P15), we can note seven subjects with a low level of values, which is 28% of tenth-grade students; thirteen (52%) students – with fairly high level; and the remaining 20% have average data on this indicator.

Continuing to look at the primary data on the emotional sphere of children, we can note that for the parameter of empathy (P16), one examinee is recorded within the low level for 16-year-olds, which is 4% of students. Within the high level, we observe twelve subjects, which, in turn, makes up 48% of tenth graders. The remaining part is occupied by schoolchildren whose level of values is at the average values for the empathy indicator, that is, 48% of students.

Thus, the majority of 16-year-olds can very well understand the emotional state of others and use these skills in communication, and many have sufficiently developed skills to express their emotions, manage their own emotional state and behavior, and also to influence the behavior of other people.

The individual data of the tenth-grade examinees for the indicator of neuroticism (P17) show a weakly pronounced scattering of the primary data. In particular, three test takers, i.e. 12% of tenth graders are found in the zone of low values; seven subjects, i.e. about 28% of students are within high values, and the remaining 60% have average values for the parameter in question.

Analyzing the spontaneous aggression indicator (P18) (see Appendix B.9), we can see that high parameters are observed in eleven subjects, i.e. 44% of the total number of tenth graders, four subjects have low parameters, which make up to 16% and consequently about 40% have a moderate value of spontaneous aggression parameter.

If we turn to the data characterizing the depressiveness index (P19), we can see the dispersion of values that ranges from 6 to 8 points. In particular, there are three tenth graders in the zone of low values, and eleven 16-year-olds are in the high-value area. In percentage terms, this is 12% and 44% of the subjects, respectively. Approximately 44% of examinees are traced within the average values of the depressiveness index.

The data of the irritability index (P20) also indicate weakly pronounced variation in individual data. Namely, ten students of the tenth grade, i.e. 40% of 16-year-olds, are found in the zone of high values; only one student is recorded in the zone of low values, which is approximately 4% in this age group; and approximately 56% have average data of the parameter under study.

It is important to consider the values of the equilibrium index (P21) for 16-year-olds in this sample. Here we see that five of the subjects have a minimum expression of this parameter and ten examinees have a fairly high representation. As a percentage, this represents 20% and 40% of the testers, and the remaining 40% are within the average values for the equilibrium parameter.

A somewhat different picture is observed for the parameter of reactive aggression (P22) (see Appendix B.9), where one examinee is recorded in the zone of low values, which amounts to 4% of tenth graders. Nineteen students are in the high-value zone, which is 76%. And about 20% of the surveyed occupy the limits of the average data.

Considering the primary values of tenth graders, we can note that the shyness indicator (P23) in its expression is reflected ambiguously in the number of its representation among 16-year-old schoolchildren. Here, twelve persons have their level expressed as much as possible and only one clearly does not have enough.

These described primary data give us grounds to say that three subgroups can be organized in the sample of children under study. That is a group of children with a high level of shyness indicator (about 48% of examinees), a group with a medium level (about 48% of tenth graders), and those with below the medium level (4% of all).

Analyzing the individual data of the emotional lability index (P24), we can state the fact that in eleven subjects it is clearly insufficiently expressed, however, in four schoolchildren this parameter is presented at a high level. Quantitatively, this may be represented as follows: at the level of low values – 44% of tenth graders, 16% of students are at the level of high values, and about 40% – at the level of average values.

On the whole, children of the age group of 16 show a tendency toward a decrease in the number of neurotic, impulsive and aggressive reactions, a decrease in the level of excitability, irritability and stabilization of the emotional state, which, in our opinion, is conditioned by the development of the ability to control oneself, understanding the motives for various actions of other people.

Considering the values of the personal self-esteem indicator (P1), we can also note certain differences in the representation of the diagnosed indicators among 17-year-old boys and girls. For example, high values of this parameter (i.e. from 95 to 100 points) are recorded in three subjects. At the same time, in one case this indicator is minimally expressed.

As for the primary data on the feeling of inferiority parameter (P4), a weakly pronounced spread in individual data is evident, mainly ranging from 0 to 2 points. At the same time, sixteen examinees are identified with a minimal representation of the parameter under study and two – with a fairly significant expression of this parameter. As can be seen from the table of individual data, there is substantial variation in the value of the self-doubt parameter (P7). In particular, eleven subjects are within the low level of the parameter in question, and eight have it in the zone of high values.

If we turn to the primary data of 17-year-old examinees, which characterize the individual values of the personal self-esteem indicator (P10), we can note seven students with low values, and six with high ones.

Each of the above-mentioned self-assessment parameters has a different quantitative representation. For example, high values are recorded in 35% of eleventh graders, and below the average level are approximately 65% of students. These data indicate that the majority of 17-year-olds rate their personal qualities and life prospects low and consider their place in society insignificant; such children, as a rule, are not confident in themselves.

Considering the values of anxiety indexes of 17-year-old boys and girls, we can note the following results of the primary data. Within the high values of the feeling of rejection parameter (P2), two of the examinees are observed, and for twenty-two students, the parameter under study is at a fairly high level. If we turn to the data characterizing family anxiety index (P5), we can find that eight students have high values and ten have rather low data. It is shown that the personal anxiety parameter (P8) has high values for eight eleventh graders and quite low for thirteen of them. Considering the individual data of the reactive anxiety parameter (P12) among 17-year-old schoolchildren, we see two examinees whose level is clearly insufficient and eighteen students with high values.

A slightly different picture in terms of individual data is observed for various parameters of personal anxiety (P13) in subjects aged 16, where low values were found in one examinee and in sixteen – within the maximum value range.

The results obtained can be interpreted by the fact that approximately 70% of eleventh graders have a high level of anxiety; about 30% have it in the range of low and below-average values.

Considering the individual values for aggression indicators, the following data can be noted. For the hostility parameter (P3), there is a weakly pronounced spread, mostly ranging from 0 to 3 points (see Appendix B.10). At the same time, in seventeen cases, the studied indicator expressed minimally, and very high in three of them.

The family aggressiveness index (P6) reveals approximately the same picture in the scattering of individual data as the previous indicator. At the same time, low values are observed in twenty-nine examinees on the studied parameter. And high values are observed for one eleventh grader.

As for the primary results for the parameter of personal aggression (P9), as can be seen from the tables of individual data for eleventh graders (see Appendix B.10), twenty-five examinees were identified within the minimum values and nine in the zone of high values.

Continuing to consider primary data of the emotional sphere in eleventh graders, we note that for 17-year-old students, the parameter of spontaneous aggression (P18) is reflected ambiguously in the number of representations. In particular, this parameter is represented at a high level for twenty-five students, and for five of them at a rather low level.

Analyzing the values of the reactive aggression parameter (P22), we can note that thirty-six students are recorded at a high level, while three eleventh graders are at a rather low level.

Each of the above-mentioned aggression parameters is also quantitatively ambiguous. We can note that approximately 46% of 17-year-old boys and girls have an overestimated level of aggression, and approximately 54% have it in the range of low and below-average values.

Considering the individual values of the neurotism index (P11), the following should be noted. Within high values on the emotional instability scale, i.e. in the concordant zone, nine examinees are observed; in the normosthenic zone, i.e. low values on the emotional instability scale, twenty-two subjects are recorded. In percentage terms, this is about 18% of the subjects in the concordant zone, 34% in the normosthenic zone, and approximately 43% in the supra-discordant zone.

It is important to consider the values of the expressivity index (P14) in this sample. Six test takers had low values, and twelve have high values, representing 12% and 23% of eleventh graders, respectively. About 75% of examinees are within the average values.

As can be seen from the presented primary data of the self-regulation parameter (P15) among eleventh-grade students (see Appendix B.10), a low level of this parameter was found in six students of the studied age, which is about 12% of all eleventh graders under study and a fairly high level is represented by eleven test takers, which is 22% of students. At the same time, about 66% of examinees have average values for the self-regulation parameter.

If we turn to the results obtained with 17-year-old children, we can see that according to the empathy index (P16), four students are in the zone of low values, which is 8% of eleventh graders. In turn, thirteen subjects are recorded within the maximum values, which is about 25% of schoolchildren. And the remaining 67% of 17-year-old boys and girls have a medium level of empathy.

For the neuroticism index (P17), we see a fairly pronounced scatter in individual data (see Appendix B.10). In particular, the studied indicator is highly expressed in nineteen cases, and in eleven, it is clearly insufficient. Quantitatively, this can be represented as 37% and 22% of eleventh graders. The rest 41% of examinees of the studied age are in the range of average values.

Considering individual values of the depressiveness parameter (P19), we see a slight spread in the primary data, mainly ranging from 6 to 8 points (see Appendix B.10). In particular, there are twenty-one maximum and only five minimum values. At the same time, in the first case indicated, this represents 40% and in the second case 10% of eleventh graders. Consequently, about 50% of schoolchildren are traced within the range of average values for the depressiveness index.

Concerning the irritability parameter (P20), eleventh graders have a range of values, mainly fluctuating from 7 to 9 points (see Appendix B.10). At the same time, its level has a maximum expression in twenty-two examinees, and in two cases, it is presented at a fairly low level. Thus, 43% of students are within the limits of high values of the studied indicator, and about 4% are in the zone of low values. The remaining 53% of children have an average level of irritability parameter data.

The range of values for the equilibrium parameter (P21) somewhat expands and ranges from 4 to 9 points. In particular, low values are observed in fourteen persons (27% of examinees); high values – in eight cases (16%), and average values are observed in 57% of 17-year-old students.

Individual data revealed by the shyness indicator (P23) are quite indicative. Thus, in the surveyed sample of 17-year-old schoolchildren, it is conditionally possible to distinguish 3 groups, that is, the group of nineteen children with a high level – 37% of eleventh graders; the group with a low level – one subject (2%); and the group with an average value for this indicator – 61% of 17-year-old schoolchildren.

On the parameter of emotional lability (P24), we can see a certain variability in the expression of differences in the age studied. In particular, twenty-two examinees in this age group show a high level of values, which is 43% of eleventh-grade students. In turn, four surveyed (about 8% of schoolchildren) have low parameters of the studied indicator. And about 49% of the subjects are presented at the level of average values by the emotional lability index.

The obtained results made it possible not only to note fluctuations in individual data but also to proceed to the necessity of optimal grouping of the diagnosed indicators, based on the proximity of their content and orientation. The grouping of these parameters has allowed us to allocate four complexes of the emotional sphere (Appendix 3 see Table 2.3.1).

The data obtained for the set of self-esteem indicators for 7-year-old children allowed us to identify 64% of examinees with high values for most of the parameters of this complex, 32% of children with low values, and 4% with medium values. Among 8-year-olds, 64% have high values for the indicators of this complex, and 36% have data below the average level. Self-esteem indicators for 9- and 11-year-olds are equally distributed across levels – 80% of test takers have high values and 20% have low values. In the group of 12-year-old children, 78% have high values for most of the parameters of this complex, 9% – average, and 13% – low. Among adolescents aged 13, 70% have high results on the indicators of this complex and 30% have below the average. Values found in 70% of 14-year-old children correspond to a high level of self-esteem indicators, in 11% – to a medium level, and in 19% – to a low level. In the group of adolescents aged 15, 51% of examinees have high values for most of the parameters of this complex, 25% – average, and 24% – low values. A total of 16% of the 16-year-olds have high data on a set of self-esteem indicators, 54% – average and 30% – low. In the group of 17-year-olds, 35% of senior schoolchildren have high values for a priority number of parameters of this complex, 10% have average and 55% have low values.

Thus, the highest self-esteem, self-confidence and minimal expression of feelings of inferiority are observed in children 9 and 11 years old. In turn, the majority of children aged 15–17 have low self-esteem.

Data obtained on a set of indicators describing anxiety in 7-year-old children showed that 43% of the subjects have high values for most of the parameters of this complex, 34% have medium values, and 23% – low values. Among children of 8 years old, 52% have high values, 18% have average values, and 30% have low values for the anxiety complex. 33% of 9-year-olds have high and average data, and 34% had low scores. Among 11-year-old children, 34% have high anxiety complex values, 45% – average values, and 21% have low values. In the group of children aged 12, 34% of the subjects have high values for most of the parameters of this complex, and 66% have average values. Among pupils aged 13, 50% have high values for indicators characterizing various manifestations of anxiety, 37% have average values, and 13% have values below the average level. The data found in 43% of 14-year-old children correspond to a high level of anxiety, in 40% – to an average level, and in 17% – to a low level. In the group of adolescents aged 15, 36% of the subjects have high values for most of the parameters of this complex, 42% – medium values, and 22% – low. At the same time, 46% of 16-year-olds have high scores for a set of anxiety indicators, 44% – average, and 10% – low. In the group of children aged 17, 46% of senior schoolchildren have high values for most of the parameters of this complex, 38% – average and 16% – low.

Thus, the highest level of anxiety is observed in children aged 8 and 13. In turn, the majority of children with low levels of anxiety are found among children of 9 years old. The average level of anxiety is most typical for children aged 12.

Individual data obtained on a set of indicators characterizing various manifestations of aggression in 7-year-old children allowed us to identify 20% of the examinees with high values for the majority of parameters of this complex and 80% with low values. Among 8-year-old children, 34% have high values in the indexes of this complex, 30% have average, and 36% – below the average. Aggression values among 9-year-old children are distributed between high (64% of subjects) and medium (36% of subjects) levels. At the same time, among 11-year-olds, 51% have high levels of aggression, 34% – on average, and 15% – below the medium level. In the group of children aged 12, 60% of the examinees have high data for most of the parameters of this complex, 12% – average and 28% – low. Among adolescents aged 13, 26% have high values for the indicators characterizing various manifestations of aggression, 22% have average values, and 52% have low values. 41% of 14-year-old children have high, 28% – average, and 31% have a low level of values for this complex. Among adolescents aged 15, 31% of the examinees have high values for most of the parameters, 41% – average, and 28% have low values. Additionally, 47% of 16-year-olds have high scores on the aggression index, 37% – average, and 16% – low. In the group of children aged 17, 36% of senior schoolchildren have high values for most of the parameters of this complex, 29% – medium, and 35% – low.

These data give us reason to note that the highest number of aggressive children is found in the groups of 9 and 12 years olds. In turn, the majority of children with low indicators of aggression were found among 7-year-old children.

Indicators combined in the self-regulation complex are diagnosed only among 11- to 17-year-old children. In the group of children aged 11, 21% of examinees have high values for most of the parameters of this complex, 72% have average values, and only 7% have low values. Among adolescents aged 12, 24% have high indicators value, 58% – average, and 18% – low. Among 13-year-olds, 21% have high self-regulation values, 64% – average, and 15% have it below the average. In the 14-year-olds group, 23% of examinees have high values for most of the parameters of this complex, 61% – average, and 18% – low. Among 15-year-old adolescents, 26% have high values for the indicators characterizing self-regulation features, 58% have average values, and 16% – low. In 34% of the group of 16-year-old, the assessments correspond to a high expression level of indicators of this complex, in 43% – to an average, and in 23% – to a low level. In the 17-year-old group, 26% of the subjects have high values for most of the parameters of this complex, 61% have average values, and 13% – low.

Thus, the majority of children of all age groups have an average level of expression of indicators of the self-regulation complex. The exception is the group of children aged 16, in which all three levels are represented approximately equally.

Summarizing the results of the performed analysis, we can draw the following conclusions.

It was established that the indicators characterizing the emotional sphere of children of different ages and genders are presented ambiguously, i.e. in each age group a certain variability in the range of their expression is noted. It is most clearly fixed in indicators of self-esteem – in pupils aged 7, 8, 11, 12, 13, 14 and 15, anxiety – in 8, 11, 14 and 17 year-olds, aggression in those aged 9, 11 and 16, depression in 12 and 13 years olds, self-regulation and empathy – in 16-year-old students, irritability – in children of 11, 13 and 15 years old, and emotional lability in 11, 13 and 17-year-old schoolchildren.

It was revealed that in each age period, there are indicators that approach the low, medium, and high levels of development of diagnosed emotional manifestations.

2.4 Dynamics of changes of emotional characteristics in children depending on age and gender

Analysis of the primary data showed that in fact, for all parameters, a clear variability in their expressiveness was revealed.

Thus, we can assume that in each age group under the survey, the genesis of the features of the emotional sphere is at different levels. The noted trends in determining the range of variability may indicate that the age groups we singled out differ in the specificity of the development of individual indicators that characterize the features of the emotional sphere of children. The results of the primary data give us reason to believe that there are significant differences in some manifestations of the emotional sphere of children of different ages. However, in order to confirm such differences, we needed to conduct an in-depth analysis of their reliability.

Considering features of changes in the emotional sphere of children, it is possible to note that, in general, on the indicator of personal self-esteem (P1), children of different ages have values that are above the average level.

Thus, we can state that all of the subjects, according to the average values of the personal self-esteem parameter, have a tendency to overestimate personal abilities. To the greatest extent, it is presented in children of 16 and 7 years old (Appendix 3 see Table 2.4.1).

Looking at the average data we can see that the difference between children of 7–8 years old is 4.20 points; between children of 8 and 9 years old is 2.78 points; 9–11 years old – 2.74 points; 11–12 years old – 3.22 points; 12–13 years old – 2.94 points; 13–14 years – 5.73 points; 14–15 years old – 1.46 points; 15–16 years old – 13.28 points, and 16–17 years old – 12.95 points. As we see, the greatest difference is observed in this indicator between children aged 15 and 16 and 16 and 17.

Further in-depth analysis shows that there are statistically reliable differences only between children aged 15 and 16 ($t = 3.34$, $p < 0.01$) and children aged 16–17 ($t = 4.33$, $p < 0.01$) (Appendix 3 see Table 2.4.2).

We explain the revealed differences, first of all, by age peculiarities associated with the difficulties of the adolescent period.

Thus, it can be argued that by the age of 16–17, personal self-esteem becomes more adequate than at the stage of adolescence.

If we turn to the data that characterize the manifestation of personal self-esteem in boys and girls, we can also see certain differences. (Appendix 3 see Table 2.4.3)

For example, the difference between boys and girls on this parameter for 7 – year-old children is 2 conditional points; for 8-year-old children – 8.1 conditional points; for 9-year-olds – 5 conditional points; for 11-year-old students – 4.3 conditional points; 12-year-old children – 13.1 points; for children aged 13 – 13.8 points; 14-year-olds – 4.6 points; for 15-year-olds – 2.7 conditional points; for 16-year-olds – 0.2 points; and for boys and girls of 17 years old – 3 conditional points. The biggest difference between boys and girls is observed at ages 12 and 13.

At the same time, the conducted in-depth statistical analysis shows that the most significant difference in the parameter of personal self-esteem between boys and girls is observed at age 8 ($t = 2.2$, $p < 0.01$) and between boys and girls aged 13 ($t = 2.0$, $p < 0.01$). Perhaps girls at the age of 9 more adequately evaluate life circumstances relative to boys. However, due to a kind of anticipatory mental development, girls at the age of 13 become less adequate in various life situations compared to boys.

Thus, the results of the analysis of average values show that the majority of children, regardless of age, slightly overestimate their abilities. Moreover, in boys, this overestimation is more pronounced. At the same time, differences between children of different ages in manifestation of personal self-esteem are not significant enough. They are most clearly shown in the transition from adolescents to young adulthood.

As for gender differences, they are also traceable only at the stage of entry into adolescence, which we explain by those physiological processes that at this stage begin to dominate over psychological ones.

For the feeling of inferiority parameter (P4), which is close to personal self-assessment, we can note that, in general, children of different ages have data below the average values. As Appendix 3, Table 2.4.1 shows, the peak growth for this parameter is presented for children aged 7.

Based on the average values, we can state the fact that the difference between children 7 and 8 years old is 0.69 points; between children 8 and 9 years old – 0.25 points; 9–11 year-olds – 0.11 points; 11–12 year-olds – 0.23 points; 12–13 year-olds – 0.33 points; 13–14 years old – 0.12 points; 14–15 years old – 0.18 points; and 15–17 years old – 0.32 points.

However, the greatest number of reliable differences are found among children aged 12–13 and 15–17.

Based on the findings, we can note that there are statistically reliable differences in this parameter only among children aged 9–11 years ($t = 3.70$, $p < 0.01$) and 12–13 ($t = 4.06$, $p < 0.01$).

It is possible that the difference detected in children aged 9–10 can be traced, primarily, in view of the difficulties associated with the transition of children from elementary school to the period of entering middle grades. And also the difference detected in children aged 9–10 can be traced, primarily, in view of the difficulties associated with the transition of children from elementary school to the period of entering middle grades and also the difficulties of the puberty period and the upcoming professional and personal self-determinations.

It is important to note that there are certain differences between boys and girls according to the average data that characterize the manifestations of the feeling of inferiority (P4). Here, the difference between boys and girls on this parameter for 7-year-old has quantitative representation at the level of 0.3 conditional points; for 8-year-olds – 0.2 points; for 9-year-olds – 0.9; for children aged 11 – 0.4; for children aged 12 – 1 conditional point; for 13-year-olds – 0.7 conditional points; for 14-year-olds – 0.6; and for 15-year-olds – 0.7 conditional points.

The greatest difference in the feeling of inferiority parameter (P4), as we see, is recorded among boys and girls aged 12. At the same time, significant differences were found only in children aged 9 ($t = 2.6$, $p < 0.01$) and 12 ($t = 3.9$, $p < 0.01$).

These differences indicate that: first, by the age of 10, the feeling of inferiority is less pronounced in girls than in boys due to age specifics. Second, in the middle of adolescence, i.e. by the age of 13, the picture changes dramatically. If we pay attention to the average values between boys and girls (Appendix 3 see Table 2.4.1), we will see that boys have a greater sense of inferiority than girls.

Summarizing the results of this study, we can see that the level of the feeling of inferiority parameter (P4) in children of different ages manifests itself to a small extent, and in boys, it is more pronounced than in girls. The biggest differences between children were recorded for the ages between 9 and 12.

Here, when looking at cross-gender differences, we can observe clear jumps at the time of transition from junior to middle school, as well as during the transition from middle school to high school.

This is explained in the first case by changes in the perception of one's place in the system of relationships, and also by changes in the social situation of development. In addition, children are at the stage of a new age period, and this, in turn, entails a number of new formations. In the second case, that is, in adolescence, it is expressed mainly due to personal instability, i.e. contradictory traits and tendencies as if fighting with each other, as well as the biological changes associated with puberty.

Considering the peculiarities of reliable differences in the emotional sphere of children of different ages, we can note that in the parameter close to self-doubt (P7), values below the average level are observed. According to the average data, it is clear that the peak of the parameter under study is recorded in children aged 8. From the presented averages, we can see that the difference between children aged 7 and 8 years is 0.4 points; 8 and 9 years old – 0.86 points; 9 and 11 years old – 0.48 points; 11 and 12 years old – 0.22 points; 12 and 13 years old – 0.81 points; 13 and 14 years old – 0.42 points; 14 and 15 years old – 0.65 points, and 15 and 17 years old – 0.2 points.

The results obtained give us reason to note that the highest difference is observed between children aged 8–9.

Statistically reliable differences in this indicator were recorded only between children aged 12 and 13 ($t = 2.80$, $p < 0.01$) and those aged between 14 and 15 ($t = 2.68$, $p < 0.01$).

These differences appear to be due to age-specific features associated with the complexities of puberty. That is, it can be argued that the parameter of self-doubt follows a decreasing line by the age of 15.

Summarizing the average values for the self-doubt parameter (P7) between boys and girls, we noted certain differences. In particular, when analyzing the difference between boys and girls according to the diagnosed indicator, we found that for children of 7 years old it is 0.2 conditional points; for 8-year-old children – 1.5 points; for 9-year-olds – 0.8 points; for 12 year-olds – 0.3 points; for 13-year-olds – 0.8 points; for 14-year-olds – 0.3 points; for 15-year-olds – 0.4; and for 17-year-olds – 0.1 points.

To the greatest extent, this difference is recorded among boys and girls of 8 years old. Here, statistical analysis showed that a significant difference is observed only among boys and girls aged 12 ($t = 3.1$, $p < 0.01$).

Thus, based on the above values, we can say that children develop self-doubt, which initially (mostly manifested in ambiguous behavior in 8-year-olds, girls, in particular) arises from the awareness of their incompetence, failure to solve some specific tasks, most often associated with learning, and then spreads to the personality as a whole. This feeling reaches its maximum level in girls at the age of 12.

Analyzing the results of the study related to the determination of reliable differences in the indicator of personal self-esteem (P10), we can see that the features of changes in the emotional sphere of children of different ages are mainly reflected in the range below the average values. That is, we can argue that the majority of the children in this parameter tend to underestimate personal abilities.

Continuing to consider the results associated with the determination of reliable differences in the diagnosed parameter of the emotional sphere of children, we see that the average values are most expressed in children of 8 years old. The resulting difference has a quantitative representation between children aged 7–8 at the level of – 0.41 points; between children 8 and 9 years old – 0.44 points; 9 and 11 years old – 0.81 points; 11 and 13 years old – 0.34 points; 13 and 14 years old – 0.28 points; 14 and 15 – 7.87 points; and between children 15 and 17 years old, the difference is 8 points. As seen, the biggest difference in this indicator can be traced among children aged 15–17. However, statistically reliable differences, as follows from in-depth analysis, were found only in children aged 14–15 ($t = 2.19$, $p < 0.01$).

These differences are explained, first of all, by the complexities of mental development during the transition period. That is, by about the age of 15, personal self-esteem becomes more adequate than at a previous age period.

Analyzing the average values between boys and girls of this indicator, it is possible to note sufficient variability in its expression. As we can see, the difference between boys and girls on the personal self-esteem parameter (P10) for 7-year-old children is 0.3 conditional points; for 8-year-old children – 0.4 points; for 9 year-olds – 0.4 points; for 11-year-olds – 0.1 points; for 13-year-olds – 0.2 points; for 14-year-olds – 0.5 points; for 15-year-old examinees – 1 point; and for 17-year-olds – 2.2 points. The greatest difference is fixed among boys and girls of 17 years old. This is confirmed by our statistical analysis, where this difference is reliable only among boys and girls aged 17 ($t = 3.3$, $p < 0.01$).

Summarizing the results of the completed study on the indicator of personal self-esteem, we assume that girls at the age of 17 assess situations more adequately than boys. If we turn to the results that characterize the average values, we can note that boys overestimate their abilities relative to girls on this parameter.

Thus, on the basis of the study, we can state that the level of the parameter of personal self-esteem (P10) in different age groups is mainly within the average and below-average values.

As for the cross-gender differences in this parameter, they are most clearly seen in adolescence.

Perhaps this is due to the fact that in this period the personal self-affirmation of boys and girls creates the prerequisites for the formation of their life positions.

When analyzing the specifics of changes in the emotional sphere of children of different ages, we can note that in terms of the feeling of rejection (P2), the values are within the range of its lower average level of expression (see Table 2.4.4).

As seen from the table, the peak growth of this parameter is found in 17-year-old subjects. From the presented average values, we can see that the difference in points in children aged 7–8 is – 0.28 points; 8–9 years old is 0.34 points; 9–11 years old – 1.38 points; 11–12 years old – 0.21 points; 12–13 years old – 1.8 points; 13–14 years old – 0.51 points; 14–15 years old – 0.36 points; and 15–17 year-olds – 2.97 points. The biggest difference is recorded between children aged 12–13 and 15–17.

Statistically reliable differences are noted here only among children aged 9–10 ($t = 3.70$, $p < 0.01$) and 12–13 ($t = 4.06$, $p < 0.01$).

We explain these results, in the first case, by factors in the organization of the educational process and informal relationships with peers, which cause an increased level of rejection feelings. In the second case, however, we attribute

TABLE 2.4.4 Statistically reliable differences in indicators describing particularities of anxiety in boys and girls

Age	*Indicators*							
statistical data	*P2*	*P5*	*P8*	*P12*	*P13*	*P17*	*P19*	*P23*
	B G	B G	B G	B G	B G	B G	B G	B G
7 y.o.				–	–	–	–	–
x	2.4 2.5	2.6 2.7	1.5 1.3					
t	= n/d	= n/d	= n/d					
8 y.o.				–	–	–	–	–
x	2.9 2.6	3.5 4.4	3.5 2.3					
t	= n/d	= n/d	= 2.0					
9 y.o.				–	–	–	–	–
x	2.8 2.1	2.0 1.9	2.7 1.8					
t	= n/d	= n/d	= 2.0					
11 y.o.								
x	5.2 5.1	3.2 4.3	1.5 1.8	32 33	42 42	5.8 5.9	6.7 7.4	7.1 7.2
t	= n/d	= 2.1	= n/d	= n/d	= n/d	= n/d	= n/d	= n/d
12 y.o.			–					
x	1.2 1.6	4.2 3.6		25 31	42 45.5	6.1 8.0	7.1 8.3	6.9 7.3
t	= n/d	= n/d		= 2.1	= n/d	= 4.7	= 3.9	= n/d
13 y.o.								
x	2.7 3.6	2.2 2.2	1.8 0.9	38.4 40.8	44 46	6.6 6.5	7.3 7.4	6.5 7.8
t	= n/d	= n/d	= 3.4	= n/d	= n/d	= n/d	= n/d	= n/d
14 y.o.								
x	1.6 1.4	3.0 2.5	2.8 2.1	42.3 42.1	39.8 48	5.6 6.8	5.8 7.5	6.4 7.0
t	= n/d	= n/d	= 2.1	= n/d	= 5.1	= 2.7	= 4.1	= n/d
15 y.o.								
x	1.8 2.7	3.6 5.4	2.1 1.7	23.9 30.9	42 42.6	5.3 6.6	6.1 7.3	6.1 6.8
t	= 2.0	= 2.0	= n/d	= 2.5	= n/d	= n/d	= n/d	= n/d

**The differences shown in the table are significant at $p < 0.05$; B – boys, G – girls.*

these differences to personal instability along with complex biological changes occurring in adolescents.

If we turn to the results that characterize the manifestations of feelings of rejection in boys and girls, we can also see certain differences. Thus, the difference between boys and girls in this parameter for children aged 7 has the following quantitative representation: 0.1 conditional points; for 8-year-olds – 0.3 conditional points; for 9-year-olds – 0.7 conditional points; for 11-year-olds – 0.1 conditional points; for 12-year-olds – 0.4 points; for 13-year-olds – 0.9 points; for children aged 14 -– 0.2; for children of 15 years old – 0.9 conditional points; and for boys and girls of 17 years old, this difference is 0.6 conditional points. The highest difference between boys and girls is observed in children between 13 and 15 years old. At the same time, a significant difference between boys and girls was found only in 15-year-old examinees ($t = 2.0$, $p < 0.01$).

Such results can be explained by the fact that in 15-year-old schoolchildren, a characteristic manifestation is the emergence of a need for psychological intimacy with another person. Its alternative is a feeling of isolation, loneliness, and a sense of rejection. If we turn to the data of statistically reliable differences in this indicator between boys and girls, we see that boys at the age of 15 have lower values for the parameter of the feeling of rejection relative to girls. Most likely, this is due to the fact that, as we pointed out above, the intimate-personal issue becomes the leading one in emotional communication with peers at this age, which is more traceable for girls than for boys.

Thus, the results of the study show that most children of different ages are within the average and below the average limits for this indicator. At the same time, the differences between the subjects of different ages in the manifestation of feelings of rejection are not significant enough. They are most clearly registered at the moment of transition from primary school age to adolescence and last approximately until the middle of it.

Based on the above data on cross-gender differences, it is clear that they are observed mainly at the end of adolescence, on the threshold of the transition to early adult life.

According to the family anxiety indicator (P5), we can note that, in general, the values presented are above the average level, i.e. we can state the fact that most of the children on the average data of this parameter have an inflated level of anxiety. Moreover, this is most pronounced in children between 11 and 15 years old.

Looking at the average data, we can see that the difference between children 7 and 8 years old is quantitatively represented by 1.34 points; between children of 8 and 9 years old, this difference is 1.92 points; between 9 and 11-year-old children – 3.19 points; between 11- and 12-year-olds – 3.84 points; 12 and 13 years old – 1.78 points; 13 and 14 years old – 1.55 points; 14 and 15 – 3.47 points; and between 15 and 17 years old, this difference is 2.49 points.

It is important to note that the biggest difference is recorded in children aged 11, 12, 14 and 15 years.

Subsequently, a more detailed analysis showed that there are statistically reliable differences between children aged 7 and 8 years ($t = 2.16$, $p < 0.01$); between children aged 8 and 9 ($t = 3.42$, $p < 0.01$); 9 and 11 years old ($t = 5.00$, $p < 0.01$); 11 and 12 years old ($t = 5.00$, $p < 0.01$); 12 and 13 years old ($t = 3.55$, $p < 0.01$); 13 and 14 years old ($t = 3.67$, $p < 0.01$); and 14 and 15 years old ($t = 5.00$, $p < 0.01$).

These differences are stated in each of the above ages by the fact that they are probably determined by the difficulties in the social development of children of primary school age that arise along with their active mastery of learning activities. Besides, it is connected with the special feeling of adulthood that occurs in adolescents at the age of 12–15. In elementary school children, the presence of certain anxiety in the family can also be substantiated by changes in self-awareness, at the level of reassessment of certain values, including some values of family interaction. Also, in children of this age group, as we know, a semantic orienting basis of action appears, which is a link between the desire to do something and unfolding actions that lead to a certain anxiety of the child in his microenvironment. As for adolescence, as such, anxiety in the family seems to manifest itself, because of conflicts arising from the influence of parental control. The most important factor confirming the change in anxiety is also the fact that difficulties and emotional breakdowns in adolescents arise with high expectations that parents will not understand and will not justify certain actions.

When analyzing the data that characterize the manifestations of anxiety in the family among boys and girls, we can also see sufficient variability in its expression. For example, the difference between boys and girls in this indicator for children of 7–8 years old is – 0.1 conditional points; for 8-year-old children – 0.9 conditional points; for children aged 9 – 0.1 conditional points; for 11-year-olds – 1.1 conditional points; for 12-year-olds – 0.6 conditional points; for children aged 14 years – 0.5 conditional points; for 15-year-olds – 1.8 conditional points. For children aged between 13 and 17, no differences were found; i.e., equal to zero. The maximum indicated difference between boys and girls is observed at the age of 15 years. This is confirmed by our in-depth statistical analysis, which showed that this difference (see Table 2.4.4.) is significant between boys and girls aged 11 ($t = 2.1$, $p < 0.01$) and 15 years ($t = 2.0$, $p < 0.01$).

The results obtained indicate a clear presence of significant differences between boys and girls aged 11 and 15 in the expression of family anxiety. Thus, for girls aged between 11 and 15, anxiety in the family can be traced to a greater extent than for boys. Probably, this occurs in them in connection with a kind of increased sensitivity to family relationships, as well as due to the outstripping of their general mental development during this period. That is, girls at this age become sensitive and less adequate than boys in assessing their own relationships with relatives.

The performed analysis also suggests that the majority of children, from 7 to 17 years old, still have an increased level of anxiety in the family, and this is probably due, primarily, to the physiological processes that dominate at this age.

Considering the parameter of personal anxiety (P8) according to the average data, we can note the values presented below the average level, i.e. we say that in the majority of children it is fixed at a minimum level.

At the same time, its highest level was noted in children of 8 years old, relative to other age groups. The difference between children aged 7 and 8 for this indicator is – 1.69 points; between children of 8 and 9 years old – 0.93 points; between children of 9 and 11 – 0.53 points; 11 and 13 year-olds – 0.16 points; 13 and 14 years old – 0.9 points; 14 and 15 – 0.34 points; and for 15 and 17 years, this difference is 0.33 points. The biggest difference was found between children aged 7 and 8 (see Table 2.4.1). A more detailed analysis showed that there are statistically reliable differences between children aged 7 and 8 ($t = 4.08$, $p < 0.01$); between children of 8 and 9 years old ($t = 1.90$, $p < 0.01$); 13 and 14 years old ($t = 3.85$, $p < 0.01$) and between children of 14 and 15 years old ($t = 2.44$, $p < 0.01$).

Such differences we can explain, first, by a minor natural crisis at age of 7, associated with a change in the perception of one's place in the system of relations when entering the school community. Within the interval between 8 and 9 years, processes of certain concealing of emotions begin to form, i.e. immediacy of emotions becomes occasional, and children begin to make certain efforts to hide their feelings. Against this background, pride and vanity are laid, the manifestation of which causes minor anxiety, which is important for self-affirmation. At 13–14 and 14–15 years, differences in the manifestation of personal anxiety are explained by contradictory trends in psychological development that arise in the teenage period and affect personal instability, which entails fluctuations in the level of this anxiety.

If we look at the average data that characterize the manifestation of the personal anxiety indicator (P8) in boys and girls, we can notice a number of distinct differences. For example, the difference between boys and girls in this parameter for children of 7 years old is 0.5 conditional points; for children aged 8 – 1.2 conditional points; for 9-year-olds – 0.9 conditional points; for 11-year-old children – 0.3 conditional points; for 13-year-olds – 0.9 conditional points; for children aged 14 – 0.7 points; for 15-year-olds – 0.4; and for 17-year-olds – 1 conditional point. To the greatest extent, this difference is observed between boys and girls of 8 years old (Appendix 3 see Table 2.4.2).

It should be noted that a significant difference was found here between boys and girls aged 8 ($t = 2.0$, $p < 0.01$); aged 9 ($t = 2.0$, $p < 0.01$); 13 ($t = 3.4$, $p < 0.01$); and 14 ($t = 2.1$, $p < 0.01$).

Thus we can assume that boys at the age of 9 have a higher level of personal anxiety than girls. Approximately the same picture is observed in children between 13 and 14 years of age.

At the same time, reliable differences between children of different ages in the manifestation of the personal anxiety index (P8) are quite significant. They are mainly observed at the beginning of primary school age and then in the middle of adolescence.

Considering the results related to the reactive anxiety indicator (P12), we note mainly the average level of expression of this parameter. Moreover, as Table 2.4.1 shows, this indicator, relative to other groups, is highly represented in the group of 14-year-olds.

At the same time, the difference in its values is clearly seen among all groups. Thus, between children 11 and 12 years old, it is 5.51 points; 12 and 13 years old – 12.65 points; 13 and 14 years old – 2.07 points; 14 and 15 years old – 3.35 points; 15 and 16 years old – 20.54 points; and 16 and 17 years old – 23.33 points. The highest difference is recorded between the subjects aged 16 and 17. At the same time, significant differences were found between children aged 11 and 12 ($t = 3.26$, $p < 0.01$); 12 and 13 years ($t = 4.58$, $p < 0.01$); 14 and 15 years ($t = 5.07$, $p < 0.01$); 15 and 16 years ($t = 3.66$, $p < 0.01$); and 16 and 17 years old ($t = 5.00$, $p < 0.01$).

The results obtained can be interpreted by the fact that these patterns in the dynamics of the manifestation of anxiety, seem to be associated with age-increasing conditions of social interaction of children's behavior. It is also possible that this is also influenced by the conditions of increasing complexity of learning activities, where there is often a feeling of uncertainty, which possibly leads to reactive anxiety.

Analyzing the data characterizing the manifestation of the parameter of reactive anxiety in boys and girls, we also found certain differences. Quantitatively, this can be represented as follows: the difference at the age of 11 is – 1 conditional point; at 12 years this difference is 6 conditional points; at 13 years – 2.4 conditional points; at the age of 14 – 0.2 points; at 15 years old – 7 points; at 16 years old – 0.7 conditional points; and at 17 years – 2.9 conditional points. The greatest difference is recorded between boys and girls at age 12. However, if we turn to statistically reliable differences, we see that they are observed only in children aged 12 ($t = 2.1$, $p < 0.01$) and 15 ($t = 2.5$, $p < 0.01$).

We can assume that girls have a higher level of reactive anxiety at the age of 12 due to their advanced mental development manifested in the physiological "development" relative to boys, i.e. their reactions in solving any task are more pronounced. Approximately the same picture is observed in girls of 15 years old, where this phase of the pubertal period reaches a new wave.

The above results of the study lead to the general conclusion that, regardless of age, most children have an adequate response in the manifestation of reactive anxiety to the current situation or the solution of any task. At the same time, anxiety is more pronounced in girls than in boys, predominantly during adolescence and at the time of transition from adolescence to adult life.

Considering the average data of the personal anxiety parameter (P13), we can note that the majority of children, regardless of age, have values that are within their average level. The maximum level of the parameter under study is expressed in subjects aged 13. At the same time, if we turn to the table of average values (Appendix 3 see Table 2.4.1), we can see that the difference between children aged 11 and 12 is 1.8 points; 12 and 13 years old – 2.43

points; between children aged 13 and 14, this difference is 1.62 points; 14 and 15 year-olds – 1.65 points; 15 and 16 years old – 3.33 points; and 16 and 17 years old – 3.18 points. The maximum difference is noted between the subjects 15 and 16 years old. However, in all cases, these statistical differences are not reliable.

If we turn to the table of average values that characterize the manifestation of personal anxiety in boys and girls, we find a certain variability in their expression. Namely, for children aged 11, the difference in this indicator is 1 conditional point; for children aged 12 – 3.5 conditional points; 13 years old – 2.4 conditional points; 14 years old – 8 points; for 15 year-olds – 0.4 points; for 16-year-olds – 0.9 conditional points; and for 17-year-old subjects – 3.9 conditional points. As seen, 14-year-old subjects have the highest difference. At the same time, as the analysis of statistically reliable differences shows, a reliable difference is recorded only in eighth-grade students, i.e. for 14-year-old test takers (Appendix 3 see Table 2.4.1).

Such results are to a certain extent consistent with the presented data on differences in reactive anxiety between boys and girls during adolescence.

Analyzing the average values for the personal anxiety parameter (P13), it can be noted that all children are relatively adequate in assessing various situations in their life path. However, in girls, anxiety is more pronounced, especially during adolescence. This was explained for the above reasons.

According to the parameter of neuroticism (P17), we can see that, in general, the values here are above the average level. Moreover, as seen from the table of average data (Appendix 3 see Table 2.4.1), the peak growth of this indicator was noted in children of 12 years old.

Considering the average values, we note that the difference between children aged 11 and 12 is 0.89 points; 12 and 13 years – 0.2 points; 13 and 14 years – 0.3 points; 14 and 15 years – 0.04 points; 15 and 16 years old – 0.32 points; and 16 and 17 years – 0.09 points. The biggest difference is recorded between children aged 11 and 12. However, reliable differences were recorded only between children aged 11 and 12 ($t = 2.22$, $p < 0.01$).

We explain these results by the fact that children of 12 years old have a rather pronounced neurotic syndrome of asthenic type with a psychosomatic character. Probably it is connected with the peculiarities of adolescent development, characterized by such traits as conflict, instability and personal inconsistency.

According to the data that characterize the manifestations of the neuroticism parameter (P17) between boys and girls, certain differences can be traced. In particular, the revealed difference for children aged 11 is 0.1 conditional points; for 12-year-old subjects – 1.9 conditional points; for 13-year-olds – 0.1 conditional points; for 14-year-olds – 1.2 points; for 15-year-olds – 1.3 points; for 16-year-olds – 1.3; and for 17-year-olds – 0.9 conditional points. The peak of growth in differences is observed between boys and girls at the age of 15 and 16. However, these differences are reliable only between boys and girls aged 12 ($t = 4.7$, $p < 0.01$) and 14 ($t = 2.7$, $p < 0.01$).

Based on the results obtained, it can be assumed that girls aged between 12 and 14 are exposed to a greater number of stresses than boys and have an exaggerated level of neuroticism.

Proceeding from the generalization of the results of the performed analysis, it is clear that the majority of children, regardless of age, have a slightly overestimated level of neuroticism. Moreover, it is expressed to a greater degree in girls. At the same time, differences between children of different ages in the manifestation of neuroticism are not significant enough. They show up most clearly in adolescence.

As for cross-gender differences, they occur only in the middle and at the end of adolescence. We attribute this to the biological processes that take place in the body of a teenager.

Considering the individual data of the parameter of depressiveness (P19) in children of different ages, we can see (Appendix 3 see Table 2.4.1) that, on the whole, they have values presented within the average and above the average level. To the greatest extent, the indicator under study is expressed in children 12 years old.

At the same time, if we turn to the average values (Appendix 3 see Table 2.4.1), we see more pronounced differences. Namely, the difference between children aged 11 and 12 has quantitative representation at the level of 0.37 points; 12 and 13 years old – 0.13 points; 13 and 14 years old – 0.63 points; 14 and 15 years old – 0.3 points; 15 and 16 years old – 0.31 points; and 16 and 17 years old – 0.1 points.

As we can see, the biggest difference is observed between children aged 13 and 14. At the same time, this difference is statistically reliable between children aged 13 and 14 ($t = 2.39$, $p < 0.01$).

Turning to the data that characterize the differences in the indicators of the emotional sphere between boys and girls on the parameter of depressiveness, we can see a certain variability in their expression. In particular, this difference for children aged 11 is 0.7 conditional points; for 12-year-olds – 1.2 conditional points; 13-year-olds – 0.1 points; 14-year-olds – 1.7 points; 15-year-olds – 1.2 points; for 16-year-old subjects – 0.8 conditional points; and for 17-year-olds – 1 conditional point.

As we see, at the age of 14, this difference is maximally expressed, and minimally in 13-year-old subjects.

At the same time, reliable differences between boys and girls were recorded only in subjects aged 12- ($t = 3.9$, $p < 0.01$), 14- ($t = 4.1$, $p < 0.01$), and 17-year-olds ($t = 2.3$, $p < 0.01$).

These differences are most likely related to the fact that gender differences, including depression, begin to show most clearly during adolescence. It can also be assumed that girls at the age of 14 have insufficiently adequate self-esteem, a lowered level of self-regulation, and a number of other features that distinguish them from boys on a depression scale.

In early adulthood, an increased level of the depression parameter is also recorded. Perhaps this is due to the emotional barriers that arise during this period among schoolchildren. In addition, it should be noted that the self-esteem in girls aged 17 is higher than that in adolescents, which may also affect their depression.

An analysis of the average values shows that the majority of children, regardless of age, show a slightly overestimated level of depression. Moreover, it is more expressed in girls than in boys. However, these data are not significant enough.

A different picture of the data is observed when considering gender differences, which are mostly recorded starting from adolescence up to high school. Perhaps this is determined by both personal and biological changes in the pubertal period.

Continuing to consider the features of differences in the emotional sphere of children of different ages, it should be noted that according to the shyness index (P23), most of the children have values above the average level. Moreover, this indicator is maximally expressed in subjects 16 years old. At the same time, based on the data presented in Table 2.4.1, we can see that the difference between children aged 11 and 12 is 0.1 points; 12 and 13 years – 0.2 points; 13 and 14 years – 0.35 points; 14 and 15 years – 0.08 points; 15 and 16 years – 0.95 points; and 16- and 17-year-olds – 0.53 points. As we can see, the highest difference is observed between children aged 16 and 17. Further analysis confirms the presence of reliable differences here ($t = 2.39$, $p < 0.01$).

Such results can be explained, first of all, by the fact that by the age of 16 schoolchildren become more confident in their statements and actions, relative to other ages.

Turning to the results characterizing the manifestation of the shyness index (P23) between boys and girls, we can also note certain differences. For example, the difference between boys and girls aged 11 is 0.1 conditional points; 12 years – 0.4 conditional points; 13 years – 1.3 conditional points; for subjects aged 14 – 0.6 points; for schoolchildren aged 15 – 0.7 points; for aged 16 – 0.2 conditional points; and in subjects aged 17 years – 0.4 conditional points.

The biggest difference is recorded between boys and girls aged 13. This difference is also statistically significant between boys and girls 13 years old ($t = 2.8$, $p < 0.01$).

It seems that girls at this age are predisposed to a more active response to common life situations that proceed according to a passive-defensive type. Higher indicators of shyness also reflect the presence of certain anxiety, constraint and self-doubt in girls aged 13, which may generate difficulties in social contact.

Thus, the results of the study show the majority of children have certain problems in communicating with both peers and adults. Differences between grades at senior school age are most clearly seen.

At the same time, when considering cross-gender differences, we should note that they are mainly observed in the middle of adolescence. Moreover, in girls, they are expressed to a much greater extent. It is also probable that it is connected not only with difficulties in communication but also with arising complexes in social contacts on the basis of expressed changes of physiological nature in adolescent girls.

Continuing to examine the features of changes in the emotional sphere of children, we can note that, in general, children of different ages have values recorded below the average level of hostility (P3), i.e. we can affirm that all children, according to the average data of this parameter, tend to be benevolent (see Table 2.4.5).

TABLE 2.4.5 Statistically reliable differences in indicators that characterize aggression features of boys and girls*

Age statistical data	*Indicators*						
	P3	*P6*	*P9*	*P11*	*P18*	*P20*	*P22*
	B G	*B G*	*B G*	*B G*	*B G*	*B G*	*B G*
8 y.o.				–	–	–	–
x	2.8 1.7	1.4 0.7	1.9 1.5				
t	= 2.6	= n/d	= n/d				
9 y.o.				–	–	–	–
x	2.0 1.4	1.8 1.1	2.0 0.7				
t	= n/d	= n/d	= 3.2				
11 y.o.							
x	2.7 2.6	2.9 1.3	0.4 0.4	14 16	6.3 7.3	7.6 7.8	7.3 1.8
t	= n/d	= 3.0	= n/d	= n/d	= n/d	= n/d	= n/d
12 y.o.			–	–			
x	2.1 0.8	3.4 0.9			5.9 5.0	7.5 7.9	8.1 7.5
t	= 3.9	= 2.1			= n/d	= n/d	= n/d
13 y.o.							
x	1.1 0.4	1.1 0.7	1.8 0.9 =	14.8 17.8	6.7 5.7	7.5 7.1	7.7 7.8
t	= n/d	= 2.1	2.1	= 2.3	= n/d	= n/d	= n/d
14 y.o.	1.4 0.8	1.6 1.5					
x	= n/d	= n/d	2.4 1.6	12.5 17.0	5.9 6.2	6.8 7.6	7.7 7.6
t			= 2.4	= 3.6	= n/d	= 2.6	= n/d
15 y.o.	–	–	–				
x				12.3 15.8	5.8 6.7	8.7 7.1	6.8 8.0
t				= n/d	= n/d	= 2.4	= n/d
16 y.o.	–	–	–				
x				11.9 13.4	5.6 5.8	7.6 6.9	7.9 8.3
t				= n/d	= n/d	= n/d	= n/d
17 y.o.							
x	1.3 0.6	2.2 1.4	2.1 0.7	11.2 16.9	6.5 7.2	7.3 7.4	8.2 7.2
t	= n/d	= n/d	= n/d	= 4.5	= n/d	= n/d	= 2.4

**The differences shown in the table are significant at $p < 0.05$ B – boys. G – girls.*

If we turn to the average values, we can see that this parameter is represented to the greatest extent in children aged 12. Analyzing these data, we note that the difference between children aged 7 and 8 is 0.15 points; between children 8 and 9 years old, this difference is 0.65 points; between children 9 and 11 years old – 0.32 points; 11 and 12 years old – 0.56 points; 12 and 13 years old – 1.6 points; 13 and 14 years old – 0.6 points; 14 and 15 years old – 0.78 points; and 15 and 17 years old, this difference is 0.97 points. As seen, the greatest difference in the average values of the hostility index is observed among children aged 12 and 13. However, this difference is reliable not only between children of these ages ($t = 3.20$, $p < 0.01$) but also between children of 8 and 9 years old ($t = 2.16$, $p < 0.01$), 13 and 14 years old ($t = 2.55$, $p < 0.01$) and 14 and 15 years old ($t = 3.12$, $p < 0.01$).

We can explain the revealed differences by the hostility parameter by the fact that in the primary school age, awareness of experiences forms reactive affective complexes which cause certain defensive aggression in the behavior of children. In adolescence, these features are observed, on the one hand, in relations with peers, who have to face certain rules of the moral "code", i.e. strictly regulated behavior and, on the other hand, in relations with adults, with adolescents' active desire to free themselves from parental control, i.e. to limit parental influence.

Having turned to the data obtained, we found that the differences in indicators between boys and girls have a certain variability. In particular, for children of 8 years old this parameter makes a difference of 1.1 conditional points; for children aged 9 years – 0.6 conditional points; for 11-year-old children – 0.1 conditional points; 12-year-olds have 1.3 conditional points; children aged 13 – 0.7 conditional points; children aged 14 – 0.5 points; 15-year-olds have 0.7 points; and children aged 17 – 0.7 conditional points. This difference was not found in children between 7 and 15 years old. The maximum difference between boys and girls, as can be seen from the data presented, is observed in children aged between 8 and 12 years.

Further analysis reveals that a reliable difference in the hostility parameter is also recorded between boys and girls aged 8 ($t = 2.6$, $p < 0.01$) and 12 ($t = 3.9$, $p < 0.01$). This may be due to the fact that boys aged between 8 and 12 develop frustration associated with personal self-assertion and problems with their active psychophysiological development.

At the same time, research results show that most children still have a low level of hostility parameter (P3). It should be noted that boys exhibit it to a somewhat greater degree than girls. The fact that there are certain differences between children in the middle of primary school age and then at the stage of adolescence points to the dynamics of changes in this parameter in view of the specific social and internal processes that the child faces.

Approximately the same trend is observed when considering the indicator of family aggressiveness (P6). From the presented table of these average values, it is clear (Appendix 3 see Table 2.4.1) that the data of this indicator are mainly at the level of average and below-average values. And, as seen from Table 2.4.1, the highest variation can be traced in relationships up to the maximum values for 11-year-old children.

If we look at the data presented in Table 2.4.1, we can see that the difference between children 7 and 8 years old is 0.06 points; between children 8 and 9 years old – 0.33 points; 9 and 11 years – 1.22 points; 11 and 12 years – 0.99 points; 12 and 13 – 0.88 points, 13 and 14 years – 0.34 points; 14 and 15 years – 0.31 points; and between children 15 and 17 years – 0.35 points. As we can see, according to the indicator of family aggressiveness, reliable differences were found between children aged 9 and 11. However, statistically reliable differences were found between children aged 9 and 11 ($t = 3.56$, $p < 0.01$); 11 and 12 years ($t = 2.05$, $p < 0.01$), and 12 and 13 years ($t = 2.02$, $p < 0.01$).

From the results obtained, it follows that the level of family aggressiveness is more pronounced in adolescence than in other age periods. Probably, it is connected with the neoplasms of this age – the growth of the spirit of independence, which makes the teenager's relations in the family very tense. During this period, the thirst for freedom from external control is combined with the growth of self-control and the beginning of conscious self-education. This increases the vulnerability of a teenager in various family circumstances.

Summarizing the average data that characterize the manifestation of the parameter of family aggressiveness (P6) in boys and girls, certain differences can be noted. Thus, the difference in this indicator for children of 7 years old is 0.3 conditional points; for children aged 8 – 0.7 conditional points; for 11-year-old children – 1.6 points; for 12-year-olds – 2.5 points; for 13-year-olds – 0.4 points; for 14-year-olds – 0.1; for 15-year-olds – 1.8; and for 17-year-olds – 0.8 conditional points. These data show that the biggest difference is recorded between boys and girls 12 years old.

A statistically reliable difference is found between boys and girls aged 12 ($t = 2.1$, $p < 0.01$). In addition, this difference was noted in children aged 11 ($t = 3.0$, $p < 0.01$) and 13 years ($t = 2.1$, $p < 0.01$). We can explain such results by the fact that boys have a greater degree of family aggressiveness parameter than girls due to the maximum expressed personal instability, as well as egocentric hobbies that alternate, which is reflected in difficulties and conflicts in relation to their parents.

These results of the study show that the majority of children, regardless of age, have a fairly low level of family aggressiveness indicator. At the same time, the tendency for differences between boys and girls is quite noticeable, primarily during the teenage years. Reliable differences between groups of children of different ages begin to be recorded on this indicator at the end of primary school age.

Analyzing the data obtained on the personal aggression index (P9), it can be noted that in the general sample, a fairly large number of children, regardless of age, have values below the average level. To the greatest extent, the indicator of personal aggression is expressed in children of 8 years old. As we can see (see Table 2.4.1), from the average data, the difference between children aged 7 and

8 is 0.44 points; between children 8 and 9, it is 0.53 points; 9 and 11 years – 0.81 points; 11 and 13 years – 1.05 points; 13 and 14 years – 0.51 points; 14 and 15 years – 0.67 points; and 15 and 17 – 0.11 points. The greatest difference, as can be seen from the presented results, is observed between children aged 11 and 13. We can state the fact that a statistically reliable difference is observed between children aged 9- and 11- ($t = 3.41$, $p < 0.01$), and 13- and 14-year-olds ($t = 2.13$, $p < 0.01$).

These results indicate that at the end of primary school age, the level of personal aggression (P9) decreases. And by the age of 15, this level begins to shift toward the minimum values.

It was found that the difference between boys and girls on personal aggression index (P9) among 7-year-old schoolchildren is 0.2 conditional points; for children aged 8 – 0.4 conditional points; for 9-year-olds – 1.3 points; for 13-year-olds – 0.9 points; for 14-year-olds – 0.8; for 15-year-olds – 0.5; and for 17-year-olds – 1.4 conditional points. At the same time, these differences were not expressed in children aged 11, 12 and 16. The maximum difference between boys and girls is observed at the age of 9–17 years.

In-depth statistical analysis shows that a reliable difference is observed between boys and girls aged 9 ($t = 3.2$, $p < 0.01$); 13 years ($t = 2.1$, $p < 0.01$); 14 years ($t = 2.4$, $p < 0.01$); and 17 years ($t = 3.1$, $p < 0.01$).

Perhaps such differences are conditioned by the fact that from the age of 10 to 12 years, the parameter of personal aggression (P9) is more expressed in boys than in girls due to their increased reactivity, dynamic against the background of the biological changes that characterize this age. Besides, at the age of 13 and 14, the indicator of personal aggression in boys may be higher also because during this period a sense of adulthood is actively developing, asserting oneself in communication among peers. We relate the increase in aggression by the age of 17 to personal feelings about the forthcoming professional self-determination.

Nevertheless, based on the data obtained, the majority of children, despite visible fluctuations, have a predominantly low level of aggression. The fluctuations themselves are most pronounced in the transition from primary school age to adolescence, as well as in the middle of adolescence. A different trend is observed in average values between boys and girls. To the greatest extent, when these results were found in children in the third grade, then these differences capture almost the entire teenage and youthful age.

The next analyzed indicator is neurotism (P11), which in children of different ages predominantly fluctuates within the average values of expression. Consequently, we can assert that the majority of children adequately react emotionally in various life situations. At the same time, as seen in Table 2.4.1, there are certain differences between different groups of children in this parameter. It is most pronounced in 11-year-old schoolchildren. If we look at the results on averages, we find that the difference between 11 and 13-year-olds is – 1.24 points; 13 and 14 years old – 1.34 points; 14 and 15 years old – 5.6 points; 15 and 16 years old – 3.56 points, and 16 add 17 years old – 1.9 points. For 12-year-old children, no difference in the average values was found. And the highest difference is observed in subjects aged 14–15.

Further analysis showed that all these differences are not statistically reliable. One of the reasons for this situation may be the significant variability of this indicator. For example, for 11-year-old subjects, the difference is 2 conditional points; for 13-year-old subjects – 3 conditional points; for 14-year-olds – 4.5 points; for 15-year-olds – 3.5 points; for children aged 16 years – 1.5 conditional points, and for 17-year-olds – 5.7 conditional points. This difference is maximally expressed between boys and girls aged 17. It should be noted that statistically reliable differences between boys and girls at the age of 13 years ($t = 2.3$, $p < 0.01$); 14 years ($t = 3.6$, $p < 0.01$); and 17 years ($t = 4.5$ $p < 0.01$) are clearly observed in terms of neuroticism.

The data obtained can be explained by the fact that at the age of 13 and 14, girls have a higher emotional sensitivity than boys. Therefore, they are less emotionally stable. The fact that girls are less emotionally stable at the age of 17, apparently, is also associated with their heightened sensitivity, and the desire to overcome a wide range of personal problems associated with assertion among peers.

These research results show that a fairly large part of the subjects on the neuroticism parameter (P11) is in the so-called "normosthenic" zone. However, girls have a slightly lower level of emotional stability compared to boys. It is most clearly traced in the middle of adolescence and at the end of senior school age.

Proceeding to consideration of the parameter of spontaneous aggression (P18), it is visible (see Appendix 3, Table 2.4.1) that basically the majority of children have data above the average values.

Based on the average data, the difference between children aged 11 and 12 is 1.29 points; 12 and 13 years old – 0.65 points; 13 and 14 years – 0.13 points; 14 and 15 years – 0.41 points; 15 and 16 years – 0.79 points; and 16 and 17 years – 1.31 points. As we can see, the greatest difference is found between the subjects aged 16 and 17.

Analysis shows that statistically reliable differences ($t = 2.53$, $p < 0.01$) on this parameter (Appendix 3 see Table 2.4.2) are observed only between children aged 11 and 12.

The revealed differences may be due to the increased level of psychopathization observed at this age, which creates the prerequisites for impulsive behavior.

According to the average data that characterize the manifestation of the parameter of spontaneous aggression (P18) between boys and girls, certain tendencies for differences can be seen. Thus, the difference between boys and girls on the parameter of spontaneous aggression for 11-year-old children is 1 conditional point; 12 years – 0.9 conditional points; 13 years –0.1 points; 14 years – 0.3 points; 15 years –0.9; for 16-year-olds –0.2 conditional points; and for 17-year-olds –0.7 conditional points. As seen (see Table 2.4.5), this difference is greatest between boys and girls aged 11.

At the same time, if we refer to the Table of statistically reliable differences (see Table 2.4.5), we see that this difference is not reliable in any of the cases.

Continuing to consider the results of studies related to the determination of differences in the emotional sphere of children of different groups, we must note that in terms of the irritability parameter (P20), the values presented above the average level are observed in most of the children we surveyed. And, as can be seen from the data shown in Table 2.4.1, this is most pronounced in 11-year-old subjects. The difference in average data between children aged 11 and 12 is 0.03 points; 12 and 13 years old – 0.34 points; 13 and 14 years – 0.06 points; 14 and 15 years – 0.08 points; 15 and 16 years – 0.12 points; and 16 and 17 years old is 0.17 points. The maximum difference is noted between children 12 and 13 years old.

However, reliable distinctions were not found among the specified age groups.

Based on the analysis of the average values characterizing the manifestation of irritability in boys and girls, certain trends for differences can be seen. Thus, the difference between boys and girls aged 11 is 0.2 conditional points; 12 years – 0.4 conditional points; 13 years – 0.4 points; 14 years – 0.8 points; 15 years – 1.1 points; 16 years – 0.7 points; and 17 years old – 0.1 conditional points. At the same time, this difference in terms of irritability is statistically reliable only between boys and girls aged 14 ($t = 2.6$, $p < 0.01$) and 15 ($t = 2.4$, $p < 0.01$).

The results obtained show that girls in adolescence, having a somewhat inflated level of emotional instability with a tendency to affective response, are still more irritable than boys.

Thus, we can state that most children, regardless of age, have a slightly elevated level of the irritability parameter, and in girls, it is more expressed than in boys. However, these differences are insignificant and are observed mainly in the middle of adolescence.

According to the reactive aggression indicator (P22), as we see (Appendix 3 see Table 2.4.1), most of the children, regardless of age, have high values according to the average data. In particular, from the presented results it can be seen that the peak of the growth of reactive aggression is recorded for 16-year-old subjects.

At the same time, if we turn to the analysis of average values, we can state that the difference in this indicator between children aged 11 and 12 is 0.12 points; 12 and 13 years old – 0.23 points; between subjects 13 and 14 years – 0.01 points; 14 and 15 year-olds – 0.12 points; 15 and 16 years – 0.38 points; and 16 and 17 years old – 0.31 points. The maximum difference is presented in 15–16-year-old examinees.

However, further analysis showed that this difference manifests itself at the level of trends, as in all cases it is not statistically reliably confirmed.

Turning to the average values that characterize the manifestation of the reactive aggression parameter (P22) between boys and girls (see Table 2.4.5), we can observe that the difference among 11-year-old children is presented at the level of 0.8 conditional points; for 12-year-olds – 0.6 conditional points; 13-year-olds have 0.1 points; 14-year-olds – 0.1 points; 15-year-olds – 1.2; 16-year-olds – 0.4; and 17-year-olds – 1 conditional point.

This difference is maximally expressed between boys and girls aged 15 years.

Statistically reliable differences between boys and girls are confirmed only at the age of 17 ($t = 2.4$, $p < 0.01$).

It is known that at this age girls have some signs of psychopathization of extratensive type. That is, a high level of the studied parameter indicates an exaggerated level of psychopathization in girls, which characterizes an aggressive attitude toward the social environment and is expressed in the desire for dominance.

Based on the results of the study, we can say that a significant proportion of children have a slightly increased level of spontaneous aggression. However, it is more expressed in girls.

At the same time, cross-gender differences are observed mainly in high school age. According to the known data, somatic shifts intensify the already frequent mood fluctuations, which lead to irascibility, as one of the factors of spontaneous aggression.

Continuing to consider features of changes in the emotional sphere of children of different ages, it can be noted that on the expressiveness parameter (P14), most children have values registered within the average values. This parameter is maximally expressed in children aged 12 years. Based on the average data presented (see Table 2.4.1), we can see a definite difference in children aged 11–12, which is – 0.41 points; 12–13 years old – 0.32 points; 13–14 years old – 0.55 points; 14–15 years old – 0.63 points; 15–16 years old – 0.19 points; and 16–17 years old – 0.15 points. As we can see, the greatest difference is observed in children aged 14–15. Based on further analysis, it was found that these differences are not statistically reliable (see Table 2.4.6).

Based on the results of the average values characterizing the manifestation of the expressiveness indicator between boys and girls, certain differences can be noted. In particular, for children aged 11, the difference is 0.6 conditional points; for children aged 12 years – 0.9 conditional points; 13-year-olds have 0.2 conditional points; 14-year-olds – 0.1 points; children of 15 years old – 0.9 conditional points; and 17-year-old subjects – 0.9 conditional points. In 16-year-old subjects, the difference was not revealed but was established between boys and girls aged 15 and 17.

As in the previous case, all these differences are not reliable.

These data indicate that expressiveness is a common feature for all children and is typical in its manifestation.

Regarding the self-regulation parameter (P15), we can note the majority of children have data at the level of average and slightly above-average values. This parameter is maximally expressed in children aged 15 years.

Looking at the average values (Appendix 3 see Table 2.4.1), one can see certain differences, based on children's age. Thus, among pupils aged 11–12 they are found at the level of 0.55 points; 12–13 years old – 0.25 points; 13–14 years – 0.76 points; 14–15 years – 0.15 points; 15–16 years – 0.86 points; and 16–17 years

TABLE 2.4.6 Statistically reliable differences in indicators characterizing peculiarities of self-regulation in boys and girls*

Age / *Statistical data*	*Indicators*									
	P14		*P15*		*P16*		*P21*		*P24*	
	B	G	B	G	B	G	B	G	B	G
1	*2*	*3*	*4*	*5*	*6*	*7*	*8*	*9*	*10*	*11*
11 y.o.										
x	6.2	6.8	6.5	7.5	7.2	7.3	6.8	6.9	5.2	7.3
t	= n/d		= n/d		= n/d		= n/d		= 3.4	
12 y.o.										
x	6.6	7.5	6.5	6.5	5.9	8.1	5.7	6.8	6.9	7.5
t	= n/d		= n/d		= 2.2		= n/d		= n/d	
13 y.o.										
x	6.7	6.5	6.5	6.0	6.5	6.5	5.7	5.4	7.0	7.4
t	= n/d		= n/d		= n/d		= n/d		= n/d	
14 y.o.										
x	6.0	6.1	7.6	6.6	6.1	7.0	5.4	5.8	5.4	7.1
t	= n/d		= 2.4		= n/d		= n/d		= 3.5	
15 y.o.										
x	6.0	6.9	6.9	7.3	6.6	7.4	5.7	5.6	5.7	6.9
t	= n/d		= n/d		= n/d		= n/d		= n/d	
16 y.o.										
x	6.5	6.5	6.3	6.4	8.5	8.1	6.5	6.3	4.4	5.6
t	= n/d		= n/d		= n/d		= n/d		= n/d	
17 y.o.										
x	6.0	6.9	7.1	6.6	7.0	7.8	5.8	5.5	6.4	7.3
t	= n/d		= n/d		= n/d		= n/d		= 2.5	

**The differences shown in the Table are significant at $p < 0.05$; B – boys, G – girls.*

– 0.15 points. The difference is greatest among children aged 15–16. However, this difference is only reliable among children aged 13–14 ($t = 2.30$, $p < 0.01$).

Apparently, children of these ages regulate their emotions quite differently in communication and thereby influence the people around them.

The average data characterizing the manifestation of the self-regulation index (P15) among boys and girls also tend to differ. In particular, the difference for children aged 11 is 8 conditional points; for children aged 13, they have 0.5 conditional points; 14-year-olds have 1 conditional point; 15-year-olds have 0.4 points; 16-year-olds have 0.1 points and 17-year-olds have 0.5 conditional points. For subjects aged 12, this difference is not evident, whereas the children aged 14 have the greatest difference in the manifestation of this parameter (see Table 2.4.6). This is confirmed by the presence of statistically reliable differences among boys and girls aged 14 ($t = 2.4$, $p < 0.01$) on self-regulation parameters.

The fact that 14-year-old boys have a higher level of self-regulation compared to girls may be related to the increased level of emotional instability of girls at this age.

Overall, these results indicate that most children, regardless of age, have average or above-average levels of self-regulation. At the same time, in boys, self-regulation is expressed to a somewhat greater degree than in girls. This parameter is most clearly manifested in the middle of adolescence.

Continuing to consider the differences in the study, we can note that the empathy indicator (P16), mainly reveals values within the average and above the average level. And, as seen from Appendix 3, Table 2.4.1, the peak growth of this parameter is recorded for children of 16 years old.

There are also some differences in dynamics, i.e. with growing age. Thus, between children aged 11–12, the difference is 0.6 points; for 12–13 years old, it is 0.14 points; for schoolchildren aged 13–14, it is 0.01 points; for 14–15 years old, it is 0.69 points; for 15–16 years, it is 1.03 points; and for 16–17 years old, it is 0.87 points. The biggest difference is observed in children aged 15–16.

However, all of these differences are not statistically reliable. They are in the nature of trends.

Based on the data presented (see Table 2.4.6), we can see that the empathy parameter (P16) between boys and girls has differences in values. In particular, the difference for children aged 11 is 0.1 conditional points; for children aged 12, it is 2.2 conditional points; for 14-year-olds, it is 0.9 points; for 15-year-olds, it is 0.8 points; and 0.4 points for 16-year-olds and 0.8 conditional points for 17-year-old subjects. The greatest difference, as we see, is observed between boys and girls 12 years old.

At the same time, statistically reliable differences were established between boys and girls aged 11 ($t = 2.2$, $p < 0.01$).

These data indicate that girls are likely to be more sensitive than boys at age 11, i.e. they are able to gain a deeper understanding of various life circumstances, as well as inspire trust in other people and thereby influence their behavior.

Thus, the results of the study show that most children, regardless of age, are able to experience and sympathize with other people and thereby inspire trust in the latter. At the same time, differences in the manifestation of empathy between children of different ages are not significant enough. As for cross-gender differences in the expression of empathy, they are observed mainly at the transitional stage from primary to secondary school age. Moreover, girls have more developed feelings of empathy and sympathy in comparison with boys.

Continuing to analyze the results of the research on the emotional sphere of children of different ages, we can note that on the equilibrium parameter (P21) most children have data within the average and above the average level. This parameter is slightly higher in children aged 11.

There is a definite difference in equilibrium index in children aged 11–12, which is 0.8 points; for 12–13 years old, it is 0.47 points; for 13–14 years old, it is 0.05 points; for 14–15 years old, it is 0.04 points; for 15–16 years old, it is

0.8 points; and for 16–17 years old, it is 0.47 points. As we can see, the greatest difference is among the subjects aged 11–12 and 15–16 years.

However, these differences are not statistically reliable in most cases (Appendix 3 see Table 2.4.2).

At the same time, certain trends toward differences in this indicator between boys and girls should be noted. Thus, for 11-year-olds, it is 0.1 conditional points; for 12-year-olds, it is 1.1 conditional points; 13-year-olds have 0.3 conditional points; 14-year-olds have 0.4 points; 15-year-olds have 0.1 points; 16-year-old subjects have 0.2 conditional points; and 17-year-olds have 0.3 conditional points. Further analysis showed that in all cases these differences are not statistically reliable.

Thus, the results of the study indicate that majority of the subjects have values above the average level on the equilibrium scale. In other words, we can say that most of the subjects have good protection against stress factors in ordinary life situations, based on self-confidence. At the same time, girls are not more protected than boys.

Considering the last indicator in the system of parameters under study, i.e. emotional lability (P24), we can note that, in general, its level is within the average and above-average values. This parameter is maximally expressed in 17-year-old subjects. At the same time, from the presented average values (see Table 2.4.1), it is seen that the difference between children aged 11–12 is 0.7 points; 12–13 years – 0.06 points; 13–14 years old – 0.84 points; 14–15 years old – 0.36 points; 15–16 – 1.63 points; and 16–17 year-olds – 1.83 points. These differences are statistically reliably confirmed only among children aged 13–14 ($t = 2.67$, $p < 0.01$), 15–16 ($t = 3.04$, $p < 0.01$) and 16–17 ($t = 3.55$, $p < 0.01$).

The results obtained can be explained by the fact that, probably, at the age of 14, 16 and 17, children develop a high level of stability of the emotional response to life circumstances.

Based on the average data characterizing the manifestation of the parameter of emotional lability between boys and girls, there are certain differences. Their quantitative representation is as follows: for children of 11 years, it is 2.1 conditional points; for 12 year-olds, it is 0.6 conditional points; for children aged 13, it is 0.4 points; for 14 years old, it is 1.7 points; for aged 15, it is 1.2 points; for 16-year-olds, it is 1.2 points; and for 17-year-olds, it is 0.9 conditional points.

These differences are statistically reliable only among boys and girls aged 11 ($t = 3.4$, $p < 0.01$), 13 ($t = 2.8$, $p < 0.01$) and 17 years ($t = 2.4$, $p < 0.01$).

Therefore, it can be argued that boys during adolescence and senior school age are more emotionally stable than girls.

Thus, the results of the study show that, regardless of age, most children have a high level of emotional lability. Moreover, it is more pronounced in girls than in boys. At the same time, reliable differences are traced mainly to the middle of adolescence and to the end of senior school age.

As for inter-gender differences, they are mainly observed in girls throughout adolescence and then at the end of senior school age, which is explained by the dominance of emotionally inadequate reactions, leading to a low level of self-control and inadequate response in various life situations.

Summarizing the above results, we can draw the following conclusion.

There are statistically reliable differences in certain indicators among children of the studied age groups. They are most expressed for

- hostility index among children aged 8–9; 12–13; 13–14 and 14–15 years,
- family anxiety parameter (P5) among 7–8; 8–9; 9–11; 11–12; 12–13; 13–14 and 14–15 year-olds,
- personal anxiety parameter (P8) among schoolchildren 7–8; 8–9; 13–14 and 14–15 years old,
- family aggressiveness (P6) for 9–11; 11–12 and 12–13 years old,
- reactive anxiety (P12), for 11–12; 12–13; 14–15; 15–16 and 16–17 years,
- emotional lability parameter (P24) for children 13–14; 15–16 and 16–17 years old.

  Statistically reliable distinctions between boys and girls of different ages on the diagnosed parameter were revealed. They are most clearly seen in
- personal anxiety parameter (P8) in children aged 8, 9, 13 and 14;
- family aggressiveness (P6) in students aged 11, 12 and 13;
- personal aggression (P9) in children aged 9, 13 and 14;
- neuroticism in subjects aged 13 and 14;
- depression in students aged 12, 14 and 17;
- emotional lability in children aged 11, 13 and 17.

2.5 Identification of the leading factors in the structure of the emotional features of a developing personality

As was shown in the previous subsection, the highlighted features of differences in the emotional sphere of children of different ages and genders have their own specifics. At the same time, for a more complete analysis of the described differences, it is important to consider those internal structural mechanisms that determine their specificity.

With this in mind, we carried out a correlation analysis of the relationships of the diagnosed indicators in each age period.

It should be noted that we assumed that if the previously identified indicators, for which reliable differences in the studied samples of subjects were recorded, confirm their dependence by connections with other indicators, then we can designate these parameters as leading in the structure of a developing personality. The latter circumstance will greatly facilitate the selection and development of conditions and methods focused on forming features of the emotional sphere of children of different ages.

Considering the interrelations (Appendix 3 see Table 2.5.1) of the indicators characterizing features of the genesis of the emotional sphere of 7-year-old children, several correlated complexes were identified. The most extensive is formed around the indicator of personal aggression (P9). Moderate correlations of this indicator with the parameters of anxiety in the family (P5, r = 0.3), personal self-esteem (P1, r = 0.2), hostility (P3, r = 0.2), self-doubt (P7, r = 0.2) and others were revealed here.

In addition, a number of correlations were established around the indicators of family aggressiveness (P6), personal anxiety and self-esteem (P8 and P10).

Thus, in the structure of indicators of the emotional sphere of 7-year-old children, the parameters of family aggressiveness, personal anxiety and self-esteem are the leading factors.

Summarizing the features of the correlational relationships between the indicators of the emotional sphere in 8-year-old children, we also revealed several relatively stable complexes of interrelations (Appendix 3 see Table 2.5.2.).

The first complex is combined by a positive correlation dependence of personal aggression data (P9) with the parameters of personal anxiety (P8, r = 0.5), feeling of inferiority (P4, r = 0.2), and has a negative correlation with family anxiety index (P5, r = 0.4) and self-doubt parameter (P7, r = 0.3).

The second complex is formed on the basis of the indicator of personal self-esteem (P10). The latter, at a fairly high level, correlates negatively with indicators of feelings of rejection (P2, r = 0.5), personal anxiety (P8, r = 0.3), hostility, personal aggression and family anxiety index (P3, P5, P9, r = 0.2).

The third complex is traced around the parameter of self-doubt (P7). Here, a number of moderate correlations of the above indicator with family anxiety index (P5, r = 0.2) and negative ones with personal self-esteem (P1, r = 0.4), feeling of rejection and inferiority (P2, r = 0.3), (P44, r = 0.3) and hostility (P3, r = 0.2) were noted.

The analysis of the data obtained shows that, as in the previous case, the factor of aggression in children of 8 years old acts as the leading one. In addition to this, important in the emotional development of children of this age are such features as multidirectional anxiety and feelings of inferiority (Appendix 3 Table 2.5.2).

Considering the features of the interrelations of indicators characterizing the development of 9-year-old children, it should be noted that no sufficiently pronounced correlations were found here (Appendix 3 see Table 2.5.3). However, there are a number of moderate correlational dependencies, mainly formed around family anxiety index (P5), personal aggression and self-esteem (P9 and P10) parameters.

The study of the results of similar correlation data obtained with 11-year-old children (fifth grade) indicates that there are fairly extensive complexes of relationships formed on the basis of three indicators. (Appendix 3 see Table 2.5.4) In particular, the most extensive complex, as we see, is observed around the emotional lability index, which at a rather high level correlates with such parameters as depressiveness (P19, r = 0.6), feeling of rejection (P2, r = 0.6), neurotism (P11, r = 0.6) and spontaneous aggression (P18, r = 0.6). At the same time, moderate correlations were found in the emotional lability index with personal anxiety

(P13, r = 0.5), neuroticism (P17, r = 0.4) and shyness (P23, r = 0.4). The indicator of emotional lability correlates negatively with hostility (P3, r = 0.3).

The next complex in this structure is formed around the parameter of depressiveness (P19). The latter at a high level correlates with indicators of neurotism (P11, r = 0.7), feelings of rejection (P2, r = 0.6) and spontaneous aggression (P18, r = 0.5). The indicator of depressiveness also correlates with personal anxiety (P13, r = 0.4), neuroticism (P17, r = 0.4), and negatively with indicators of personal self-esteem (P10, r = 0.4) and aggression (P9, r = 0.3).

The third complex is formed around the indicator of irritability (P20), which at a fairly high level correlates with the parameters of spontaneous aggression (P18, r = 0.6), family anxiety index (P5, r = 0.5), and negatively correlates with indicators of personal aggression (P9, r = 0.6) and reactive anxiety (P12, r = 0.5). In addition, a number of moderate correlations of this indicator were also revealed here. In particular, between indicators of anxiety (P2, r = 0.4) and depressiveness (P19, r = 0.3).

Based on the considered results, we can state that high values of indicators of emotional lability, depression and irritability are essential features in the emotional sphere of a developing personality in children of this age.

Analyzing results of the study of the correlations between indicators characterizing the developmental features of the emotional sphere of 12-year-old children, we note here several sets of relationships (Appendix 3 see Table 2.5.5).

Most vividly it is expressed around the indicator of emotional lability (P24), which at a high level correlates with the parameters of depressiveness (P19, r = 0.6), neuroticism (P17, r = 0.5) and negatively with the index of self-doubt (P7, r = 0.5).

In addition, there are correlations of this indicator with the parameters of reactive anxiety (P12, r = 0.4) and irritability (P20, r = 0.4).

Along with the presence of connections in the indicator of emotional lability, correlations around the parameter of equilibrium (P21) were also revealed. In particular, this indicator is highly correlated with the feeling of rejection (P2, r = 0.5).

Moderate connections are noted here between the parameters of equilibrium and expressivity (P14, r = 0.4), self-regulation (P15, r = 0.4), irritability (P20, r = 0.4) and spontaneous aggression (P18, r = 0.3).

In the same structure, a number of other correlation dependencies were also revealed. Most clearly it is recorded around the indicators of reactive aggression (P22), neuroticism (P17) and a number of others.

Thus, based on the analysis of the data obtained, we can assume that the leading factors in children of twelve years of age are equilibrium and emotional lability. At the same time, it is impossible not to note the big role of reactive aggression and neuroticism in the formation of the emotional sphere of a developing personality.

Moving on to the next age group (Appendix 3 see Table 2.5.6), we can note that in the structure of the correlation dependencies of the diagnosed indicators, the leading position among 13-year-old children is occupied by the parameter of emotional lability (P24). The latter at a high level interacts with indicators of depressiveness (P19, r = 0.6), personal anxiety (P13, r = 0.6), neurotism (P11, r = 0.5) and neuroticism (P17, r = 0.5).

The second set of correlations is formed around the parameter of equilibrium (P21). Here, a number of moderate dependencies were found for the indicator of depressiveness (P19, r = 0.4), reactive anxiety (P12, r = 0.3), neuroticism (P17, r = 0.3), neurotism (P11, r = 0.3), expressiveness (P14, r = 0.3), as well as negative ones with an indicator of personal self-esteem (P1, r = 0.4).

The latter complex in this age group is fixed on the basis of the parameter of depressiveness (P19), which closely correlates with the indicators of neuroticism (P17, r = 0.6), personal anxiety (P13, r = 0.6) and neurotism (P11, r = 0.5).

In the same structure, other correlations were established around the data of empathy (P16), shyness (P23) and anxiety (P8).

The results obtained indicate that the leading factors in the structure of the development of the emotional sphere of 13-year-old children are emotional lability, reactive aggression and depressiveness.

Summarizing the features of the connections between the parameters of the emotional sphere in 14-year-old children, we have identified four relatively stable complexes.

The first is fixed by a positive correlation dependence of the data on the indicator of emotional lability with the parameters of depressiveness (P19, r = 0.8), neuroticism (P17, r = 0.5) and personal anxiety (P13, r = 0.5). And this indicator negatively correlates with the parameter of self-regulation (P15, r = 0.3).

The next complex clusters around the parameter of shyness (P23), which is closely correlated with the index of depressiveness (P19, r = 0.6). Moderate connections can be traced on this indicator with neuroticism (P17, r = 0.4), as well as feelings of inferiority (P4), spontaneous aggression (P18), irritability (P20), equilibrium (P21) and reactive aggression (P22). The above indicator is also related to the shyness parameter (P23), where r = 0.3 ($P < 0.05$).

The third complex is formed around the parameter of depressiveness (P19), which correlates at a fairly high level with the indicator of neuroticism (P17, r = 0.5), and also negatively with the indicators of self-regulation (P15, r = 0.3) and self-esteem (P1, r = 0.2).

The fourth complex is established around the indicator of empathy (P16). However, a number of correlations of this parameter with expressivity (P14, r = 0.4), self-regulation (P15, r = 0.3), neurotism (P11, r = 0.3) and other parameters that were found here (see Appendix B.1) are moderate.

In addition to the above correlations, other relationships were found around the indicators of equilibrium (P21), self-regulation (P15), neuroticism (P17) and spontaneous aggression (P18).

Considering the results of the correlation relationships of the diagnosed indicators in children of fourteen years old, it should be noted that such parameters as emotional lability, shyness, depressiveness and empathy have the largest number of correlation relationships. Consequently, there is reason to believe that these features dominate and probably determine the nature of changes in the development of the emotional sphere of children of this age period.

At the same time, we cannot ignore the fact that self-regulation, equilibrium, neuroticism and spontaneous aggression also play a significant role in the emotional regulation of the behavior of children of fourteen years of age.

The study of the correlation relationships of indicators characterizing the features of the emotional sphere in 15-year-old children showed that the most extensive complex is formed on the basis of the shyness parameter (P23). The latter at a fairly high level correlates with personal anxiety (P13, $r = 0.6$) and depressiveness (P19, $r = 0.6$). Relatively moderate correlations are also recorded between indicators of shyness, neuroticism (P17, $r = 0.4$) and various manifestations of anxiety (P5, P8, $r = 0.3$), aggression (P3, P18, $r = 0.2$), and negative – with self-regulation (P15, $r = 0.3$).

The second complex is formed around the indicator of reactive aggression (P22), which at a fairly high level correlates with the indicators of depressiveness, spontaneous aggression and neuroticism (P17, P18, P19, P22, $r = 0.4$). Also, at a high level, the above indicator (reactive aggression) interacts negatively with the hostility parameter (P3, $r = 0.5$).

The third most extensive complex is established around the indicator of emotional lability (P24), which at a high level correlates with indicators of depressiveness (P19, $r = 0.7$), neuroticism (P17, $r = 0.6$), spontaneous aggression (P18, $r = 0.5$), shyness (P23, $r = 0.5$) and others.

Here we can also see (see Appendix B.2) the fourth and fifth complexes, which are united by relations around the indicators of empathy (P16) and spontaneous aggression (P18).

The obtained data of the correlation relationships of indicators characterizing the manifestations of the emotional sphere of 15-year-old children indicate that shyness, reactive and spontaneous aggression, emotional lability and empathy are quite significantly represented in relation to other manifestations of the emotional sphere.

Analysis of the correlations between the indicators that characterize the emotional sphere of 16-year-old children (Appendix 3 see Table 2.5.7) allows us to note the presence of moderate correlations between the depressiveness index and the parameters of neurotism (P11), personal anxiety (P13) and self-regulation (P15) at the level $r = 0.4$ ($P < 0.01$).

In addition, the indices of personal anxiety (P13) and self-regulation (P15) correlate in the same structure at a sufficiently high level. The former also closely interacts with reactive anxiety (P12, $r = 0.7$) and neurotism (P11, $r = 0.5$), and the latter – with expressivity (P14, $r = 0.7$) and personal anxiety (P13, $r = 0.5$).

The presence of such a pattern of connections gives grounds to assume that the dominant parameter in the structure of emotional characteristics of the development of 16-year-old children is the parameter of depressiveness.

Considering the results of the correlation analysis of indicators that characterize the features of the emotional sphere in children aged 17 years (eleventh grade), we find three sets of relationships (Appendix 3 see Table 2.5.8).

First, this is the range of indicators that can be traced around the parameter of emotional lability (P24). The latter at a fairly high level correlates with depressiveness (P19, r = 0.7), neuroticism (P17, r = 0.6), neurotism (P11, r = 0.6) and shyness (P13, r = 0.5), and negatively – with various manifestations of aggression and anxiety.

Second, this is a galaxy of correlation relationships, which is mainly formed around the irritability parameter (P20). It also found a number of moderate correlations with neuroticism (P17, r = 0.3) and neurotism (P11, r = 0.4).

Third, it is the series of correlations formed around the indicator of depressiveness, which, in turn, correlates at a fairly high level with the indicators of neurotism (P11, r = 0.6) and neuroticism (P17, r = 0.5), as well as reactive and personal anxiety (P12, P13, r = 0.3).

The data obtained give grounds to believe that emotional lability is the leading one among young men in the structure of other features of their emotional sphere. At the same time, depressiveness and irritability, neuroticism and shyness also play a significant role in the emotional regulation of the behavior of 17-year-old children.

These results give us grounds to state:

- First, the specificity of the correlation relationships of the diagnosed indicators of the features of the emotional sphere of children from 7 to 17 years of age has a number of differences that manifest themselves at the level of trends regarding the expansion of the number and density of connections in our study.
- Second, the indicators of emotional lability, multidirectional aggression and depressiveness are dominant in terms of the number of identified correlations with other parameters.

2.6 Prognostic tendencies in the genesis of the emotional sphere of children and youth

The features of the expression of diagnosed indicators of the emotional sphere in children of different ages and genders, outlined in the previous sections, represent important material that can be used as a basis for determining typical tendencies in the predictive development of the emotional sphere of children.

Before we start the generalized analysis of the most important tendencies in the genesis of the emotional sphere of children, it is necessary to define the starting positions on which these tendencies will be fixed. To such positions, we have attributed:

- first, the identification of the greatest values in the growth or decline of the diagnosed indicators of emotional features in children with age changes;

- second, the identification of the most significant reliable differences in the diagnosed indicators of emotional characteristics that are observed among children of different ages;
- third, to determine the nature of the shifting of correlational relationships, taking into account the age features of the children.

The implementation of such a systematic analysis, from our point of view, allows us to present relatively holistic information about those patterns that can be described at the level of prognostic trends in the genesis of the emotional sphere of children.

Taking into account the first position, it is possible to note that at the age of 7–9 years, there is relative stabilization in the genesis of emotional processes. At the same time, active change in the features of the emotional sphere of schoolchildren begins to shift distinctly between the age of 11 and 12. In particular, certain peaks of growth are recorded in such parameters as anxiety in the family, family aggressiveness, self-regulation, empathy, irritability and equilibrium at the age of 11 years.

The same patterns were noted at age 12 on feelings of rejection and inferiority, hostility, as well as features of expressiveness, neuroticism and irritability.

At ages 13, 14, 15 and 17, high values are recorded mainly on the indicators of personal self-esteem, feelings of rejection, personal anxiety, multidirectional aggression, neurotism, expressiveness, self-regulation, empathy, spontaneous aggression and emotional lability.

Data analysis also shows that pronounced growth peaks are observed in the parameters of personal self-esteem, equilibrium, reactive aggression and shyness even at the age of 16.

Thus, based on the identified features, it can be noted that the likelihood of increased anxiety is quite significant at the age of 8, at 11–14 and at 17.

Tendencies of inflated self-esteem are possible at ages 7, 8, 12, 15 and 16. At the same time, the likelihood of nervous breakdowns in schoolchildren is most significant in middle adolescence, i.e. at 12 and 13 years. High empathic experiences are most likely to occur at ages 11 and 15. Sufficiently high self-regulation of emotional behavior begins to manifest itself at 11, 13, 15 and 16 years of age. The possibility of depression, as well as severe irritability, is more likely at age of 12. Increased signs of shy behavior may occur at 16 years of age.

The level of slightly increased aggressiveness is likely at the ages of 11, 12, 14 and 17.

Considering the results of the obtained data, and with regard to the second position, we can note that the pronounced differences in indicators between children of different ages are mostly recorded in the parameter of anxiety in the family (for 7 age groups). Statistically significant differences were found in this parameter among children aged 7–8; 8–9; 9–11; 11–12; 12–13; 13–14; and 14–15 years old. Therefore, we can clearly state that anxiety tends to change with age.

The self-regulation index also shows reliable differences (for 5 age groups) among children aged 11–12; 12–13; 14–15; 15–16; and 16–17 years old. Such data indicate that the probability of stabilization or formation of self-regulation has several periods, which are likely during transitions from one specified age to another.

At the same time, on the parameter of hostility, differences are recorded (for 4 age groups) among children aged 8–9 years; 12–13 years; 13–14 years; and 14–15 years old. Less pronounced differences (for three age categories) were found for the indicators of family aggressiveness, personal anxiety and emotional lability. For two age categories, significant differences were recorded on the parameters of personal self-esteem, feelings of rejection, self-doubt and personal self-esteem. One age group showed significant differences in feelings of inferiority, personal self-esteem, self-regulation, neuroticism, spontaneous aggression, depressiveness and shyness.

Thus, we see that the anxiety parameter is quite predictive in the dynamics of changes in the features of the emotional sphere. At the same time, it may be assumed that the greatest increase in changes in indicators of personal self-esteem, family aggressiveness and emotional lability is to be expected in the transition from age of 11 to 12, from 14 to 15 years and from 15 to 16 years.

The observed decreases in the level of hostility and multidirectional anxiety indicate certain trends in the stabilization of the above features of the emotional sphere from the age of 8 to 9, from 9 to 11, from 12 to 13 and from 14 to 15.

The expression of such tendencies in the dynamics of changes in the diagnosed indicators will be more significant if it is also supported by internal correlations of the diagnosed indicators. The greatest correlations between the studied parameters are observed at the age of 12, 13 and 15 and the lowest at 11, 14 and 17 years of age. At the same time, at the ages of 7, 8, 9 and 16, there are only tendencies to form complex interrelationships.

Based on the above data, we can note that such indicators as family aggressiveness, neurotism and personal anxiety could be exactly those features that probably influence the entire structure of the emotional stability of the child's personality development.

We can also state that stability in the genesis of the emotional sphere and balance in its manifestations are most likely during the transition from 11 to 12 years of age; from 12 to 13, from 13 to 14 and from 15 to 16 years of age, while imbalance is most clearly recorded in the period from 7 to 8 years, from 8 to 9, from 9 to 11 and also from 16 to 17. Such periods as 12, 13 and 15 years old are essential in the formation of the emotional sphere.

It is necessary to keep in mind that the high level of family aggression, personal anxiety and neurotism is apparently caused by personal instability, which is typical for this age period. A special form of self-awareness – a sense of adulthood – appears. Aggression toward adults, especially relatives, arises as a result of a discrepancy between the child's increased needs and the "outdated" attitude toward the child on the part of the parents.

Starting from senior school age, the importance of own values increases and anxiety associated with self-esteem grows. The latter tends to be higher in early adulthood than in adolescence.

During the period of primary school age, the dominance of anxiety is connected, firstly, with the entrance of children into a new activity, which, in our opinion, has set quite considerable demands on schoolchildren. Secondly, this is a consequence of natural protective mechanisms associated with the social and psychological conditions of adaptation to a new environment and formation of the personal status in it.

Such results have an important theoretical – as a prognostic basis for the characterization of the genesis of the emotional sphere – and practical importance associated with taking into account the identified patterns in the organization of the educational process and psycho-corrective work.

Discovered data on anxiety retain its position regarding the dynamics of changes in this indicator. However, unlike the previous data, this trend has an indirect character to the increase. That is, in some cases, anxiety progresses from age to age (from 7 to 8, from 9 to 11, from 11 to 12, from 15 to 16 and from 16 to 17 years), in others, it has a decreasing character (from 8 to 9 years). A similar trend is recorded for the aggression indicator, which also tends to increase (mostly from the age of 7 to 12, from 13 to 14 and from 15 to 17 years) and to decrease from 8 to 9 and from 12 to 13 years.

Depressiveness has increased from 11 to 12 and decreased from 15 to 17.

The availability and construction of such a prognostic model is an essential point in the preparation of various scientific and methodological manuals, and recommendations, and also in the organization of the educational process and special psycho-corrective work.

Thus, when analyzing prognostic tendencies, it is important to consider the fact that in 7–9-year-old children a relative stabilization of the functioning of emotional processes is observed. At the same time for 11–12-year-old schoolchildren, there are certain changes, which are mainly characterized by an increase in the expression of anxiety in the family, self-regulation, empathy, irritability, equilibrium and family aggressiveness.

In addition, family anxiety index, self-regulation and hostility indicators can act as certain criteria for differentiation of various age groups.

To this, it is necessary to add that family aggressiveness, neurotism and personal anxiety in most cases are the leading parameters in the manifestation of the emotional sphere of a developing personality.

Proceeding from the generalization of the results obtained, it is possible to make certain clarifications and additions to the data on the development of the emotional sphere of contemporary children.

Based on the available data in the special and methodological literature (Weiner, 1997; Questions of the psychology of moral education; Kulagina, 1996; Mukhina, 1985; Stavitskaya, 1991), it was established that an essential attribute of the development of the emotional sphere of children from 7 to 11 years old is the relative stabilization of the functioning of emotional processes. Increased emotional sensitivity and switchability, a high level of empathy and a low level of anxiety are characteristics of this age period.

In our research, these data are supplemented by the fact that children of 6 and 7 years old have inflated personal self-esteem. Along with this, only 7-year-olds showed an exaggerated level of inferiority, and an underestimated level of personal aggression and anxiety, but this indicator is not stable.

In 8-year-old children, an exaggerated level of personal anxiety is typical; in 8 and 9-year-olds, self-doubt is typical, and at the same time, an underestimated level of feelings of inferiority and personal self-esteem.

As research in the scientific literature shows (Abramova, 2000; Vasilishina, 2000), that high levels of anxiety associated with self-esteem, which is most pronounced in 12- and 16-year-old schoolchildren, are characteristic of adolescent children. Starting from the age of 13 and 14, the number of personality disorders increases sharply. The level of emotional sensitivity and self-doubt increases. At the age of 14, a high level of self-regulation is pronounced, especially in boys. In addition, in adolescence, a high level of reflection and empathy is also noted.

The obtained data are supplemented by the fact that starting from the age of 11, stability in the genesis of emotional processes and balance in its manifestations are fixed. Based on our study, this characteristic can be clarified by the fact that contemporary 11-year-old children are commonly driven by a somewhat overestimated level of family aggressiveness and anxiety, irritability and, at the same time, equilibrium. An underestimated level of inferiority feelings and lack of self-confidence was also recorded here.

At the age of 13, high values were recorded for the parameters of neurotism, personal anxiety and emotional lability, and low values for multidirectional aggressiveness, especially in the family. On the basis of the results of our research, a balance in the manifestation of emotional processes is on the contrary fixed in 14-year-old schoolchildren. Along with this, an exaggerated level of personal aggression, and reactive and personal anxiety was found. And such features of the emotional sphere as anxiety in the family generally lose their dominant force. As clarifying and complementary to the data of this characteristic, based on the conducted research, is that contemporary 15-year-old schoolchildren are characterized by an overestimated level of expressiveness, personal self-esteem and anxiety, self-regulation, anxiety in the family and a low level of multidirectional aggression.

Generalization of latest works (Abramova, 2000; Brushlnisky, 1979; Vasilishina, 2000; Questions of the psychology of moral education; Cohn, 1989; Kulagina, 1996; Morgun, Tkacheva, 1981) on senior school (adolescent) age shows that the characteristic features of this age period are increased emotionality, which is reflected in the development of feelings of friendship and love. As in the middle grades (teenage), there is also a high level of empathy. Scientific literature data show (Abramova, 2000; Brushlnisky, 1979; Cohn, 1989), that the level of anxiety by the age of 16 (tenth grade) falls and rises again by the age of 17. This is probably due to changes in the self-esteem of these students. In general, this period is characterized by personal stabilization and a high level of equilibrium. Compared to teenage, in adolescence, there is a high level of communication. It is also necessary to note here a decrease in self-doubt, internal self-doubt and anxiety, feelings of dependence and inferiority.

The results of our research allow us to additionally note exaggerated reactive aggression, shyness and a lowered level of neurotism in contemporary 16-year-old schoolchildren; for 17-year-olds, an exaggerated level of feelings of rejection, reactive anxiety and such features of the emotional sphere as family aggression and hostility generally lose their dominant force altogether.

Based on the data obtained, it is important to deepen research (Chebykin, 2021; Chebykin, Kichuk, 2022) on the emotional health of young people under conditions of the COVID-19 epidemic as well as during the military situation in Ukraine.

2.7 Conclusions

In general, summarizing the results obtained in this section, we can draw the following general conclusions.

1 It is established that in schoolchildren of different ages the development of many manifestations of the emotional sphere has considerable variability. The maximum values for anxiety indicators were revealed in schoolchildren aged 8, 11, 14 and 17 years. At the same time, the minimum values were recorded for the parameters of shyness in children aged 12 and 14, and neuroticism in subjects aged 12 and 16.

2 It was revealed that such emotional characteristics as neuroticism, depressiveness, empathy and self-regulation do not change significantly with age. At the same time, such features as hostility, various manifestations of anxiety, family aggressiveness and emotional lability change with age, which is confirmed by statistically reliable differences ($P < 0.05$) revealed when comparing indicators characterizing these features in children of different ages.

3 It is shown that the sensitive periods in changes of separate manifestations of the emotional sphere are those: from 12 to 13 years, where there is an increase in feelings of rejection, hostility, and a decrease in various manifestations of anxiety; from 13 to 14 years – an increase in personal anxiety, self-regulation, depressiveness and emotional lability, a decrease in hostility and personal aggression; and from 14 to 15 years – an increase in various manifestations of anxiety, personal self-esteem, and a decrease in hostility and self-doubt.

4 Certain differences were found in the expression of hostility index at the level of statistically reliable differences ($P < 0.05$) between boys and girls of 8 and 12 years old; personal anxiety and self-regulation in children and

adolescents aged 8, 13 and 14; various manifestations of aggression at 9, 11, 12, 13, 14 and 17 years of age; self-doubt and empathy in 12-year-old students; neurotism in 12 and 14 years; neuroticism in 12 and 14 years; and shyness in 13-year-olds. In other cases, differences were found at the trend level for one indicator.

5 Based on the results of the analysis of the relationship of indicators characterizing emotional characteristics of children of different ages, it was established that the dominant features are: in children of 7 and 8 years old – various manifestations of aggression; in 11-year-olds – emotional lability, depression and irritability; teenagers aged 12 and 13 also have emotional lability and equilibrium; adolescents aged 16 have emotional lability and expressiveness; boys and girls of 15 years – shyness, reactive aggression and emotional lability; boys and girls of 17 years – emotional lability, irritability and depressiveness.

6 It was noted that children
   - at age 7 have an overestimated level of inferiority feelings,
   - at 8 and 9 years – underestimated personal aggression and anxiety, low level of feelings of inferiority and personal self-esteem;
   - at age 11 have an overestimated level of family aggressiveness and anxiety;
   - at age 13 have an increased level of neurotism, personal anxiety, emotional lability and a decrease in multidirectional aggression;
   - at age 14 have an overestimated level of personal aggression and various manifestations of anxiety;
   - at age 15 have an increase in the level of expressiveness, anxiety, self-regulation and a decreased level of aggression;
   - at age 16 have an increased level of reactive aggression, shyness and a decreased level of neurotism,
   - at age 17 have an increased level of feelings of rejection and reactive anxiety.

The conducted research made it possible to identify several theoretical and experimental tasks for further understanding of the problem of the genesis of the emotional sphere in childhood, adolescence and young adulthood. To such priority tasks we include: the study of the emotional sphere of children exposed to the coronavirus epidemic, as well as the influence of various social networks, etc.

References

Abolin, L.M. (1987). *Psychological mechanisms of human emotional stability*. Kazan: Kazan University Press.

Abramova, G.S. (2000). *Age psychology*. Moscow: Academ. Project, Ekaterinburg: Business Book.

Anokhin, P.K. (1964). *Emotions*. In: Big Medical Encyclopedia: Vol. 35. Moscow: Medicine, 339–357.

Aristotle. (1927). *Poetics*. Leningrad: Academia.

Arnold, M.B. (1969). *Emotion, motivation and limbic system*. Annals of the New York Academy of Sciences, 159, 3.

Avdeeva, N.N., Meshcheryakova, S.Y. (1991). *You and the baby: the origins of communication*. Moscow: Pedagogika.

Bauer, T.D. (1985). *Psychological development of the infant*. Moscow: Progress.

Bogomolova, N.N. (1991). *Social psychology of the press, radio and television*. Moscow: Moscow State University Publishing House.

Bozhovich, L.I. (1972). *Initial experiences as a subject of psychology*. Voprosy Psychologii, 1, 130–134.

Breslav, G.M. (1984). *Emotional processes*. Riga: Riga State University publishing house.

Brushlnisky, A.V. (1979). *Thinking and prognostication (logical and psychological analysis)*. Moscow: Mysl.

Bukin, V.R. (1976). *Art and social psychology*. Leningrad: Znanie.

Chebykin, O.Y. (1992). *Emotional regulation of educational and cognitive activity*. Odessa: Publishing House Academy of Sciences Society of Psychologists of the USSR.

Chebykin, O.Y., Melnichuk, I.V (2004). *Genesis of the emotional peculiarities in children of different ages and gender*. UNC APN of Ukraine.

Chebykin, O.Y. (2021). *Conceptual approaches to the possibilities of studying the foundations of emotional health of participants in educational activities in a coronavirus pandemic*. Science and Education, 4, 23–29.

Chebykin, O., Kichuk, A. (2022). Research of interrelation of features of psychoemotional health with data of vital activity in youth. *Science and Education*, 1, 22–29.

Chomskaya, E.D., Batova, N.Y. (1992). *Brain and emotions: neuropsychological research*. Moscow: Publishing House of Moscow University.

Cohn, I.S. (1989). *The psychology of early adolescence: A book for the teacher*. Moscow: Prosveshcheniye.

Darwin, C. (1953). *Expression of emotions in animals and men*. Collected works, Vol. 5. Moscow.

Davydov, V.V. (1986). *Problems of developing education*. Moscow: Pedagogika.

Dembo, E.L. (1948). *Motivational theory of emotions*. Psychological Review, 55, 6.

Descartes, R. (1950). *Passions of the soul*. Selected works. Moscow: Gospolitizdat, 593–700.

Dodonov, B.I. (1982). In the world of emotions. Kiev: Politizdat

Dodonov, B.I. (1978). *Emotions as a value*. Moscow: Politizdat.

Dodonov, B.I. (1987). *In the world of emotions*. Kiev: Politizdat.

Elkonin, D.B. (1960). *Children's psychology*. Moscow: Uchpedgiz.

Flegontova, S.M. (1975). *Social psychology and art*. Textbook. Leningrad: Leningrad State University publishing house.

Galperin, P.Y. (1976). *Introduction to psychology*. Moscow: Moscow State University.

Galunov, V.I. (1978). *Speech, emotions, personality: problems and prospects*. Textbook. Leningrad, Leningrad State University, 3–13.

Gelgorn, E., Lufborrow, J. (1966). *Emotions and emotional disorders*. Moscow: Mir Publishing House.

Gromova, E.A. (1980). *Emotional memory and its mechanisms*. Moscow: Nauka.

Grote, N. (1879–1880). *Psychology of feelings in its history and main foundations*. St. Petersburg: St. Petersburg Publishing, 418–497.

Ilyin, E.P. (2001). *Emotions and feelings*. St. Petersburg: Peter.

Ilyuchenyuk, R.Y. (1988). *Emotions and memory: (reality and myths)*. Novosibirsk: Novosibirsk Publishing House.

Isaev, D.N. (2000). *Psychosomatic disorders in children: a guide for physicians*. St. Petersburg: Peter.

Izard, K.E. (1980). *Human emotions*. Moscow: Publishing House of Moscow University.

Izard, K. (2000). *Psychology of emotions*. St. Petersburg: Peter.

James, W. (1984). *What is emotion*. In: Psychology of emotions. Texts. V.K. Vilyunas, Y.B. Gippenreiter (ed.). Moscow: Publishing House of Moscow State University, 83–92.

Kalin, V.K. (1983). *Will, emotions, intelligence*. In: Emotional-volitional regulation of behavior and activity: conference proceedings. Simferopol.

Kennon, W. (1927). *Physiology of emotions*. Leningrad: Priboy.

Klapared, E. (1984). *Feelings and emotions*. In: Psychology of emotions. Texts. V.K. Vilyunas, Y.B. Gippenreiter (ed.). Moscow: Publishing House of Moscow State University, 93–102.

Kolot, S.A. (1999). *Formation of the culture of the emotional sphere of personality at the level of socio-psychological training*. Science and Education, 3–4, 68–71.

Kopina, O.S. (1982). *Study of the emotional regulation of mental activity*: Dissertation abstract. Moscow.

Kovalev, A.G. (1971). *Education of feelings*. Moscow: Pedagogika.

Krutetsky, V.A. (1977). *Psychological mechanisms of education of adolescents in the family*. Moscow: Znanie.

Kulagina, I.Y. (1996). *Age psychology: the development of the child from birth to seventeen years*. Moscow: Sphera.

Kulchitskaya, E.I. (1981). *Education of feelings in a child*. Kiev: Institute of psychology publishing.

Leeper, R.W. (1984). *Motivational theory of emotions*. In: Psychology of emotions. Texts. V.K. Vilyunas, Y.B. Gippenreiter (ed.). Moscow: Publishing House of Moscow State University, 138–151.

Leontiev, A.N. (1983). *Selected psychological works*, Vol. 2. Moscow: Pedagogika.

Lichko, A.E. (1983). *Psychopathy and character accentuations in adolescents*. Leningrad: Medicine.

Lindsley, D.B. (1960). *Emotions*. In: Experimental psychology. Moscow: Inostrannaya Literatura 629–684.

Lisina, M.I. (1983). *Education of young children in the family*. Kiev: Znanie.

Lobzin, V.S., Polyakova, A.A. (1984). *Possibilities of physiological self-regulation of emotions*. Leningrad: LDNTP.

Lomov, B.F. (1984). *Methodological and theoretical problems of psychology*. Moscow: Nauka.

Marshak, S.Y. (1961). *Education by word*. Moscow: Sovetsky pisatel, 439–539.

Melnichuk I., Chebykin A. (2021). *Some methods of studying emotional and personal characteristics of young peopleю (scientific and methodological recommendations)*. Odessa: Ushinsky University.

Morgun, V.F., Tkacheva, N.Y. (1981). *The problem of periodization of personality development in psychology*. Moscow: Publishing House of Moscow State University.

Morozova, N.G. (1979). *To the teacher about cognitive interest*. Moscow: Znanie.

Mukhina, V.S. (1985). *Child psychology*. Moscow: Prosveshcheniye.

Naem, J. (1984). *Psychology and psychiatry in the USA*. Moscow: Progress.

Nagaev, V.V., Bendas, T.V. (1982). *Psychology of feelings and its education. Textbook for the special course*. Perm: Perm University.

Nosenko, E.L., Egorova, S.N. (1996). *Memory and emotional state*. Dnepropetrovsk: Dnipropetrovsk State University Press.

Olshannikova, A.E. (1978). *To the psychological diagnostics of emotionality. In: Problems of general, age and pedagogical psychology*. Moscow: Pedagogika, 40–51.

Olshannikova, A.E. (1983). *Emotions and education*. Moscow: Znanie.

Petrazhitsky, L.I. (1993). *Psychology of emotions*. Texts. Moscow: Moscow State University publishing house.

Plutchik, R. (1962). *The emotions: Facts, theories and new model*. New-York: Random House.

Psychological Dictionary (1997). V.P. Zinchenko, B.G. Meshcheryakova (ed.). 2nd ed. Moscow: Pedagogika-Press.

Questions of the psychology of moral education. In: book. Levitova, I.A. Pedagogical psychology of a child. Moscow: Prosveschenie, 207–246.

Reikovsky, Y. (1979). *Experimental psychology of emotions*. Moscow: Progress.

Reinvald, N.I. (1987). *Psychology of personality*. Moscow: Publishing House of UDN.

Romanova, A.V. (1983). *Interrelation of mental and physical development of children in the family*. Leningrad: Znanie.

Rubinstein, S.L. (1959). *Being and consciousness*. Moscow: Publishing House of the AN USSR.

Rubinstein, S.L. (1976). *Problems of general psychology*. Moscow: Pedagogika.

Rubinstein, S.L. (1999). *Fundamentals of general psychology*. Moscow, 1946 (Re-edition. St. Petersburg: Peter, 1999).

Sannikova, O.P. (1984). *Emotionality and regulation of communication activity*. Voprosy Psychologii, 3, 124–128.

Schopenhauer, A. (2000). *Aphorisms and truths*. Moscow: Eksmo-press; Kharkov: Folio.

Semenov, V.E. (1988). *Social psychology of art*. Leningrad: Publishing House of Leningrad State University.

Sermyagina, O.S. (1991). *Emotional relationships in the family (social-psychological research)*. P.Y Gozman (ed.). Kishinev: Shtiintsa.

Shepel, V.M. (1987). *Socio-psychological problems of education*. Moscow: Moskovskij rabochij.

Shingarov, G.K. (1971). *Emotions and feelings as a form of reality reflection*. Moscow: Nauka.

Shlyakhova, N.M. (1981). *Emotions and artistic creativity*. Kiev: Iskusstvo.

Simonov, P.V. (1966). *What is an emotion?* Moscow: Nauka.

Simonov, P.V. (1984). *The theory of reflection and psychophysiology of emotions*. Moscow: Publishing House of Moscow University, 29–46.

Smirnova, E.O., Lagutina, A.E. (1991). *Awareness of experience of children in the family and in kindergarten*. Voprosy Psychologii, 6, 30–37.

Spinoza, B.O. (1984). *The origin and nature of affects*. In: Psychology of emotions. Texts. Moscow: Publishing House of Moscow University, 29–46.

Stavitskaya, S.O. (1991). *Psychological and pedagogical conditions for the suppression of personal anxiety in children of primary school age*: Dissertation abstract. Kiev.

Tikhomirov, O.K. (1969). *The structure of mental activity of a man*. Moscow: Publishing House of Moscow University.

Tikhomirov, O.K., Klochko, V.E. (1980). *Emotional regulation of mental activity*. Voprosy Psychologii, 5, 23–31.

Vasiliev, I.A. (1974). *To the analysis of the emergence of intellectual emotions*. In: Psychological study of intellectual activity. Moscow: Publishing House of Moscow State University, 50–53.

Vasiliev, I.A. (1998). *The role of intellectual emotions in regulation of mental activity*. Journal of Psychology, 4, 49–60.

Vasiliev, I.A., Popluzhny V.L., Tikhomirov O.K. (1980). *Emotions and thinking*. Moscow: Publishing House of Moscow State University.

Vasilishina, T.V. (2000). *Empathy as a factor in the effectiveness of pedagogical communication*: Dissertation abstract. Kiev.

Vilyunas, V.K. (1976). *Psychology of emotional phenomena*. Moscow: Publishing House of Moscow State University.

Vilyunas, V.K. (1984). *The main problems of the psychological theory of emotion*. In: Psychology of emotions. Texts. Moscow: Publishing House of Moscow State University, 3–28.

Vilyunas, V.K. (1990). *Psychological mechanisms of human motivation*. Moscow: Publishing House of Moscow State University.

Viskovatova, T.P. (1976). *Mental retardation in children due to the influence of small doses of natural and anthropogenic factors*. Odessa: YuUPU.

Vygotsky, L.S. (1970). *Spinoza and his doctrine of emotions in the light of modern psychoneurology*. Voprosy Psichologii, 6.

Vygotsky, L.S. (1991). *Pedagogical psychology*. Moscow: Pedagogika.

Weiner, M.E. (1997). *To the teacher about the emotional development of a junior schoolboy*. Nachalnaja Schkola, 3, 21–23.

Woodworth, R. (1950). *Experimental psychology*. Moscow: Inostrannaya literatura.

Wundt, W. (1912). *Introduction to psychology*. Moscow: Kosmos.

Wundt, W. (1984). *Psychology of emotional unrest*. In: Psychology of emotions. Texts. V.K. Vilyunas, Y.B. Gippenreiter (ed.). Moscow: Publishing House of Moscow State University, 47–63.

Yakobson, P.M. (1966). *The emotional life of a schoolboy*. Moscow: Prosveshcheniye.

Yakovleva, E.L. (1997). *Emotional mechanisms of personal and creative development*. Voprosy Psychologii, 4, 11–14.

Zaporozhets, A.V., Neverovich, Y.Z. (1974). *About genesis, function and structure of emotional processes in a child*. Voprosy Psychologii, 6, 35–50.

Zemskaya, M. (1986). *Family and personality*. L.V. Vasilyeva (ed.). Moscow: Progress.

Zinchenko, V.P. (1995). *Affect and intelligence in education*. Moscow: Trivola.

3

DIAGNOSTICS OF THE DEVELOPMENT OF EMOTIONAL MATURITY IN ADOLESCENCE AND EARLY ADULTHOOD

The problem of emotional maturity has been studied by domestic and foreign psychologists (such as A. Reber, A. Sukharev, O. Chebykin, C. Lambert, W. Menninger, etc.), psychophysiologists (P. Fress, P. Simonov and others) and psychotherapists (D. Abrahamsen, C.E. FitzMaurice and others).

A significant contribution to solving the problem of emotional maturity of a person was made by O. Chebykin, A. Maurer, J. Murray and others, whose works have shown the general concepts of its research and formation.

The results of research by G. Breslav, O. Zaporozhets, O. Kulchytska, E. Nosenko, A. Olshannikova, E. Chomskaya, O. Yakovleva and others, focused on revealing certain patterns of formation of the emotional sphere, and by K. Abulkhanova-Slavskaya, L. Antsiferova, L. Bozhovich, B. Bratusya, A. Maslow and V. Morgun, which reveal the meaning of the concepts of "maturity" and "personal maturity", and also by O. Asmolov, L. Vygotsky, G. Craig, I. Cohn, O. Leontiev, D. Elkonin and others, related to the determination of the factors of personality development, actualize the problem of in-depth understanding of emotional maturity. After all, according to V. Vilyunas, O. Leontiev, P. Fress and others, the study of emotional maturity belongs to the undeveloped areas of psychology. At present, the psychological content of emotional maturity and the main features that characterize this phenomenon are still insufficiently defined.

In age and pedagogical psychology, the problem of diagnosing emotional maturity is also of paramount importance. According to L. Bozhovych, R. Granovska, I. Cohn, A. Olshannikova, L. Potapchuk, O. Tolstykh and others, this period can be considered optimal for the formation of these emotions.

Emotional maturity can be viewed as an integrative property of a personality characterized by the development and adequacy of emotional response in various living conditions. In this case, the main components in its structure may be such properties as intensity, self-regulation and empathy. Taking into account the

DOI: 10.4324/9781003330943-3

given properties the methodology of emotional maturity diagnostics is presented. The peculiarities of the development of emotional maturity in adolescents and young adults from 11 to 23 years are described. We also gave characteristics of types of emotional maturity (such as expressive, self-regulatory, empathic, harmonious, self-regulatory-empathic, expressive-empathic and expressive-self-regulatory).

The first part of the chapter summarizes approaches to clarify the psychological content of emotional maturity, tendencies of its recognition and characteristic features. The methodology for examining emotional maturity is presented. The final part presents empirical results concerning the development of emotional maturity, taking into account the age and gender differences between adolescents and young adults.

We believe that the presented results can be useful both for specialists in the field of development of the emotional sphere and for practicing psychologists in the education system.

3.1 Clarification of the psychological content of emotional maturity of a person

At the present time in the field of studying emotional phenomena a rich research material has been accumulated. These include works on the development of emotions (Zaporozhets, Neverovich, 1974; Kolot, 1999; Kulchitskaya, 1996; Melnichuk, 2003; Donaldson, Westerman, 1986; Okano, 1994; Russell, 1991 and others), individual-specific features of the emotional response (Kuznetsov, 2001; Malimon, 2003; Nebylitsyn, 1971; Olshannikova, 1977; Rusalov, 1989; Sannikova, 1984; Cunningham, 1977; etc.), brain organization of emotions (Bekhtereva, Smirnov, 1975; Vartanyan, Petrov, 1989; Denisova, 1978; Simonov, 1981; etc.), and the pathology of emotions (Kirillova, Kurek, 2002; Kulibaly, 1995; Lebedinsky, Bardyshevskaya, 2002; Chomskaya, 2002; etc.).

It should be noted that when examining emotional phenomena, experts point to the difficulties related to attributing them to a certain class of mental formations (Vilyunas, 1984; Wundt, 1984; Kulchitskaya, 2003; Leontiev, 1984; Chomskaya, 2002; etc.), with terminological discrepancies in the terminology used by the authors in their descriptions (Vilyunas, 1984; Denisova, 1978; Russell, 1991), and by specifying their features and approaches to their classification (Vilyunas, 1976; Ilyin, 2001a,b; Leontiev, 1984). In particular, authors have defined emotional processes (Wundt, 1984; Izard, 1980; etc.), emotional reactions (Reikovsky, 1979; Smirnov, Trokhachev, 1974; etc.), emotional states (Anokhin, 1964; Yakobson, 1966; etc.), emotional personality traits (Ilyin, 2001), emotional relationships (Gozman, 1987; Myasishchev, 1960), emotional - personal qualities (Chomskaya, Batova, 1992; etc.). In our opinion, the phenomenon of emotional maturity can be referred to as the last class.

A summary of the literature available shows that many works (Sukharev, 2001; Shtepa, 2004; Menninger, 1967) use the term "emotional maturity", but do not describe the semantic meaning of this notion, which significantly complicates the process of its understanding.

In its turn, when examining such psychological phenomena as emotional intelligence (Goleman, 1996; Salovey, Mayer, 1990), emotional flexibility (Zavalkevich, 2004; Mitina, Asmakovets, 2001), emotional competence (Kunitsyna et al., 2001; Libin, 2000; Lambert, 1998), emotional literacy (Yakovleva, 1997; Goleman, 2000) scientists identify a number of characteristics inherent to emotional maturity.

An attempt to specify the notion of "emotional maturity" is carried out only in some works (Luk, 1982; Maurer, 1990; Reber, 2000; Fress, 1975; Murray, 1996; etc.).

In general, there are three approaches to understanding the concept of emotional maturity. Representatives of the first approach (Reber, 2000; Fress, 1975; etc.) understand emotional maturity as one of the characteristics of an adult, i.e. a biologically mature person, and define it as the compliance of a person's emotional reactivity with adult norms in a given society. Thus, P. Fress uses this term to denote the tendency for the total frequency of emotional reactions to decrease with age. The author explains this tendency through the development in adults of the ability to anticipate emotional situations and inhibit emotional manifestations. Thus, emotional maturity, according to P. Fress, is a set of characteristics of emotional response inherent in an adult person, which consist of the development of self-control, the ability to anticipate the consequences of a certain event, as well as mastering the reactions that are adequate to different situations encountered by a person. Similar ideas are found in the works of Reber (2000) and Lambert (1998), who use this term to denote the ability to control one's emotions and control their external manifestations.

In our opinion, this view of emotional maturity is incomplete. On the other hand, it should be agreed that these emotional manifestations may be signs of emotional maturity of a person.

In the opinion of the second group of authors (Luk, 1982; Maslow, 1999; Yakovleva, 1997; Menninger, 1967 and others), emotional maturity allows emotional reactions to meet not only the expectations of society but also the needs, values and interests of the subject. Representatives of this tendency believe that emotional maturity characterizes internally non-contradictory personality, which is capable to recognize and express his/her own emotions adequately to the experience that arises.

One can agree with the above-mentioned experts that the ability to recognize the emotions of both – own and others – and the adequacy of emotional response is an important characteristic in the content of emotional maturity.

Representatives of the third school of thought (Isaev, 1982; Maksimova et al., 1996; Maurer, 1990; Chudina, 2003; Murray, 1996 and others) approach the understanding of emotional maturity of a person as a characteristic of various emotional manifestations inherent in a certain age period of a person, ensuring the successful performance of activities. In the works of these authors, it is confirmed that such features as the inability to control emotions, the inability to find an adequate explanation and realistic expression, along with increased emotional excitability, impulsiveness, inhibition, the predominance of game motivation, and high suggestibility may be signs of emotional immaturity. In turn, the general indicator of maturity – immaturity of the representatives of this school is the compliance of emotional behavior with the idea of the norm for a certain age.

The conducted research allows us to state that all representatives of the above-mentioned scientific directions in "emotional maturity" phenomenon consider the ability to adequate emotional reactions, given a certain age-specific period of the personality's life, i.e. its development in specific social conditions.

As for discrepancies, they can be defined only at the level of tendencies when different properties of the emotional order (expressiveness, emotional sensitivity, etc.) are included in the content of the notion of emotional maturity.

Certainly, the definition of emotional maturity cannot go beyond the context of the maturity of the person in general. However, the latter concept has a broader meaning and includes in addition to emotional a lot of other human characteristics that have an indirect relation to emotional maturity. At the same time, the phenomenon of personality maturity should serve as a system-forming basis for defining the notion of emotional maturity.

According to a number of authors (Abramova, 2003; Bratus, 1980; Gezzel, 2002; Krupnik, Lebedeva, 2000; Morgun, 1977; Orban-Lembrik, 2003; Pasichnyak, 1999; etc.) maturity is understood as one of the ontogenesis periods characterized by the tendency to achieve the highest level of development of all human abilities. Other specialists (Reber, 2000: 287; Shtepa, 2004) in determining maturity focus on the compliance of biological (physiological) and psychological characteristics of a man with the age standards accepted in a particular society. Some authors (Anziferova, 1980; Asmolov, 1984; Golovakha, Kronik, 2003; Morgun, Tkacheva, 1981; etc.) consider the regularities of maturity formation at the level of versatility, multidimensionality, and hierarchy of this process. Researchers (Abulkhanova-Slavskaya, 2003; Bozhovich, 1995; Luk, 1982; Maslow, 1999; Obukhovsky, 1972; Potapchuk, 2001; etc.) describe certain psychological criteria of the maturity of a person, such as functional autonomy, realism, ability to discern ideal and real goals, high level of reflection, self-control and flexibility of behavior, developed sense of responsibility, strong and consistent values orientations, the need to find meaning in life, care for others, tolerance for own and others' shortcomings, the ability to actively participate in the life of society and effective use of their knowledge and potential, psychological closeness with other people, constructive solution of various life problems, etc.

The research of Bratus (1980), Gorbatkov (2001), Dyachenko, Kandybovich (2001: 90), Lebedinsky (1985), Mironenko (2001), Sadokova (2001), etc. allows us to assume that the formation of emotional maturity, as well as other types of psychological maturity of a person (maturity of sensory, mnemonic and intellectual functions), is based on physiological development, and affects the moral, ideological and professional maturity of a person.

Speaking about maturity, both general and emotional, scientists (Koblyanskaya, 1995; Kunitsyna et al. 2001; Libin, 2000; Makarenko, 2001; Cherevko, 2001; etc.) use the term "competence" and understand it as a complex integrative property of a person, characterized by a system of knowledge about social reality and about oneself, as the use of that system of knowledge in life. In our opinion, this concept to the greatest extent allows us to consider the meaningful signs of emotional maturity at the level of adequacy of the emotional response of a person to certain social conditions.

In this sense, we find the works dedicated to emotional intelligence (Nosenko, Kovriga, 2003; Salovey, Mayer, 1990) are interesting. Among them, the most generalizing is the research conducted by (Nosenko, Kovriga, 2003), who understand emotional intelligence

> ... as a form of revealing a positive attitude to the world (assessing it as one in which a person can exercise successful life); others (as worthy of benevolence); oneself (as capable to independently determine one's own life goals and actively act in the direction of their implementation and worthy of self-esteem).
>
> *p. 109*

As we see, the mentioned approach reveals the possibility of considering the specificity of emotional intelligence as a certain characteristic property of the intellectual-emotional order with a functionally positive orientation of the personality.

Important for our study is the authors' statement that emotional behavior, adequate to the situation, provides the formation of a system of social skills and the presence of appropriate guidelines in the subject about the possibility of an alternative behavior in specific life situations (Nosenko, Kovriga, 2003: 113).

Taking into consideration these and other research (Kulchitskaya, 1996; Kunitsyna et al., 2001; Rusalov, 1989; Sannikova, 2003; Chirikova, 1976; Russell, 1991; etc.), we came to the conclusion that human emotions have both natural, i.e. psychophysiological and social basis in their development. The natural basis grounds on those psychophysiological properties that reflect the adequacy of their dynamics and ontogenetic development in accordance with age, and the social basis reflects the acquired experience of the emotional attitude of the developing personality to the world around them.

The latter gives grounds to consider emotional maturity as an integrative quality of personality, which characterizes the degree of development of the emotional sphere at the level of adequacy of emotional response in certain sociocultural conditions.

Thus, this definition describes emotional maturity as (1) an integrative phenomenon of a purely emotional order; (2) a certain level of human emotional development; and (3) personality quality, which characterizes the adequacy of emotional response.

Proceeding from these provisions, we try to search for specific properties and signs of their manifestation.

3.2 Generalization of the main tendencies in the knowledge of emotional maturity

A summary of the information available to us has shown that the main trends in the study of emotional maturity can be considered in several ways.

The first direction includes works related to identifying specific features of the emotional maturity of a person (Reber, 2000; Sukharev, 2001; Menninger, 1967; Lambert, 1998 and others).

The second line of research includes studies devoted to identifying the conditions for the formation of emotional maturity (Milrud, 1987; Chebykin, 1989a,b; Griffith, 1999; Cardwell, Dunn, 1986; etc.).

Coming to the third, there are works that describe both goal-directed and spontaneous formation of emotional maturity (Abdyukova, 2000; Andreeva, 2002; etc.).

Moreover, it is advisable to look at the studies devoted to the identification of neoplasms in the emotional sphere that is important for the adequacy of emotional response in a certain age period (Bozhovich, 1995; Breslav, 1990; Bylkina, Lyusin, 2000; Zaporozhets, Neverovich, 1974; Kulchitskaya, 1996; Lebedinsky, 1985; Bischof-Köhler, 1994; Donaldson, Westerman, 1986), as well as works that examine the phenomenon of emotional immaturity (Zakharov, 1988; Maksimova et al., 1996; *Psychology of personality*: Dictionary, 2001; etc.).

Consider more closely the trends presented.

When studying the works of the first group (Sukharev, 2001; Goleman, 2000) and others, it was found that authors mostly study emotional maturity indirectly or fragmentarily, and in some cases conflate it with other emotional phenomena.

Characteristics in this aspect may be studies in which emotional maturity is considered in connection with emotional literacy (Yakovleva, 1997; Goleman, 2000; etc.), emotional competence (Moloney, 2001 and others), emotional intelligence (Salovey, Mayer, 1990 and others). However, in some cases, researchers attribute similar signs to both emotional maturity and other properties.

In particular, in some works, the authors (Lambert, 1998; Moloney, 2001) define emotional maturity and emotional competence as self-awareness, the ability to be the master of one's emotions, to have the courage to make difficult decisions, to anticipate possible disadvantages, to influence the directivity of others' actions, the ability to combine the efforts of different people and make a highly productive team, to resolve interpersonal conflicts in such a way that participants do not feel resentment, to inspire self-respect, and the ability to encourage people to work within their capabilities, etc.

However, if we turn to the definition of emotional competence and emotional maturity given in the previous section, it becomes clear that the above features are largely consistent with the first of them.

D. Goleman (1996) attributes the same features to emotional maturity and emotional intelligence. He believes (Goleman, 2000) that emotional maturity is a set of competencies that allow one to work effectively in any environment.

However, if we refer to the works on emotional intelligence (Nosenko, Kovriga, 2003; Salovey, Mayer, 1990), it becomes clear that this is about the intellectual use of emotions in behavior, i.e. emotional intelligence.

The common thing in all of the above studies is that some authors conflate emotional, social and intellectual phenomena, bringing some confusion into the differentiation of these concepts. However, the works of Nosenko, Kovriga, (2003) have shown quite thoroughly that emotional intelligence is one of the forms of intelligence detection, namely its detection in the emotional sphere of the personality. Emotional maturity, in its turn, reflects the level of adequacy of emotional response in certain conditions.

Also within the first group, there are works (Sukharev, 2001; Menninger, 1967; etc.) that directly study the features of emotional maturity, but in fact, talk about other phenomena.

Thus, Menninger (1967) and Murray (1996) consider features of emotional maturity, such as:

a a wide range of emotions;
b clear, undistorted perception of reality and the ability to interact constructively with it;
c ability to adapt to changes;
d ability to adequately perceive oneself, others and events;
e ability to interact with people consistently, with mutual satisfaction and appreciation;
f ability to take into account the needs of others;
g ability to love;
h ability to accept expressions of love from others;
i ability to enjoy life;
j self-confidence and self-esteem;
k ability to be honest with oneself;
l integrity;
m reflexivity;
n resolution;
o trust in intuition;
p sense of humor;
q openness to the new;
r ability to recognize own imperfection;
s ability to learn from your own and others' mistakes;
t compassion;
u ability to restrain impulsiveness.

In our opinion, some of the above traits ("i", "j", "l", "m", "n", "r", "s") rather refer to the traits of personal maturity, consistent with the results of research of Anziferova (1980), Asmolov (1984), Craig (2000) and Obukhovsky (1972), who studied personal maturity. Other features ("c", "e", "f"), according to the works of Koblyanskaya (1995) and Cherevko (2001), are referred to the social competence of a person. The third ("b", "o", "q"), according to the research of Luk (1982) and Maslow (1999), are referred to the characteristics of a personality associated with creativity.

The problem of emotional maturity is also considered in the aspect of a child's readiness for school (Maurer, 1990). According to A. Maurer, emotional maturity is manifested in the reduction of impulsive behavior, in the ability to perform for a long time not very diligent work (i.e. in the development of arbitrary behavior), the need for communication with peers, the ability to obey orders and follow instructions, the ability to communicate and cooperate, establish positive attitudes toward peers, adults, tasks. As the author shows, emotionally mature children are characterized by a return to the environment with an orientation toward activity and an outlet to meet others, emotionally connected to the environment, freely enter into pleasant, warm relationships with adults and peers, and evoke the same attitude toward themselves. They are inherent harmony movements, gestures, facial expressions and the adequacy of verbal expressions.

In our opinion, this approach combines the concepts of "emotional" and "social maturity". However, the first includes the reduction of impulsive behavior and the development of its arbitrariness, lack of emotional tension, rigidity, the adequacy of expression of their emotional state, and the second includes the need to communicate with peers, the ability to obey orders and follow instructions, communicate and cooperate, etc.

The study of the works of the other trend (Cardwell, Dunn, 1986; Griffith, 1999; etc.) showed that in the formation of emotional maturity the authors include the development of self-awareness, self-understanding, self-acceptance, altruism, cooperation, awareness of the meaning of life, improvement of emotional control, development of the sense of personal identity, and expansion of social contacts. And self-awareness is assigned a central role here. Thus, these scientists believe that emotional maturity is the result of long-term purposeful work of a person aimed at harmonization, improvement of one's inner world, as well as an increase in the level of social competence.

At the same time, studies of external conditions are important in this area (Al-Hadidi Saud, 2001; Chebykin, 1989a; Lebedinsky, Bardyshevskaya, 2002; Jacobson, 1977; Okano, 1994; Russell, 1991; etc.), which influence the development of the emotional sphere. A generalization of these and other works have shown that such conditions are considered at the level of traditions (Al-Hadidi Saud, 2001; Okano, 1994), rituals (Lebedinsky, Bardyshevskaya, 2002), ethnocultural factors (Yakobson, 1977; Russell, 1991), corresponding goals and approaches in education (Yakovleva, 1997), the conditions of professional activity (Kochnev, 1986; Milrud, 1987; Chebykin, 1989), etc. Experts note that the very way of life, traditions, rituals, celebrations, games and professional activities contain complex external psychotechnical methods of influencing their emotions.

Mastering and implementing these methods allow a person to develop a certain emotional culture.

Considering the role of such conditions, it should be noted that the social environment unequally affects different emotional manifestations. Some authors (Kunitsyna et al., 2001; Yakobson, 1977; Russell, 1991; etc.) show that emotions are most susceptible to this influence implemented in communication.

The third trend includes works of socio-psychological nature (Abdyukova, 2000; Andreeva, 2002; Kunitsyna et al., 2001; Repnova, 2003; Sergeeva, 2001; etc.), in which the formation of emotional maturity is studied in the aspect of a purposeful influence on the personality in cases of its spontaneous formation. It is proved that the socialization of emotions can be carried out under the influence of unconscious mechanisms, such as suggestion, influence, psychological contamination and identification, and also of observable ones, such as beliefs, group influence and the influence of authority.

The study by K.E. FitzMaurice (Donaldson, Westerman, 1986; Field, et al., 1982), in which the author identifies 6 levels (or stages) of emotional maturity formation, is important from the point of view of systematization and adequacy of the purposeful development of emotional maturity. These are as follows:

The first level is *emotional responsibility:* thinking that any external forces (such as people, places, things, destiny and alcohol) are responsible for the emotional state, but not the person himself.

The second is *emotional honesty:* a person's willingness to acknowledge his/her own feelings, which is associated with overcoming conscious or unconscious attitudes of inferiority, which prohibit experiencing these or other feelings.

Third is *emotional openness:* a person's readiness and ability to adequately express their own feelings, self-disclosure and learning to experience and express any emotion without suppression or imitation.

The fourth is an *emotional statement*: The main task of this level is to learn to expect and achieve the satisfaction of one's own needs and desires, to express them freely, that is, to value and respect one's own feelings. According to the author, this is achieved by understanding the relationship between the repression of feelings, stress and illness.

Fifth is *emotional understanding:* awareness and acceptance of emotional responsibility and irresponsibility, the transition from identification with external objects or internal images that dictate the rules of behavior, to identification with the real self.

Sixth is *emotional alienation:* alienation from the burden of inadequate ideas about oneself, self-esteem and evaluations of others. It should be noted that the author considers the conditions for the formation of emotional maturity only at the level of psychological counseling, for which he proposes various techniques to influence the system of attitudes, self-esteem, etc., i.e. the correction of self-awareness as an internal condition for emotional maturity.

Proceeding from the aim of our research, there are important data (Bozhovich, 1995; Breslav, 1990; Bylkina, Lyusin, 2000; Zaporozhets, Neverovich, 1974; Kulchitskaya, 1996; Lebedinsky, 1985; Olshannikova, 1983; Bischof-Köhler, 1994; Donaldson, Westerman, 1986; Spitz, 1946; etc.), which indicate new developments in the emotional sphere that occur during a certain age period, as well as the information about the formation of those personality traits that are important for the adequacy of emotional response in various life situations. Summarizing the research of these scientists allowed us to establish certain characteristics of the emotional sphere, the formation of which depends on the successful adaptation of a child to society. The first position is taken by the expressive experience that a child acquires in his or her interactions with the environment. The second position is taken by the ways of adequate emotional regulation of a child. The third position includes the emergence of gnostic and aesthetic feelings, i.e. the higher senses that allow individuals to realize their humanistic values and to be actively involved in social and labor activity.

The generalization of these and other studies has also allowed us to identify a number of areas in which the development of the emotional sphere of man throughout life is taking place.

The *first direction* is the differentiation of emotions, which is understood as:

a enrichment of the qualitative palette of experiences, the emergence of a multitude of variants of emotions (Ilyin, 2001);
b change in the content of emotions, that is, the complication of emotion-generating objects, and expansion of the number of such objects (Olshannikova, 1983; Reikovsky, 1979);
c change of emotional expression, that is, from simpler but generalized forms to more complex and specific ones (Izard, 1980).

The *second direction* is the development of emotional empathy as the ability to respond emotionally to the experience of another person (Gavrilova, 1974; Strelkova, 1987; Bischof-Köhler, 1994). The development of empathy can be characterized as follows:

a from the emotional contamination of another person's mood to the separation in the mind of the emotions of another person from one's own experiences (Bischof-Köhler, 1994);
b from empathy based on identification with another person, to compassion, which is based on the need for the well-being of another person (Gavrilova, 1974);
c from passive sympathy for another person to taking into account in one's own behavior the other person's feelings and desires (Breslav, 1990; Gippenreiter et al. 1993; Zaporozhets, Neverovich, 1974; Kotirlo, Ladivir, 1985).

The *third direction* is inextricably linked with the previous, that is, the development of the ability to adequately perceive, evaluate and understand one's own emotions and the emotions of other people (Bazhin, Korneva, 1981; Kurek, 1996; Fetisova, 1981), which has the following features:

a from the inability to recognize emotion (4–5 years) to engaging more additional information that consolidates into a complete picture (according to various authors, that is, after 6–7 years (Bylkina, Lyusin, 2000; Shchetinina, 1984), or 10–11 years (Donaldson, Westerman, 1986));
b the ability to recognize emotions of different modalities is not formed simultaneously (Fress, 1975);
c along with the development of the ability to recognize and interpret emotions, the ability to use this knowledge in communication is improved (Labunskaya, 1987, 1989).

The *fourth direction* – the development of emotional expression – is also closely related to the previous ones. It includes:

a mastering the forms of expression of emotions commonly accepted in this culture (Reikovsky, 1979);
b creating a "language" of emotions that enriches the spontaneous expressive movements and makes them more diverse (Fress, 1975);
c development of the ability to use the emotional expression as a means of communication (Ananiev, 1996; Luk, 1982; Maurer, 1990);
d emergence of the ability to detach expressive means from experiences (Ilyin, 2001);
e emergence and development of the ability to express emotions in an optimal and purposeful way (Sukharev, 2001; Field et al., 1982).

The authors assert that the acquisition of such skills is achieved by accumulating experience in perceiving and understanding expressive information according to certain communication situations.

The *fifth direction* is the emergence and development of the ability to understand and reflect the emotional states (Bozhovich, 1977; Kunitsyna et al., 2001; Yakovleva, 1997), which includes:

a ability to analyze one's own emotions, as well as the causes of their occurrence;
b ability to anticipate situations that can cause certain emotions;
c ability to predict the consequences of certain emotional reactions.

The *sixth direction* is the emergence and development of emotional self-regulation, which includes:

a formation of the ability to the self-control of emotions, which some authors understand as the ability to control excessively strong emotions (Reber, 2000;

Fress, 1975), while others speak about controlling emotions whose expression differs from the behavioral norms of a certain culture (Kunitsyna et al. 2001);

b mastering the ability to mask and simulate emotions (Ilyin, 2001; Chebykin, Pavlova, (2009);

c development of the ability to arbitrarily control one's own emotions, i.e. to control the expression, experience and generation of emotions in accordance with the appropriateness (Bozhovich, 1995; Simonov, 1981);

d mastering cultural psychotechnical methods of stabilization and tonization of one's emotional state, i.e. formation of socially adequate ways of obtaining emotional impressions (Ananiev, 1996; Lebedinsky, 1990).

In some works (Zueva, 1995; Starodubova, 2001; Winnicott, 1958), emotional maturity is considered a category polar to emotional immaturity.

A generalization of works that use the concept of "emotional immaturity", showed that scientists (Breslav, 1990; Zakharov, 1988; Maksimova et al., 1996; etc.) understand it as a special nature of the emotional response, which corresponds to the idea of a norm for an earlier age period, i.e. inability to control emotions, inability to find an adequate explanation and realistic expression of them. Among the signs of emotional immaturity, we see an increased emotional restlessness, impulsiveness, liability, inhibition, underdevelopment of emotional perception, weak empathy, high sensitivity, low capacity to volitional control of emotional impulses, lack of voluntary self-containment, high suggestibility, dependence on the opinion of other people.

From our point of view, the use of the category "immaturity" is not correct enough, because it characterizes the absolute inadequacy of the development of the emotional sphere, rather than the quality of its development. Therefore, when studying emotional maturity, it seems to us reasonable to look at it not on the polar scale of maturity–immaturity, but on a unidirectional way – from the minimum to the maximum degree of its development.

The considered research allowed us to allocate some tendencies in studying the emotional maturity of the person.

Some scientists tend to note similar features in such phenomena as the emotional, personal and social maturity of a person as a result of their close integration and interaction. Other authors often equate the concepts of emotional maturity, emotional competence and emotional intelligence, which can be explained by a certain intellectualization of the emotional sphere with age. In the opinion of the majority of the authors, the conditions for the formation of emotional maturity are related to the natural features of development and assimilation of sociocultural experience. And finally, the conditions for the formation of emotional maturity are associated with various psychological techniques.

Based on the data obtained, the important signs of emotional maturity include:

- the ability to respond emotionally to the experience of others;
- the ability to use the emotional expression as a means of communication, purposefully express emotions and arbitrarily control their manifestation;

- the ability to adequately perceive, evaluate and understand one's own emotions and the emotions of others, awareness, the reflection of emotional states, self-control of emotions, etc.

These all can be reduced to the features of self-regulation, empathy and expression.

3.3 Factors that determine the formation of emotional maturity

The question of factors that determine the development of personality, including the formation of its emotional maturity is considered in numerous studies by both domestic (Asmolov, 2001; Bozhovich, 1977; Vygotsky, 1984; Govorun, 2002; Cohn, 1988; Lebedinsky, Bardyshevskaya, 2002; Leontiev, 1975a,b; Morgun, Tkacheva, 1981; Olshannikova, 1977; Elkonin, 1989; etc.) and foreign authors (Craig, 2000; Oudshoorn, 2002; Cantwel, Tarjan, 1979; Rutter, 1966) and others).

According to Bratus (1986), Gorbatkov (2001), Craig (2000), Maurer (1990), Mironenko (2001), Sadokova (2001), etc., one of the characteristics of the formation of the general maturity of the personality is its emotional maturity, the most intensive formation of which occurs during preadolescent and adolescence age. Therefore, we considered the factors of formation of emotional maturity in the aspect of personality development in general, conditionally dividing factors into internal and external.

Among the internal factors of personality development, we include individual human characteristics, both hereditary and those that are formed under the influence of prenatal and postnatal development (Denisova, 1978; Oudshoorn, 2002; Rutter, 1966 and others). At the same time, some experts point out their genetic conditioning (Ravych-Shcherbo, 1999; Rutter, 1966; etc.), features of physiological maturation of the organism (Isaev, 1982; Lebedinsky, Bardyshevskaya, 2002; etc.) and mental development of personality (Vygotsky, 1984; Cohn, 1989; etc.).

Characterizing the external conditions of personality formation, the authors (Abdyukova, 2000; Abramenkova, 2002; Belinskaya, Tikhomandritskaya, 2001; Bronfenbrenner, 1976; Craig, 2000; Krysko, 2001: 588; etc.) present various models and classifications of them -

- ecological model of Bronfenbrenner (1976),
- the model of the psychological space of the child's interaction with the world by Abramenkova (Abramenkova, 2002),
- classification of four groups of realities of human existence proposed by Mukhina (Mukhina, 2000), and
- examined by Craig (Craig, 2000) the classification of three types of factors influencing the development of personality, such as normative-age, normative-historical and non-normative.

Summarizing these and other research, we propose to divide all external influences into factors that indirectly determine the formation of emotional maturity at the macro level, and factors that directly influence this process at the micro level. The first one includes cultural and economic conditions of socialization of adolescents and young people, which were considered by Abramenkova (2002), Andreeva et al. (1997), Belinskaya, Tikhomandritskaya (2001), Cole (1997), Newcomb (2002), Perepelytsya (1990), Rice (2000), Tolstykh (2002), Horney (2002) and others. The second one includes the quality of family interaction (Diduk, 2001; Zavatska, 2002; Maksymenko, Rakytyanska, 2000; Makushina, 2002; Eidemiller, Yustytsky, 1989; Yakovleva, 1997; etc.), circle of communication (Goshovsky, 1995; Kulagina, Kolyutsky, 2003; Kulachkivska, 1986; Petrovsky, 1981; Umansky, 1980; etc.) and the frequency of social contacts (Granovska, 1997; Cohn, 1989; Mukhina, 1985; Olshannikova, 1983; etc.).

Let's consider each of these factors in detail. We consider the factor "personality traits" to be a prerequisite for development at the level of psychophysiological and individual-typological features of personality (Danilova, Krylova, 1997; Mendelevich, 1998; Moskvin, 1988; etc.). Those who work in the field of differential psychology and psychophysiology (Isaev, 2000; Kochnev, 1986; Rusalov, 1989; etc.) note that the dynamic features of the personality may create a positive or negative impact on the formation of emotional maturity. The complex of favorable preconditions includes activity, the rhythmicity of physiological functions, good adaptability to new things, more or less high lability of emotional arousal, dynamic inhibition of the consequences of emotional stimuli, low intensity of reactions to changes in the environment (Isaev, 2000; Kochnev, 1986). Among individual features that can negatively influence the formation of emotional maturity, scientists (Isaev, 2000; Rusalov, 1989) distinguish a low threshold of sensitivity to stimuli, high intensity of reactions, difficulties in adapting to new experiences, and the prevalence of negative emotions.

However, in the opinion of many experts in the field of psychology of individual differences (Asmolov, 1984; Ilyin, 2001; Nebilitsyn, 1971; Olshannikova, 1977; Ravich-Shcherbo, 1999; Teplov, 2002; Chebykin, Abolin, 1984; etc.), individual-typological manifestations of nervous processes may not be positive or negative, but create an individual and unique reaction style. The authors claim that individual characteristics determine the formal and dynamic aspects of a person's behavior and, only by engaging in activities, influence the formation of personality, including the formation of emotional maturity.

The consolidation of works devoted to this problem (Ilyin, 2001; Isaev, 1982; Kochnev, 1986; Sannikova, 1984; etc.) allows us to conclude that the influence of individual-typological features on the formation of emotional maturity can be carried out in several ways, namely, they determine the speed of adaptation to new situations, sensitivity to environmental influences, intensiveness of reaction to these influences and impose their effect on the way of communication, determining, in particular, greater or lesser activity in establishing contacts.

In our opinion, the internal factors that significantly influence the formation of emotional maturity in adolescence should include the time of onset and speed of pubescent maturation. Some authors (Craig, 2000; Lichko, 1983; Newcomb, 2002; etc.) point out the adverse effects of this process of delayed or insufficient physical development for boys, as well as accelerated maturation for girls.

Apart from those mentioned above, the results of child development achieved at previous stages, i.e. age-related psychological neoplasms, should also be included in the determination of emotional maturity in adolescence (Anziferova, 1980; Bozhovich, 1995; Dashkevich, 1986; Lomov, 1984 and others).

First of all, we are talking about the development of self-awareness, which can be considered one of the most important factors in the formation of emotional maturity of adolescents, and about the psychological conditions of its formation. Specialists (Burns, 1986; Cohn, 1989; Elkonin, 1971; Makushina, 2002; Pasichniak, 1999; etc.) point out the emergence of a special form of self-awareness – "self-concept" at the end of adolescence.

The psychological conditions of its formation in the cognitive sphere are the emergence of time perspective (Bozhovich, 1995; Klee, 1991; Greene, 1990; etc.), the development of formal thinking (Geiko, 2002; Piaget, 1994), the formation of reflection (Burns, 1986; Remshmidt, 2002; etc.), and at the end of adolescence, an increase of the individual component in thinking (Vygotsky, 1984).

Psychological conditions in the personal sphere include the emergence of a number of needs, the satisfaction of which is of direct importance for the formation of emotional maturity of the individual, such as the need for adequate self-identification (Mukhina, 1985; Pasichniak, 1999), the need for interaction with peers (Davydov, 1974; Morgun, Tkacheva, 1981; Elkonin, 1971; etc.), and the need for support from significant adults (Chesnokova, Yaremchuk, 2002; etc.).

Some authors (Valion, 2000; Goshovsky, 1995; Kotirlo, Ladivir, 1985; Slutsky, 1996; Sukholenova, 2000; and others) indicate that the deprivation of basic needs leads to emotional immaturity, which manifests itself in a poor repertoire of emotional interaction, delays in the formation of social skills, and sometimes in severe disorders of emotional development.

In turn, the timely formation of adequate "self-concept" leads to the emergence in older adolescents of a desire for self-development, self-education, ability to make independent decisions, awareness of one's own individuality, finding of psychological autonomy, formation of one's own system of norms and values, development of self-control as a competent regulation of one's own behavior, and improving the ability to more subtly and differently feel the experiences of other persons (Abulkhanova-Slavskaya, 2003; Burns, 1986; Granovska, 1997; etc.).

Significant internal factors are portrayed in the formation of emotional maturity in adolescence, such as a new development in personal and professional self-determination, the successful formation of which leads to the general stabilization of the personality of young people, their self-understanding, self-esteem, self-acceptance, development of self-regulation, improvement of control over their emotions and formation of emotional maturity in general (Cardwell, Dunn, 1986; Murray, 1996; etc.).

Psychological conditions for the formation of personal and professional self-determination are: the emergence of the desire to understand oneself and others (Craig, 2000; Mukhina, 2000), to know the meaning of what is happening, and the meaning of one's own existence; and formation of a life plan (Kulagina, Kolyutsky, 2003), the emergence of autonomous morality and moral steadiness and independence from the group (Sadokova, 2001).

Consideration of external factors that mediate the formation of emotional maturity on the macro level, allows us to conclude that those factors include the level of stability of the state's economic policy (Andreeva, et al., 1997; Mukhina, 2000; Newcomb, 2002) and the speed of change in the system of social roles (Lopukhova, 2001; Remshmidt, 2002; etc.).

In turn, the factor "the level of stability of state's economic policy" affects the immediate conditions of personality development, such as the material status of the family (Newcomb, 2002), the length of the working day of parents, and accordingly, the time they spend with their children (Rais, 2000) and the choice to live in a certain city, district or educational institution for a child (Cohn, 1989), etc.

Regarding the factor "speed of change in the system of social roles", authors (Lopukhova, 2001; Remshmidt, 2002; etc.) believe that accelerated social changes cause differences in cultural and historical experience and contemporary social expectations, and lead to ambiguity in the demands placed by different socialization institutions on the emotional maturity of a person.

Microsocial factors of emotional maturity in adolescence, according to a number of scientists (Eidemiller, Yustitsky, 1989; Craig, 2000; Makushina, 2002; Satir, 1999; Tolstykh, 2002; Yakovleva, 1997; etc.), primarily related to the attitude of parents and other significant adults to those changes that have occurred in the personality of the adolescent, stimulating their independence and discipline, supporting adequate emotional reactions, giving the example of emotionally mature behavior. These influences, which may conditionally be combined into a factor "quality of family interaction", determine the level of development of the ability to adequately interpret the emotional state of partners, freely convey their own emotions, and encourage the expansion of social contacts, which in turn is the most important condition for the formation of the emotional maturity of the individual.

The factor "circle of communication" (Kulagina, Kolyutsky, 2003; Petrovsky, 1981; Umansky, 1980; etc.) in adolescence is determined by the presence or absence of a reference group of peers, as well as its level of social development, i.e. the degree of psychological integrity of the members of this group, its organization and moral conjugacy.

Studying external factors of formation of emotional maturity in early adulthood, it should be noted that it differs from adolescents by reduction of the role of factors related to family upbringing, and by the increased role of "circle of communication" and "frequency of social contacts" factors (Granovska, 1997; Ljutak, 2001; Mukhina, 2000; Olshannikova, 1983; etc.). The latter create favorable conditions for mastering and appropriation of various patterns of emotional response in different life circumstances.

Thus, the factors that determine the formation of a personality have been widely studied in the literature, but the factors of formation of emotional maturity in adolescence and young adulthood have been studied fragmentarily.

On the basis of the literature available to us, the factors that determine the formation of emotional maturity of the individual in adolescence and young adulthood can be divided into internal and external. The internal factors include individual characteristics (hereditary and congenital) of a person, individual and typological features of personality, as well as factors of neoplasms of children (formation of an adequate "self-concept") and young people (personal and professional self-determination).

External factors of formation of emotional maturity of the individual in adolescence and young adulthood include social influences, such as the level of stability in social environment, the speed of changes in the system of social roles, the quality of family interaction, circle of communication and frequency of social contacts.

3.4 Identification of the main structural components of emotional maturity

Beginning with the main components of the structure of emotional maturity, it should be noted that we understand it as a certain integrative feature that gives a relatively holistic view of the formation of the emotional sphere of a person. At the same time, we understand that all the signs of emotional development are directly or indirectly related to each other, interact and interplay with each other.

At the same time, modern psychology (Vecker, 2000; Lomov, 1984; Petrovsky, Yaroshevsky, 1999; etc.) has clearly revealed the idea that each mental process in its structure contains both significant properties and less important, which can characterize it as a whole. The search for such properties is the subject of many studies aimed at the recognition of both emotions and their individual characteristics.

Summarizing the most essential features in the structure of the emotional sphere has allowed us to reveal a number of them. In particular, the most widespread in this sense are studies of emotionality (Olshannikova, 1977; Pereverzeva, 1981; Rusalov, 1989; Sannikova, 2003; Fress, 1975; etc.), emotional agitation (Nebylitsyn, 1971; Pereverzeva, 1981; etc.), sensitivity (Ilyin, 2001; etc.) and emotional stability (Abolin, 1987; Dyachenko, Ponomarenko, 1990; Zhorov, Shulga, 1987; Chebykin, 1989; etc.).

Thus, emotionality as an integrative characteristic of a personality is considered by scientists in two aspects. First, it is understood as a quality of temperament, i.e., a totality of features that describe the dynamics of the emergence, continuation and termination of various emotional processes and states (Nebylitsyn, 1971; Pereverzeva, 1981; Fress, 1975). Second, it is defined in a slightly broader way – as an integral structural formation of personality, including in its properties in addition to dynamic ones, qualitative and semantic characteristics (Gorbatkov, 2001; Olshannikova; Sannikova, 2003 and others).

Close to emotionality are the concepts of "emotional agitation", "sensitivity" and "emotional stability". Emotional agitation is understood as a person's affective perception, and sensitivity to emotionally stimulating influences (Nebylitsyn, 1971). In turn, emotional sensitivity (susceptibility) is seen as the lightness, speed and flexibility of emotional response (Zavalkevich, 2004).

Considering emotional stability as an integral property of the psyche, scientists understand it as the ability to overcome the state of excessive emotional disturbance when performing a difficult activity (Dyachenko, Ponomarenko, 1990; Chebykin, 1995; Kotova, 2001). It is studied at the level of insensitivity to frequent changes of emotions (Aminov, 1988; Chernikova, 1962; etc.), resistance to emotional conditions (Smirnov, Trokhachev, 1974; Chebykin, Abolin, 1984; etc.) and the ability to maintain adequate functioning under various stressors (Pisarenko, V.M., 1986; etc.).

We believe that the vast majority of these properties, although they are the most essential characteristics of the person's emotional sphere, at the same time, they reflect its dynamic features, which narrows their importance in assessing the emotional maturity of the individual.

Summarizing these and other research works, as well as taking into account the specifics and meaning of the concept "emotional maturity", we focused on the search for those properties that would allow us to evaluate emotional maturity at the level of purely natural, dynamic and inherited traits and socially acquired in the process of people's life activity.

Following the ideas of Chebykin, Pavlova (2009) and taking into account the conducted research, we have determined that the features of emotional expressiveness, emotional self-regulation and empathy can be referred to such properties. These qualities, in our opinion, are the integrative characteristics that can characterize the formation of emotional maturity of a man and are its structural components (see Figure 3.4.1.).

To prove the above, we should note that emotional expressiveness is an emotional reaction of hereditary nature (Ananiev, 1996; Vitt, 1991; Reikovsky, 1979); at the same time, it can change depending on the social conditions of life activity (Yakobson, 1977; Field et al., 1982). It reflects both in external expressive facial expressions, pantomime, expressive actions and intonationally true emotional state that arises in a person in specific conditions.

It has been proved (Zakharov, 1988; Maurer, 1990; Kurek, 1996) that deviations in the development of expressiveness, i.e. inadequate expressive response is an important feature in the assessment of emotional maturity. At the same time, the inclinations that a person has can contribute to the essential development of emotional expression, the highest achievement of which is the actor's activity (Kochnev, 1986; Yakobson, 1977; etc.).

Mental self-regulation is considered to be an essential component of all conscious mental phenomena inherent to man (Apetik, 2001; Boryshevsky et al., 1995; Vershinin, 1986; Kirichenko, 2001; Morosanova, 2002). In the opinion of Abulkhanova-Slavskaya, 2003; Buchek, 1994; Krauklis, 1963, it is a condition for adequate mental representation by the person of their own subjective world and its relationship with objective reality. In the broadest sense, this process is understood as a function of the brain that involves controlling an individual's actions, states and inclinations and is aimed at achieving tactical and strategic behavioral goals (Krauklis, 1963; Konopkin, 1980; Yurkevich, 1972). Some authors understand emotional self-regulation as the control of emotions according to the situation and suitability, the ability to cope with one's emotions in socially accepted ways (Reikovsky, 1979; Chebykin, 1986; Thompson, 1994; etc.).

Some studies (Konopkin, 1980; Krauklis, 1963) show that since birth a human being is endowed with physiological and psychological mechanisms of adaptation to the physical conditions of life and activity. Psychological mechanisms improve with age, and new ones associated with the formation of conscious, arbitrary self-regulation of behavior (Bekh, 1986; Kirichenko, 2001) emerge. But innate features remain associated with the individual style of self-regulation, i.e. typical of a person's individual ways of regulation, which are steadily manifested in various activity situations and types of mental activity (Konopkin, 1980; Morosanova, 2002).

Empathy is defined by the authors as the ability to understand the world of other people's experiences (Shchetinina, 1984), to respond emotionally to their experiences (Gavrilova, 1974; Kotirlo, Ladyvir, 1985), as well as using these abilities in communication (Breslav, 1986; Chebykin, 1989; etc.). The development

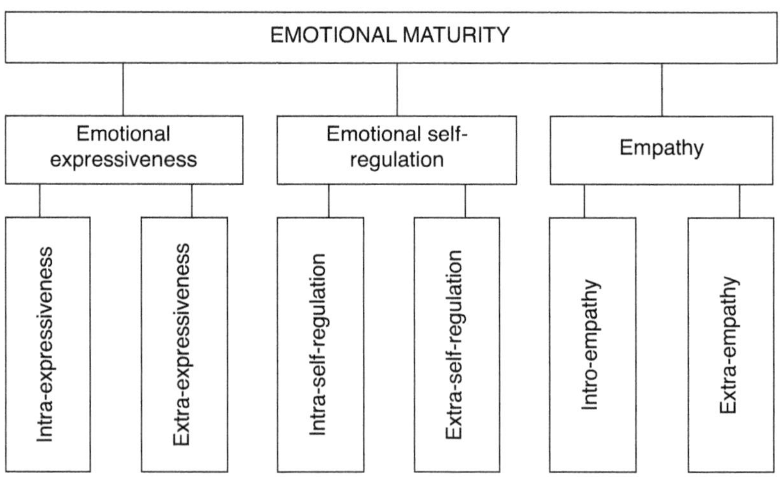

FIGURE 3.4.1 The main structural components of emotional maturity.

of the ability to empathize occurs through the action of such mechanisms as emotional contamination, imitation and identification (Vasilishina, 2000; Krotenko, 2001; Zhuravlova, Chebykin, 2021), which with age are increasingly intertwined with cognitive formations (Gavrilova, 1984; Strelkova, 1987). While a number of scientists (Krotenko, 2001; etc.) trace the relationship between the ability to empathize and some innate properties (gender, temperament, emotional excitability, sensitivity), other authors (Gavrilova, 1974; Kulchytska, 1996; and others) point out the dependence of this experience on the previous emotional experience of the subject and a number of social factors that determine this emotional experience. In particular, according to (Alpatova, 2002; Vasilishina, 1999; Kairis, 2001; Solodukhova, 1996; Chebykin, 1992), high-level empathy is formed in pedagogical activity.

In literature, one can find statements that can be used to explain how each of these components affects the manifestation of others. Thus, in the process of recognizing the expression of a communication partner, apart from everything else, one uses one's own experience as a set of parameters (Kurek, 1996;). In turn, self-regulation is carried out by constantly comparing the perceived information with the current emotional state and internal plan of activities. Only with a constant supply of material for this juxtaposition is it possible to achieve the adequacy of self-regulation (Krauklis, 1963). The greatest dependence of emotional expressiveness on self-regulation is observed in the case of the arbitrary expression of emotions, and in the case of the restraint of undesirable emotional manifestations. It should also be noted that essential in the development of empathic abilities is the expressive experience that a person acquires in communication with others (Chebykin, 1989; Shchetinina, 1984). In turn, the development of these abilities leads to the creation of a specific "language" of emotions, which is used in communication (Luk, 1982; etc.).

However, the results of some experimental studies indicate that these components may be independent of each other. Thus, Cunningham (1977) in his research established a negative relationship between the ability to perceive and express certain emotional states. In some pathopsychological studies (Bazhin, Korneva, 1981; Ganina, Korneva, 1984; Chomskaya, Batova, 1992), it has been found that in cases of "emotional coldness" and "dissociation of intelligence and affect", the accurate perception of another person's emotional state is not accompanied by an expressive reaction. And in the case of "emotional blindness", adequate perception of emotional stimuli is impaired, but the ability to experience and express emotions remains.

These data allow us to admit the relative independence of the components of emotional maturity and the indirectness of their manifestation in the mental state and actual emotional experiences of the individual.

Referring to the data (Kunitsyna et al. 2001; Lebedinsky, Bardyshevskaya, 2002; Libin, 2000; Rusalov, 1989; Chirikova, 1976; Yakovleva, 1997; Goleman, 1996; Mayer, Salovey, 1993; Russell, 1991; etc.) about the fact that emotions that arise in a person to social objects are manifested differently than to themselves, we are tempted to look at the formation of emotional maturity separately on the personal and interpersonal levels.

We consider the personal level of manifestation of emotional maturity as a result of the internal activity of the personality (Konyukhov, 1996: 42), aimed at mastering oneself and the transformation of the inner world. The interpersonal level is seen as the result of external activity aimed at the transformation of the external world and manifested in communication (Mukhina, 2000). We will further call these levels of manifestation of the components of emotional maturity as *introspectivity* (i.e., focused on the internal state of consciousness) and *extraspectivity* (i.e., focused on the external social environment). But unlike the usage of the Latin prefixes "intro- (inside)" and "extra- (outside)", which some authors (Gray, 1968; Gurevich, 1970; Zhorov, Ermolaeva-Tomina, 1971; Rusalov, 1987; etc.) use to denote opposite poles of one property, in our case these prefixes characterize different levels of manifestation of each component of emotional maturity, which are mutually complementary to each other.

Using the above-mentioned terminology, *introexpressiveness* is regarded as an involuntary manifestation of emotions in facial expressions, gestures and intonation, which, in addition to other things, fulfill the function of relaxation, relief and regulation of the excitement process caused by emotional experience. Therefore, despite the fact that the expression of emotions is primarily related to the communicative function, we believe it is possible to interpret the involuntary expression of emotional states as an action aimed at organizing internal activity.

That is, the features of personal level of emotional expressiveness are variability and eloquence of facial expressions, movements, gestures, intonation, lack of rigidity, and vice versa, the ability to adequately express emotions without suppression.

In turn, purposeful expression of certain emotions, the use of special techniques to more accurately express the real or desired emotional state, is used only in communication. Therefore, the ability to involve expressive means in communication, intentionally and purposefully express the emotional state, detach expression from experiences, to mask, to replace expression of one feeling with another one, we consider these as being signs of extraexpressiveness.

The personal level of emotional self-regulation is manifested in the ability to regulate one's own reactions, states and processes according to the situation and expediency. It is achieved by means of improvement of techniques for restraining unwanted reactions and stimulating of desired activity.

Therefore, the signs of *intro-self-regulation* can be considered as the ability to restrain too strong, undesirable emotional manifestations, arbitrarily and indirectly control the expression, experience and generation of emotions, mastering the techniques of stabilization and tonization of the emotional state according to the situation and expediency.

We define *extra-self-regulation* as the ability to influence other people's behavior, possession of the means of direct and indirect influence on the interlocutor, namely the ability to create specific emotional situations that help increase the efficiency of cooperative activities, possession of various means to help focus attention, arouse interest in recipients for certain objects and events, restrain their unwanted emotional reactions if they interfere with activity, etc.

Introempathy is viewed as the ability to understand the emotional state of the people involved, to sympathize and empathize with them, and to understand the causes of their behavior. Signs of this level are high sensitivity to other people's experiences, accurate identification of their emotions, personality traits and attitudes by verbal and nonverbal characteristics ofbehavior, understanding the mood of communication partners, and predicting their emotional reactions that may occur in a given case. *Extraempathy* is characterized by the ability to adequately use empathic abilities as a means of regulating relations in communication.

Summarizing the results of the study, the structure of emotional maturity as an integrative quality of personality that characterizes the degree of emotional sphere development at the level of adequacy of emotional response in certain sociocultural conditions can be represented at the level of emotional expressiveness, emotional self-regulation and empathy. Each of these components has specific features at the personal and interpersonal level of manifestation.

The research shows that the problem of emotional maturity is viewed ambiguously in modern psychology. In general, we can distinguish three consistent approaches to understanding the concept of emotional maturity:

- as conformity of emotional manifestations of an adult, i.e. biologically mature person to the norms of a given society;
- as the correspondence of emotional manifestations of an adult not only to society's expectations but also to the needs, values and interests of the subject;
- as conformity of emotional behavior to the notion of the norm for a certain age.

From the point of view of the goal and objectives of our study, emotional maturity can be interpreted as an integrative quality of personality that characterizes the degree of development of the emotional sphere at the level of adequacy of emotional response in certain sociocultural conditions. Important signs of emotional maturity include:

- the ability to respond emotionally to the experiences of others;
- the ability to use the emotional expression as a means of communication, to express emotions in a targeted way, and arbitrarily control their manifestation;
- the ability to adequately perceive, evaluate and understand one's own emotions and the emotions of others, awareness, a reflection of emotional states, self-control of emotions, etc.

Factors that determine the formation of emotional maturity of the individual in adolescence and young adulthood can be divided into internal and external. The internal factors of emotional maturity of a person in adolescence and young adulthood include individual characteristics, individually typological characteristics, the formation of adequate "self-concept" in adolescents, and personal and professional self-determination of young adults. External factors include the level of social and environmental stability, the speed of changes in the system of social roles, the quality of family interaction, the circle of communication and the frequency of social contacts.

The main components of emotional maturity may include features of emotional expressiveness, emotional self-regulation and empathy, which have specific features at the personal and interpersonal levels of manifestation.

3.5 Investigation of emotional maturity in adolescence and young adulthood

As was shown in the previous section, emotional maturity is primarily a phenomenon of the emotional order, characterized by emotional expressiveness, emotional self-regulation and empathy. By identifying the features of the manifestation of these qualities, as well as their interrelation with other personality traits, we can reveal both individual and age-specific regularities of emotional maturity in adolescence and early adulthood.

Proceeding from the above, we have set the following research objectives:

1. To select and adapt methods that meet the goals of our study and allow us to diagnose the examined properties.
2. To conduct the empirical study of the manifestation of these properties in adolescents and young adults.
3. To identify differences in the formation of emotional maturity with consideration of subjects' age and gender.
4. To investigate the most essential interrelations between the main properties of emotional maturity and other personality traits.
5. To establish regularities in the formation of emotional maturity, with consideration of age and gender of the developing personality.
6. Characterize the most essential types of emotional maturity.
7. The organization and implementation of an empirical study of the formation of emotional maturity in adolescence and early adulthood included three stages: preparation, examination, and processing and interpretation of the obtained data.

At the first (preparatory) stage, the planning of the content side of the research, determination of the representative sampling, search, adaptation and approbation of the appropriate methodological apparatus were carried out.

The purpose and objectives of our study determined the composition of the sample, which was to be representative of age and gender. The sample consisted of 400 test takers, including 225 adolescents and 175 young men.

The selection of methods for empirical research was made with the regard, first, to its compactness and accessibility, second, the diagnostic ability to obtain both quantitative and qualitative indicators, and third, objectivity, i.e. independence of results from the researcher's influence. Taking into account these principles, we created a psychodiagnostic complex, which includes four methods:

- Diagnostics of emotional maturity of the individual by O.Y. Chebykin,
- Personality Inventory by G. Eisenk,
- T.V. Dembo's "Placing oneself on a scale",
- form "B" Freiburg Personality Inventory (FPI), the use of which allowed to diagnose the features of personality's emotional maturity and its components:
- emotional expressiveness ("Ex" index),
- emotional self-regulation ("S" index) and
- empathy ("Em" index), and also to examine them in the system of personality traits of adolescents and young adults, such as
- extravertedness ("E" index),
- neurotism ("N" index),
- personal self-esteem ("SE" index),
- neuroticism (F1 index),
- spontaneous aggression (F2 index),
- depressiveness (F3 index),
- irritability (F4 index),
- sociability (F5 index),
- equilibrium (F6 index),
- reactive aggression (F7 index),
- shyness (F8 index),
- openness (F9 index),
- extraversion-introversion (F10 index),
- emotional lability (F11 index),
- masculinity-feminism (F12 index).

The second stage of the study is the implementation of the planned actions and carrying out empirical procedures. The diagnostic part of the study was conducted in schools of Odessa and Odessa region, as well as at the K.D. Ushynsky South Ukrainian State Pedagogical University.

In the third stage we carried out mathematical and theoretical analysis and systematization of the data obtained in empirical research, and the psychological explanation of the revealed facts and regularities is given. During the processing of the obtained data we used the following statistical methods: calculation of the average sampling value (x), modes (Mo) and median (Me) of the distribution, standard deviation (σ), which was specified when calculating the coefficient of variability (CV) (Kulikov, 1995); using Student's t-criterion (t) to determine the consistency of differences between the compared samples, as well as Pearson's coefficient of momentum extraction (r) for correlation analysis (Andrienko, 1999); determination of the correlation divergence coefficient (CDC) when comparing correlation matrices in groups of members of different genders (Schmidt, 1964); and conducting factor analysis using the method of principal components with Varimax-rotation (Okun, 1974). The correlation and factor analysis was performed using SPSS 9.0 for Windows, while other indicators were calculated using Microsoft Excel.

The preceding analysis has shown that at this time in both domestic and foreign literature available we could not find special methods that would allow us to investigate emotional maturity. Most of the authors (Luk, 1982; Maurer, 1990; Murray, 1996; Lambert, 1998; etc.), as a rule, characterize its peculiarities at the theoretical level by hypothetically defined indicators. At the same time, the methodological basis on which these techniques are based does not correspond to the analysis of indicators of emotional maturity in the context of the chosen theoretical and methodological model presented above.

Therefore, the method "Diagnostics of emotional maturity of the individual" by Chebykin, Pavlova, 2009 is undoubtedly the most adequate for studying emotional maturity. The Manual contains 42 questions divided into three main scales (Appendix 4). Each of them, in turn, is divided into two subscales. It allows us to evaluate emotional maturity on the basis of the following data:

- General indicator ("Ex") of developmental capacity to adequately reflect one's own expressive manifestations of emotions, to perceive them in other people and influence them (which is composed of the index ("IEx") of the development of the ability to adequately express own expression of emotions and influence them and the index ("EEx") of the development of the ability to adequately perceive expression of emotions in other people and influence on them).
- General indicator ("S") of the development of ability for self-regulation of emotions, to perceive it in other people and influence it (which is composed of the index ("IS") of development of adequate manifestation of own self-regulation and influence on it and the index ("ES") of development of adequacy of perceiving self-regulation in other people and influence on them).
- General indicator of development ("Em") of the capacity to adequately reflect one's own empathic behavior, perceive other people and influence them (which is composed of the index ("IEm") of the development of adequacy to display own empathy and influence on it, and the index ("EEm") of development to adequately perceive empathy of other people and influence on them).
- Integrated indicator ("EZ"), which characterizes the general development of emotional maturity on the basis of data of expressiveness of self-regulation and empathy.

Each item of the technique has equal diagnostic value in terms of determining the indicator of emotional maturity of a person, which is why the response is measured on a dichotomous scale, according to the key of the questionnaire. The integral parameter of emotional maturity is defined as the sum of the points of the three main scales. Thus, the maximum score of each subscale is 6 points, the scale is 12 points and the integral parameter ("EZ") is 36 points.

We adapted the methodology in order to create a bilingual questionnaire that can accurately assess the emotional maturity of the tested. Based on the peculiarities of the sample of subjects, the adaptation tasks included: (1) translating the questionnaire into Ukrainian, checking the comprehensibility, reliability and validity of this version of the questionnaire; and (2) specifying the boundaries of high, medium and low levels in relation to the age of the sample takers.

The first stage of the work on the adaptation of the questionnaire was to translate the contents of its items into Ukrainian. In order to preserve the semantics of the original version of the methodology, we sought to slightly change the vocabulary and phrases. To test the simplicity and clarity of each question, a questionnaire was presented to students majoring in psychology. As a result, some issues were replaced by other versions, but the number of items remained unchanged. In addition, the name of scales and subscales of the questionnaire was slightly adjusted to comply with the model of emotional maturity that we had defined.

The next stage of work on the methodology was to check the reliability and validity of the Ukrainian version of the questionnaire. At this stage, 186 subjects – students of grades 5–11 and students who have a good command of Russian and Ukrainian languages – were tested.

The empirical validity of the new version of the instrument was checked by the method of parallel forms (Avanesov, 1982). The essence of it lies in the fact that both variants of the questionnaire were tested. However, we expected that the test results of the majority of the test takers would not change. It should be noted that the use of this method in this case slightly disturbs the external validity of testing – the technique is not included in the group of achievement tests, does not provide correct and incorrect answers, the time between two tests was 14 days, and the order of presentation of the two forms of questionnaire in different age groups alternated. All this, in our opinion, eliminates the impact of the previous testing on the next one. As a result of the test, we formed two matrices of individual data and calculated the correlation coefficient of the Pearson moment acquisition (see Table 3.5.1).

As seen from the table, the data obtained during testing using the Ukrainian version of the questionnaire, in all respects are quite strongly correlated with the estimates obtained using the original questionnaire ($p < 0.001$). Such data demonstrate a high empirical validity of the new version of the instrument.

The internal consistency, or homogeneity, of the test, was checked by calculating Cronbach's α-coefficient (Avanesov, 1982) on the same sample of subjects (186 people). The information on internal consistency turned out to be ambiguous (see Table 3.5.2).

TABLE 3.5.1 Information on the empirical validity of the Ukrainian version of the methodology for diagnosing the emotional maturity of a person (186 tested)

№.	*Symbol*	*Index*	*Value of correlation coefficient (r)*
1.	Ex	Emotional expressiveness	0.918
2.	IEx	Introexpressiveness	0.846
3.	EEx	Extraexpressiveness	0.914
4.	S	Emotional self-regulation	0.782
5.	IS	Intro-self-regulation	0.806
6.	ES	Extra-self-regulation	0.816
7.	Em	Empathy	0.894
8.	IEm	Introempathy	0.882
9.	EEm	Extraempathy	0.877
10.	EZ	Integrative parameter of emotional maturity	0.877

TABLE 3.5.2 Psychometric indicators of internal consistency of "Diagnostics of emotional maturity of a person" methodology (186 subjects)

№.	*Index*	*Number of points*	*Index dispersion (D)*	*Cronbach α-coefficient values*
1.	EZ	36	18.5	0.758
2.	Ex	12	4.14	0.613
3.	IEx	6	1.43	0.450
4.	EEx	6	1.85	0.564
5.	S	12	4.04	0.581
6.	IS	6	1.46	0.431
7.	ES	6	1.57	0.436
8.	Em	12	4.21	0.775
9.	IEm	6	1.48	0.415
10.	EEm	6	1.96	0.712

Thus, the calculated values of the coefficient α for the indicators "EZ", "Em" and "EEm" are at a fairly high level (0.712–0.775). In turn, such subscales as "IEx", "IS", "ES" and "IEm" showed moderate values of this coefficient (0.415–0.450). The results obtained suggest a moderate internal consistency of these subscales. Other indicators of the methodology can be considered internally reliable and consistent.

Verification of the retest reliability of the new version of the questionnaire was carried out on a sample of 69 subjects – students of 5–10 grades. The interval between tests was 6 months. A correlation analysis performed using Pearson's coefficient was conducted for the test results (see Table 3.5.3).

TABLE 3.5.3 Information about the retest reliability of the Ukrainian version of the method for diagnosing the emotional maturity of a person (69 subjects)

№.	*Symbol*	*Index*	*Value of correlation coefficient (r)*
1.	Ex	Emotional expressiveness	0.92
2.	IEx	Introexpressiveness	0.83
3.	EEx	Extraexpressiveness	0.88
4.	S	Emotional self-regulation	0.86
5.	IS	Intro-self-regulation	0.85
6.	ES	Extra-self-regulation	0.79
7.	Em	Empathy	0.87
8.	IEm	Introempathy	0.86
9.	EEm	Extraempathy	0.75
10.	EZ	Integrative parameter of emotional maturity	0.9

The obtained data in the range of 0.75–0.92 ($p < 0.001$) indicate a sufficient correspondence between the results of the two tests. It should be noted that in the re-testing the results were the least consistent with the indicators "ES" ($r = 0.79$) and "EEm" ($r = 0.75$), which indicates moderate stability of this index.

Discriminativity of the items of the new version of the questionnaire was calculated according to the algorithm of four-cell correlation (Shmelev, Pokhilko, 1985) on a sample of 118 tested.

For this purpose, 27% of respondents (32 people each) with the highest and lowest values of the integrative parameter "EZ" were selected from the main sample. According to the results of the calculation of the four-cell correlation coefficients for each questionnaire item, we have found that the level of significance of different items is unequal (see Table 3.5.4).

Thus, for items "6+", "7+", "28+", "30+" and "39+", which diagnose the manifestations of the index "ES", items "4+", "12+", "21+", "23+", "25-" and "40+" (index "S") and items"8+", "11+", "35+" and "38+" (index Em) the value of the coefficient is within the range of 0.281–0.326 at $p < 0.05$. For other items of the questionnaire indexes, the values of their discriminativity were found to be rather regular, their values being in the range of 0.338–0.574 at $p < 0.01$.

These data allow us to state that, in general, the questionnaire items have a sufficiently high discriminatory capacity to differentiate the levels of expression of emotional maturity of a person.

Therefore, according to the results of the statistical testing, the Ukrainian version of the questionnaire on emotional maturity diagnostics by O. Chebykin meets the requirements for validity and reliability.

The last stage of work on the methodology was to determine the boundaries of the levels of expression of the studied indexes in different age groups. At this stage, 400 subjects aged 11–23 years were examined. The obtained data

TABLE 3.5.4 Information about the discriminative reliability of the Ukrainian version of the methodology for diagnosing the emotional maturity of a person (64 subjects)

Ex				*S*				*Em*			
IEx		*EEx*		*IS*		*ES*		*IEm*		*EEm*	
1+	0.358	2+	0.382	3+	0.574	4+	0.313	8+	0.284	13+	0.452
6+	0.281	18+	0.531	12+	0.316	5+	0.472	10+	0.536	14+	0.433
7+	0.298	20+	0.416	17-	0.350	29+	0.460	11+	0.294	26+	0.513
30+	0.326	28+	0.281	21+	0.291	36+	0.406	16+	0.378	27+	0.472
39+	0.299	32+	0.445	23+	0.313	37-	0.389	22+	0.376	35+	0.313
41+	0.538	42+	0.526	25-	0.316	40+	0.295	34+	0.378	38+	0.293

TABLE 3.5.5 Conditional limits of levels of emotional maturity indicators

Age	*index*	*Limits of levels of expression of indicators of emotional maturity in points*									
		Ex	*IEx*	*EEx*	*S*	*IS*	*ES*	*Em*	*IEm*	*EEm*	*EZ*
11–13	H	9–12	6	5–6	9–12	5–6	6	10–12	6	6	25–32
y.o.	M	5–8	3–5	2–4	5–8	2–4	3–5	5–9	2–5	2–5	16–24
	L	0–4	0–2	0–1	0–4	0–1	0–2	0–4	0–1	0–1	0–15
14–15	H	9–12	5–6	5–6	10–12	5–6	6	10–12	6	6	26–32
y.o.	M	4–8	2–4	2–4	5–9	2–4	3–5	4–9	2–5	2–5	15–25
	L	0–3	0–1	0–1	0–4	0–1	0–2	0–3	0–1	0–1	0–14
16–17	H	9–12	6	5–6	10–12	5–6	6	11–12	6	6	26–32
y.o.	M	5–8	3–5	2–4	5–9	2–4	3–5	6–10	3–5	3–5	17–25
	L	0–4	0–2	0–1	0–4	0–1	0–2	0–5	0–2	0–2	0–16
18–23	H	11–12	6	6	11–12	6	6	11–12	6	6	29–32
y.o.	M	6–10	3–5	3–5	6–10	2–5	3–5	7–10	3–5	3–5	20–28
	L	0–5	0–2	0–2	0–5	0–1	0–2	0–6	0–2	0–2	0–19

allowed us to determine the average sample values and standard deviations for 4 age groups and to outline the boundaries of the average level. Further on the statistical limits of the average level were rounded to whole values, which allows us to determine the conditional limits of high, medium and low levels of indicator diversity, convenient for the interpretation of individual estimates (see Table 3.5.5).

3.5.1 Analysis of individual indicators that reflect the characteristics of emotional maturity in the sample

As a result of the empirical research we received primary data on the expressiveness of emotional maturity in 8 age groups. Referring to the individual data on the indicators of emotional maturity of **children aged eleven**, we found that the indicator "Ex" in the sample has a fairly low variability (σ = 1.14; CV = 17.5). The data varies within the range of 4–9 points, but most of them are grouped within the average level of expressiveness (Appendix 5 see Table 3.5.6).

As seen from the table, only 3.6% of subjects have low levels, and 3.6% have high levels. In addition, the most common estimates are 6–7 points (64% of respondents).

The average sample value of this indicator is also in the marked range (x = 6.5) and coincides with the median (Me = 6.5). The most widespread estimation on "Ex" is 6 points. This nature of the distribution indicates that most of the tested 11-year-olds are emotionally impaired.

The signs of external manifestation of emotions in facial expressions, movements and intonation ("IEx") are also within the conditional average level (x = 3.79) and have low variability (σ = 0.79; CV = 20.8). The values of this subscale fluctuate in the range of 3–5 points, i.e. all the tested have a medium level of its intensity. Individual values that characterize the ability to transfer one's emotional mood to others ("EEx" index) have a significant variance (σ = 0.94; CV = 34.5), and they are within the low-medium levels (0–4 points). At the same time, only 7.1% of test takers showed an insufficient level of "EEx" manifestation, and the rest of the subjects (92.9%) have an acceptable level. The average value (x = 2.71) is also within the average level. Moreover, it was found that within the limits of the general indicator that characterizes emotional expressiveness, the variability of which is at a sufficient level, two individual characteristics are formed differently. In the majority of subjects (64.3%) the values for "IEx" exceed those for "EEx". In some 11-year-old children (25%) the data on these subscales are identical, only in 10.7% of the subjects their "EEx" is higher than "IEx". Thus, 11-year-old children have a higher level of involuntary expression of emotions in facial expressions, movements and intonation than their ability to convey the emotional state to the other children.

Regarding individual data of the indicator "S" in the group of 11-year-old children, we note that they are distributed in the interval from 4 to 10 points, but most of them (78.6%) can be taken as average. It was also found that the most widespread assessment of 8 points (Mo = 8) coincides with the upper boundary of the average level, and the average sample value (x = 7.07) is also within this interval. The given data testify about the moderate level of formation of self-regulation at this age.

The data on the subscale, which determines the ability to control one's own emotions ("IS" index), indicate that among 11-year-old children there are those who have a fairly high level of its expression (7.1% of respondents have scores of 5 points), and those who do not know how to regulate their emotions (10.3% of respondents have scores equal to 1 point). But most of the evaluations are average (82.2%). Such data, as well as indicators of the central trend (Mo = 3; Me = 3; x = 2.93), testify to a sufficient level of formation of the ability to regulate own emotions.

"ES" features are also characterized by a wide range of estimates (from 2 to 6 points). However, in contrast to "IS", a few more values (10.7%) correspond to a high level of expressiveness (see Table 3.5.1). Besides, other indicators of the central tendency also have higher values (Mo = 5; Me = 4). However, the majority of respondents also showed medium values of "ES". That is, in general, 11-year-olds have a sufficient ability to influence the behavior of other people.

The comparison of individual values for "IS" and "ES" revealed that in 71.4% of test takers the "ES" exceeds the "IS" one. Only 28.6% of subjects have the same manifestation of these characteristics or exceed the level of "IS". This indicates that in children of 11 years old the ability to regulate their own emotions is lower than the ability to influence the behavior of others.

The individual data obtained on the indicator "Em" are distributed in the range from 3 to 11 points and characterized by medium variability ($\sigma = 1.60$; CV = 22.1). Most of the values (85.7%) are within 5–9 points. A high level is attributed to 10.7% of the evaluations, and only 3.6% to a low level. According to these data, the expressiveness of empathy in the group is sufficient.

Regarding the analysis of individual components of the "Em" index at this age, the ability to adequately perceive the emotional state of others ("IEm") is represented by data in the range from 2 to 6 points. The most widespread is the score of 4 points (Mo = 4). The average value of "IEm" ($x = 3.86$) in the sample corresponds to the average level of expression of this feature, which includes 92.9% of responses. The high level of "IEm" is 7.1% of the evaluations, and there are no low evaluations. On the basis of such information, we can make an assumption that 11-year-old children are quite good at understanding the emotional state of other people and the motives behind their behavior.

The data that characterize the ability to influence the behavior of others by understanding the emotional and motivational factors of their behavior ("EEm"), have a slightly lower level of formation. The values are distributed in the range from 1 to 5 points. The most widespread, as in the case of "IEm", is the assessment of 4 points, but 7.1% of respondents demonstrated low indicators, and the high level is absent here.

Comparison of data on the manifestations of "IEm" and "EEm" indexes revealed that in children of this age the scores for "IEm" are often higher than for "EEm" (57%), 25% of subjects have the same variability of these indicators, and only 17% have higher scores than "EEm". That is, 11-year-old children have a better ability to understand the emotional state of others and understand the emotional and motivational factors of their behavior than the ability to use these skills in communication.

Almost all individual values of the integrative parameter "EZ", which characterizes the overall adequacy of emotional response, are within the average level of 16–24 points (only 14.3% of respondents have an assessment above the average). The maximum score in the sample is 29 points, the minimum is 16. It was also found that the data for "EZ" is close to the normal distribution, the center of the sample is marked at a point which is approximately equal to 21 points ($x = 20.8$; $Mo = 21$; $Me = 21$).

It should be noted that not all components of emotional maturity in 11 years are equally formed. The share of the "Ex" indicator in the overall assessment of emotional maturity is 31%, the "S" indicator is 34%, and the "Em" indicator is 35%. This data allows us to assume that in 11-year-old children the development of empathy is ahead of the formation of emotional expressiveness and emotional self-regulation.

Analysis of individual indicators obtained in children aged **twelve years** showed that this sampling is characterized by greater variability of data than the previous one. Therefore, the measures of the central tendency are less likely to reflect the real distribution. Thus, both low and high results were obtained for the "Ex" indicator (Appendix 5 see Table 3.5.7).

Such a distribution of individual data causes high fluctuation in the manifestation of the indicator "Ex" at this age ($\sigma = 2.02$; $CV = 29.2$). However, based on primary statistics data ($x = 6.91$; $Mo = 6$; $Me = 7$), we can make an assumption about the average variability of emotional expressiveness in 12-year-old children.

It was also found that the manifestations of involuntary expression of emotions in mimics, gestures and intonation ("IEx") in the group are within the conditional average level ($x = 3.70$). The values of this subscale vary between 2–6 points, most of the tested (78.3%) have a medium level of severity, and the rest – either low (13%) or high (8.7%). The individual data that characterize the ability to convey one's emotional mood to the recipients (signs of "EEx") have a range of values from the minimum of 0 points to the maximum possible 6 points. Most often there is a score of 3 points (43% of subjects), which corresponds to the average level of their severity. The average value of "EEx" ($x = 3.30$) in the sample is also within the average norm, which was conditionally selected by us. As a result of comparison of individual values for "IEx" and "EEx" it was established that at the age of twelve within the limits of general index "Ex", the expressiveness of which is at a sufficient level, the formation of its two separate characteristics is balanced. This can be explained, first of all, due to the growing ability to arbitrarily express emotional state and to use expression in communication.

The indicator "S" is represented by data ranging from 2 to 10 points. 65.2% of answers belong to the medium level (see Appendix 5, Table 3.5.7). The average sample ($x = 6.52$) is slightly lower than the mode and median in the group ($Mo = 7$; $Me = 7$), which is conditioned by the presence of a certain number of children with a low level of index severity. The latter (a low level of index severity) can be explained by the fact that the age of 12, according to the data of specialists [Olshannikova, 1977] and others, is characterized by the onset of adolescent age crisis, which increases impulsive behavior and reduces the ability to control own feelings.

An analysis of data on the subscale "IS" shows that most 12-year-old children have a good ability to satisfactorily control their own emotions (78.3%). But a fairly large proportion of subjects showed low values of this feature (17.4%). Only

4.3% of the responses were of a high level. The most common subscale score is 3 points (Mo = 3). Unlike "IS", the scores that characterize the level of ability to influence the behavior of other people ("ES") are slightly higher (x=3.78; Mo=4; Mo=4). A comparison of individual values for "IS" and "ES" revealed that 65% of subjects had "ES" scores exceeding "IS". In 22% of subjects, there is a similar expressiveness of these indicators. The "IS" level is exceeded by 13%. So, as in the group of 11-year-old children, the ability to control their own emotions is formed significantly less than the ability to regulate the behavior of other people in 12-year-olds.

The most unevenly distributed assessments of the indicator "Em" (σ = 2.57; CV = 38.6). They vary from 1 to 11 points, and the most frequently encountered scores were 4 and 9 points (22% of observations). Data falling within the interval between them (5–8 points) belong to only 39% of respondents. Therefore, the average score (x = 6.65) only approximately characterizes the level of "Em". As the general indicator "Em", two of its components have high indicators of variability; for "EEm" (σ = 1.5; CV = 47.2) they are much higher than for "IEm" (σ = 1.31; CV = 37.7).

Referring to the individual values of "IEm", which characterize the ability to adequately perceive the emotional state of others, we should note that there is a small number of responses to the low and high levels (see Appendix 5, Table 3.5.7). Most of them belong to the medium level of "IEm" expression (87%). The average value of the indicator (x = 3.48) also corresponds to the average level. The expressiveness of "EEm" is slightly lower (x = 3.17). The individual values that characterize this feature are distributed in the range from 0 to 6 points, low scores are observed in 13% of the tested, and high in 4.4%. By comparing the data on the expressiveness of indicators "IEm" and "EEm", it was possible to determine that children of this age do not have a significant discrepancy between the ability to understand the emotional state of the respondents and the ability to influence their behavior.

The characteristics of the intensity of the integrative parameter "EZ" in the group of 12-year-olds reflect the peculiarities of data distribution that are typical for its components, namely: individual data have a great variability (from 8 points, corresponding to low "EZ" level and up to 29 points – for a high "EZ"). But the highest frequency of tests (65.2%) is found in the interval from 16 to 24 points. This interval corresponds to the average level of expression of the "EZ", which was conditionally determined by us. The average value (x = 20.1) also corresponds to the indicated interval. The low and high levels are 17.4% each.

The above data allow us to state that at the age of 12, which is characterized by the beginning of the adolescent crisis, there is either an increase in emotional maturity due to the formation of abilities to regulate own emotions and to adequately express their state in communication, or a decrease in the adequacy of emotional reactions.

Besides, it should be noted that at this age the formation of emotional expressiveness is slightly ahead of the development of other emotions. Thus, the share of the "Ex" index in the integrative parameter of emotional maturity is 35%, the indicator "S" is 32% and the indicator "Em" is 33%. These data do not contradict the assumption that in children aged 12 the adequacy of emotional response is ensured primarily through the formation of emotional expression.

Examining the primary data characterizing peculiarities of emotional maturity in **13-year-old children**, we have found that for the "Ex" index they have some discordance ($\sigma = 1.92$; CV = 29.1) and range from 2 to 10 points. However, 91% of tests are described within 4–9 points. The most common assessment is 7 points (Mo = 7), which coincides with the sampling median (Me = 7). According to our conditionally determined levels, individual data of 15.6% of subjects indicate the low severity of this indicator (Appendix 5 see Table 3.5.8).

As can be seen from the table, average scores are observed in 64.4% of respondents, and high in 20%. All these data allow us to conclude that for 13 years olds in general a sufficient level of formation of emotional expressiveness is formed.

At the level of the components of this scale, it was established that the features of external manifestation of emotions in facial expressions, gestures and intonation ("IEx") are within the conditional average (x = 3.60). The values of this subscale vary from 2 to 6 points with moderate variability ($\sigma = 1.14$; CV = 31.6). The majority of tested (77.8%) have a medium level of expression of this indicator, the rest have either low (15.6%) or high scores "IEx" (6.7%). That is, the manifestations of involuntary emotions at age 13 do not change.

Individual data that characterize the ability to convey one's emotional mood to the recipients ("EEx") have a significant range of values, covering all acceptable estimates (0–6 points). The most typical results for this group are 3 and 4 points (29% of tests). The majority of respondents (86.7%) show a medium level of expression of "EEx", only 4.4% of responses belong to the low level and 8.9% to the high. The average value of this indicator (x = 3) indicates that at the age of 13, the level of arbitrary expression of emotions decreases slightly.

A comparison of individual values for the indicators "IEx" and "EEx" revealed that 54% of the subjects had "IEx" scores higher than "EEx". In 22% of subjects, there is a similar expressiveness of these indicators. The EEx level is exceeded by 24%. Thus, it was found that within the limits of the general indicator that characterizes emotional expressiveness, the level of involuntary expression of emotions in facial expressions, gestures and intonation is expressed more intensely than the ability to arbitrarily use the emotional expression in communication.

Further analysis showed that data on the indicator "S" ranged from 3 to 10 points. The variability of this indicator ($\sigma = 1.76$; CV = 28.1) is slightly less than that of other indicators in the sample. Thus, most values (80%) are in the range of 5–8 points and correspond to the average level of expressiveness. But 15.6% of tests are below the defined limits, and only 4.4% correspond to a high level. It should be noted that the average sample value of "S" (x = 6.27) is slightly lower than this figure in the sample of children 12 years of age. That is, the decrease in the level of emotional self-regulation, which was recorded in the previous age group, continues to occur at the age of 13.

An analysis of the features that make up the scale "S", allows us to note that they have different weights. Thus, the average data on the subscale "IS" (x = 2.49) are lower than in the sample of 12-year-old children, and although most indicators (73.3%) are in the range of 2–4 points, 22.2% of responses are low, and only 4.4% are high. In turn, the data on the "ES" index have a distribution with a maximum point of 6 points, a minimum of 2 points. They have much less variability (σ = 1.02; CV = 27) than in "IS" and are located mainly in the range of 2–4 points (84.4% of tests). Only 13.3% of respondents have low individual assessments. The average value (x = 3.78) and other indicators of the distribution center (Me = 4; Mo = 4) correspond to the upper limit of the average level and do not differ from similar indicators in the 12-year group.

The comparison of individual values for the "IS" and "ES" indicators revealed that in 77.8% of test takers, the "ES" scores exceed the "IS" ones. In 13.3% of samples, there is the same severity of these indicators and the excess of "IS" level exists only in 8.9% of cases. That is, as in previous groups, in the sample of 13-year-olds, the intensity of the ability to regulate own emotions is lower than the ability to control the behavior of others.

Referring to the individual data of the indicator "Em", we can see that they are distributed in the range from 2 to 10 points and are characterized by average variability (σ = 1.87; CV = 28.7). Most of the values (84.4%) are defined as 5–9 points, which corresponds to the average level. Such data, as well as primary statistics, testify to a sufficient development of empathy in 13-year-olds. Regarding the analysis of individual components of the indicator "Em" in the group, the "IEm" index is represented by data belonging to the range from 1 to 6 points and distributed with average variability (σ = 1.2; CV = 36.5). The most widespread is the assessment of 3 points (Mo = 3), and most values (91.1%) are in the range of 2–5 points. Low and high scores were achieved by 4.4% of test takers. It should be noted that the average value of this indicator (x = 3.29), compared with the group of 12-year-old children, appears to be slightly lower.

The indicator "EEm" is slightly different from "IEm". The data characterizing this feature are distributed in the range from 0 to 6 points, and the average sample equals 3.2 points. As in the case of "IEm", most data (91.1%) are grouped within 2–5 points, and the rest of the estimates (4.4%) are high or low.

By comparing the individual data for "IEm" and "EEm", it was possible to determine that 42.2% of cases showed an excess of "IEm" estimates. The same intensity in both features was observed in 26.7% of those tested. The overestimation of "EEm" scores was observed in 31.1% of cases. These data allow us to conclude that at the age of 13 the ability to influence the behavior of others is approaching the level of formation of the ability to understand the emotional state of others.

The data on the integrative parameter of emotional maturity ("EZ") of 13-year-old children are notably wide. They are characterized by a minimum score of 8 points and a maximum of 27 points. But the variability of the data in the sample is quite moderate (σ = 4.09; CV = 21.1). Most values (77.8%) are within the range of 16–24 points. The peculiarity of the data distribution for this index is its bimodality, with modes at points 18 and 22. However, the average value (x = 19.38) indicates a certain decrease in the level of emotional maturity of children of this age. The examination of the percentage representation in the integrative indicator of its individual components suggested that the formation of emotional maturity at the age of 13 is more balanced. The formation of components of emotional expressiveness and empathy at this age does not appear to be significantly higher than the formation of emotional self-regulation.

Turning to the study of individual data obtained from the examination of **14-year-olds**, it should be recalled that in the groups of 14–15 year-olds, the conditional boundaries of levels are slightly different than in the previous age groups.

The analysis of individual data of the "Ex" indicator according to the levels we defined showed that most of the responses can be evaluated as average (Appendix 5 see Table 3.5.9).

As seen from the table, low and high estimates are approximately equally represented. The average sample value (x = 6.05) compared to the previous groups decreases here. Considering the expressiveness of this indicator in the dynamics, we can assume that the level of emotional expressiveness decreases with age.

For its part, the "IEx" subscale includes both low and maximum possible scores (from 1 to 6 points). The majority of test takers (84.7%) received scores in the range of 2–4 points - a conditional average level of "IEx". Low scores are observed in only 3.8%, and high in 11.5% of respondents. The average (x = 3.31) fairly accurately reflects the value of the distribution center, which has two adjacent modes (Mo1 = 3; Mo2 = 4). The data that determines the center of distribution (x = 2.73; Me = 3; Mo = 4) by the indicator "EEx" show that it differs from the normal one. This is due to the fact that the low level is characterized by a significant percentage of estimates (20.5%). Medium intensity occurs in 71.8% of cases, and high in 7.7% of cases. Such distribution of the data significantly differs from the distribution of "IEx".

Comparison of individual data on the severity of indicators "IEx" and "EEx" allowed us to determine that in children of this age the scores for "IEx" are often higher than for "EEx" (55.1%), in 24.4% of those tested the intensity of these indicators is the same, and only in 20.5%, there is an excess of "EEx". That is, the majority of 14-year-olds have a significantly higher level of involuntary expression of emotions in facial expressions, gestures and intonation than the ability to use expressive means in communication.

Further analysis showed that the data for the indicator "S" are distributed somewhat more densely than for "Ex" (σ = 1.99; CV = 28.2). They are located in the range from 3 to 11 points, and most of the estimates (78.2%) are within 5–9 points, which corresponds to the average level. Only 9% of responses are low. The rest of the subjects (12.8%) received high estimates on the scale. Note that the average score of "S" (x = 7.06) is much higher than the average in groups of children 12 and 13 years old. This allows us to assume that the level of emotional self-regulation which decreased during previous years, began to increase at the age of 14.

It was also found that "IS" features are represented by data that belong to the range of 1–6 points. The most common assessment is 3 points (Mo = 3), and most of the values (83.3%) are in the range of 2–4 points. The rest of the data correspond to either low (3.8%) or high (12.8%). In turn, individual assessments for "ES" in 73.1% of respondents belong to the average level, and the number of samples with low assessments (16.7%) is significantly higher than for the "IS". It should be noted that the average value of "IS" (x = 3.24), as in the case of the general indicator "S", significantly exceeds similar estimates of the previous groups. However, the average sample score of "ES" (x = 3.82) exceeds the average values of this characteristic only a little bit in the groups of children 12 and 13 years old. It should be added that in 51.3% of the subjects, the "ES" scores exceed the "IS". In 25.6% of the samples, there was similar severity of these characteristics, and the "IS" level was exceeded in 23.1% of cases.

The obtained data allow us to specify that the increase in the level of emotional self-regulation at the age of 14 is due to the intensive formation in this period of abilities to control emotions. However, as in previous groups, in the sample of 14-year-olds, these abilities are worse developed than the ability to influence other people's behavior.

The average value of the indicator "Em" (x = 6.58) in a group of 14-year-olds is between two adjacent modes (Mo1 = 6; Mo2 = 7). The presence of a bimodal distribution causes a fairly large variability of individual estimates in the sample (σ = 2.24; CV = 34.1). However, the majority of respondents (79.5%) have a medium level of expression of "Em" (4–9 points), and the rest have either low (7.7%) or high scores (12.8%).

Analysis of the data on the features that make up the scale "Em" allows us to note that the average value on the subscale "IEm" (x = 3.44) is within the average level, and compared with the previous group, increases slightly. Most indicators (93.6%) are within the average boundaries, the rest are low (1.3%) or high (5.1%). Data characterizing the expressiveness of "EEm" have a distribution with a maximum point of 6 points and minimum 0 points. The highest frequency weight is 2 points (Mo = 2), which corresponds to the lower limit of the average level. Estimates of 79.5% of the subjects belong to the average level, but there were more children with low "EEm" (12.8%) than those with high "EEm" (7.7%).

A comparison of individual data for "IEm" and "EEm" revealed that 44.9% of cases have an overestimation of "IEm" scores, and 26.9% of test takers have the same intensity of these characteristics. An excess of "EEm" estimates occurs in 28.2% of cases. This data suggest that children of this age have an insignificant difference in their ability to use empathic skills in communication compared with the ability to understand the emotional state of their peers.

On the basis of the data obtained, we can assume that in the formation of the empathic component of emotional maturity at the age of 14 there are no significant changes. It is possible to notice only a tendency to increase the level of understanding of the emotional state of respondents. According to V.A. Labunskaya (Labunskaya, 1987), significant changes in the manifestation of empathy at the interpersonal level occur only in adolescence.

Regarding the expressiveness of the integrative parameter "EZ", most of the data for it are in the range of 15–25 points (73.1% of estimates). High scores were obtained in 11.5% and low scores in 15.4% of cases. The average sample value (x = 19.69) differs slightly from the similar estimate in the previous group.

The representation of individual components of emotional maturity in the integrative parameter in the group of 14-year-old children is unequal. The contribution of the "Ex" indicator to the overall assessment is 31%, the "S" indicator is 36%, and the "Em" indicator is 33%. Such data allow us to state that at the age of 14 the adequacy of emotional response is ensured primarily by the formation of emotional self-regulation, and the significance of the expressive component in this process decreases.

This can be explained by the fact that in older adolescents, the period of stabilization in the physiological maturation of the organism begins, as discussed in (Lichko, 1983; Oudshoorn, 2002). In the mental sphere, as indicated by (Abulkhanova-Slavskaya, 2003; Burns, 1986; Olshannikova, 1983), during this period there are changes associated with the formation of reflection, growth of the desire for self-development, formation of the own system of norms and values, development of self-control as a conscious regulation of one's behavior.

The analysis of individual values and primary statistics data in a sample of **15-year-olds** showed that according to the "Ex" indicator, they have moderate variability (σ = 1.7; CV = 25.6). In particular, scores vary from 2 to 10 points. However, most subjects have a medium intensity of this indicator (Appendix 5 see Table 3.5.10).

As can be seen from the table, low scores are found here only in 2% of respondents. The average value of this indicator (x = 6.67) is slightly higher than the average score found in 14-year-old children. Such data allow us to conclude that at the age of 15 the level of emotional expressiveness increases.

A detailed study of the expressiveness of the components of the "Ex" index shows that signs of the external manifestations of emotions in facial expressions, gestures and intonation ("IEx") in 15 years are almost unchanged. Thus, the average value (x = 3.24) is within the conditional average level. The majority of respondents (84.3%) also have scores of 2–4 points, and 15.7% of responses correspond to the high level. The average value of "EEx" (x = 3.43), in its turn, characterizes a significant increase in the ability to use the emotional expression in communication. Other characteristics of the distribution center (Me = 4; Mo = 4), which correspond to the upper limit of the average level, also confirm the assumption. It is worth paying attention to the fact that at the age of 15 the ability to use expressive means in communication for the first time reaches the level of involuntary expression of emotions in facial expressions, gestures and intonation.

These data allow us to conclude that at the age of 15 there is an intensive form of the expressive component of emotional maturity, primarily due to the development of abilities to freely express the desired emotions. In our opinion, this is possible due to the progressive formation of emotional self-regulation, which was recorded in the previous age group. That is, at the age of 15 teenagers are already quite masterful in controlling their own emotions and can express them according to purpose and expediency.

The data on the expressiveness of the indicator "S" in the group of 15 years are in the range from 3 to 12 points. Most of the values (80.4%) are within the average level. The average sample value equals 7.18 points. A small number of individual values (7.8%) refers to a low level, to a high level of 11.8% of estimates. As can be seen, comparing these data with the corresponding estimates in previous groups, the sufficient level of emotional self-regulation, determined in 14-year-old subjects, is also acceptable in the group of 15-year-old adolescents.

Examination of individual features of the indicator "S" allows us to note that they have different weights. Thus, the average value for "IS" is 2.88 points, and most of the individual values (80.4%) are in the range of average values (2–4 points). Only 9.8% of individual assessments can be attributed to the high level of expressiveness of this indicator, and 7.8% to the low level. As opposed to "IS", the average severity of the interpersonal level of emotional self-regulation ("ES") is significantly higher ($x = 4.29$). Here, 21.6% of estimates correspond to the high level, and 68.6% to the average. Only 9.8% of those tested belong to a low level.

A comparison of individual values of "IS" and "ES" showed that most of the test takers (74.5%) had more "EU" scores than "IS" ones. This ratio of expressiveness of the ability to control emotions and regulate the behavior of others indicates a significant excess of the latter.

The individual data obtained by the indicator "Em" are distributed in the range from 2 to 12 points and are characterized by high variability ($\sigma = 2.44$; $CV = 33.9$). Most of the values (76.5%) are within the middle level, while 15.7% of the data are high. Only 7.8% of the values correspond to the low level. The average sample value ($x = 7.22$) greatly exceeds the corresponding figure in the group of 14-year-old children. That is, at the age of 15 there is a tendency for a significant increase in empathy. Following D.B. Elkonin (Elkonin, 1971), who considered this age as the boundary between adolescence and young adult age, we can assume that a certain trend is connected with the increase of sociability, generally focused on communication, as well as development of a qualitatively new type of communication – interpersonal, in the process of which empathic adolescent personality experience is acquired.

Showed personal and interpersonal levels of expression of the empathy component are divided differently. While the estimates for "IEm" are grouped tightly, and most of the values (84.3%) are within the average level, the distribution of data for "EEm" is much wider – the average level of expression is represented by only 66.7% of the data, the rest are high (13.7%) and low (19.6%). The observed discrepancies in the distribution of individual assessments were confirmed by the evaluation of the variability of indicators, which in the case of "EEm" is much higher. These facts can be interpreted as the initial, unstable phase of formation of interpersonal level of empathy manifestation. We can assume that in the future the data on this indicator attain equilibrium and range mainly within the middle level. Moreover, based on a comparison of individual data on the intensity of "IEm" and "EEm" in 15-year-old adolescents, it can be assumed that within the overall indicator "Em" both of its constituent parts are equally expressed.

Summing up the results obtained in the group of 15-year-old adolescents, we note that the data characterizing the integrative parameter "EZ", in comparison with the previous groups, also grew significantly (x = 21.1). Examination of the correlation between main components of emotional maturity indicates that such growth is caused primarily by the formation of empathy and emotional self-regulation. Thus, the representation in the integrative parameter of emotional maturity of the indicator "Ex" is 32%, and indicators "S" and "Em" are 34% each. However, these differences are not significant enough, which does not allow us to distinguish one or another component as a leading one.

These facts allow us to characterize the age of 15 years as sensitive for the improvement of skills to arbitrarily express the desired emotions, the gradual increase in empathy, and the further formation of emotional self-regulation.

According to a research on emotional maturity in **16-year-olds**, we found that in general, the "Ex" index in the sample has the same peculiarities as in the previous group. Data range from 3 to 11 points and have moderate variability (σ = 1.79; CV = 27.5). The most common score is 7 (Mo = 7), which coincides with the sample median (Me = 7), but the average value of this indicator (x = 6.51) is lower than the center of distribution. This is caused by the fact that more individual values are attributed to the low level of indicator expressiveness than to the high one (Appendix 5 see Table 3.5.11).

According to the data given in the table, 16-year-old children are generally characterized by moderate expression of emotional expression. At the level of the components of the "Ex" indicator it was established that external manifestation of emotions in facial expressions, gestures and intonation ("IEx") are within the conditional average level (x = 3.44). Individual values of this subscale range from 2 to 6 points. In turn, most of the individual indicators that characterize the ability to convey one's emotional mood to the recipients ("EEx") are in the range of 2–4 points (78% of respondents). The average value (x = 3.07) corresponds to the lower limit of the average level and approaches the median of the distribution (Me = 3). All this allows us to conclude that the ability to convey the emotional mood in 16-year-olds is slightly lower than in the previous group, which is also reflected in a decrease in the overall level of emotional expressiveness.

The indicator "S" in the group of 16-year-olds is represented by data that range from 3 to 10 points. Individual values are distributed in a rather condensed way (σ = 1.79; CV = 27.3). The low level was reached by 22% of the scores in the sample. Only 2.4% of test takers have a high level, and the rest of 16-year-olds (75.6%) have an average level of intensity. The mean sample value (x = 6.56) indicates that the level of self-regulation in 16-year-old boys decreases compared to the previous age group.

A detailed examination of the expression of personal and interpersonal levels of emotional self-regulation showed that the data on the subscale "IS" have low variability ($\sigma = 1$; CV = 35.3). Most of the assessments are concentrated in the range of 2–4 points with a clearly visible center, which corresponds to 3 points (Mo = 3; Me = 3). The low level of this indicator occurs in 9.8% of cases, and high in 4.9%. The average value coincides with other indicators of the central trend in the sample (x = 2.83) and hardly differs from the same indicator in the group of 15-year-old children. The ability to influence the behavior of others ("ES") is characterized by data, most of which (73.2%) also correspond to the average level. However, a certain proportion of young people in the group (19.5%) demonstrated low scores. These data, as well as the average sample value (x = 3.73) allow us to assume that the weakening of emotional self-regulation at the age of 16 is primarily conditioned by a decrease in the ability to influence the behavior of other people. However, the comparison of individual values for the "IS" and "ES" indexes revealed that in 56.1% of the tested, the "ES" scores exceed the "IS" ones. In 29.31% of cases, there is a similar diversity of these characteristics, the "IS" level was found to be exceeded by 14.6%. That is, the ability to regulate own emotions remains lower than the ability to influence the behavior of other people in 16-year-olds.

The individual data obtained for the "Em" index are distributed in the range from 4 to 11 points and have fairly low variability ($\sigma = 1.87$; CV = 23.6). Most of them are grouped in the interval of 6–10 points (82.9% of values). Worth to note that only 7.3% of respondents have scores lower than 6. The average sample value (x = 7.9) increases significantly compared to the previous group. The "IEm" parameter is represented by data that are distributed similarly to the general "Em" index. Most scores correspond to either average (78% of the assessments fall into the 3–5 point range), or a high level (14.7%, which equals to 6 points) of this feature manifestation. The mode (Mo = 4) and the average value (x = 4.15) are higher than in the previous group. In turn, EEm data is also increasing. The average sample score here is 3.83 points, and the highest frequency weight gain is 3–5 points (82.9%), which corresponds to the average level. A comparison of individual data on the manifestation of "IEm" and "EEm" in the group of 16-year-olds permits us to assume that within the limits of the general indicator "Em" both of its components are formed quite evenly.

Most of the individual values of the indicator that characterizes the general adequacy of emotional response (integrative parameter "EZ") are in the interval of 17–25 points (82.9%). Only 4.9% of respondents have a low level of "EZ" expression and 17.1% have a high one. The average value of the "EZ" index (x = 21) indicates that in the period from 15 to 16 years the overall adequacy of emotional response does not change. That is, young people of 16 years old have a generally average level of emotional maturity.

However, as shown above, some changes took place in the formation of features and components of emotional maturity, which are reflected in the decrease in the level of emotional self-regulation and expressiveness and the increase in the level of empathy.

Examining in more detail how these components correlate at age 16, we found that the contribution of the "Ex" indicator to the overall assessment is 31%, the "S" indicator is 31%, and the "Em" indicator is 38%. Thus, the level of empathy in 16-year-olds far exceeds emotional expressiveness and emotional self-regulation. These data confirm our assumption that at the beginning of adolescence the adequacy of emotional response is ensured primarily by empathic abilities.

According to the survey of **17-year-olds**, all indicators of emotional maturity, compared to the previous group, are growing. Examination of the percentage of each of the studied indicators in the group allows us to note that a significant proportion of young people demonstrated an average level of expression of indicators under study (Appendix 5 see Table 3.5.12).

As can be seen from the table, the largest range of estimates is determined by the indicator "Ex". The range that outlines the expressiveness of the indicator in the sample is 3–11 points. Low and high values here comprise a significant part of the sample, and average estimates, compared to other indicators, are rare (64.6%).

The features that make up this scale have approximately the same weight. Most respondents have average scores (78%). The average values and medians on these subscales also do not differ ($x = 3.52$; $Me = 3$ for "IEx"; $x = 3.17$; $Me = 3$ for "EEx"). The only difference between them lies in the fact that the "IEx" subscale has the highest frequency value of 3 points ($Mo = 3$), and the "EEx" subscale has two adjacent modes ($Mo1 = 2$; $Mo2 = 3$). In turn, high clearness of signs of the interpersonal level of manifestation of emotional expressiveness (16.7%) is observed more often than the high intensity of personal level (8.3%).

These data allow us to conclude that at the age of 17 there is an increase in the ability to express own emotions, while the signs of personal and interpersonal levels of manifestation of these abilities are more balanced than in previous years.

Data that characterize the level of emotional self-regulation in 17-year-old teenagers have fairly low variability ($\sigma = 1.82$; $CV = 25.5$). Most of the scores are of medium intensity (83.4%), and high and low evaluations have 8.3% of respondents. The average value of the indicator ($x = 7.13$) significantly exceeds this estimate in the group of 16-year-old subjects.

The "IS" data indicate that most of the representatives of this age are able to satisfactorily regulate their own emotions (79.2%). Other subjects showed low (8.3%) or high (12.5%) indicators. The most widespread assessment on the subscale is 3 points ($Mo = 3$; $Me = 3$). The average value of "IS" also correlates with other indicators of the central trend in the sample ($x = 3$). The level of ability to influence other people's behavior ("ES") is higher than "IS" ($x = 4.25$; $Mo = 4$; $Me = 4$). Only 4.2% of responses in the group were attributed to the low level of the indicator expression, 79.2% of respondents have an average level, and 16.6% have a high level. Comparison of individual values for "IS" and "ES" also indicates a significant difference in their expressiveness: 72.9% of the tested subjects had scores for "ES" exceeding "IS". In 20.8% of subjects, there is a similar severity of these features. The "IS" level was exceeded in 6.3% of cases. So, despite the growth of emotional self-regulation in general, the ability to control own emotions in 17-year-olds remains much more poorly formed than the ability to regulate the behavior of others.

Individual data obtained for the indicator "Em" are distributed in the range from 4 to 12 points and characterized by low variability (σ = 1.82; CV = 23.6). The average value in the sample (x = 7.71) is slightly lower than in the previous group. Most of the values (81.3%) are defined by the limits of the average level. A total of 10.4% of assessments belong to the low level and 8.3% to the high level.

In the analysis of individual components of "Em" indicator at this age group, the ability to adequately perceive the emotional state of other respondents ("IEm") is represented by data that belong to the range from 1 to 6 points and have moderate variability (σ = 1.24; CV = 32.4). The most widespread score is 4 points (Mo = 4). The average value of this indicator (x = 3.83) in the sample of 17-year-olds corresponds to the middle level, to which 75% of responses belong. The low and high levels of "IEm" are 12.5% each. The "EEm" indicators are represented by data distributed in the range from 2 to 6 points. The sample average belongs to the middle-level range (x = 3.88). A comparison of the data on the expressiveness of "IEm" and "EEm" allowed us to determine that they do not differ in general.

Turning to the analysis of individual values of the integrative parameter "EZ", we note that most of them are also within the average level. Only 18.8% of those tested had a score above the average level and 10.4% had a lower one. The maximum in the sample is 29 points, the minimum is 13. It was also found that the average value of emotional maturity (x = 21.52) is slightly increasing.

We should pay attention to the fact that not all components of emotional maturity at the age of 17 are formed evenly. The share of "Ex" in the overall assessment of emotional maturity is 31%, the "S" index is 33%, and "Em" is 36%. Thus, as in the previous group, 17-year-olds have a better ability to understand the emotional state of others, and to understand the emotional and motivational factors of their behavior than the ability to control their own emotions and adequately express them in communication.

Representatives **aged 18–23** have the highest expressiveness in all indicators of emotional maturity when compared with other age groups. Thus, the data for the indicator "Ex" are distributed in the range of 4–12 points, and the average value (x = 7.91) exceeds by more than 1 point compared to the analogous evaluation in the group of 17 years. Most estimates can be attributed to the average level of severity (Appendix 5 see Table 3.5.13).

On the level of the components of "Ex" index, it was found that the average value of "IEx" (x = 3.62) does not differ in this estimation in 17-year-olds. Individual values vary between 1 and 6 points and are distributed with average variability (σ = 1.26; CV = 34.8). The most common result is 4 points (Mo = 4;

Me = 4). 19.8% of the values correspond to the low level of "IEx", 74.4% to the average level, and 5.8% to the high.

Individual indicators that characterize the ability to transfer one's emotional mood ("EEx") are also distributed in the range from 1 to 6 points, but with significantly less variability ($\sigma = 1.1$; CV = 25.7). Only 3.5% of the estimates in the sample correspond to a low level. The remaining values are medium (80.2%) or high (16.3%). The average value ($x = 4.29$) significantly exceeds the same estimate in the previous group. Comparison of individual assessments for "IEx" and "EEx" allowed us to find out that within the limits of the general indicator that characterizes emotional expressiveness, personal and interpersonal levels of its manifestation are not equally expressed. In the majority of respondents (51.2%) the scores for "EEx" exceed those for "IEx"; in some cases (29.1%) the data on these scales coincide, and in 19.7% of the respondents the scores for "IEx" exceed "EEx".

These data indicate that in late adolescence, the adequacy of emotional expression develops, primarily due to the ability to express emotions arbitrarily, taking into account the situation of communication and own needs.

The indicator of emotional self-regulation ("S") is represented by data ranging from 3 to 12. A total of 79.1% of responses belong to the average level, 9.3% to the high, and 11.6% to the low. The average sample value ($x = 7.83$) exceeds the similar estimate in the group of 17 years. Data on the subscale "IS" indicate that persons of this age are most often found to be able to regulate their own emotions satisfactorily (90.7%). The average value of "IS" is 3.3 points. Unlike "IS", data on the formation of the ability to influence the behavior of others ("ES") are more varied. Only 66.3% of the evaluations are at the average level, and a high level is presented in 25.6% of the samples. The average score on the scale is 4.51 points. A comparison of individual values for the "IS" and "ES" indicators allowed us to establish that 72% of subjects had scores for "ES" that exceeded "IS". The same intensity of both indicators and exceeding the level of "IS" is determined in an equal number of test takers (14% of cases each). Thus, in young people aged 18–23, as in other age groups, the ability to control their own emotions is formed worse than the ability to influence the behavior of other people.

Individual data obtained by the indicator "Em" are distributed in the range from 2 to 12 points and have low variability ($\sigma = 1.73$; CV = 19.9). It should be noted that only 9.3% of respondents have estimates that correspond to the relatively low level of this indicator manifestation. The average level is represented by 77.9% of respondents, and 12.8% have high scores. The average sample value ($x = 8.69$) is more than 1 point higher than the same estimate in the 17-year-olds group, which gives grounds to assume a significant increase in empathic abilities in late adolescence.

Features of personal and interpersonal levels of manifestation of the indicator "Em" are distributed similarly. Thus, those of "IEm" are represented by data, most of which correspond to a high (20.9%) or medium (67.4%) level of expressiveness. The most widespread is 5 points (Mo = 5), which corresponds to the upper limit of the conditional average. "EEm" data are also mostly in the high (19.8%) and medium (73.3%) levels of intensity. Only 7% of respondents have low scores. A comparison of individual data for "IEm" and "EEm" indicators in the group of 18–23 years old allows assuming that within the limits of the general indicator that characterizes empathy, both of its components are formed fairly evenly.

The characteristics of the expressiveness of the integrative parameter "EZ" in the group of late adolescents reflect the peculiarities of data distribution that are typical for its components, namely: individual data have low variability (σ = 3.62; CV = 14.8), values vary from 13 up to 31 points. Low scores are uncommon (8.1% of scores). 76.7% of the obtained values belong to the average level of expressiveness of this indicator, and 15.1% of estimates correspond to the high level. The average sample value (x = 24.42) is much higher than this value in the group of 17-year-olds.

Summarizing the data on the intensity of emotional maturity in young people of 18–23 years, we focus on the fact that certain changes have occurred in its components, which are reflected in the growth of levels of emotional expressiveness, self-regulation and empathy. Given this, certain interest is devoted to the role of these components in the general adequacy of the emotional reaction. After all, not all components of emotional maturity are formed evenly. The share of "Ex" in the overall assessment of emotional maturity is 31%, "S" 33% and "Em" 36%. Thus, the level of empathy at this age far exceeds emotional expressiveness and emotional self-regulation.

Summarizing the information obtained in the process of analyzing individual data, we present a description of the development of the basic properties of emotional maturity in representatives of each age group.

Thus, 11-year-olds are characterized by a moderate level of emotional expressiveness and emotional self-regulation, and sufficient empathy, the development of which precedes the formation of other components. Twelve-year-old children have a tendency to have a lower level of emotional self-regulation and empathy and a higher level of emotional expressiveness. Adolescents of 13 years old are characterized by the moderate intensity of all three properties. As 14-year-olds, they have an increase in emotional self-regulation and a decrease in emotional expressiveness. The level of empathy in them almost does not change. However, at the age of 15, there is a tendency for empathy to increase, the development of which reaches the level of emotional self-regulation. The intensity of emotional expressiveness at this age also grows slightly. At the age of sixteen, there is also an increase in empathic abilities, and at the same time, a decrease in emotional self-regulation. Seventeen-year-olds are characterized by a fairly high level of empathy and a moderate degree of emotional expressiveness and emotional self-regulation. Young men aged 18–23 have a significant increase in all the properties of emotional maturity.

However, the information about changes in the formation of the main properties of emotional maturity of each age group has a hypothetical nature. To confirm the probability of these trends in the development of these properties, additional research should be conducted.

Almost in all age groups, the indicators that characterize features of emotional maturity of the person are generally in line with the average norms of expression. These data indicate that the majority of healthy adolescents and young people of any age have no fundamental differences in the formation of emotional maturity. However, in each age group, there are subjects whose data are close to low or high levels. In our opinion, this variability can be explained by individual peculiarities of the formation of emotional maturity, related to natural, psychophysiological conditioning (predominance of one of the components of emotional maturity and compensation for underdevelopment of others), or social conditioning (the nature of social environment, the frequency of social contacts). We believe that this issue needs further study and special explanation.

There is a certain imbalance in the formation of components of emotional maturity in some age groups. It is expressed in the excess of emotionality at 11, 16, 17 and 18–23 years, and emotional self-regulation at the age of 14. The most even formation of all three components of emotional maturity was observed at the ages 12, 13 and 15.

3.5.2 Distinctions in the development of emotional maturity depending on age

The analysis of the individual data concerning the expressiveness of indicators that characterize the main components of emotional maturity of a person, allows us to assume the presence of significant differences among the representatives of different age groups. In order to confirm such discrepancies, we need to conduct a more in-depth examination.

Considering the peculiarities of changes in the expressiveness of the components of emotional maturity, we can note that in general, most of the representatives of different age groups have values that correspond to the average level of its intensity on the indicator "Ex". However, the comparison of the average group data revealed some differences between different age groups (Appendix 5 see Table 3.5.14).

As shown in the table, the difference between the average values in the groups of 11 and 12 years old is 0.41 points, in the groups of 12 and 13 years old is 0.31 points, in 13 and 14 years is 0.55 points, in 14 and 15 years is 0.62 points, in 15 and 16 years is 0.15 points, in 16 and 17 years is 0.18 points, in groups of 17 and 18–23 years old is 1.22 points. Only the differences between the groups 17 and 18–23 years old, where $t = 3.4$, $p < 0.01$, were confirmed to be statistically reliable. At the level of two signs that characterize the general indicator "Ex" there were also revealed some age-related changes.

According to the "IEx" index between the groups of 11 and 12-year-olds, the difference between the average values is 0.09 points, between groups of 12 and 13-year-olds is 0.1 points, 13 and 14-year-olds is 0.29 points, 14 and 15-year-olds is 0.07 points, 15 and 16-year-olds is 0.2 points, 16 and 17-year-olds is 0.08 points, and 17 and 18–23-year-olds is 0.1 points.

Statistically reliable discrepancies in the expressiveness of this parameter between the age groups were not found. Unlike "IEx", the signs of the interpersonal level of emotional expression ("EEx") differ by greater age variability. Here, the difference in the average values between the groups of 11 and 12-year-olds is 0.59 points, between the groups of 12 and 13-year-olds is 0.3 points, 13 and 14 year-olds is 0.27 points, 14 and 15-year-olds is 0.7 points, 15 and 16-year-olds is 0.36 points, 16 and 17-year-olds is 0.09 points, and 17 and 18–23-year-olds is 1.12 points. Statistically valid differences are between the groups of 14 and 15 years old, where $t = 3.05$, $p < 0.01$, and between groups 17 and 18–23 years, where $t = 5.36$, $p < 0.001$.

Therefore, we can assert that during the period from 11 to 14 years, the level of involuntary expression, as well as purposeful expression in facial expressions, intonation and gestures in communication does not change significantly. Further, there is a significant increase in the activity of expression in interaction with other people. At the age of 18–23 years, the manifestation of expressiveness increases significantly. All these changes in general emotional expressiveness are conditioned by acquiring skills of purposeful use of facial expressions, intonation and gestures in communication. The level of involuntary expression does not change with age.

As in the case of "Ex" for the indicator "S" in different age groups individual evaluations were obtained, most of which can be attributed to the average level of its intensity. The difference between the average values in the samples of 11 and 12-year-olds was 0.55 points, 12 and 13 years – 0.26 points, 13 and 14 years – 0.8 points, 14 and 15 years – 0.11 points, 15 and 16 years – 0.62 points, 16 and 17 years – 0.56 points, 17 years and 18–23 – 0.7 points.

As seen from Appendix 5, Table 3.5.14, statistically significant are only the differences between groups 13 and 14-year-olds, where $t = 2.3$, $p < 0.05$, and between groups 17 and 18–23-year-olds, where $t = 2.03$, $p < 0.05$. At the level of two signs that characterize the general indicator "S", some age-related changes were identified. According to the indicator "IS" between groups 11 and 12-year-olds there is a difference between the average values of 0.19 points, between groups 12 and 13 years – 0.25 points, 13 and 14 years – 0.75 points, 14 and 15 years – 0.36 points, 15 and 16 years – 0.05 points, 16 and 17 years – 0.17 points, and 17 and 18–23-year-olds – 0.33 points. Statistically valid differences in the strength of this parameter were found only between the groups of 13 and 14-year-olds, where $t = 3.47$, $p < 0.01$. More variable in terms of age are the signs of "ES" – here the difference in average values between the groups of 11 and 12-year-olds is 0.36 points, between the groups of 12 and 13 years there are no differences, between 13 and 14-year-olds – only 0.04 points, 14 and 15 years – 0.47 points, 15 and 16 years – 0.56 points, 16 and 17 years – 0.52 points, 17 years and 18–23 – 0.27 points, 18–23 and 24–45 years – 1.22 points. Statistically valid are the differences between the groups of 15 and 16 years old, where $t = 2.1$, $p < 0.05$, and also 16 and 17 years old, where $t = 2.02$, $p < 0.05$.

These data show that from the age of 11 to 13 years, both the ability to control emotions and the ability to influence the behavior of others do not change significantly. At the age of fourteen there is a significant increase in the level of regulation of own emotions, which is reflected in changes in the general indicator "S". In the meantime, there are essential fluctuations in the dynamics of the tendency to influence other people, however, this does not affect the state of the indicator that characterizes the overall emotional self-regulation. In late adolescence, the degree of self-regulation increases notably.

Despite the fact that in most age groups there is a tendency to a certain excess of the general level of "Em" over other components of emotional maturity, the indicator "Em" has signs of dynamics similar to "Ex". A comparison of the average values given in Appendix 5, Table 3.5.14 revealed a difference between the groups of 11 and 12 years of 0.6 points, 12 and 13 years – 0.14 points, 13 and 14 years – 0.07 points, 14 and 15 years – 0.64 points, 15 and 16 years – 0.69 points, 16 and 17 years – 0.19 points, 17 and 18–23-year-olds – 0.98 points. Characteristically, the value of this indicator is gradually increasing, but only between 17 and 18–23 years there is a statistically considerable increase in the level of its strength ($t = 3.01$, $p <0.01$).

There are no significant age-related changes at the level of "IEm". In contrast to this subscale, "EEm" has the same age dynamics as the general indicator that characterizes empathy. Here, the difference in average values between the groups of 11 and 12-year-olds is 0.08 points, between the groups of 12 and 13 years – 0.03 points, 13 and 14 years – 0.06 points, 14 and 15 years – 0.27 points, 15 and 16 years – 0.42 points, 16 and 17 years – 0.05 points, and 17 and 18–23-year-olds – 0.58 points. Statistically valid are the differences between the groups of 17 and 18–23 years, where $t = 2.86$, $p <0.01$.

These data allow us to state that during the period from 11 to 17 years the ability to adequately perceive the emotional state of the interlocutor, the ability to understand the motivational and emotional factors of his/her behavior, as well as the ability to use this knowledge to interact with people does not change significantly. Then, in late adolescence, there is a significant increase in the ability to use empathy in interaction with others, which is reflected in the increase in the overall indicator that characterizes empathy.

The intensity of the integrative parameter "EZ", which characterizes emotional maturity, repeats the general patterns of the dynamics of most of its components. Thus, at the level of average values the divergence between the groups of 11 and 12-year-olds is 0.73 points, between groups of 12 and 13 years – 0.71 points, 13 and 14 years – 0.31 points, 14 and 15 years – 1.37 points, 15 and 16 years – 0.08 points, 16 and 17 years – 0.55 points, 17 and 18–23-year-olds – 2.9 points. Only the differences between the groups of 17 and 18–23 years are statistically essential, where $t = 4.21$, $p <0.001$.

Thus, the formation of emotional maturity of a person is marked by a significant increase, which falls in the period of late adolescence and consists of an essential raise in the overall adequacy of emotional response. Moreover, at the age of 14, there is a jump in the level of emotional self-regulation, namely, the ability to control emotions, and at the age of 15, there is also an increase in the ability to freely express emotions in communication.

The most stable period in terms of the formation of emotional maturity can be considered the period of 11–13 years, during which there are no dynamics of all the studied characteristics. Also, similar values were obtained in the periods 14–15 and 16–17 years.

3.5.3 The relationship between indicators of emotional maturity and personal characteristics in surveyed subjects, depending on age

A previous analysis of correlations between indicators of emotional maturity in a group of **11-year-old children** showed that the integrative parameter "EZ is quite closely ($p < 0.01$) associated with indicators that determine emotional expression ("Ex"), emotional self-regulation ("S)" and empathy ("Em"), as well as with subscales that characterize the features of introexpressiveness ("IEx"), extra-self-regulation ("ES"), intro- and extraempathy ("IEm" and "EEm").

Significant correlations are also observed between the indicator "Ex" and characteristics of "IEx" and "EEx" ($p < 0.01$), the indicator "S" and signs "IS" and "ES" ($p < 0.01$), the indicator "Em" and signs "IEm" and "EEm" ($p < 0.01$).

As seen from these data, the hierarchical structure of an individual's emotional maturity is quite closely linked in a group of 11-year-olds. However, the relationships between individual components and features are not formalized. According to the results of factor analysis, we obtained a structure that differs essentially from the model we defined at the theoretical level (see Figure 3.5.1).

Factor analysis of data obtained in a group of 11-year-old children showed the following nature of the factor distribution: nine indicators characterizing the emotional maturity of a person were grouped into three factors similar in content to our theoretically determined components of emotional maturity; however, only factors F1 ($r = 0.79$) and F2 ($r = 0.52$) have a significant relationship with the integrative parameter "EZ".

The first factor included: the indicator "Em" and features that reflect the expressiveness of both personal and interpersonal levels of its manifestation; signs of personal involuntary expression of emotions "IEx"; signs of interpersonal manifestation of emotional self-regulation "ES". In our opinion, the factor reflects the priority role of empathy in the formation of emotional maturity of a person at the age of eleven and its impact on the formation of expressiveness and the ability to regulate the emotions of others. The second factor is influenced by such indexes as "IS" and "S", it conveys the content of self-regulation of emotions. The third factor included indicators "EEx" and "Ex", which reflect the

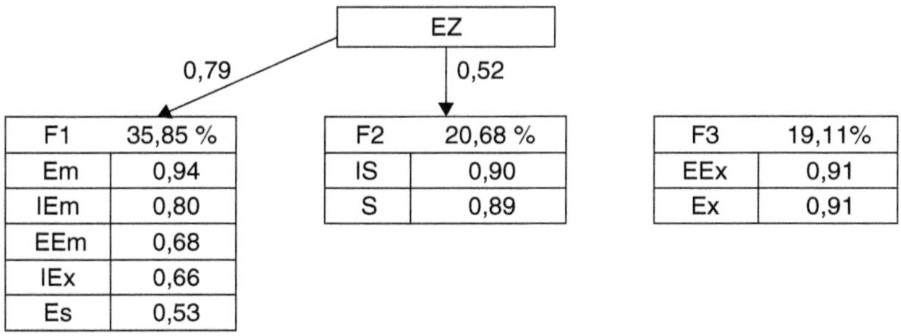

FIGURE 3.5.1 The structure of emotional maturity in a group of 11-year-old children (5 rotations).

external manifestation of emotions in facial expressions, gestures, postures and movements of a person which is, in this case, of arbitrary nature. As we can see, in children of this age, expressiveness is weakly related to the emotional maturity of the person in general.

Examination of the relationship between indicators of emotional maturity and personal characteristics of 11-year-old children allowed us to find the following significant correlations: between signs of "IEx" and the indicator "F2" ($r = 0.397$, $p < 0.05$); between signs of "IS" and indicators "F8" ($r = -0.483$, $p < 0.05$) and "E" ($r = 0.435$, $p < 0.05$); and between signs of "ES" and the indicator "F12", which has a negative value ($r = -0.485$, $p < 0.05$). Such data demonstrate that a fairly high level of spontaneous expression of emotions in children at this age is associated with increased spontaneous aggression and impulsive behavior. The ability to control emotions in children aged 11, does not score high in the majority of those examined, directly depends on their level of extroversion, and is hampered by high shyness, anxiety, insecurity and related difficulties in social contacts. Eleven-year-olds have a high ability to influence the emotional state of others due to low levels of masculinity.

In the group of 11-year-olds, it consisted of 5 factors that have different weights in the total dispersion of the indicators being studied.

Thus, the first factor has the highest percentage in the total dispersion (20.02%) and is bipolar. It includes indicators that characterize negative emotional manifestations, such as depression ("F3"), emotional lability ("F11"), neurotism ("N"), spontaneous aggression ("F2"), shyness ("F8"), irritability ("F4") and neuroticism ("F1"). At the other pole there is only one indicator "L" with a factor intensity (–0.68), which reflects the level of social desirability of the answers of the "EPI" questionnaire and is interpreted in this case as openness in communication. We called the factor a "factor of negative emotional manifestations".

The second factor (16.55%) has one pole. It consisted of: the integrative parameter of emotional maturity ("EZ"), an indicator of empathy ("Em") and the manifestations of its signs on the personal ("IEm") and interpersonal ("EEm") levels, signs of involuntary expression of emotions ("IEx"), and ability to influence the emotional state of others ("ES"), as well as the indicator ("F6"), which reflects the degree of a balance. This factor was called the "empathy" factor. Its content confirms the assumption of its leading role in the formation of emotional maturity in children of the studied age, as well as indicates the importance of balance in this process.

The third factor (12.92%) is also unipolar. It combines interrelated indicators of masculine behavior ("F12"), extraversion ("E" and "F10") and reactive aggressiveness ("F7").

The fourth factor (9.32%) has two poles. The first of them focuses on an indicator that reflects the strength of emotional self-regulation ("S") with a factor weight (0.76) and signs of personality level of its manifestation ("IS") with a factor weight (0.62). On the other pole – an indicator that tells about the level of sociability ("F5") with a factor weight (–0.62). The nature of the factor allows us to call it "emotional self-regulation" and draw attention to the negative relationship of this component of emotional maturity with social activity.

The fifth factor (8.90%) is also bipolar. The first pole encloses such indicators as "EEx" with factor weight (0.86) and "Ex" – (0.77). The other contains the indicator "SE" with a factor weight (–0.61). This one can be called the factor of "emotional expressiveness". Its content indicates the connection between this component of emotional maturity and specifically the interpersonal level of its manifestation with the inability to adequately assess oneself.

Examination of the factor structure found in the group of 11-year-old children allows us to conclude that emotional maturity is not a leading component in the formation of the emotional sphere of a person, but occupies a very important place in this process. At this age, it is not a fully formed structure, its components are more or less separated. The development of children's empathy is a key factor in the formation of emotional maturity.

The previous analysis of correlations between indicators of emotional maturity in the group of **12-year-old children** showed that the integrative parameter "EZ", which characterizes emotional maturity, as in the previous group has a significant link with indicators of emotional expressiveness, emotional self-regulation and empathy.

Besides, it was determined that are correlations of the indicator "Ex" with the signs "IEx" ($r = 0.832$; $p < 0.01$), "EEx" ($r = 0.803$; $p < 0.01$) and "ES" ($r=0.426$; 0.878; $p<0.01$), indicator "S" with signs "IS" ($r = 0.878$; $p < 0.01$), "ES" ($r = 0.812$; $p < 0.01$) and "EEx" ($r = 0.443$; $p < 0.05$), and the indicator "Em" with the signs "IEm" ($r = 0.903$; $p < 0.01$) and "EEm" ($r = 0.926$; $p < 0.01$).

The results of in-depth factor analysis conducted separately for the indicators of emotional maturity of the personality revealed that a group of schoolchildren 12 years of age has a more tense structure (see Figure 3.5.2).

As can be seen in the figure, indicators that characterize the emotional maturity of a person are grouped into three factors (see Figure 3.5.2). The first factor included: the indicator "Em" and signs that reflect the expressiveness of both personal and interpersonal levels of its manifestation. As in the previous group, the

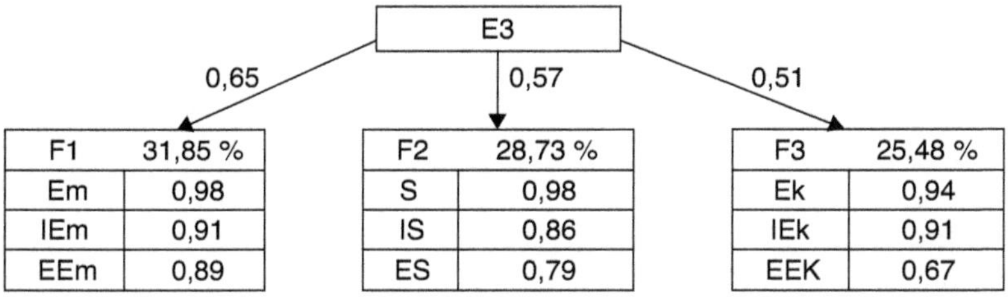

FIGURE 3.5.2 The structure of emotional maturity.

factor that can be called "empathy" reflects the priority role of this component in the formation of emotional maturity of 12-year-old children.

The second factor is influenced by such indicators as "S", "IS" and "ES", it conveys the content of features of emotional self-regulation. The third factor includes indicators "Ex", "IEx" and "EEx", which are related to the component "emotional expressiveness". The integrative parameter "EZ" significantly correlates with each of these factors, namely, with "empathy" (r = 0.65), "emotional self-regulation" (r = 0.57) and "emotional expressiveness" (r = 0.51).

Examination of interrelations between indicators of emotional maturity and personal characteristics of 12-year-olds allowed us to find reliable correlations between the index "Ex" and indicators "F4" (r = 0.541, p <0.01), "F6" (r = 0.420, p <0.05) and "F12" (r = 0.492, p <0.05); "S" with indicators "F6" (r = 0.459, p <0.05) and "F7" (r = 0.467, p <0.05); and "Em" with indicator "F5" (r = 0.541, p <0.01). Also with "F5" correlate the integrative parameter "EZ" (r = 0.510, p <0.05) and the signs of "EEm" (r = 0.506, p <0.05).

"IEx" signs are significantly related to the indicators "F2" (r = 0.556, p <0.01), "F4" (r = 0.688, p <0.01), "F10" (r = 0.496, p <0.05), "F12" (r = 0.551, p <0.01), and signs of "IS" – with indicators "F6" (r = −0.432, p <0.05) and "F7" (r = 0.458, p <0.05).

These data indicate that the formation of emotional maturity, empathy and the ability to use empathic abilities in communication is related to the level of camaraderie. In addition, it should be pointed out about the importance of balance in the formation of emotional expressiveness and self-regulation, in a particular personalized level of emotionality. In turn, emotional expressiveness, namely, its involuntary manifestation is closely related to irritability and also with masculine characteristic features.

The in-depth factor analysis of emotional maturity and personal qualities of those surveyed in the group of 12 years, consists of 5 factors.

The first factor (19.83%) has one pole. It includes such indicators of personal manifestations as extroversion, irritability, spontaneous aggressiveness, masculinity and related emotional expressiveness, particularly, the personal level of its manifestation. We called this factor "impulsive communicative activity". Its content shows that in children 12 years of age the adequacy of orientation in emotional communication is ensured by the expression of emotions, especially their involuntary manifestation, and associated with them extroversion, irritability, significant manifestation of masculine traits, and decreased impulsive behavior.

The second factor (19.17%) is also unipolar. It includes an integrative parameter of emotional maturity ("EZ"), indicators of empathy ("Em") and the manifestation of its signs on personal ("IEm") and interpersonal ("Em") levels, and also the indicator ("F5"), that reflects the level of camaraderie. The factor named "empathy" factor indicates a close relationship between the formation of empathy and emotional maturity in general with activity in social contacts.

The third factor (13.38%) combines interrelated indicators that characterize the manifestation of emotional self-regulation ("S") and its signs at personal ("IS") and interpersonal ("ES") levels, signs of emotional expressiveness, which is arbitrary ("EEx"), and also of self-esteem ("SE"). The nature of the factor allows us to call it "emotional self-regulation" and to pay attention to the interrelation of this component of emotional maturity of a person with the level of adequacy of the assessment of own abilities.

The fourth factor (11.12%) has two poles. The first is "F7" with factor weight (0.63) and "F6" (0.56). The second indicator is "F8" with a factor weight (−0.78).

The fifth factor (11.03%) unites such indicators as "F11" with a factor weight (0.86), "F3" (0.83) and "F1" (0.73). It can be called a factor of "emotional instability" because it conveys the relationship of such features as emotional lability, depression and neuroticism.

The analysis of the factor structure found in the group of 12-year-old children allows us to conclude that emotional maturity begins to play a more important role in the formation of emotional sphere of the personality. In turn, the importance of negative emotional experiences decreases.

As previously set, in the group of **13-year-olds**, the integrative parameter of emotional maturity, as in previous groups, is closely related to indicators of emotional expressiveness, emotional self-regulation and empathy, as well as subscales that characterize features of personal and interpersonal levels of manifestation of these properties.

According to the table, the indicator "Ex", in its turn, significantly correlates with the signs "IEx" ($r = 0.715$; $p < 0.01$), "EEx" ($r = 0.814$; $p < 0.01$), with the indicator "Em" ($r = 0.571$; $p < 0.01$) and its signs "IEm" ($r = 0.317$; $p < 0.05$) and "EEm" ($r = 0.528$; $p < 0.01$), and also with "ES" ($r = 0.324$; $p < 0.05$). The indicator "S" is related to the signs "IS" ($r = 0.832$; $p < 0.01$) and "ES" ($r = 0.767$; $p < 0.01$). The indicator "Em" shows correlations with "IEm" ($r = 0.735$; $p < 0.01$), "EEm" ($r = 0.769$; $p < 0.01$), "IEx" ($r = 0.356$; $p < 0.05$) and "EEx" ($r = 0.508$; $p < 0.01$).

According to these data, the group of 13-year-old adolescents has a closer connection between the components of emotional maturity and the levels of its manifestation. The nature of this connection points to the special role that the component of emotional expressiveness plays in the formation of emotional maturity of 13-year-olds, especially its signs that characterize the ability to accurately convey emotional state in communication. In-depth factor analysis, conducted separately for indicators of the emotional maturity of the individual, allows us to confirm this statement (see Figure 3.5.3).

The indicators of emotional maturity were grouped into three factors. The first factor included the indicator "Ex" and the signs of "EEx" and "EEm", which reflect the strength of the interpersonal level of emotional expression and empathy. The factor was conditionally called "emotional expressiveness". The content of this factor indicates that the adequacy of emotional response in 13-year-olds is ensured through the ability to understand and use the expression in communication. The second factor is influenced by such indicators as "S", "IS" and "ES", it conveys the content of signs of emotional self-regulation. The third factor includes indicators "IEm", "Em" and "IEx" related to the component "empathy". The integrative parameter "EZ" significantly correlates with each of these factors, namely, with the factor "emotional expressiveness" ($r = 0.67$), "emotional self-regulation" ($r = 0.48$) and "empathy" ($r = 0.57$).

The analysis of the correlation in the group of 13-year-old children allowed us to determine the indicators characterizing extra-introversion ("E", "F10") are most closely related to the indicators that characterize emotional maturity. It significantly correlates with the integrative parameter of emotional maturity ("EZ"), indicators of emotional expressiveness ("Ex"), extraexpressiveness ("EEx"), empathy ("Em"), extraempathy ("EEm") and emotional self-regulation ("S", "IS" and "ES").

Along with the above mentioned, the following correlations were found: between "IEx" signs and F6 indicator ($r = 0.376$, $p < 0.05$) and F12 ($r = 0.359$, $p < 0.05$); signs of "ES" and indicator "F4" ($r = 0.305$, $p < 0.05$); and between indicators "S" and "N" ($r = -0.309$, $p < 0.05$).

These data testify to the fact that in the formation of emotional maturity at the age of 13 a special role begins to play the extroversion of the personality, its orientation toward social relationships and activity in communication.

Factor analysis in a group of 13-year-old adolescents revealed 4 factors with significant weight. The first factor (20.26%) has one pole and includes six indicators that characterize empathic abilities ("IEm") and the ability to use them in communication ("EEm"), contagiousness of emotional expressiveness for recipients ("EEx"), general level of empathy ("Em"), emotional expressiveness ("ES")

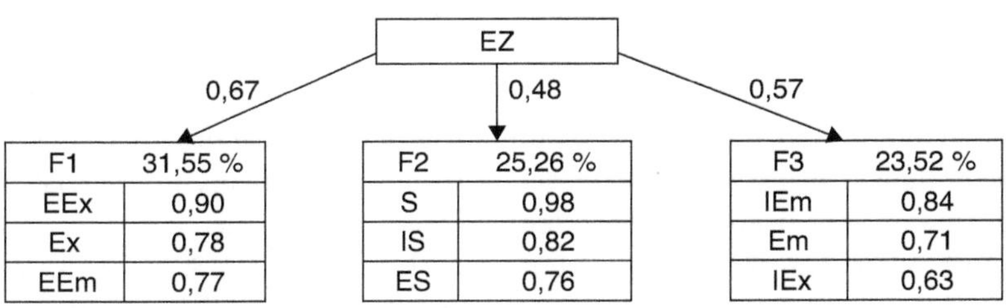

FIGURE 3.5.3 The structure of emotional maturity in the group of 13-year-old children (6 rotations).

and emotional maturity ("EZ"). We called this factor "emotional maturity." Its content indicates that the formation of emotional maturity in 13-year-old children develops due to integration of expressive and empathic abilities, along with the development of skills to use in communication. The second factor (18.02%) is also unipolar. It consists of indicators "S" with weight (0.88), signs "IS" (0.80), "ES" (0.75) and indicator "E" (0.69). This factor called "emotional self-regulation", indicates that the formation of this component of emotional maturity in 13-year-olds depends on the level of their extroversion.

The third factor (13.25%) has one pole and includes indicators that determine the level of irritability ("F4"), depression ("F3"), neurotism ("N"), neuroticism ("F1"), emotional lability ("F11") and spontaneous aggression ("F2"). We called it "negative emotional manifestations" factor. It should be noted that a similar factor was identified in the group of 11-year-old children, but its indicators took first place in the factor distribution. The fourth factor (10.72%) has two poles. One of them concentrates on indicators that characterize the level of comradeship ("F5"), extra-introversion ("F10"), personal self-esteem ("SE") and signs of the personal level of emotional expressiveness "IEx". At the other pole are "F8" with a factor weight (−0.66), which characterizes shyness, and "F6" (−0.47), which determines the level of composure. The factor called "social activity" demonstrates the relationship between activity in establishing social contacts, high self-esteem and the clarity of the expression of emotions in behavior.

Further analysis of correlations between indicators of emotional maturity in the group of **14-year-old children** showed that the integrative parameter characterizing emotional maturity ("EZ") has correlations with indicators of emotional expressiveness ("Ex", "IEx", "EEx"), emotional self-regulation ("S", "IS", "ES") and empathy ("Em", "IEm", "EEm "), which are significant with a high level of probability ($p < 0.01$).

There is also a close correlation between the components and levels of its manifestation within the structure of emotional maturity. Thus, the indicator "Ex" correlates with the signs "IEx" ($r = 0.823$) and "EEx" ($r = 0.895$), as well as with the indicators "S" ($r = 0.338$), "Em" ($r = 0.419$) and signs "ES" ($r = 0.339$) and "EEm" ($r = 0.376$) with a high level of significance ($p < 0.01$).

These data allow us to state that in the group of children aged 14 years the structural interrelationships revealed are not only of a dependent nature but also tightly integrate the main components of emotional maturity between each other.

It should be noted that the relationship between the signs that characterize personal and interpersonal levels of the components of emotional maturity has its own specifics: signs that determine one level of various components are correlated but not related to signs from the second level of other components. An exception is a relationship between the signs of "IEm" and "EEx" ($r = 0.278$; $p < 0.05$), which testifies that the ability to understand the emotional state of the interlocutor is formed in interaction with the natural expressiveness of the personality.

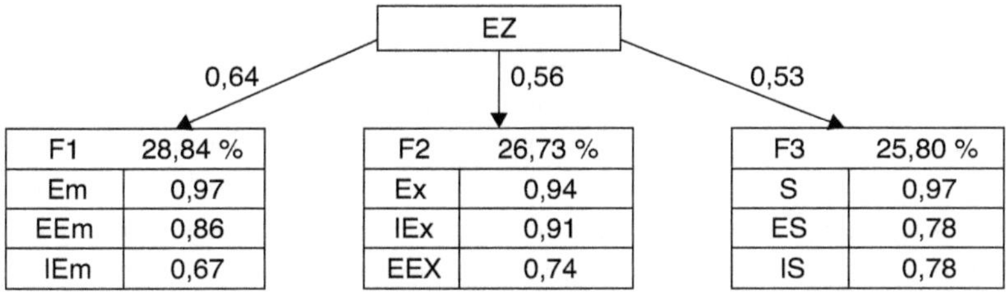

FIGURE 3.5.4 The structure of emotional maturity in the group of 14-year-old children (4 rotations).

The in-depth factor structure of indicators of emotional maturity of the person in the group of 14-year-old children most precisely coincides with the content of our theoretical model (see Figure 3.5.4).

As you can see in the figure, indicators that characterize the emotional maturity of a person are grouped into three factors. The first factor included the indicator "Em" and signs that reflect the interpersonal ("EEm") and personal ("IEm") levels of its manifestation. The factor conveys the content of the component "empathy". The second factor is influenced by such indicators as "Ex", "IEx" and "EEx", which are related to the component "emotional expressiveness". The third factor includes indicators "S", "ES" and "IS" and conveys the content of signs of emotional self-regulation. The integrative parameter "EZ" significantly correlates with each of these factors, namely, with the factor "empathy" ($r = 0.64$), "emotional expressiveness" ($r = 0.56$) and "emotional self-regulation" ($r = 0.53$).

Examination of interrelations between indicators of emotional maturity and personal characteristics of 14-year-olds allowed us to find the following significant correlations: the indicator "Ex", which characterizes emotional expressiveness, with indicators of self-esteem ("SE": $r = 0.261$), extra-introversion "E": $r = 0.333$) and neurotism ("N": $r = 0.280$); an indicator of emotional self-regulation ("S") with indicators of neuroticism ("F1": $r = -0.368$), depressiveness ("F3": $r = -0.345$), comradeship ("F5": $r = 0.294$), emotional lability (F11 ": $R = -0.318$), self-esteem ("SE": $r = 0.302$) and extra-introversion ("E": $r = 0.306$); "Em" indicator with comradeship indicator ("F5": $r = 0.252$), composure ("F6": $r = 0.244$), extra-introversion ("E": $r = 0.370$) and neurotism "N" ($r = 0.320$). It is noteworthy that the signs that characterize the interpersonal level of manifestation of indicators of emotional maturity demonstrate the same pattern of interconnections with personal characteristics (see Table 3.5.21).

In turn, the integrative parameter "EZ", which characterizes emotional maturity, also correlates with "F5" ($r = 0.293$, $p < 0.01$), "SE" ($r = 0.262$, $p < 0.05$), "E" ($r = 0.447$, $p < 0.01$) and "N" ($r = 0.274$, $p < 0.05$).

These data indicate that emotional maturity in 14-year-old adolescents is closely linked to social activity, self-esteem, extraversion and neurotism.

However, only the level of extraversion has a positive influence on the formation of all three components of emotional maturity. Neurotism is associated only with emotional expressiveness and empathy. Self-esteem does not affect the development of empathy, and comradeship is not associated with emotional expressiveness. Moreover, the increase in emotional self-regulation observed at this age is associated with a decrease in depression and emotional lability in adolescents and is negatively related to the level of neurotism.

The in-depth factor structure, representing the interrelation of indicators of emotional maturity and personal qualities of 14-year-olds examined in the group is composed of 5 factors.

The first factor has the highest percentage of the total dispersion (16.50%). As in previous groups, it includes indicators that characterize negative emotional manifestations, such as depression ("F3"), emotional lability ("F11"), shyness ("F8"), neuroticism ("F1"), irritability ("F4"), spontaneous aggression ("F2"). It is important here that the values of "F3" and "F11", which have the most significant factor influence, in the period from 13 to 14 years decrease to the limits of average severity. This factor was called the "reduction of negative emotional manifestations". The second factor (13.97%) included: the integrative parameter of emotional maturity ("EZ"), indicators of empathy ("Em"), and the manifestation of its signs on personal ("IEm") and interpersonal ("EEm") levels, and also indicators that characterize the intensity of neurotism ("N") and extraversion ("E"). The content of this factor called "empathy" points to the close relationship between the development of empathy and emotional maturity in general with extraversion and neurotism.

The third factor (13.84%) called "social activity", consists of indicators that characterize the level of extra-introversion ("F10"), comradeship ("F5"), masculinity ("F12"), reactive aggression ("F7"), balance ("F6") and openness ("F9"). The fourth factor (11.86%) combines indicators that determine the level of expressiveness ("Ex") and its manifestation at the personal ("IEx") and interpersonal ("EEx") levels, as well as an indicator that characterizes personal self-esteem ("SE"). This factor can be called "emotional expressiveness". Its content indicates the connection between this component of emotional maturity and adequate self-esteem. The fifth factor (10.01%) combines such indicators as "S" with factor weight (0.85), signs "IS" (0.89) and "ES" (0.51). This factor is named "emotional self-regulation".

The presence of such a picture of the factor distribution allows us to assume that emotional maturity can not be considered as a leading in the formation of the emotional sphere of the personality of 14-year-old children, but it is a fairly integral and orderly formation. As in the previous age groups, empathy dominates in the formation of emotional maturity of the personality.

In the group of **15-year-olds**, the integrative parameter "EZ" also demonstrates significant relations (probability level - $p < 0.01$) with indicators of emotional expressiveness ("Ex"), emotional self-regulation ("S") and empathy "Em", as well as with subscales that characterize the signs of their manifestation at personal and interpersonal levels.

The indicator "Ex", in its turn, correlates with the signs "IEx" (r = 0.719), "EEx" (r = 0.734), indicator "Em" (r = 0.478), and the signs "IEm" (r = 0.386) and "EEm" (r = 0.376) at the level of not less than (p <0.01). Indicator "S" is associated with the signs "IS" (r = 0.773; p <0.01) and "ES" (r = 0.829; p <0.01), as well as with "Em" (r = 0.309, p <0.05). The indicator "Em" shows correlations with the characteristics of "IEm" (r = 0.723; p <0.01), "EEm" (r = 0.851; p <0.01), "IEx" (r = 0.398; p <0.01), "EEx" (r = 0.298; p <0.05) and "ES" (r = 0.341; p <0.05).

There is a connection between some features of emotional maturity. According to these data, the relationship between the components of emotional maturity and the levels of their manifestation in the group of 15-year-olds is less close than in the previous group. The nature of this connection indicates the special role of empathy, which unites other components and their characteristics.

The in-depth factor analysis conducted separately for indicators of the emotional maturity of the individual revealed 3 factors in its structure. The integrative parameter "EZ" significantly correlates with each of these factors (see Figure 3.5.5).

The first factor includes indicator "Em", signs "IEm" and "IEx". In our opinion, the content of the factor called "empathy" indicates that the formation of empathy, namely the ability to understand the emotional state of a partner, occurs in interaction with the natural expressiveness of a person.

The second factor contains indicator "S" and signs that reflect the expressiveness of personal and interpersonal levels of its manifestation; it corresponds to the content of the component "emotional self-regulation".

The third factor includes indicators "EEx", "Ex" and "EEm". The factor "emotional expressiveness" at this age reflects the relationship between the ability to adequately express emotions in facial expressions, gestures, postures, movements and the ability to use empathy to increase the efficiency of communication.

Further examination of the results of correlation analysis allowed the establishment of a fairly wide range of relationships between indicators of emotional maturity and emotionally specific features.

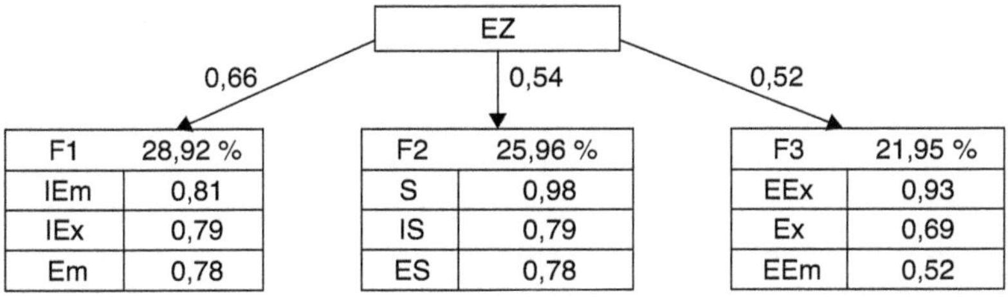

FIGURE 3.5.5 The structure of emotional maturity in the group of children aged 15 (7 rotations).

First, the complex created around the indicator "F5" (comradeship) significantly correlates with the integrative parameter "EZ" ($r = 0.646$), indicators "Ex" ($r = 0.539$), "S" ($r = 0.376$) and "Em" ($r = 0.542$) and the signs "EEx" ($r = 0.587$), "ES" ($r = 0.484$) and "EEm" ($r = 0.533$) at the level of probability ($p < 0.01$) and also with "IEm" ($r = 0.301$; $p < 0.05$). Second, the complex which is formed around the indicator "F10" (extra-introversion), is also associated with "EZ" ($r = 0.495$), "Ex" ($r = 0.444$), "Em" ($r = 0.429$), "EEx" ($r = 0.433$), "EEm" ($r = 0.388$) at the correlation level ($p < 0.01$), and with "ES" ($r = 0.303$) and "IEm" ($r = 0.283$) at the level ($p < 0.05$).

Third, it is a complex around the indicator "SE" (self-esteem), which correlates with "EZ" ($r = 0.305$), "Em" ($r = 0.284$), "ES" ($r = 0.333$) and "IEm" ($r = 0.316$) at the level ($p < 0.05$), and with the indicator "S" ($r = 0.373$; $p < 0.01$). Fourth, the complex forms around indicator "E" (extra-introversion), which has significant links with "EZ" ($r = 0.443$), "Ex" ($r = 0.422$) and "EEx" ($r = 0.415$), "ES" ($r = 0.478$) on a correlational level ($p < 0.01$), and with "S" ($r = 0.369$) at the level ($p < 0.05$).

Proceeding from the examined data, we can conclude that the formation of emotional maturity of 15-year-olds is significantly associated with such personal characteristics as extroversion, camaraderie and activity in communication.

According to the in-depth results of factor analysis conducted in a group of 15-year-old adolescents, 5 factors were identified, each of which has only one pole. The first factor (18.13%) combines indicators that characterize such personal manifestations as emotional lability ("F11"), depression ("F3"), neurotism ("N"), shyness ("F8"), neuroticism ("F1"), openness ("F9") and spontaneous aggressiveness ("F2"). The factor called "negative emotional manifestations", as in most groups of adolescents, occupies a significant place in the overall distribution of personality traits.

The second factor (17.04%) included indicators that determine: masculinity ("F12"), extroversion ("F10" and "E"), reactive aggression ("F7"), camaraderie ("F5") and steadiness ("F6"). The factor called "masculinity" indicates that children with a masculine type of mental activity are more sociable, active, optimistic, self-confident and balanced. The third factor (12.64%) – "empathy" – contains empathy index ("Em") and manifestations of its signs at personal ("IEm") and interpersonal ("EEm") levels, the integrative parameter of emotional maturity ("EZ"), as well as the indicator ("SE"), which reflects the level of adequacy of self-esteem of examined persons.

The fourth factor is represented by indicators that characterize the formation of emotional self-regulation "S", and the manifestation of its signs on the personal "IS" and interpersonal "ES" levels. This factor is what we called "emotional self-regulation". The fifth factor (10.44%) – "emotional expressiveness" – combines indicators that determine the level of expressiveness ("Ex") and its manifestation at personal ("IEx") and interpersonal ("EEx") levels.

The nature of the factor distribution reveals that in adolescents aged 15 years emotional maturity is quite separate from other emotionality and personality traits. The formation of its components occurs independently, isolated from one another. Empathy remains a property that integrates other components and signs of emotional maturity.

The previous examination of the results of correlations in a group of **16-year-olds** showed that the integrative parameter "EZ" has a significant connection with indicators of emotional expressiveness ("Ex"), emotional self-regulation ("S") and empathy ("Em"), as well as with "IEx", "EEx", "IS", "ES" and "EEm" at the level ($p < 0.01$).

Regarding the indicators that characterize the components of emotional maturity, the correlation is observed only between "Ex" and "S" ($r = 0.688$; $p < 0.01$). Correlations of the "Ex" indicator with the signs "IEx" ($r = 0.748$), "EEx" ($r = 0.800$), "IS" ($r = 0.400$), "ES" ($r = 0.669$) are probable at the level of ($p < 0.01$), and with "EEm" at ($r = 0.321$; $p < 0.05$). The indicator "S" shows correlations with the signs "IS" ($r = 0.741$), "ES" ($r = 0.843$), "IEx" ($r = 0.610$) and "EEx" ($r = 0.465$) at the level ($p < 0.01$), and the indicator "Em" shows correlations only with the signs "IEm" ($r = 0.776$) and "EEm" ($r = 0.714$).

The obtained results allow us to assume that the "empathy" component is becoming more and more intensive at this age. For its part, emotional self-regulation, the level of which level slightly decreases in adolescents at the age of 16 years, is closely related to emotional expressiveness. The in-depth factor analysis clarifies this relationship (see Figure 3.5.6).

The analysis of the factor structure showed that the indicator "S" is closely integrated with such scales as "IS" and "IEx" in the first factor. The second factor is represented by the indicators "EEx", "Ex" and "ES". The third factor contains indicators "Em", "IEm" and "EEm". This can be interpreted as a priority of changes in the organization of internal emotional activity at this age. In turn, the indicators representing the content of the second factor at the age of 16 years decrease to some extent, i.e. the external manifestation of emotionality and self-regulation becomes weaker.

Beginning with the examination of individual correlates of emotional maturity indicators in 16-year-olds, we can notice that the correlation dependencies have a moderate character here.

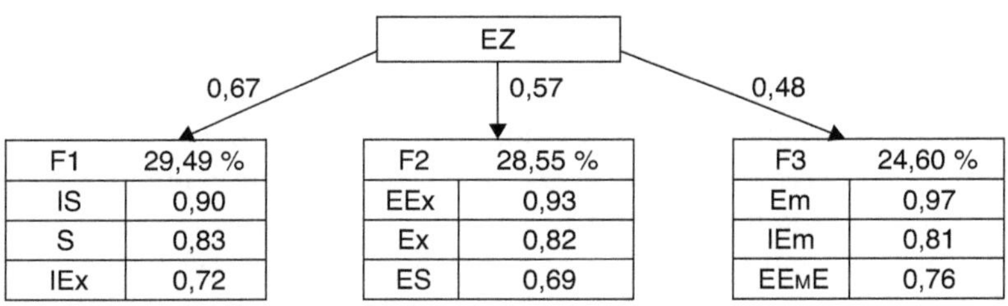

FIGURE 3.5.6 The structure of emotional maturity in the group of children aged 16 (5 rotations).

Only the following correlations are reliable at a sufficient level of significance ($p < 0.05$): between the signs of "IEx (introexpressiveness) and indicators "F1" (neuroticism) and "F3" (depressivity); signs of "EEx" (extraexpressiveness) and indicator self-esteem ("SE"); signs of "ES" (extra-self-regulation) and indicators "F5" (sociability) and "F9" (openness).

These interrelations indicate that the involuntary manifestation of emotions at the age of sixteen is often influenced by neurotic and depressive states. Emotional expressiveness, which is of an arbitrary, purposeful nature, develops due to the increase in self-esteem which is typical for young people of this age. And the ability to regulate other people's emotions deteriorates with a decrease in the level of camaraderie and the emergence of some secrecy in the relationship.

The factor structure that reflects the interrelation of indicators of emotional maturity and the personal qualities of those surveyed in the group of 16-year-olds, differs in some respects from the previous ones, indicating significant changes in the formation of the emotional sphere in general. The analysis procedure allowed us to identify 4 factors that have a significant factor weight.

The first factor (20.83%) combines indicators that characterize the integrative parameter of emotional maturity ("EZ"), emotional expressiveness ("Ex"), self-regulation ("S"), and its manifestation on personal ("IEx" and "IS") and interpersonal ("EEx" and "ES") levels. This factor is called "emotional maturity". The second factor (13.46%) called "empathy" is bipolar. On the first pole are concentrated the indicator "Em" with factor weight (0.96), the signs "EEm" – (0.77) and "IEm" – (0.75). On the other pole is the indicator "F3" with a factor weight (–0.51). The content of this factor confirms the separation of empathy from other components of emotional maturity, as well as the importance of its formation for the reduction of signs of depression in the emotional state and behavior of 16-year-olds.

The third factor (13.01%) also has two poles. The first has the indices "F12" with factor weight (0.65), "SE" (0.63) and "F5" (0.58). On the second, indicator for "F8" with factor weight is (–0.60), and for "F1", it is (–0.55). The factor called "masculinity" allows us to make assumptions about a direct connection between the type of mental activity with self-esteem and companionship, and implicit with shyness and neuroticism. The fourth factor (11.08%) is bipolar. The first pole is represented by indicators that characterize openness ("F9"), emotional lability ("F11"), spontaneous aggression ("F2") and extravertedness ("F10"). On the other pole, the indicator "F6" with a factor weight (−0.61), determines the level of equilibrium. The factor called "openness" characterizes the decrease in the desire for a reliable, open relationship with the people involved at the age of 16, which is associated with a decrease in emotional lability, impulsivity and a slight increase in equilibrium, and also depends on extra-introversion.

The obtained results of correlation and factor analysis allowed us to conclude that 16-year-olds acquire significant changes in both the structure of emotional maturity and its participation in the formation of the emotional and personal sphere in general. Thus, in contrast to the previous years, there is a decrease in the importance of features associated with communicative activities, and the activation of the role of those involved in the organization of internal activities. This age feature can be explained by the development of reflection and the emergence of the desire to understand, first of all, oneself, and the decrease of impulsive tendencies in behavior, which is determined in the course of the personal research, and together with them the general communicative activity, invertedness in communication, and increased level of competence in everyday life situations.

The nature of the relationship between emotional maturity in **17-year-olds**, as in the previous group, is distinguished by the absence of close intercomponent relationships that are inherent in the emotional maturity of adolescents. However, hierarchical relations remain quite significant.

Thus, the integrative parameter "EZ" has a tight relationship with the indicators "Ex" ($r = 0.740$), "S" ($r = 0.530$), "Em" ($r = 0.764$), "IEx" ($r = 0.619$), "EEx" ($r = 0.580$), "IS" ($r = 0.421$), "ES" ($r = 0.410$), "IEm" ($r = 0.681$) and "EEm" ($r = 0.505$). Correlations are also valid for the indicator "Ex" with the signs "IEx" ($r = 0.828$), "EEx" ($r = 0.795$) and "IEm" ($r = 0.523$); indicators "S" with signs "IS" ($r = 0.772$) and "EC" ($r = 0.794$); and indicators "Em" with "IEm" ($r = 0.824$), and "EEm" ($r = 0.749$) and "IEx" ($r = 0.374$). These correlations are reliable at the level ($p <0.01$).

Regarding intercomponent relations, they are inherent only to the indicators "Ex" and "Em" ($r = 0.451$; $p <0.01$), as well as to their signs "IEx" and "IEm" ($r = 0.547$; $p <0.01$).

The obtained results allow us to assume that the formation of emotional self-regulation at this age is self-dependent. In turn, emotional expressiveness and empathy are closely related, primarily due to the interaction of personal levels of manifestation of these characteristics.

The in-depth factor analysis of emotional maturity in 17-year-olds also differs from the previous ones, primarily in that it consists of four factors (see Figure 3.5.7).

The first factor is represented by indicators that characterize emotional self-regulation ("S") and the levels of its manifestation. The second factor contains signs of the personal level of emotional expressiveness ("IEx") and empathy

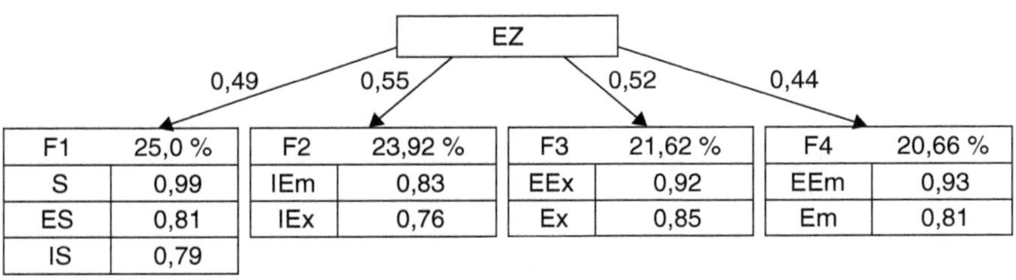

FIGURE 3.5.7 The structure of emotional maturity in the group of 17-year-olds (7 rotations).

("IEm"), it can be called the "emotional sensitivity" factor. The third and fourth factors included indicators that characterize the general emotional expressiveness ("Ex") and empathy ("Em") and their signs at the interpersonal level of manifestation. These factors we call "emotional expressiveness" and "empathy".

Such features of the factor distribution indicate that the leading role in the formation of emotional maturity in 17-year-olds plays the desire to improve skills of self-regulation of own emotions and regulation of emotional states of other people. In addition, at this age occurs the formation of the properties responsible for the adequacy of perception of nonverbal information about other people's emotions, formation of compassion and empathy, which requires increased expression of own feelings.

Further consideration of correlations in the group of 17-year-olds allowed us to identify a fairly large set of indicators associated with signs of the interpersonal level of emotional self-regulation, and this relationship is mostly negative.

These are "F1" (neuroticism), "F3" (depression), "F8" (shyness) and "N" (neurotism). Indicators "F10" and "E" (extra-introversion) show direct correlations with "ES". Moreover, the following significant correlations were found: "Ex" with "F7" (reactive aggression); "S" with "F8" (shyness), "E" (extra-introversion) and "N" (neurotism); "Em" with "N" (neurotism) and some others. The integrative parameter "EZ" has no significant correlations with the diagnosed indicators of the emotional and personal sphere.

The identified peculiarities of the interrelationship indicate that the intensive development of the interpersonal level of emotional self-regulation is based on extraversion and is complicated by such negative emotional and personal traits as neuroticism, depression, shyness and neurotism. In turn, empathy at high neurotism develops normally.

The procedure of data reduction allowed us to identify 7 factors, 4 of which have a significant weight. The first factor (17.90%) – "emotional maturity" – includes the integrative parameter of emotional maturity ("EZ"), indicators of empathy ("Em"), emotional expressiveness ("Ex"), and their manifestation on the personal ("IEx" and "IEm") and interpersonal ("EEx" and "EEm") levels. The second factor (15.93%) corresponds to a very widespread complex, which we found in groups of 11-, 13- and 15-year-olds and called "negative emotional manifestations". It includes indicators that characterize emotional lability ("F11"), depression ("F3"), irritability ("F4"), neurotism ("N"), neuroticism ("F1"), openness ("F9"), spontaneous aggression: ("F2").

The third factor (15.75%) has two poles. The first one focuses on indicators that determine extra- or introversion ("F10" and "E"), masculinity or feminism ("F12"), as well as the level of comradeship ("F5"), reactive aggression ("F7") and self-esteem ("SE"). At the other pole is the factor "F8" with a factor weight (−0.54), which characterizes shyness. The factor called "activity" reflects the interrelation of activity in social contact with masculinity, reactive aggression and self-esteem.

The fourth factor (10.13%) consists of such indicators as "IS" with factor weight (0.83), "S" (0.77) and "ES" (0.46). This is definitely a factor of "self-regulation". As we can see, in 17-year-olds it occupies a special place in the structure of emotional and personal characteristics.

A preliminary correlational analysis of indicators that characterize the emotional maturity of young people **aged 18–23** were found at a high level of reliability ($p < 0.01$), which does not distinguish young adults from the representatives of previously examined groups. The same, as for the last two groups, is the characteristic of weakening intercomponent relationships while maintaining intensive hierarchical correlations. Among specific features of the relationship should be noted the following correlations: indicator "S" and signs "EEm" ($r = 0.379$), indicator "Em" and signs "ES" ($r = 0.287$), as well as between the signs "ES" and "EEm" ($r = 0.457$).

The presented data allow us to ascertain that the links between the components of emotional maturity become weaker with age. However, for young people aged 18–23 years, the interconnection between the ability to regulate other people's emotional states and the ability to use empathic abilities in communication is characteristic.

Factor analysis, conducted separately for indicators of emotional maturity, allows us to clarify the nature of this relationship (see Figure 3.5.8).

As can be seen in the figure, the first factor combines indicators "S", "ES", "IS" and "EEm". This factor we may call "emotional self-regulation", its content indicates that at the age of 18–23 years emotional maturity occurs primarily due to improved self-regulation and strengthening of its connection with the acquisition of the ability to use empathy in communication.

The second factor consists of the indicators "Ex", "IEx" and "EEx", the content of which corresponds to the component "emotional expressiveness". The third factor includes indicators "Em" and "IEm", which by its content could be called "empathy". The integrative parameter "EZ" significantly correlates with each of these factors.

The correlation analysis allows us to establish interrelations of the integrative parameter "EZ", which characterizes emotional maturity, with the indicators

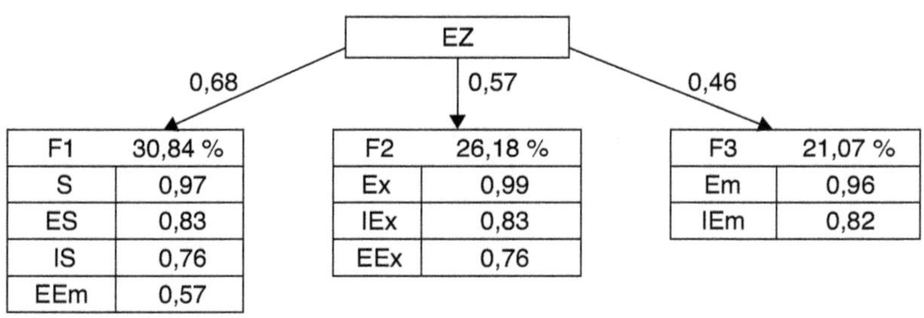

FIGURE 3.5.8 The structure of emotional maturity in the group of young men aged 18–23 (5 rotations).

"E" and "F10" (extra-introversion). A rather wide complex of interrelations is observed in the indicator "IS", namely, it is negatively correlates with "F8" (shyness), and directly with "E", "F10" (extra-introversion), "F5" (comradeship), "F7" (reactive aggression). In addition, a number of individual correlations have been also identified.

Proceeding from the examined data, we can conclude that in young people aged 18–23, the formation of emotional maturity in general and emotional self-regulation in particular is significantly connected with the level of their extraversion and camaraderie. Emotional expressiveness is significantly influenced by neurotism.

The closest ties with the emotional and personal sphere at this age are observed in the signs of personal manifestation of self-regulation, which testifies to the dependence on the ability to control own emotions on the level of comradeship, extravertedness, masculinity and shyness. Moreover, the latter trait negatively affects the formation of these abilities.

Further on, in order to simplify the description of correlations, a factor analysis was carried out, which resulted in 5 factors being determined. Although the first three of them demonstrated the highest weight, we will consider them all, because the last two contain indicators of emotional maturity of the personality.

The first factor (22.24%) has two poles. One concentrates indicators of extra- or introversion ("F10"), masculinity or feminism ("F12"), as well as the level of comradeship ("F5"), balance ("F6") and reactive aggression ("F7"). The others are "F1", with factor weight (−0.67), which characterizes neuroticism, and "F8" (−0.60), which characterizes shyness. This factor called "activity", reflects the interrelation of activity in social contacts with masculinity, reactive aggression and the negative impact on the activity of neurotism and shyness.

The second factor (18.25%) has only one pole, it includes indicators characterizing emotional self-regulation ("S") and levels of its manifestation ("ES" and "IS"), signs of the interpersonal level of empathy "EEm", and also extra-introversion ("E"). It was called the factor of "emotional self-regulation", which characterizes the leading role in its formation of the ability to influence the emotional state of other people, using empathic abilities in communication, as well as the connection of these skills with extraversion.

The third factor (15.34%) comprises indicators that characterize such personal manifestations as irritability ("F4"), depressiveness ("F3"), emotional lability ("F11"), openness ("F9"), neurotism ("N") and spontaneous aggression ("F2"). The factor called "negative emotional manifestations", as in most previous groups, conveys negative emotional factors of impulsive behavior. As seen, this age group occupies a less significant position in the structure of the emotional and personal sphere than in many younger groups.

The fourth factor (11.61%) contains indicators "Ex" with factor weight (0.94), "IEx" (0.90) and "EEx" (0.56). As for its content, it corresponds to the component of "emotional expressiveness".

The fifth factor (8.70%) consists of two indicators, "Em" with factor weight (0.82) and "IEm" with factor weight (0.90). It conveys the meaning of the "empathy" component.

The identified peculiarities of the structural interconnections allow us to conclude that at 18–23 years of age, there is a continuation of the loosening of the links between the components of emotional maturity and the complexes of interactions with extraversion and camaraderie typical for the previous groups are preserved.

Summarizing the data of correlation and factor analyses allowed us to distinguish:

Firstly, all the age groups we studied are characterized by a significant intensity of interrelations between the integrative parameter that characterizes emotional maturity, and its components and signs. However, the intensity of intercomponent relationships has certain age dynamics – they are almost absent in the pre-teenage period (11–12 years), which can be explained by their immaturity; then up to the age of 14 these connections strengthen, gaining maximum integration of the structure due to the interaction of personal and interpersonal components; then the weakening occurs again, which characterizes the independence and autonomy of the further formation of each component.

Secondly, the tendency to the interconnection of the indicator that characterizes emotional expressiveness with signs of interpersonal levels of emotional maturity observed at the age of 13, 14 and 15 years, and the indicator that characterizes empathy with signs of personal level (13 and 15 years) was noted. This trend indicates that the formation of abilities that ensure the adequacy of emotional regulation of the internal state is due to the development of empathy. In turn, the formation of abilities to adequately regulate emotions in communication depends on the level of expressiveness.

Thirdly, it was found that the integrative parameter describing emotional maturity is most closely connected with the empathy index at the age of 11, 12, 14 and 15 years, with the index of emotional self-regulation at the ages 16, 17 and 18–23, and with the index of emotional expressiveness at the age of 13. These data indicate that emotional maturity is ensured primarily through empathy in adolescence, and emotional self-regulation is dominant in young adulthood.

Fourthly, in all age groups we studied, the components of emotional maturity are associated with extraversion and camaraderie, at the age of 12 and 13, balance is significant in the development of emotional maturity, and at 14, 15 and 16 years – personal self-esteem. Shyness at 11, 17 and 18–23 years, irritability at 12 and 13 years, and neuroticism at 16, 17 and 18–23 years have a negative impact on the formation of components of emotional maturity.

Fifthly, at different periods of age emotional maturity takes different weights in the structure of emotional and personal characteristics. Thus, at the age of

11, 14 and 15 years it is less significant than the characteristics of negative emotional manifestations, at 12 and 18–23 years its values outweigh the characteristics of personality activity. Emotional maturity is most important at the age of 13, 16 and 17.

3.5.4 Disparities in the values of indicators of emotional maturity, depending on subjects' gender

Starting with the comparison of males and females in terms of emotional maturity, we proceeded from the data of some authors (e.g. Vasiliev et al., 1997; Kagan, 2000; Kovalev, 1996; Melnichuk, 2003; Prichozhan, 2000; Sukhanova, 2001; Chomskaya, Batova, 1992), who pointed to certain differences in the emotional sphere of the representatives of the male and female constitution. However, data regarding gender differences in the formation of characteristics of emotional maturity, are of limited nature.

A review of the results of our own research showed that in some cases the differences exist only at the level of tendencies. For their part, some indicators show considerable variability in many age groups, which indicates a strong dependence of some features on the gender of the tested.

Thus, the comparison of individual data according to the "Ex" indicator, revealed some differences between the boys and girls. In particular, girls are more likely to show high scores on the "Ex" at the ages of 11, 12, 13, 15 and 17 years. The average values also prevail in the groups of girls at the age of 11 by 0.58 points, at the age of 12 by 0.9 points, at 14 by 0.2 points, at 15 years by 0.89 points, at 16 by 0.08 points, at the age of 17 by 0.96 points, and in groups of boys at the age of 13 by 0.18 points and at 18–23 years by 0.21 points. However, a statistical verification of the significance of these differences revealed their lack of validity (see Appendix 5, Table 3.5.15).

The intensity of "IEx" attributes in general has the same features of gender differences as "Ex" itself; namely, at the age of 11, 12, 15 and 17 years, high scores are more often received by girls.

However, the maximum and minimum values in the groups of boys and girls do not differ. Comparison of average scores showed that they are higher in the groups of girls at age of 11 years by 0.06 points, at 12 years by 0.28 points, at 14 years by 0.05 points, at 15 years by 0.52 points, at 16 years by 0.13 points, at 17 years by 0.96 points, and in groups of boys at age of 13 years by 0.36 points, and in 18–23 years by 0.25 points. Only differences in the group of 17 years are statistically valid, where $t = 2.75$, $p < 0.01$. As can be seen from the table, the expressiveness of "EEx" attributes in the representatives of different genders does not differ significantly.

The data obtained allow us to assert that in general the formation of emotional expression does not depend on gender, although there is some tendency for girls to show more pronounced emotions in facial expressions, intonations and gestures than boys. This tendency gains significant value only in the involuntary manifestation of emotional expressiveness at 17 years.

According to the indicator "S", the highest individual valuations are more frequent in boys at 13, 14, 16 and 18–23 years, and in girls at 11 and 17 years. In some cases, the indicators of the central tendency also differ significantly. Thus, at the age of 14, the assessment most frequently encountered in the sample (Mo) is 9 points for boys and only 6 points for girls, the difference between mods is 3 points for boys aged 16 and 17, and at the age 18–23, 2 points.

The comparison of the average values of the indicator "S" showed that they are higher in the groups of girls at 11 years by 1 point and at the age of 15 years by 0.44 points (see Table 3.5.16).

In turn, this index exceeds in groups of boys at 12 years by 0.03 points, at 13 years by 0.57 points, at 14 years by 1.07 points, at 16 years by 0.13 points, at 17 years by 0.5 points and in 18–23 years by 0.97 points. Only the differences between the groups at 14 years old, where $t = 2.43$, $p < 0.05$, and at 18–23 years, where $t = 2.20$, $p < 0.05$ are statistically valid. The indicator that characterizes the personal level of emotional self-regulation ("IS") also has some gender differences. Individual assessments are slightly higher for girls aged 11 and 17, and for boys aged 12, 13, 14 and 18–23. Average values in the groups of boys at the age of 13 are higher by 0.7 points, at 14 years by 0.53 points, at 18–23 years by 0.52 points, and in the groups of girls at 11 years by 0.46 points. In the rest of the age groups, the difference between the average scores of boys and girls is almost non-existent.

TABLE 3.5.16 Gender differences in the severity of indicators of emotional self-regulation

Age	*Statistical index*	*Index; gender*					
		S		*IS*		*ES*	
		male	*female*	*male*	*female*	*male*	*female*
11 y.o.	X	6.50	7.50	2.67	3.13	3.83	4.38
	T	1.69		1.06		1.31	
12 y.o.	X	6.53	6.50	2.73	2.75	3.80	3.75
	T	0.03		0.02		0.09	
13 y.o.	X	6.52	5.95	2.80	2.10	3.72	3.85
	T	1.09		2.11*		0.41	
14 y.o.	X	7.64	6.57	3.53	3.00	4.11	3.57
	T	2.43*		2.14*		1.71	
15 y.o.	X	6.85	7.29	2.92	2.87	3.92	4.42
	T	0.73		0.16		1.12	
16 y.o.	X	6.63	6.50	2.84	2.82	3.79	3.68
	T	0.24		0.08		0.28	
17 y.o.	X	7.38	6.88	2.92	3.08	4.50	4.00
	T	0.95		0.52		1.52	
18–23 y.o.	X	8.38	7.42	3.62	3.10	4.76	4.33
	T	2.20*		1.90		1.59	

Statistical verification showed that differences are likely in the groups of 13-year-olds, where t = 2.11, $p < 0.05$, and 14-year-olds, where t = 2.14, $p < 0.05$. Individual data and average values of the "ES" indicator in the group of girls are higher at the age of 11, 13 and 15. In boys, they predominate at 14, 17 and 18–23 years. However, statistically reliable discrepancies in the expressiveness of these features between the groups we studied have not been found.

These data indicate that in early adolescence (11 years) girls' ability to regulate their own emotions and ability to influence the behavior of others is slightly higher than that of boys. At the end of this period, at the age of 13–14, boys develop more emotional self-regulation, especially the ability to control emotions. Young men aged 18–23 also have a greater formation of emotional self-regulation than young women of this age.

When comparing individual data by the "Em" index, the following differences were established between boys and girls – the latter have higher scores at the ages of 12, 14, 15, 17 and 18–23. Average values in these age groups are also higher in girls, namely: at 12 years by 2.26 points, at 14 years by 0.92 points, at 15 years by 0.8 points, at 17 years by 0.92 points, and at 18–23 years by 0.73 points. In other age groups, there is a slight increase in average scores in the boys' samples (see Table 3.5.17).

Statistically confirmed were gender differences in groups of 14-year-olds, where t = 2.8, $p < 0.01$, 15 years, where t = 2.4, $p < 0.05$, 17-year-olds, where t = 3, $p < 0.01$, and 18–23-year-olds, where t = 2.91, $p < 0.01$. Individual values of the indicator that characterizes the interpersonal level of empathy ("EEm") are

TABLE 3.5.17 Gender differences in the severity of indicators of empathy

Age	*Statistical index*	*Index; gender*					
		Em		*IEm*		*EEm*	
		male	*female*	*Male*	*female*	*male*	*female*
11 y.o.	X	7.17	7.31	3.83	3.88	3.33	3.19
	t	0.24		0.10		0.38	
12 y.o.	X	5.87	8.13	3.13	4.13	2.73	4.00
	t	2.22*		1.88		2.09*	
13 y.o.	X	6.52	6.50	3.44	3.10	3.08	3.35
	t	0.04		0.97		0.69	
14 y.o.	X	6.08	7.00	3.06	3.76	3.03	3.24
	t	1.83		2.80**		0.57	
15 y.o.	X	6.62	7.42	3.08	4.05	3.54	3.37
	t	0.97		2.40*		0.28	
16 y.o.	X	8.00	7.82	4.26	4.05	3.95	3.73
	t	0.31		0.62		0.56	
17 y.o.	X	7.25	8.17	3.33	4.33	3.92	3.83
	t	1.78		3.00**		0.27	
18–23 y.o.	X	8.27	9.00	3.76	4.59	4.51	4.41
	t	1.92		2.91**		0.39	

more often higher in boys aged 14, 15, 16, 17 and 18–23 years. Only the samples of 12 and 13-year-old girls demonstrate higher scores. When comparing the average values in the groups of representatives of different gender, we obtained the same results: namely, for boys aged 14 years, the average score is higher by 0.21 points, at 15 years by 0.17 points, at 16 years by 0.22 points, at 17 years by 0.09 points, at 18–23 years by 0.1 points, and for girls of 12 years old it is higher by 1.27 points, and at 13 years by 0.29 points. However, only differences at 12 years old are statistically valid, where $t = 2.09$, $p < 0.05$.

Based on the studied data, we can conclude that the formation of empathy in different genders does not occur in the same way: in general, the ability to empathize in girls is formed slightly higher than in boys, much higher aged girls develop the ability for compassion and sympathy for another person, understanding the motives of their behavior, while boys tend to overdevelop the ability to use such information in communication.

Comparison of individual data and average values of the integrative parameter "EZ" showed that there are small differences between boys and girls in their expressiveness, but they do not reach reliable values (see Table 3.5.18).

The data in the table show that the formation of emotional maturity in general does not depend on the gender of a person.

Summarizing the data, we can conclude that the formation of emotional maturity does not depend on gender. However, the data obtained during the research allows us to assume that males and females choose different ways to achieve the adequacy of emotional reactions. Thus, girls are the most active in forming skills for sympathy and compassion, understanding of the emotional state and motives of the communication partner's behavior. Boys are more successful in forming abilities to regulate emotions.

3.5.5 Relationships between emotional maturity indicators and personality traits of the respondents, depending on the gender

The analysis of the correlation structure of emotional maturity in **11-year-old** boys showed that it is composed of weakly related indicators. Thus, the integrative parameter "EZ" has significant correlations only with the indicators "S" ($r = 0.756$; $p < 0.01$) and "Em" ($r = 0.668$; $p < 0.05$), as well as with the subscales characterizing attributes "IEx" ($r = 0.732$; $p < 0.01$), "ES" ($r = 0.785$; $p < 0.01$) and "EEm" ($r = 0.671$; $p < 0.05$). Moreover, were found the correlations that reflect hierarchical relations of the indicator "Ex" with attributes of "EEx" ($r = 0.703$; $p < 0.05$), the indicator "S" with attributes of "IS" ($r = 0.783$; $p < 0.01$) and "ES" ($r = 0.643$; $p < 0.01$), and indicators "Em" with attributes "IEm" ($r = 0.839$; $p < 0.01$) and "EEm" ($r = 0.693$; $p < 0.05$). Intercomponent relationships are presented only between attributes of "ES" and "EEm" ($r = 0.706$; $p < 0.05$).

The interrelations between the indicators that characterize emotional maturity and other emotionally specific properties are of particular interest due to their small number. Among the important correlations, first of all, it is necessary to note the links of the indicator "F11" with the integrative parameter "EZ"

TABLE 3.5.18 Gender differences in the expressiveness of the integrative parameter of emotional maturity of the individual

Statistical index	*Age, gender*													
	11 years		*12 years*		*13 years*		*14 years*		*15 years*		*16 years*		*17 years*		*18–23 years*	
	male	*fem*	*male*	*fem*	*male*	*fem*	*male*	*fem*	*male*	*fem*	*male*	*fem*	*male*	*fem*	*male*	*fem*
X	19.83	21.56	19	22.13	19.72	18.95	19.67	19.71	19.46	21.61	21.11	20.86	20.83	22.21	24.68	24.22
t	1.53		1.38		0.62		0.04		1.27		0.20		1.25		0.57	

(r = 0.636; p <0.05), the indicator "Em" (r = 0.855; p <0.01) and with attributes of "IEm" (r = 0.717; p <0.01) and "EEm" (r = 0.593; p <0.05). Significant correlations between some signs of emotional maturity with personality traits have also been identified.

The observed peculiarities of emotional maturity indicators correlation in the group of 11-year-old boys indicate weak interrelations both within the structure of emotional maturity itself and the personality traits of the examined persons. Specific for the group being analyzed is the relationship between empathy and emotional maturity with emotional lability.

Moving on to the analysis of the correlation structure of emotional maturity in 11-year-old girls, we note that the hierarchical links of the integrative parameter "EZ" with the components of emotional maturity and the levels of their manifestation are tighter than in the group of boys. Examination of intercomponent relations shows that, as in the group of boys, they have limited character and are manifested only in the correlations of the indicator "S" with attributes "IEm" (r = 0.533; p <0.05).

The strongest relationship with personal characteristics is observed in the indicator "IS". It significantly correlates with "F2" (r = −0.521), "F3" (r = −0.535), "F8" (r = −0.618) at the level (p <0.05), and also with "F9" (r = −0.678), "F11" (r = −0.684) and "E" (r = 0.793) at the level (p <0.01). Such character and direction of interconnection testify about the negative impact on the formation of the ability to regulate own emotions of depressiveness, shyness, spontaneous aggression and emotional lability, as well as the direct dependence of this ability on the level of intro-extraversion.

Regarding the integrative parameter "EZ", 11-year-old girls have only negative connections with the indicators "F7" (r = −0.562) and "F8" (r = −0.542) at the level (p <0.05). Therefore, the formation of emotional maturity of 11-year-old girls is significantly hampered by their reactive aggressiveness and shyness. And this is reflected, above all, at the level of emotional self-regulation.

Comparison of correlations between indicators of emotional maturity in boys and girls of 11 years old showed that the most significant difference between the groups is observed in the indicators "IEm", where the correlation divergence coefficient (CDC) is 0.082 points, "EEx" (CDC = 0.071), "Ex" (CDC = 0.061) and "IS" (CDC = 0.057). The correlations of other indicators of emotional maturity in boys and girls are slightly less different.

These data indicate that in 11-year-old boys and girls the ability to understand the emotional state of other people, to adequately express their own emotions, and to regulate their emotional state is formed under the influence of various factors.

A more detailed study of these differences showed that in the indicator "IEm" they are defined by 13 others: "F11" (0.90), "F7" (0.80), "SE" (0.73), "F10" 0.72), "F8" (0.66), "F3" (0.65), "EEx" (0.63), "F9" (0.58), "Ex" (0.57), "F12" (0.57), "S" (0.53), etc. Particular attention should be paid to the discrepancies between the correlations of this characteristic and the indicator "S", where correlations have a high level of significance in girls, and not in boys, as well as "F9", "F11" and "SE", where correlations are significant only in the group of boys.

So, we can assert that despite the absence of gender differences in the expressiveness of the indicator that characterizes the ability to understand the emotional state of other people, its formation is influenced by different properties; namely in girls, it depends on the level of emotional self-regulation, and in boys, it is connected with inadequate self-esteem, emotional lability and openness in relationships.

Regarding the differences in the correlations of the indicator "EEx", they are defined in 12 correlations: with the indicators "N" (0.71), "F12" (0.64), "IEm" (0.63), "F4" (0.63), "F11" (0.59), "F10" (0.56), "F2" (0.55) and others. Among them are also indicators ("F2"), which in boys correlate with "EEx" at a high level of significance, and in girls are not associated with this feature. These data indicate that, unlike girls, in 11-year-old boys at the interpersonal level emotional expressiveness is associated with spontaneous aggression. Considering gender differences in the correlations of the indicator "Ex", we can recognize that they are similar to those in "EEx". Such deviations are determined by 10 indicators: "F1" (0.77), "N" (0.74), "F4" (0.74), "F10" (0.65), "F2" (0.61)), "SE" (0.58), "IEm" (0.57), "F8" (0.53) and others. The opposite relationship is found in the "F4" indicator, which significantly correlates with "Ex" in the group of girls, and in the group of boys, it has a small correlation with a negative sign. Thus, emotional expressiveness in girls is manifested in a shaky emotional state and is associated with a tendency to affective reactions.

Determination of deviations in the correlations of the indicator "IS" showed that they occur with 8 other ones: "E" (0.89), "F9" (0.71), "F5" (0.67), "F11" (0.62), "F1" (0.57), "F2" (0.57), etc. Particular attention should be paid to the discrepancies between the correlations of this feature with indicators "F2", "F9", "F11" and "E", where the correlations in girls have a high level of significance, but not in boys. These data testify to the above-mentioned specificity of interrelations of this feature in the group of girls.

A more detailed examination of the differences in correlations of the integrative parameter "EZ" showed that they differ slightly in the groups of boys and girls aged 11 years (CDC = 0.027). There are deviations in correlations with only 3 indicators: "F7" (0.53), "F8" (0.90), where in girls they have a high level of significance, and "F11" (0.80), where the correlation is significant only in boys. These data show that the formation of emotional maturity in 11-year-old boys and girls is influenced by different personality traits. Namely, in girls, it is associated with the lack of desire for domination, a non-aggressive attitude to the social environment and is hampered by shyness and self-doubt. In boys, the formation of emotional maturity is carried out under the significant influence of emotional lability, i.e. instability of emotional state, which is manifested in frequent mood swings, irritability, restlessness and lack of self-regulation.

The correlation analysis of indicators in the group of **12-year-old** boys showed that the integrative parameter "EZ" is more closely connected to the components of emotional maturity and attributes of their manifestation than in the previous group. There are also significant correlations of the "Ex" indicator with attributes "IEx" (r = 0.866), and "EEx" (r = 0.772) at the level of p <0.01, indicator "S" with attributes "IS" (r = 0.884), "ES" (r = 0.845) at the level of p <0.01, and "EEm" (r = 0.557; p <0.05), and the indicator "Em" with signs "IEm" (r = 0.893) and "EEm" (r = 0.913) at the level of p <0.01. These data indicate that the structure of emotional maturity in 12-year-old boys is more consistent than in previous age. As for the connections between the components of emotional maturity, they have not yet been formed.

Two correlation complexes have been established at the level of interrelations between indicators of emotional maturity and other emotional and personal properties. The first is formed by indicators "F1", "F5", "EZ" and "IS". The correlations of "F1" and "F5" are negative (r = −0.536; p <0.05). Accordingly, "F1" shows a negative relation with "EZ" (r = −0.579), "S" (r = −0.555) and "IS" (r = −0.588) at the level of p <0.05, and correlations of indicator "F5" with "EZ" and "IS" are positive. The second complex is formed by indicators "Em", "F3" and "F11". Here, the relation between "F3" and "F11" (r = 0.693; p 0.01) is positive, while in turn, each of them is negatively related to "Em".

The correlations of emotional maturity with personality traits in the group of 12-year-old boys indicate that the formation of emotional maturity, and in particular the ability to regulate emotions, depends on the balance between neuroticism and comradeship. In other words, high social activity spurs this process, while certain neuroticism, on the contrary, slows it down. Also, weak formation of empathy is connected with high depressivity and emotional lability.

Analyzing the correlation structure of emotional maturity in 12-year-old girls, we found that the hierarchical relationships of the integrative parameter of the EZ with components of emotional maturity and the levels of their manifestation are limited here, and significant correlations are only with "Ex" (r = 0.948; p <0.01), "Em" (r = 0.739; p <0.05), "EEx" (r = 0.838; p <0.01) and "IEm" (r = 0.746; p <0.05). However, the links between components of emotional maturity are slightly tighter than in the group of boys. Thus, the indicator "Ex" is significantly correlated with "Em" (r = 0.786; p <0.05) and "IEm" (r = 0.860; p <0.01), while attributes of "EEx" have probable correlations with "ES" (r = 0.732; p <0.05) and "IEm" (r = 0.755; p <0.05).

The established features of the correlation structure of emotional maturity indicators in the group of 12-year-old girls show that the formation of intercomponent relations in girls begins earlier than in boys, it is based on the intensive development of empathic abilities at this age, which is the basis for the formation of interpersonal levels of emotional expressiveness and emotional self-regulation.

Further analysis showed that indicators "F6" (r = 0.737) and "F10" (r = 0.756) have a significant connection with the integrative parameter "EZ". The indicator "F6", in its turn, correlates with "S" (r = 0.880), "IS" (r = 0.724), and "ES" (r = 0.739), and "F10" with "Ex" (r = 0.775) and "ES" (r = 0.808). Besides, indicator "S" has negative correlations with "F3" (r = −0.756) and "F8" (r = −0.790). Also, the correlations between some signs of emotional maturity with personality traits were found. The correlations indicate that such personality traits as balance and extroversion play crucial roles in the formation of emotional maturity in girls of 12 years of age. Namely, the success of the formation of emotional self-regulation depends on the first property, and emotional expressiveness depends on the second one. Moreover, excessive depressivity and shyness can inhibit the formation of emotional self-regulation.

The comparison of correlations of emotional maturity in boys and girls of 12 years old showed that a significant difference between groups is observed in the indicators "Em" (CDC = 0.081) and "S" (CDC = 0.070), "IS" (CDC = 0.057), "ES" (CDC = 0.076), "IEm" (CDC = 0.069), "EEm" (CDC = 0.062) and "EZ" (CDC = 0.061). Correlations of other indicators of emotional maturity in boys and girls are slightly less different (Table 2.3).

These data show that in 12-year-old boys and girls the formation of emotional maturity in general, as well as empathy and emotional self-regulation in particular, is influenced by various factors.

A more detailed analysis of these differences showed that in the indicator "Em" they are linked with 10 indicators: "F4" (1.10), "IEx" (0.90), "F2" (0.87), "Ex" 0.71), "F11" (0.70), "F12" (0.60), "F3" (0.51) and others. A similar picture is observed when analyzing the differences in "IEm" and "EEm" attributes. Particular attention should be paid to the discrepancies in correlations of these indicators with "F3" and "F11", where correlations have a high level of significance in boys and express a negative nature of the relationship, and not in girls. Otherwise, in "Ex" indicator correlations are significant only in the group of girls. These data confirm the previously identified characteristics of the correlation structure in the group and allow us to assume that very low empathy scores, found in 12-year-old boys in comparison to their female peers may be caused by high depressiveness, emotional lability, and the influence of other negative emotional and personal characteristics.

Regarding differences in the correlation links of the indicator "S", they are defined in 9 correlations: with indicators "F7" (0.82), "F8" (0.81), "F6" (0.78), "F12" (0.77), "F10" (0.61), "EEm" (0.60), "SE" (0.55) and others. Among them, there are also such indicators ("EEm") which correlate with "S" at a high level of reliability in boys, and not in girls. On the contrary, "F6", "F7" and "F8" indicators have significant correlations with "S" only in the group of girls. The attributes "IS" and "ES" in general have the same differences in correlation structures.

These data show that, unlike boys, 12-year-old girls develop emotional self-regulation under the influence of balance and reactive aggression, and are inhibited by excessive shyness. In boys, this component of emotional maturity is closely connected with the ability to use empathy in communication.

The determination of gender differences in the correlations of the integrative parameter "EZ" showed that they are observed in 8 indicators: "F4" (0.82), "F12" (0.73), "F6" (0.72), "F2" 0.70), "F7" (0.65), "F10" (0.60) and others. Particular attention should be paid to the discrepancies between correlations of the

"EZ" with the indicators "F4", "F6" and "F10", where girls have a high level of significance, and boys do not. Such data indicate that irritability, balance and extroversion are specific personality traits that affect girls' emotional maturity.

The analysis of the correlation structure of emotional maturity in a group of **13-year-old** boys showed the strengthening in both hierarchical and inter-component connections. Thus, the integrative parameter "EZ" has significant correlations with the indicators "Ex" (r = 0.826), "Em" (r = 0.818) and attributes "IEx" (r = 0.624), "EEx" (r = 0.724), "IEm "(r = 0.657), "EEm "(r = 0.598) at the level of $p < 0.01$, and also with the indicator" S "(r = 0.405) and the signs "ES "(r = 0.404) at the level of $p < 0.05$. Besides, the correlations that reflect hierarchical relationships of indicators "Ex", "S" and "Em" with attributes of personal and interpersonal levels of their manifestation were also revealed. Among the interrelations between components of emotional maturity, first of all, we should mention the correlations of signs "EEx" with "IEm" (r = 0.435; $p < 0.05$) and "EEm" (r = 0.683; $p < 0.01$), which cause corresponding correlations between the indicators "Ex" and "Em" (r = 0.713; $p < 0.01$).

The identified peculiarities of the correlation structure of emotional maturity indicators in the group of 13-year-old boys testify that the improvement of the ability to arbitrarily and purposefully express emotions according to the situation is due to the formation of empathic abilities.

Examination of interrelations between the indicators that characterize emotional maturity with other emotional and personal features allowed us to identify the following significant correlations: "Ex" with "F6" (r = 0.444) and "F10" (r = 0.412); indicator "S" with "F4" (r = 0.406) and "E" (r = 0.495), indicators "Em" with "F2" (r = 0.435), "F4" (r = 0.402) and "F6" r = 0.507), the integrative parameter "EZ" with "F2" (r = 0.401), "F4" (r = 0.560), "F6" (r = 0.433) and "E" (r = 0.568). Some important correlations of emotional maturity signs with the same personality traits have also been identified. According to such data, the peculiarities of emotional maturity in 13-year-old boys are formed under the influence of such emotional and personal characteristics as spontaneous aggression, irritability, balance and extroversion.

Thirteen-year-old girls, like boys of this age, have close hierarchical relationships in the structure of emotional maturity. The integrative parameter "EZ" has correlations with indicators "Ex" (r = 0.839), "S" (r = 0.829) and "Em" (r = 0.733), "IEx" (r = 0.530), "EEx" (r = 0.671), "IS" (r = 0.596), "ES" (r = 0.709) and "EEm" (r = 0.657). Within the structure of emotional maturity, indicator "Ex" correlates with attributes "IEx" (r = 0.597) and "EEx" (r = 0.824), and also with indicator "S" (r = 0.612) and attributes "ES" (r = 0.611) with a high level of significance ($p < 0.01$). Indicator "S" has a strong correlation with "IS" (r = 0.752) and "ES" (r = 0.828), as well as with the attributes "EEx" (r = 0.469). Indicator "Em" is related only to attributes "IEm" (r = 0.673) and "EEm" (r = 0.808) at the level $p < 0.01$. It should be noted that the signs that determine one level of manifestation of different components correlate with each other and are not related to the signs of the other level of other components. So, attributes

"IS" are related to "IEx" and "IEm", while attributes "ES" are related to "EEx" and "EEm". These data allow us to state that in the group of 13-year-old girls emotional self-regulation plays the leading role in the process of integrating the main components of emotional maturity into a single structure.

Further study of the correlation structure in the group of 13-year-old girls showed that there is little correlation between indicators that characterize emotional maturity and other emotional and personal characteristics. Among the important correlations, first of all, it is necessary to identify the connections of the indicator "E" with the integrative parameter "EZ" ($r = 0.612$) with the value of $p < 0.01$, indicators "Ex" ($r = 0.485$), "S" ($r = 0.548$), as well as with attributes "ES" ($r = 0.531$) and "EEm" ($r = 0.491$) at the level of reliability $p < 0.05$. In addition, negative correlations of "S" with "F11" ($r = -0.464$) and "N" ($r = -0.495$), "Em" with "F4" ($r = -0.453$), and some others were determined.

Such character and direction of the relationship indicate the dependence of emotional maturity, emotional expressiveness and self-regulation in girls of this age on the level of their extravertedness, and also the negative impact on the formation of emotional self-regulation of such emotional and personal characteristics as emotional lability and neurotism.

A comparison of correlation structures in 13-year-old boys and girls showed that the difference between the groups is relatively small. Significant differences are observed only in the indicators "Em" (CDC = 0.056) and "IEm" (CDC = 0.078). Correlations between other indicators of emotional maturity in boys and girls are much smaller. These data prove that boys and girls aged 13 in general develop emotional maturity under the influence of the same determinants, with the exception of empathy, namely, the personal level of its manifestation, the formation of which in different gender groups is influenced by different factors.

A closer examination of these differences showed that in the indicator "Em" they are manifested with 9 indicators: "F4" (0.86), "F6" (0.74), "SE" (0.72), "F8" (0.70), "F2" (0.65), "EEx" (0.43) and others. A similar picture is observed if we analyze the differences in the correlations of "IEm" attributes. Particular attention should be paid to the discrepancies in correlations of these indicators with "F2", "F6" and "EEx", where correlations have a high level of significance in boys, and girls do not, and also "F4", where correlations are significant in both groups, but in the group of boys the connection has a positive direction, and in girls' group, it shows a negative relationship. These data indicate that spontaneous aggression, irritability and balance have a specific influence on the formation of empathy in 13-year-old boys. In contrast to them, in girls, the formation of empathy is inhibited by high irritability.

It is also worth mentioning that gender differences in correlations of the integrative parameter "EZ" are observed only in 5 indicators: "F4" (0.75), "F2" (0.58), "F6" (0.52), "N" (0.48) and "F3" (0.43). Particular attention should be paid to the discrepancies between the correlations of the "EZ" with indicators "F2", "F4" and "F6", where in boys they have a high level of significance, and in girls not. This data points to the fact that spontaneous aggression, irritability and balance are specific to 13-year-old boys' personal characteristics that influence the formation of emotional maturity.

In the group of **14-year-old** boys, the integrative parameter "EZ" has significant connections with indicators "Ex" (r = 0.800), "S" (r = 0.713) and "Em" (r = 0.799), as well as with subscales that characterize attributes "IEx" (r = 0.657), "EEx" (r = 0.789), "ES" (r = 0.620), "IEm" (r = 0.504) and "EEm" (r = 0.722) with a high level of correlation ($p < 0.01$), and with "IS" (r = 0.417) with a level of $p < 0.05$. Each of the components of emotional maturity demonstrates the same close hierarchical interaction. Within the structure of emotional maturity, there is also a closer relationship between the components and levels of their manifestation. Thus, the indicator "Ex" correlates with attributes "IEx" (r = 0.882) and "EEx" (r = 0.929), as well as with the indicators "S" (r = 0.331), "Em" (r = 0.467) and attributes "IEm" (r = 0.363) and "EEm" (r = 0.383). Indicator "S" has a tight relationship with "IS" (r = 0.661) and "ES" (r = 0.812), as well as with the indicator "Em" (r = 0.377), and attributes "EEx" (r = 0.413) and "EEm" (r = 0.395). The indicator "Em" is related both to attributes "IEm" (r = 0.644) and "EEm" (r = 0.896) and to "IEx" (r = 0.401), "EEx" (r = 0.444) and "ES" (r = 0.371).

These data allow us to state that in the group of 14-year-old boys the revealed structural relationships are not only of a dependent nature but also quite closely integrate the main components of emotional maturity.

Further study of the results of correlation analysis in this group allowed us to establish a fairly wide range of interrelations between indicators of emotional maturity and emotionally specific characteristics. First, it is a complex formed around the parameter "E", which has significant links with "EZ" (r = 0.574), "Ex" (r = 0.410), "S" (r = 0.484), "Em" (r = 0.442), "EEx" (r = 0.445), "ES" (r = 0.578) and "EEm" (r = 0.457) at a high level of reliability ($p < 0.01$). Secondly, the complex around the indicator "SE", which correlates with "EZ" (r = 0.492), "Ex" (r = 0.390), "S" (r = 0.430), "EEx" (r = 0.403), "ES" (r = 0.540) and "EEm" (r = 0.392) at a reliability level of not less than $p < 0.05$. Thirdly, the complex formed around indicator "F5" significantly correlated with the "EZ" (r = 0.425), indicators "S" (r = 0.390) and "Em" (r = 0.384) and attributes "ES" (r = 0.483) and "EM" (r = 0.446). Fourthly, the complex formed around indicator "F3", which has negative links with the "EZ" (r = −0.433), "S" (r = −0.474), "Em" (r = −0.331) and "ES" (r = −0.525). Besides the integrative parameter "EZ", indicator "S" and attributes "ES" show significant correlations with "F1" and "F11".

Proceeding from the examined data we can conclude that the development of emotional maturity in 14-year-old boys is undoubtedly associated with such personality traits as extravertedness, self-esteem, sociability and activity in communication, and is inhibited by excessive depressiveness, neuroticism and emotional lability.

Starting to examine the features of correlations that reflect the formation of the structure of emotional maturity in the group of 14-year-old girls, it is worth noting that it does not differ from the structure of their peers. That is, both subordinate and intercomponent connections are widely represented. The only difference between these two groups is the absence of intercomponent connections in the "IEx" attributes and the presence of correlations between "IS" and "IEm" attributes ($r = 0.337$; $p < 0.05$). These data allow us to assume the absence of differences in the formation of the structure of emotional maturity in 14-year-old boys and girls.

Further examination of correlations in the group of 14-year-old girls showed that the indicators of emotional maturity are less correlated with personal characteristics than in the boys' group. Attention is drawn only to the active relationship with indicator "N" of the integrative parameter "EZ" ($r = 0.349$; $p < 0.05$), indicators "Ex" ($r = 0.350$; $p < 0.05$) and "Em" ($r = 0.350$; $p < 0.05$), as well as attributes "EEx" ($r = 0.485$; $p < 0.01$) and "EEm" ($r = 0.353$; $p < 0.05$) is worth attention. Moreover, it should be noted that indicators "Ex", "EEx" and "EEm" have a predominant number of significant correlations with indicators of emotional and personal spheres.

The identified features of the relationship demonstrate that the level of emotional maturity in 14-year-old girls in general, and emotional expressiveness and empathy in particular, depends significantly on such a parameter as neurotism. In addition, there is a tendency to increase the level of emotional expressiveness and empathy in those girls who are capable of impulsive behavior, and depressive states, and are prone to affective reactions. Moreover, the influence of these personal manifestations is significantly more pronounced in the formation of interpersonal levels of these components.

The comparison of correlations between indicators of emotional maturity in boys and girls aged 14 showed that there is little difference between the groups in indicators "EZ" (CDC = 0.039), "ES" (CDC = 0.038) and "S" (CDC = 0.035). Correlations of other indicators of emotional maturity in boys and girls have slightly smaller differences, and in the indicators "IS" (CDC = 0.008), "EEm" (CDC = 0.008) and "IEm" (CDC = 0.015), they are almost absent.

A more detailed examination of these differences showed that in the indicator "EZ" they are defined with 8 indicators: "F11" (0.69), "F3" (0.62), "F1" (0.55), "F2" 0.53), "SE" (0.47) and others. The same differences in content are also found in parameters "S" and "ES". Particular attention should be paid to the discrepancies between correlations of these indicators with "F2", where correlations have a high level of significance in girls and not in boys, as well as "F1", "F3", "F11", and "SE" and "E". where correlations are significant only in the group of boys. These data demonstrate a link specific for girls between emotional maturity and spontaneous aggression, and impulsive behavior. In turn, the dependence of emotional maturity on extroversion and personal self-esteem is special for boys. Moreover, for boys at this age, it is characterized by a decrease in the level of neuroticism, depressiveness and emotional lability, which occurs, in our opinion, due to the formation of emotional self-regulation becomes a tendency.

The study of the correlation structure of emotional maturity in **15-year-old** boys showed that the integrative parameter "EZ" has significant correlations with most indicators of emotional maturity, namely with "Ex" ($r = 0.806$) "S" ($r = 0.734$), "Em" ($r = 0.892$), "EEx" ($r = 0.778$), "ES" ($r = 0.792$), "IEm" ($r = 0.792$) and "EEm" ($r = 0.727$), which are determined with a high level of reliability ($p < 0.01$). Also, we revealed hierarchical correlations of the indicator "Ex" with attributes "IEx" ($r = 0.736$) and "EEx" ($r = 0.879$) at the level of $p < 0.01$, of the indicator "S" with attributes "IS" ($r = 0.656$; $p < 0.05$) and "ES" ($r = 0.824$; $p < 0.01$), and "Em" with attributes "IEm" ($r = 0.739$) and "EEm" ($r = 0.907$) at the level of $p < 0.01$. Intercomponent links are represented by correlations of the indicator "Em" with "Ex" ($r = 0.589$; $p < 0.05$), "EEx" ($r = 0.586$; $p < 0.05$) and "ES" ($r = 0.733$; $p < 0.01$), attributes "IEm" with indicator "S" ($r = 0.700$; $p < 0.01$) and attributes "EEx" ($r = 0.686$; $p < 0.01$) with "ES" ($r = 0.613$; $p < 0.05$).

According to these data, the link between the components of emotional maturity and levels of their manifestation in the group of 15-year-old boys is less tight than in the previous age group. The nature of this connection indicates the special role of empathy, which unites other components, primarily due to its interrelation with the attributes of interpersonal level of emotional expressiveness and self-regulation.

The study of the results of correlation analysis allowed us to establish two sets of interrelations between indicators of emotional maturity and emotional and personality traits. The first complex is formed around the indicator "SE", which correlates with "EZ" ($r = 0.696$) and "S" ($r = 0.835$) at the level of $p < 0.01$, and also with "IS" ($r = 0.652$), "ES" ($r = 0.609$) and "IEm" ($r = 0.651$) at the level ($p < 0.05$). The second complex is less extensive than the first, it is formed around the indicator "F5", which significantly correlates with the integrative parameter "EZ" ($r = 0.685$; $p < 0.05$) and attributes "ES" ($r = 0.754$; $p < 0.01$). Proceeding from the examined data, we can conclude that the formation of emotional maturity in 15-year-old boys depends on the level of adequacy of their self-esteem, as well as on camaraderie and on activity in communication.

The structure of emotional maturity in 15-year-old girls as well as in boys is characterized by very close hierarchical links. Certain intercomponent correlations were identified: between "Ex" and "Em" ($r = 0.404$) and "EEm" ($r = 0.351$), as well as between attributes of "IEx" and "Em" ($r = 0.397$) and also "IEm" ($r = 0.504$), which have a sufficient level of reliability ($p < 0.05$). These data allow us to conclude that the structure of emotional maturity in girls of 15 years old, as well as in boys of this age is generally orderly, but the relationship between individual components of emotional maturity and their levels of manifestation is less tight than in 14-year-old boys and girls. Intercomponent relations are preserved only in the indicators that characterize emotional expressiveness and empathy.

In contrast to the characteristics of relationships within the structure of emotional maturity, where deep differences between boys and girls were not found, the correlations of these indicators with emotional and personal characteristics vary in some way, primarily in their number. In the group of girls, we can distinguish at least 3 big complexes of such interconnections: the first formed around the indicator “F5”, which significantly correlates with the integrative parameter “EZ” (r = 0.628; p <0.01), indicators “Ex” (r = 0.503; p <0.01), “S” (r = 0.331; p <0.05), “Em” (r = 0.527; p <0.01) and attributes “EEx” (r = 0.597; p <0.01), “ES” (r = 0.403; p <0.01), “EEm” (r = 0.616; p <0.01). The second is around “F10”, which is also related to “EZ” (r = 0.563), “Ex” (r = 0.499), “Em” (r = 0.501), “EEx” (r = 0.548), and with “EEm” (r = 0.511) at the level of reliability (p <0.01); the third is a complex formed around the indicator “E”, that has strong links with “EZ” (r = 0.495), “Ex” (r = 0.552), “S” (r = 0.429), “EEx” (r = 0.612) and “ES” (r = 0.522) at the level p <0.01.

These complexes reveal a number of positive connections that reflect the influence on the formation of emotional maturity of such personality traits as extravertedness and companionship. In particular, it is determined that they stimulate the formation, first of all, of those signs of emotional maturity that characterize the interpersonal levels of manifestation of its components.

In addition to the above, there are indicators that establish negative relationships with certain components of emotional maturity and signs of their manifestation. These are indicators “F3” and “F8” and “N”, which are negatively connected with “S” and “ES”, and positively with “IEx”. This character of the connection allows us to assume that the spontaneous expression of emotions in 15-year-old girls is influenced by such negative emotional and personality traits as depressiveness, anxiety and neurotism, which, in turn, complicates the formation of emotional self-regulation.

Comparison of correlations of emotional maturity in 15-year-old boys and girls showed that there is a great difference between the groups according to attributes of “EEx” (CDC = 0.073), “ES” (CDC = 0.064) and “IEm” (CDC = 0.061). The correlations between other indicators of emotional maturity in boys and girls have a little less difference.

A more detailed examination of these differences showed that in the indicator “EEx they are linked with 13 indicators: “IEm” (0.85), “F2” (0.69), “SE” (0.65), “F6” (0.62), “F7” (0.51), “F10” (0.48), “E” (0.47), “Em” (0.45) and others. Particular attention should be paid to the discrepancies between correlations of these indicators with “Em” and “IEm”, where correlations have a high level of significance in boys, and not in girls, and also to “F7”, “F10” and “E”, where correlations are valid only in a group of girls. These data show that the formation of the ability to arbitrarily express emotions according to the situation and competence in 15-year-old boys is influenced by empathic qualities, and in girls by extrovertedness and reactive aggression.

Examination of the differences in correlations of the indicator “ES” showed that they are determined by 12 indicators: “F11” (0.60), “IEm” (0.59), “Em” (0.56) “N” (0.55), “F8” (0.50), “F1” (0.50), “F3” (0.46), “EM” (0.40) and others. Among them are also such indicators (“Em”, “IEm”, “EEm”) which correlate with “ES” at a high level of significance in boys, but not in girls. On the contrary, indicators “F1”, “F3”, “F8”, “F11” and “N” have significant negative correlations with “ES” only in the group of girls. These indicate that, unlike boys, the ability of 15-year-old girls to influence other people's emotional states is complicated due to their excessive neuroticism, depressiveness, shyness, emotional lability and neurotism. In boys, these abilities are closely linked with empathy.

Regarding the differences in the correlations of "IEm" attribute, they are defined in 11 correlations: with the indicators "F12" (0.61), "S" (0.60), "ES" (0.60), "IEx" (0.49), "F8" (0.49), "SE" (0.36) and others. The most significant, in our opinion, is the data on differences in correlations with the indicators "S", "ES" and "SE", where they have a high level of significance in boys, and not in girls. Such data indicate that the specific determinants of the formation of abilities to understand the emotional state of a partner, to empathize, and to sympathize with him or her in boys are emotional self-regulation and personal self-esteem. In addition, it should be noted that gender differences in the correlations of the integrative parameter "EZ" are insignificant (CDC = 0.22), they are observed for only 3 indicators: "F6" (0.52), "SE" (0.49) and "EEx"(0.42). Particular attention should be paid to the differences in correlation between the integrative parameter "EZ" and the indicator "SE", which has a high level of significance only in the boys. This means that the dependence of the formation of emotional maturity on personal self-esteem is specific for 15-year-old boys.

The analysis of correlations of indicators characterizing the emotional maturity of **16-year-olds** showed that the integrative parameter "EZ" with high significance ($p < 0.01$) correlates with indicators "Ex" ($r = 0.603$), "S" ($r = 0.730$), and attributes "IEx" ($r = 0.575$) and "IS" ($r = 0.597$), and moderately ($p < 0.05$) with indicator "Em" ($r = 0.547$) and attributes "ES" ($R = 0.530$) and "EM" ($r = 0.465$). Besides, were found correlations that reflect the hierarchical relations of the indicator "Ex" with attributes "IEx" ($r = 0.630$) and "EEx" ($r = 0.749$), the indicator "S" with attributes "IS" ($r = 0.734$) and "ES" ($r = 0.800$), the indicator "Em" with attributes "IEm" ($r = 0.781$) and "EEm" ($r = 0.632$), which are significant at $p < 0.01$. Intercomponent connections in the structure of emotional maturity of 16-year-old boys do not exist.

As can be seen from these data, 16-year-old boys, while maintaining a close hierarchical structure, have looser intercomponent connections, which indicates the independence and self-sufficiency of the formation of each of the components of emotional maturity.

The study of the relationship between indicators of emotional maturity and emotional and personal characteristics of young people of this age allowed us to establish that they have a limited number. Significant correlations were found only between indicators "Em" and "F4" ($r = 0.781$; $p < 0.01$), between attributes "IEx" and indicators "F1" ($r = 0.482$; $p < 0.05$), "F2" ($r = 0.477$; $p < 0.05$), "F3" ($r = 0.571$; $p < 0.05$) and "SE" ($r = -0.798$; $p < 0.01$), between attributes "IEm" and "F1" ($r = -0.541$; $p < 0.05$), between those of "EEm" and the indicator "F4" ($r = 0.491$; $p < 0.05$). Such data show a certain independence of emotional self-regulation from the personal qualities of the examined persons. The level of irritability in young people of this age has a significant impact on the development of empathy, and the involuntary expression of emotions depends on neuroticism, reactive aggression and depressiveness.

For girls at the age of 16, the defined structure of emotional maturity is more integrated. In addition to fairly tight hierarchical links, there is an interaction of some components and their features at personal and interpersonal levels. Thus, the indicator "Ex" correlates with "S" ($r = 0.806$; $p < 0.01$) and its attributes "IS" ($r = 0.492$; $p < 0.05$) and "ES" ($r = 0.783$; $p < 0.01$). The indicator "S", in turn, is connected with "IEx" ($r = 0.728$; $p < 0.01$) and "EEx" ($r = 0.587$; $p < 0.01$), the above-mentioned attributes also have a close relationship.

When interpreting the received data, we should pay attention to the relative isolation of the indicator that characterizes the formation of empathy, which may indicate the independence and self-sufficiency of its formation in young people of this age. In turn, the formation of emotional expressiveness and self-regulation takes place with an active interplay of these qualities on each other.

A crucial feature of the correlation structure in 16-year-olds is the absence of any significant interrelations between emotional maturity and emotional-personal properties.

A comparison of the correlations between indicators of emotional maturity in 16-year-old boys and girls showed no significant differences. A moderate difference between the groups is observed only for indicators "S", where the correlation divergence coefficient (CDC) equals 0.041 points, "IEx" (CDC = 0.036) and "EEx" (CDC = 0.037). These data indicate that young boys and girls 16 years of age develop their emotional maturity under the influence of the same determinants, except for emotional self-regulation, as well as personal and interpersonal levels of emotional expressiveness, which develop under the influence of different factors in different gender groups.

A more detailed analysis of these differences showed that for the indicator "S" they are correlated with 9 indicators: "F1" (0.62), "F4" (0.41), "EEm" (0.40), "F3" 0.39), "Ex" (0.38), "EEx" (0.36), "IEx" (0.35) and others. Moreover, the correlations of this indicator with "Ex", "IEx" and "EEx" in girls have a high level of significance, but not in boys. These data correspond to the above-mentioned features of the structure of emotional maturity inherent to 16-year-old girls. Regarding differences in the correlations of the indicator "IEx", they are defined in 7 correlations: with the indexes "SE" (0.75), "F2" (0.50), "F3" (0.41), "IS" (0.38), "S" (0.35) and others. Among them, there are such indicators ("F2", "F3",and "SE"), which in boys correlate with "IEx" at a high level of significance, and in girls are not associated with this feature, and vice versa, indicators "S" and "IS" significantly correlate with "IEx" only in girls. Gender differences in the correlations of the indicator "EEx" are manifested with the same indicators as in "IEx".

As we can see, in general, differences in the determination of emotional maturity in young men and women of 16 years old are almost non-existent. The only exception is a specific relationship between the indicator that characterizes emotional self-regulation and some negative emotional manifestations in young men, as well as the interaction of indicators that characterize emotional expressiveness and self-regulation in girls.

The analysis of correlations between indicators in the group of **17-year-old** boys showed that the integrative parameter "EZ" to great extent ($p < 0.01$) correlates with indicators "Ex" ($r = 0.759$), "S" ($r = 0.604$) and "Em "($r = 0.811$), as well as with the attributes "IEx" ($r = 0.739$), "EEx" ($r = 0.582$), "IEm" ($r = 0.736$) and "EEm" ($r = 0.572$). There are also significant correlations of the indicator "Ex" with the attributes "IEx" ($r = 0.849$) and "EEx" ($r = 0.880$), the indicator "S" with "IS" ($r = 0.720$) and "ES" ($r = 0.654$), and the indicator "Em" with attributes "IEm" ($r = 0.779$) and "EEm" ($r = 0.822$) at the level of $p < 0.01$.

Intercomponent interactions are represented by correlations formed around the attributes of personal levels of empathy and emotional expressiveness. Thus, the features of "IEm" show moderate relationships ($p < 0.05$) with "IEx" ($r = 0.445$), "Ex" ($r = 0.418$) and "S" ($r = 0.430$), in turn, attributes of "IEx" are significantly connected with "IS" ($r = 0.405$). As a result, the correlation between "Ex" and "Em" also appeared significant ($r = 0.430$; $p < 0.05$).

These peculiarities of interrelations indicate some separation of emotional self-regulation from other components of emotional maturity, as well as the leading role of personal levels of emotional expressiveness and empathy for the formation of the structure of emotional maturity of 17-year-old boys.

Regarding the interrelations of indicators of emotional maturity with other emotional and personal characteristics, they are established with only two indicators: "SE", with which negative correlations are defined in indicators "S" ($r = -0.487$) and "IS" ($r = -0.481$), and also in "F5", which correlates with "Em" ($r = 0.423$). All correlations have a sufficient level of reliability ($p < 0.05$).

These correlations indicate that young people with low self-esteem have a rather intensive formation of emotional self-regulation, in particular the ability to control their own emotions. In addition, the dependence of empathy formation on the level of camaraderie, and social activity of young people is determined.

Analyzing the correlation structure of emotional maturity in 17-year-old girls, we found that the integrative parameter "EZ" significantly correlates with all components of emotional maturity and levels of their manifestation. However, the connections between the components of emotional maturity are even more limited. As in the group of boys of the same age, there is a link between indicators "Ex" and "Em" ($r = 0.405$; $p < 0.05$), but it is based only on the correlation of individual levels of the mentioned components ($r = 0.479$; $p < 0.05$).

The established peculiarities of the correlation structure of emotional maturity in the group of 17-year-old girls showed that in the process of becoming emotionally mature there is an interplay of empathic skills and spontaneous expression of emotions in behavior, which is the basis for further improvement of emotional expressiveness and empathy.

Further analysis revealed the following correlations: "N" with "S", "IS" and "ES", "E" with "S", and "EEx" and "ES", and also between indicators "F4" and "S". According to these data, such personality traits as balance and extroversion, as well as a relatively low level of neurotism play key role in the formation of emotional self-regulation.

A comparison of correlation structures in 17-year-old boys and girls showed that the difference between the two groups is relatively small. Significant differences are observed only in indicators "S" (CDC = 0.059) and "IS" (CDC = 0.065). Correlations of other indicators of emotional maturity differ insignificantly. These data suggest that the determinants of emotional maturity in young men and women aged 17 do not generally differ, with the exception of emotional self-regulation, namely, the personal level of its manifestation, which develops in different gender groups under the influence of different factors.

A detailed examination of these differences showed that in indicator "S" they are defined by 13 indicators: "F6" (0.61), "N" (0.55), "F5" (0.54), "F9" (0.50), "SE" (0.49) and others. A similar picture is observed when analyzing the differences in the correlations of "IS" attributes. There are also discrepancies in correlations with 13 indicators: "N" (0.65), "F5" (0.58), "F3" (0.56), "F6" (F6) (0.55), "SE" (0.54), "F10" (0.51) and others. Particular attention should be paid to the differences between these indicators with "SE", where boys have a high level of significance and negative, and not in girls, as well as "N", "E" and "F6", where correlations are significant only in girls. These data indicate that lowered self-esteem is a specific determinant in the formation of emotional self-regulation in 17-year-old boys. In girls, the formation of this component of emotional maturity develops successfully in interaction with such aspects of the personality as extravertedness, emotional stability and balance.

In the group of young people **aged 18–23**, the integrative parameter "EZ" has significant connections with indicators "Ex" (r = 0.561), "S" (r = 0.683) and "Em" (r = 0.666), as well as with subscales, which characterize the attributes of "IEx" (r = 0.434), "EEx" (r = 0.447), "IS" (r = 0.560), "ES" (r = 0.754) and "EEm" (r = 0.732) with high-reliability level ($p < 0.01$). Each of the components of emotional maturity demonstrates the same close hierarchical interaction.

Within the structure of emotional maturity, there is also an interrelation between indicator "S" and attributes of "IEm" (r = −0.327; $p < 0.05$) and "EEm" (r = 0.617; $p < 0.01$); "ES" correlates with the indicator "Em" (r = 0.468; $p < 0.01$) and with attributes of "EEm" (r = 0.758; $p < 0.01$). These data allow us to state that in the group of young people aged 18–23, the identified intercomponent connections are represented by the interaction of interpersonal levels of emotional self-regulation and empathy.

Further study of the results of correlation analysis in this group allowed us to establish that the "IS" attributes correlate more closely with other indicators of emotional maturity with emotional and personal characteristics such as "F5" (r = 0.339), "F7" (r = 0.374), "F8" (r = −0.377), "F10" (r = 0.370), "F12" (r = 0.371) and "E" (r = 0.344), with which correlations were established at a sufficient level of significance ($p < 0.05$). As a rule, indicators of emotional maturity are closely related to those of "F7", "F12" and "E". This can be noted by analyzing correlations of the integrative parameter "EZ", as well as indicators "S", "ES" and "EEm".

Proceeding from the examined data, the formation of emotional maturity in young people aged 18–23 is associated with such personality traits as extravertedness, masculinity and reactive aggressiveness.

Determining the correlation features of the relations that reflect the formation of the structure of emotional maturity in the group of girls aged 18–23, showed that hierarchical relations at all levels have a sufficient indicator of reliability. The distinctive feature of this group is the absence of any significant correlations that would characterize the intercomponent relationship.

Regarding the interrelations between the indicators of emotional maturity and other emotional and personal characteristics, they are found in only two indicators: "IS" correlates with "F1" ($r = -0.316$; $p <0.05$), "F5" ($r = 0.380$; $p <0.01$), "F8" ($r = -0.377$; $p <0.01$), "F10" ($r = 0.321$; $p <0.05$), "F12" ($r = 0.410$; $p < 0.01$) and "N" ($r = -0.318$; $p <0.05$), and also "S", which is associated with "F5" ($r = 0.284$; $p <0.05$), "F8" ($r = -0.374$; $p <0.01$) and "F11" ($r = -0.301$; $p <0.05$).

The observed peculiarities of the interconnection show that in girls aged 18–23, the formation of emotional self-regulation, including the ability to control emotions depends on companionship and extravertedness, and is hampered by excessive neuroticism, emotional instability and shyness.

A comparison of the correlations between the indicators of emotional maturity in young men and women aged 18–23 showed that a significant difference between the groups is observed only for the indicator "EEm" (CDC = 0.056). Correlations between other indicators of emotional maturity have insignificant differences.

These data testify to the fact that in young people of 18–23 years old in general, the formation of emotional maturity occurs under the influence of the same determinants, with the exception of the interpersonal level of empathy, the formation of which in different gender groups is influenced by different factors.

A detailed examination of these differences showed that the most important of them are differences in correlations with "F8" (0.65), "S" (0.45), "ES" (0.56), "E" (0.48) and "F7" (0.30), where those indicators reach a high level of significance for boys and not for girls.

These data allow us to conclude that the influence of emotional self-regulation, reactive aggressiveness and extravertedness on the ability to use empathy skills in interaction is specific for 18–23-year-old boys, as well as the negative influence of shyness.

Thus, the conducted analysis of correlation structures in these groups allows us to conclude that, despite the number of gender differences in the expressiveness of emotional maturity, its formation in boys and girls has both age-specific features and is influenced by specific factors.

The most significant gender differences are manifested in the relationship of empathy, which in boys is more often associated with emotional lability, depressiveness and irritability, while the smallest differences are found in the determination of emotional expressiveness.

There is a tendency to decrease with age the differences in the factors of formation of both emotional maturity in general and its main components. That is, in the process of developing abilities that ensure the adequacy of emotional response, differences in the personal determination are smoothed out.

The relationship between extravertedness and camaraderie and emotional maturity is equally manifested in both boys and girls, which allows us to determine that the impact of these properties on the formation of emotional maturity is one of the general patterns of this process.

Independence from the gender of the tested is also defined in the formation of the structure of emotional maturity, especially on the level of interrelations between its components, which allows attributing changes in intercomponent interactions to the age-specific patterns of emotional maturity.

3.5.6 Main tendencies in the development of emotional maturity in adolescents and young adults and their types

A summary of the information about the dynamics of indicators that characterize the main components of emotional maturity, allows us to identify certain trends in their formation. Thus, in the period from 11 to 13 years, there is a certain fluctuation of indicators of emotional maturity, but in general, they are all within 6–7.5 points (see Figure 3.5.9).

As can be seen in the figure during this period there is a tendency for the self-regulatory and empathic components to weaken and for the emotional expressiveness to increase. It was mentioned above that the increase in the level of emotional expressiveness at this age is connected with increased activity directed to the external social environment. This is observed not only in the interaction of emotional expressiveness with interpersonal levels of other components but also in its significant interrelation with the person's extroversion. At the end of this period, there is a decrease in the level of emotional expressiveness, stabilization of all three components, and their equal participation in the organization of the adequacy of emotional reactions. That is why we defined the period that corresponds to early adolescence as a stage of expressive organization of emotional maturity.

To clarify the information about the peculiarities of emotional maturity manifestation during this period, we compared groups of children aged 11–13 who received high and low scores on the integrative parameter of emotional maturity (see Table 3.5.19).

As can be seen from the table, 11–13-year-olds with a high level of emotional maturity are significantly more developed than their peers in terms of emotional expressiveness, emotional self-regulation and empathy. In addition, there is a significant increase in the level of comradeship ("F5"), balance ("F6") and extravertedness ("F10" and "E").

These data indicate that already at the stage of expressive organization of emotional maturity, i.e. at the age of 11–13 years, there are individual variations

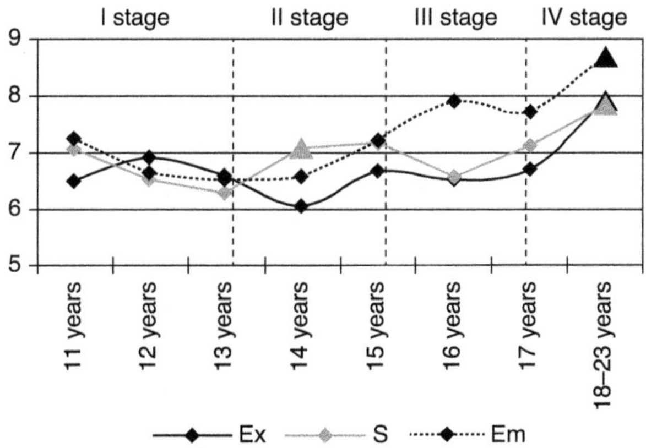

FIGURE 3.5.9 Age dynamics of indicators that characterize the main components of emotional maturity of the individual.

from low to high levels of emotional maturity, which are also differentiated by a similar level of camaraderie, balance and extraversion.

Turning back to Figure 3.5.9, we note that further, at the age of 14–15 years, which corresponds to the older adolescent period, there is a tendency to reduce the expressive regulation of emotional response, but at the same time there is a significant increase in the level of emotional self-regulation. The expressiveness of empathy in this period also tends to increase. We assumed that such a picture of the formation of emotional maturity can be an indicator of the successful progression of mental development of older adolescents, indicating the manifestation of social consciousness, and the desire for self-improvement and self-education. It should be noted that along with the growth of abilities to self-regulation in older adolescents there is a decrease in negative emotional manifestations, such as neuroticism, depressiveness and emotional lability, which also indicates the successful development of the personality of older adolescents.

Generally, it can be asserted that at this stage the role of expressive regulation of behavior is loosened, which characterizes the unconscious (intuitive) level of adequate emotional response, and at the same time, the increasing the importance of conscious regulation of their own emotions and behavior.

As for adolescents who have a high or low level of the integrative parameter "EZ", in them, as well as in younger children, the essential differentiation on all indicators of emotional maturity (see Table 3.5.20) was determined.

According to the data given in the table, the most explicitly by expressiveness level groups differ on the indicator "EZ" that characterizes the level of empathy formation ("Em") and also attributes of interpersonal level of emotional self-regulation ("ES") and empathy ("EEm"). Moreover, valid differences between groups of children aged 14–15 with high and low levels of emotional maturity were found in indicators of companionship ("F5"), self-esteem ("SE") and extraversion ("F10", "E"). This may indicate that those adolescents who have a high

TABLE 3.5.19 Expressiveness of indicators that characterize the features of emotional maturity and personality traits in children 11–13 years with high and low levels of emotional maturity

Level of emotional maturity	*Ex*	*S*	*Em*	*IEx*	*EEx*	*IS*	*ES*	*IEm*	*EEm*	*EZ*	*F5*	*F6*	*F10*	*E*
Low	4.2	4.4	3.6	2.8	1.6	1.7	2.7	2.0	1.6	12.2	3.5	5.9	4.6	10.8
high	8.8	8.2	9.3	4.9	3.8	3.5	4.7	4.8	4.5	26.3	4.7	7.7	6.3	16.0
T	7.15*★	4.84*★	6.83*★	5.97*★	3.53*★	3.20*★	4.85*★	5.82*★	6.41*★	6.12*★	2.08★	2.72*★	2.53★	2.44★

TABLE 3.5.20 Expressiveness of indicators that characterize the features of emotional maturity and personality traits in adolescents 14–15 years with high and low levels of emotional maturity

Level of emotional maturity	*Ex*	*S*	*Em*	*IEx*	*EEx*	*IS*	*ES*	*IEm*	*EEm*	*EZ*	*F5*	*F10*	*SE*	*E*
low	3.4	4.7	3.9	2.4	1.0	2.3	2.4	2.3	1.5	12.0	3.4	5.1	56.1	11.7
high	8.3	9.3	9.7	4.2	4.1	3.9	5.4	4.8	4.9	27.4	6.1	6.7	71.4	19.3
t	6.87**	6.94**	7.12**	4.81**	6.35**	4.64**	5.96**	5.81**	6.47**	6.24**	4.30**	2.81**	3.36**	3.92**

level of emotional maturity also have a higher level of communicative activity, they focus on social relations and self-confidence in contrast to peers with a low level of emotional maturity.

The third period, 16–17 years, is characterized by a tendency to increase the level of empathy, while the importance of emotional self-regulation in the organization of adequate emotional response decreases. The correlation study shows that there are certain changes in the very structure of emotional maturity in early adolescence, which consist in decreasing the importance of features related to communication activities and increasing the role of abilities involved in the organization of internal activity of the individual. Such changes are probably related to the development of reflection (Vygotsky, 1984), the desire to understand oneself, to know your one's own inner world (Granovska, 1997; Mukhina, 2000), and the trustworthy and candid interaction with recipients (Olshannikova, 1983).

The comparison of indicators that characterize the peculiarities of the manifestation of emotional maturity and personality traits of young people aged 16–17 with high and low levels of emotional maturity confirmed our assumption (see Table 3.5.21).

As we can see, among the personality traits we study, significant differences in the groups of young people are found only in the intensity of balance ("F6") and self-esteem ("SE"). Moreover, it should be noted that young men with a high level of emotional maturity show much lower self-esteem than their peers with a low level. This can be explained by the fact that young people with a high level of emotional maturity in this period have a faster and more active reconstruction of self-awareness associated with new developments of this period.

The fourth period for persons aged 18–23 years, is characterized by a significant increase in all components of emotional maturity while maintaining the leading role of empathy in the organization of adequate emotional response.

Regarding differences between groups with low and high levels of emotional maturity during this period, it should be noted that they are essential only in the intensity of indicators that characterize individual components and levels of their manifestation (see Table 3.5.22).

TABLE 3.5.21 Expressiveness of indicators characterizing the features of emotional maturity and personality traits in young people aged 16–17 with high and low levels of emotional maturity

Level of emotional maturity	*Ex*	*S*	*Em*	*IEx*	*EEx*	*IS*	*ES*	*IEm*	*EEm*	*EZ*
Low	5.3	5.3	6.7	2.6	2.7	2.3	2.4	3.6	3.1	17.3
high	9.9	9.6	10.4	4.8	5.2	4.1	5.6	5.2	5.3	29.9
T	5.36**	3.85**	2.79*	3.82**	4.74**	2.93**	5.41**	2.01*	2.69*	7.0**

According to these data, young men aged 18–23 with high and low levels of emotional maturity differ significantly only in the formation of emotional expressiveness, emotional self-regulation and empathy.

These data, as well as the results of preceding examination of correlations in young people of this age, allow us to determine the specificity of this stage, which consists in the isolated, autonomous formation of each component of emotional maturity and call it the stage of autonomous emotional maturity.

Thus, the identification of tendencies in the formation of the main components of emotional maturity of a person, taking into account previously obtained information allowed us to nominally distinguish four stages in the formation of this integrative quality:

I – stage of expressive organization of emotional maturity (11–13 years);
II – stage of self-regulation improvement (14–15 years);
III – stage of improving the personal level of emotional maturity (16–17 years);
IV – stage of autonomously balanced and relatively stable manifestation of emotional maturity (18–23 years).

The foregoing subsections have looked at the general age and gender features of the formation of emotional maturity in adolescence and young adult age. However, they do not describe all the variability of specific forms of achieving the adequacy of emotional response. Nevertheless, the psychologist encounters them in practical activity. Therefore, we made an attempt to create a more or less generalized typology of individual options for the formation of emotional maturity of a person.

The basis for its creation was the idea of the formation of emotional maturity as a process of mastering the individual stereotypes of emotional reactions, formed in a particular sociocultural environment on the basis of individual characteristics and innate self-regulatory mechanisms.

Proceeding from the results of theoretical analysis of works (Budnitska, 2001; Abolin, 1974; Dodonov, 1972; Dorfman, 1989; Zaika, Kartashov, 1993; Kulchitskaya, 2003; Libin, 2000; Moskvin, 1988; Pereverzeva, 1989; Miller, 1988), in which the individual specificity of emotional response is considered, we assumed that its adequacy can be achieved in different ways. The formation of a particular type of emotional maturity may have been due to different relations of two groups of factors: (1) the predominance of one of the emotional properties (emotional agitation (impulsivity), emotional stability, emotional sensitivity, etc.); and (2) the nature of the social environment, which provides examples of emotional response, approves or denies certain emotional reactions of the individual.

When identifying the types of emotional maturity, a purely pragmatic approach of relying on the dominant component of its structure was taken as a basis. The real possibility of the relations of such components allowed us to identify 7 types of emotional maturity (see Figure 3.5.10).

The first type is characterized by the domination of emotional expressiveness in the organization of adequate emotional responses. The data of some authors (Vysotskaya, 1979) allow us to assume that in unbalanced individuals with high emotional excitability, the impulsiveness of the formation of emotional expressiveness will compensate for the lack of expressiveness of other components.

The second type is characterized by a greater expression of emotional self-regulation, the formation of which predominates in individuals balanced and emotionally stable (Reikovsky, 1979; Chebykin, Abolin, 1984).

The third type is associated with the predominance of empathy in the formation of emotional maturity. It is more likely to be formed in people with high emotional sensitivity (Manerov, 1990; Tsagarelli, 1981).

Another group of factors primarily affects the level of emotional maturity in general. However, it should be noted that the formation of one or another type occurs when interacting with patterns of the emotional response of people from the closest social group, each of which also has its own individual peculiarities of emotional maturity.

The other types are variants of emotional maturity development, in which either the harmonious manifestation of two of the components and their predominance over the third (fifth, sixth and seventh types), or an equal expressiveness of all components regardless of level of formation (fourth type) are defined.

According to the above-mentioned ideas, all the tested were divided into groups that correspond to each of the above types of emotional maturity. Among the adolescents and young people we surveyed, the first type was identified in

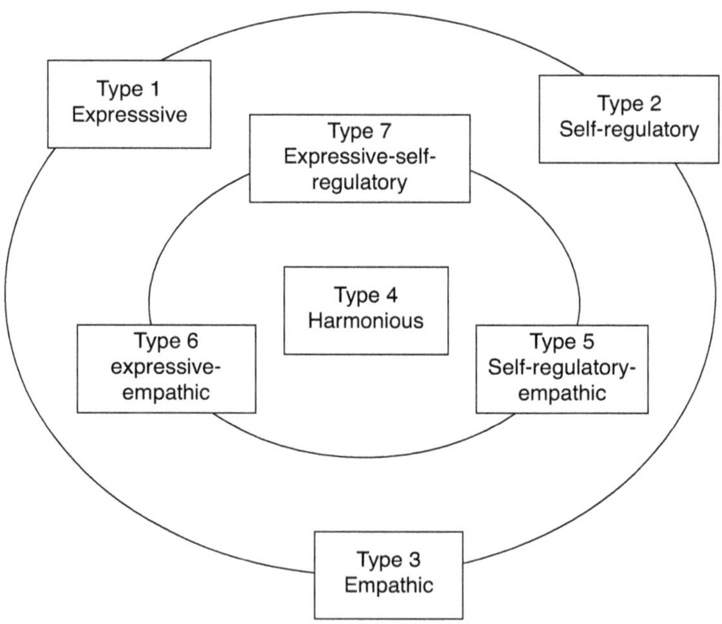

FIGURE 3.5.10 Model of the main types of emotional maturity of a person.

TABLE 3.5.22 Expressiveness of indicators that characterize the features of emotional maturity and personality traits in young men 18–23 years old with high and low levels of emotional maturity

Level of emotional maturity	*Ex*	*S*	*Em*	*IEx*	*EEx*	*IS*	*ES*	*IEm*	*EEm*	*EZ*	*F5*	*F6*	*SE*	*E*
low	*4.2*	*4.4*	*5.4*	*2.3*	*1.9*	*2.0*	*2.4*	*2.9*	*2.5*	*14.0*	*4.4*	*4.8*	*72.3*	*17.6*
high	8.3	9.4	9.7	4.2	4.1	3.9	5.4	4.8	4.9	27.4	5.1	6.1	59.0	18.1
t	6.33**	6.63**	5.67**	6.85**	3.99**	4.0**	6.22**	6.26**	4.68**	5.84**	0.61	2.07*	2.06*	0.22

18.75% of all subjects, the second in 25%, the third in 30.5%, the fourth in 3.5%; the fifth in 10%, the sixth in 7.25% and the seventh in 5%. The given data indicate that types with a predominance of one of the components of emotional maturity in the sample are much more frequent than mixed ones. The most widespread is the empathic type. Expressive-self-regulatory and harmonious types are almost exceptional, the first of which is based on a purely empirical assumption about the possibility of existence in some individuals of the same intensity of opposite emotional properties (emotional excitability, impulsivity emotional stability, balance), and the other indicates the absence of prevalence of one of the emotional qualities over the others in the individuals of this group.

Turning to the analysis of the defined typological groups, we should point out that the first three groups show a significant dominance of the leading indicator over others. Thus, with rather high estimates of the indicator "Ex" in the expressive group, the values of the indicators "S" and "Em" are markedly lower. The same picture is observed in self-regulatory and empathic groups. Regarding mixed types, it should be noted that the average values of all indicators in these groups are lower than in the previous ones. The only exception is the expressive-empathic group, where the estimates of "Ex" and "Em" are at the border of medium and high levels.

A certain interest is committed to the value of the integrative parameter "EZ" in the defined groups, as it is an indicator of the effectiveness of a particular type of emotional maturity in general. The data obtained for this parameter indicate unequal levels of its expression (see Table 3.5.23).

Thus, the highest average values of the integrative parameter "EZ" were found in the harmonious (group 4: x = 22.43) and expressive-empathic (group 6: x = 22.45) groups, the lowest average values are obtained in the expressive-self-regulatory group 7: x = 19.65); in the other groups the estimates occupy an intermediate position between these values.

Statistical verification of differences in the intensity of the parameter "EZ" between groups showed high validity only between the expressive-self-regulatory, empathic ($t = 2.01$; $p < 0.05$) and expressive-empathic ($t = 2.11$; $p < 0.05$) groups.

These data allow us to conclude that individuals with an empathic and expressive-empathic type of emotional maturity achieve a higher level of adequacy of emotional reactions than those belonging to the expressive-self-regulatory type.

TABLE 3.5.23 Intensity of integrative parameter of emotional maturity in different typological groups

Mean value (x), standard deviation (σ)	*Typological groups*						
	1	*2*	*3*	*4*	*5*	*6*	*7*
X	20.95	21.01	21.96	22.43	20.28	22.45	19.65
Σ	4.77	4.56	3.91	4.62	5.08	4.30	4.53

In general, the most effective formation of emotional maturity is found in people with a harmonious and expressive-empathic type.

In order to determine the specific symptom complexes of emotionally specific properties attributed to each of the identified types of emotional maturity for each typological group, the interrelations between indicators that characterize them were analyzed by correlation and factor analysis.

The obtained results showed that the most important in the formation of emotional maturity of persons of expressive type is the factor of "emotional instability"(see Table 3.5.24).

As seen from the table, this factor is formed by indicators that characterize neuroticism ("F1"), neurotism ("N"), emotional lability ("F11") and depressiveness ("F3"). The other factor of "social activity" (18.79%) consists of indicators that characterize the level of extraversion ("E" and "F10"), reactive aggression ("F7") and comradeship ("F5"). The third and fourth factors have a low percentage of general dispersion, the indicators that comprise them have no significant connections with the indicators of emotional maturity.

Note. * factor has a negative relationship with the indicators of emotional maturity.

These data indicate that in individuals belonging to the expressive type are characterized by, first, emotional instability – it is expressed in a certain anxiety, neuroticism, frequent mood swings, irritability, agitation, lack of self-regulation and sometimes signs of depressive syndrome in the emotional state.

Secondly, the outward orientation of activity, which is characterized by a pronounced extroversion of a personality, the need for communication and constant readiness for its satisfaction, as well as a certain desire for domination.

The study of correlation and factor data in the self-regulatory typological group showed that the most important factor here is "social activity" (see Table 3.5.24). The factor is formed from indicators that characterize extraversion ("F10" and "4E"), comradeship ("F5"), expressiveness of masculine traits ("F12"), reactive aggression ("F7") and balance ("F6"). As can be seen from these data, the composition of the factor in the self-regulatory group differs somewhat from the analogous in the expressive group primarily in that it contains properties such as balance and masculinity.

The second factor – "passivity" – consists of indicators that characterize the level of shyness ("F8"), neurotism ("H"), depressiveness ("F3") and neuroticism ("F1"). According to the data of correlation analysis, these indicators demonstrate in the first place a negative connection with the indicator "S", so the interpretation of this factor is the opposite. In other words, the self-regulatory type is characterized by a rather low level of these properties. Also, a negative connection with the indicators of emotional maturity was demonstrated by the indicators included in the third factor "imbalance". These are indicators that characterize irritability ("F4"), emotional lability ("F11") and spontaneous aggression ("F2").

These data point to the fact that a high level of activity and balance are characteristic of the self-regulatory type. This is expressed in extravertedness, emotional

TABLE 3.5.24 The content of factors associated with indicators of emotional maturity in representatives of various typological groups

Typological group													
Expressive		*Self-regulatory*		*Empathic*		*Harmonious*		*Self-regulatory-empathic*		*Expressive and empathic*		*Expressive-self-regulatory*	
Name of the factor	Indicator (factor load))	Name of the factor	Indicator (factor load)	Name of the factor	Indicator (factor load)	Name of the factor	Indicator (factor load)	Name of the factor	Indicator (factor load)	Name of the factor	Indicator (factor load)	Name of the factor	Indicator (factor load)
Emotional instability 9.79 %	F1 (0.90) H (0.81) F11 (0.68) F3 (0.59)	Social activity 23.99 %	F10 (0.85) F5 (0.74) F12 (0.73) F7 (0.69) E (0.65) F6 (0.58)	Emotional volatility* 24.10 %	F11 (0.85) F1 (0.80) H (0.78) F3 (0.73) F8 (0.60) F4 (0.50)	Equilibrium 35.98 %	F6 (0.95) F10 (0.90) CO (0.85) F5 (0.77) F2 (−0.93)	Emotional imbalance * 25.24 %	F3 (0.92) F11 (0.84) H (0.75) F2 (0.65) F1 (0.62)	Emotional instability 32.2 %	F3 (0.81) F1 (0.79) F4 (0.70) F8 (0.60)	Impulsiveness 5.87 %	F2 (0.89) E (0.85) H (0.65) F8 (−0.72)
Social activity 18.79 %	E (0.86) F10 (0.79) F7 (0.66) F5 (0.60)	Passivity* 19.34 %	F8 (0.80) H (0.75) F3 (0.71) F1 (0.58)	Social activity 20.06 %	F10 (0.77) F12 (0.73) F7 (0.69) E (0.68) F5 (0.65)	Aggressiveness* 21.56 %	F7 (0.89) F1 (0.89) F4 (0.85)	Balance in communication 18.36%	F6 (0.80) E (0.69) F10 (0.68) F5 (0.66)	comradeship 19.08 %	F5 (0.81) F10 (0.77) H (−0.67)		
		Unbalance* 14.05 %	F4 (0.72) F11 (0.63) F2 (0.61)			18.81 Emotional instability *	H (0.91) F11 (0.67) E (−0.78)						

stability, camaraderie, commitment to domination, self-confidence, optimism and protection against the effects of stress factors in everyday life situations.

The factor analysis in the group of representatives of the **empathic type** allowed us to identify 4 factors, two of which have a significant weight (see Table 3.5.24). The table shows that the factor of "emotional instability" is also related to the empathic group. It consists of indicators that characterize emotional lability ("F11"), neuroticism ("F1"), neurotism ("N"), depressivity ("F3"), shyness ("F8") and irritability ("F4"). Correlation analysis data show a negative relationship between some of these indicators ("F3", "F8") and indicators of emotional maturity. This allows us to characterize the representatives of the empathic group as persons with unstable emotional states together with insufficient self-regulation and irritability, i.e. signs that characterize the asthenic type of emotional response. The other factor of "social activity" (20.06%) consists of indicators that characterize the intensity of extra-introversion ("F10" and "E"), masculinity ("F12"), reactive aggression ("F7") and comradeship ("F5"). These data show that individuals of the empathic group, as well as expressive persons, have an outward orientation of activity, i.e. pronounced extroversion and social activity.

The factor of "balance" (35.98%) is the most important in the formation of emotional maturity of persons of **harmonious type**. It has two poles (see Table 3.5.24). As can be seen from the table, the first pole is formed from indicators that characterize balance itself ("F6"), extraversion ("F10"), personal self-esteem ("SE") and camaraderie ("F5"). The other pole is formed by an indicator that determines the level of spontaneous aggression ("F2" with a factor weight of 0.93). These data indicate that people with harmonious development of all components of emotional maturity are characterized by a balanced emotional state, non-impulsiveness, personality orientation to social objects, the adequacy of self-assessment, and his/her place among others.

The other factor "aggression" (21.56%) consists of indicators that characterize reactive aggressivity ("F7"), neuroticism ("F1") and irritability ("F4"). The negative nature of the connection between these indicators and attributes of "EEm" indicates the absence of aggressive tendencies in behavior of representatives of the harmonious group, which contributes to the establishment of emotional contacts with communication partners.

The third factor of "emotional instability" (18.81%) is bipolar. The first pole is formed by indicators that determine the level of neurotism ("N") and emotional lability ("F11"). The second is the extraversion ("E") index. Correlation analysis data also point to the negative relationship between this factor and emotional maturity.

Such peculiarities of the factor distribution in a harmonious group allow characterizing its representatives as well-balanced, emotionally stable, and devoid of a tendency to react aggressively.

In the **self-regulatory-empathic group**, factor analysis revealed two important factors that describe 43.6% of the dispersion of the studied characteristics (see Table 3.5.24). The first factor of "emotional imbalance" (25.24%) consists of indicators that characterize depressiveness ("F3"), emotional lability ("F11"), neurotism ("N"), spontaneous aggression ("F2") and neuroticism ("F1"). Low individual and group estimates of these indicators allow us to assume that the low level of depressiveness, emotional lability, neurotism and impulsiveness that is inherent to the representatives of this group. The second-factor "balance in communication" (18.36%) is formed from the balance ("F6"), extravertedness ("E" and "F10") and comradeship ("F5") indicators. This factor is opposite in content to the first factor. In addition, the indicators it comprises show strong positive connections with the components of emotional maturity. This fact confirms the assumption that the representatives of this group possess emotional equilibrium and focuses on the fact that it is based on self-confidence, optimism, high social activity and mastery of communication skills.

Turning to the examination of correlation and factor structures obtained in expressive-empathic and expressive-self-regulatory groups, it is worth noting that the interpretation of their meaning is somewhat complicated by the absence of significant correlations with emotional maturity and requires additional consideration of individual and group assessments.

Thus, in the expressive-empathic group, the first factor of "emotional instability" (32.20%) is formed by indicators that characterize depressiveness ("F3"), neuroticism ("F1"), shyness ("F8") and irritability ("F4") (see Table 3.5.24). These indicators do not show any significant correlation with indicators of emotional maturity, but according to the analysis of its average estimates, the expressiveness of these indicators in the group is high enough to consider representatives of the expressive-empathetic group as persons with unstable emotional state, passive-defensive type of emotional response to these or other stressful situations, irritability and neuroticism.

The second-factor "camaraderie" (19.08%) has two poles. The first is represented by indicators that characterize the level of sociability ("F5" – 0.81) and extraversion ("F10" – 0.77), and the second is by the indicator of neurotism ("N" – 0.67). The content of this factor allows us to assume that in general the representatives of this group are characterized by high companionship, which is expressed in the focus of the individual on the external social environment, a high need for social contacts, and the real possibility of satisfying it.

The first-factor "impulsiveness" (25.87%), defined in the **expressive-self-regulatory group**, is quite specific (see Table 3.5.24). As seen from the table, the factor has two poles, the first of which is formed by indicators characterizing spontaneous aggression ("F2"), extraversion ("E") and neurotism ("N"), the second pole is represented by only one indicator "F8" with significant factor weight (−0.72). According to the content of this factor, the representatives of the expressive-self-regulatory type have a certain impulsiveness of behavior, high emotional tension, even anxiety, and at the same time, general orientation toward the social environment. The other factor – "emotional lability", composed of indicators that characterize emotional lability ("F11"), repressiveness ("F3") and neuroticism ("F1") – indicates the presence of certain emotional nervousness, mood-altering tendencies in individuals with the expressive-self-regulatory type of emotional maturity.

Summarizing the obtained information allowed us to give a brief description of each type of emotional maturity of the individual:

- Expressive type, which is found in 18.75% of adolescents and young adults, is characterized by the domination of emotional expressiveness over other components of emotional maturity, the general development of which is moderate. Representatives of this type express emotional instability (frequent mood swings, excessive agitation, irritability, lack of self-regulation) and outward-directed activity (extrovertedness, the need for communication, the desire for domination).
- Self-regulatory type found in 25% of the studied sample is distinguished by the domination of emotional self-regulation with the moderate formation of other components of emotional maturity. Representatives of this type are characterized by a high level of activity and balance, expressed in extravertedness, emotional stability, camaraderie, self-confidence and optimism.
- Empathic type that occurs most often – in 30.5% of cases – is characterized by the domination of empathy and a higher level of formation of emotional maturity in general than the previous types. Representatives of this type have inherent emotional lability, anxiety and resistance to stressful reactions, along with extroversion and camaraderie.
- Harmonious type was detected only in 3.5% of adolescents and young adults, who were characterized by the same intensity of all components of emotional maturity, with a rather high overall adequacy of emotional response. People belonging to the harmonious type are characterized by balance, emotional stability, nonaggressiveness, focus on social objects, and an adequate assessment of own capabilities and one's place, among others.
- Self-regulatory-empathic type is observed in 10% of test takers, which is characterized by the domination of emotional self-regulation and empathy with moderate overall adequacy of emotional response. Individuals belonging to this type have a certain emotional balance, based on self-confidence, optimism, high social activity and communication skills.
- Expressive-empathic type is found in 7.25% of respondents, and features the domination of emotional expressiveness and empathy over emotional self-regulation, and a high level of formation of emotional maturity in general, emotional instability, orientation to the external social environment, need for communication and camaraderie.
- Expressive self-regulatory type, which was detected in 5% of tested individuals, is characterized by the lowest level of emotional maturity, which includes emotional expressiveness and self-regulation in its structure. Representatives of this type show certain impulsive behavior, high emotional tension and even anxiety, and at the same time, they are oriented toward social connection.

The given results allowed us to adapt the "Diagnosis of emotional maturity" questionnaire, which consisted in creating a Ukrainian-language version and developing scales for determining the standard values of diagnosed indicators in relation to the age of the tested persons. It was also shown that there are certain age differences in the formation of emotional maturity of a person.

Thus, statistically proven differences are observed

- between adolescents aged 13 and 14 in the ability to control their own emotions;
- between 14- and 15-year-olds in the ability to arbitrarily express emotions in communication;
- between 17- and 18–23-year-olds for all the components of emotional maturity;

We have also identified certain age dynamics in the formation of relationships between the components of emotional maturity: from minor correlations at the age of 11–12 years, to their strengthening at the age of 13–14 years, and further weakening in 15, 16, 17 and 18–23 years;

We have found the connection between components of emotional maturity with extraversion and comradeship in all age groups studied, which indicates their importance for the development of these abilities. Such a trait as the balance is getting a positive value for the formation of emotional maturity at the age of 12 and 13 years, while personal self-esteem is at the age of 14, 15 and 16 years. Shyness at 11, 17 and 18–23 years, irritability at 12 and 13 years, and neuroticism at 16, 17 and 18–23 years cause negative influence on the formation of components of emotional maturity.

Also, it was established that the general level of emotional maturity does not differ fundamentally in persons of different sexes. As for its individual components, there are certain differences in their manifestation, namely: girls are more active in the ability to empathize and sympathize, they better understand the emotional state and motives of the partner's behavior in communication; boys are more successful in developing the ability to regulate their own emotions.

The obtained data allow us not only to assume that males and females choose different ways to achieve adequacy of emotional response but also describe gender differences, manifested at the level of interrelations between the components of emotional maturity and emotional and personal characteristics. They are most significant in the interrelations of empathy, which in boys is more often associated with emotional lability, depressiveness and irritability.

The smallest differences were identified in the determination of emotional expressiveness; as well as the tendency for decreasing with age of gender differences in relation to emotional maturity. Thus, in the process of developing abilities that ensure the adequacy of emotional response, the differences in personal determinants are smoothed out. It was shown that the connection of extravertedness and comradeship with the emotional maturity of a person is equally common for both boys and girls.

It was found that age-related changes in the intercomponent interactions of emotional maturity are independent of the gender of the tested persons.

Conditional stages in the formation of the emotional maturity of a person are presented. They are characterized:

- by the domination of the expressive organization of emotional maturity at the first stage (11–13 years);
- by the improvement of conscious regulation of emotional response at the second stage (14–15 years);
- the third stage (16–17 years) shows a significant improvement in the personal level of emotional maturity;
- the fourth stage (18–23 years) is a period of autonomously balanced and relatively stable manifestation of emotional maturity.

The change of stages is marked by significant leaps in the dynamics of the corresponding components of emotional maturity.

We have identified a typological model of emotional maturity, that includes 7 types, namely expressive, self-regulatory, empathic, harmonious, self-regulatory-empathic, expressive-empathic and expressive-self-regulatory.

We have shown that the most widespread of them are empathic (30.5%) and self-regulatory (25%) types. Expressive-self-regulatory (5%) and harmonious (3.5%) types are rare. Representatives of different types have different general levels of development of emotional maturity, and the most effective development is found in persons belonging to the harmonious and expressive-empathic type. Insufficient adequacy of emotional response can be observed in representatives of expressive-self-regulatory type. Emotional instability is essential for the expressive type; self-regulatory and self-regulatory-empathic types are characterized by balance and self-confidence; empathic and expressive-empathic types by emotional lability; expressive-self-regulatory type by impulsive behavior and anxiety; and harmonious type by emotional stability and nonaggressiveness. Common to all types of emotional maturity is the orientation of a person to the social environment and the need for communication.

3.6 Conclusions

Summarizing all obtained data, the following general conclusions can be made:

1 It was proved that emotional maturity in modern psychology is viewed ambiguously. We can distinguish three consistent approaches to understanding the concept of emotional maturity:
   - as the conformity of emotional manifestations of an adult, i.e. biologically mature person, to the norms of a given society;

- as conformity of emotional manifestations of an adult person not only to the expectations of society but also to the needs, values and interests of the subject;
- as the correspondence of emotional behavior to the beliefs about the norm for a certain age.

In general, we can define emotional maturity as an integrative quality of personality, which characterizes the degree of development of the emotional sphere at the level of adequacy of emotional reactions in certain sociocultural conditions. To the greatest extent, it is reflected in the peculiarities of the manifestation of emotional expressiveness, emotional self-regulation and empathy. These properties are part of the structure of emotional maturity and are its main components.

2 In the context of the theoretical and methodological model presented in the research the methodology of emotionality maturity diagnostics was suggested. The latter allows estimating its general index on the basis of:
   - expressiveness, with a consideration of its own adequacy, reflecting its emergences, as well as perceiving them in people and influencing it;
   - self-regulation at the level of its own development, as well as perceiving and influencing it in people;
   - empathy at the level of adequacy of reflection of its own manifestations, as well as perceiving it in people and influencing it in them.

3 An empirical study of the emotional maturity of adolescents and young adults has revealed certain age-related differences in its formation, which indicate a tendency for the level of its individual properties to increase with age: from 13 to 14 years, at the level of controlling own emotions; from 14 to 15 years, at the level of arbitrary expression of emotion in communication; and from 17 to 18–23 years, at the level of all components of emotional maturity.

4 There are gender differences in the manifestation of signs of emotional maturity, namely girls are most active in the formation of empathy and sympathy, understanding of emotional state and motives of behavior of a communication partner; boys are in the regulation of their own emotions. Gender differences are also manifested at the level of interconnection of the main components of emotional maturity and emotional and personal characteristics. They are most significant in the interrelations of empathy, which is more often connected with emotional lability, depression and irritability in boys than in girls. The smallest differences are found in the determination of emotional expressiveness.

5 The conducted research on age and gender differences in the context of the manifestation of attributes of emotional maturity during adolescence and early adulthood made it possible to distinguish the main stages of its formation:
   - the first stage (11–13 years) is represented by the domination of expressiveness;

- the second stage (14–15 years) is represented by the domination of self-regulation;
- the third stage (16–17 years) shows a significant improvement in the personal level of emotional maturity;
- the fourth stage (18–23 years) is a period of autonomously balanced and relatively stable manifestation of emotional maturity.

6 The results of the research give us grounds to state that it is possible to create a typological model of the emotional maturity of a person, which includes 7 types, namely expressive, self-regulatory, empathic, harmonious, self-regulatory-empathic, expressive-empathic and expressive-self-regulatory. The most common of these are empathic (30.5%) and self-regulatory (25%) types. Expressive-self-regulatory (5%) and harmonious (3.5%) types are rare.

It was shown that emotional instability is typical for the expressive type; the self-regulatory and self-regulatory-empathic are characterized by balance and self-confidence; empathic and expressive-empathic – by emotional lability; expressive-self-regulatory – by impulsiveness of behavior and anxiety; and harmonious – by emotional stability and nonaggressiveness. All types of emotional maturity evince the orientation of the individual toward the social environment and the need for communication.

7 Certain regularities in the formation of emotional maturity in adolescence and early adulthood, which exhibit the corresponding evidence of mental development, were determined, namely:
   1 irregularity of the formation of emotional maturity, which is manifested in the imbalance in the development of the basic properties and levels of their manifestation, as expressed in the stages of its formation;
   2 integration and subsequent attainment of autonomy of individual components of emotional maturity, which is reflected in the age dynamics of formation of links between the components of emotional maturity: from insignificant correlations at the age of 11–12 years, to their strengthening at the age of 13–14 years, and further weakening at the age of 15, 16, 17 and 18–23;
   3 connection with certain personal qualities, namely, extroversion and camaraderie. In the study, it manifests itself regardless of age, gender and type of emotional maturity.

This study does not cover all aspects of the problem under consideration. In our opinion, the following areas of further work may be promising: (a) theoretical and experimental disclosure of the cognitive aspect of the formation of emotional maturity, i.e. study of patterns and mechanisms of realizing one's own emotions and the emotions of other people; (b) study of conditions and ways of forming emotional maturity in psychological and pedagogical process; (c) widening the range of research of this property, i.e. examining the prerequisites of the formation of emotional maturity in childhood and the dynamics of its signs in adulthood and old age, etc.

References

Abdyukova, N.V. (2000). *Psychological peculiarities of contemporary pre-adult socialization*: Dissertation abstract. Kiev.

Abolin, L.M. (1974). Ballance *of psychological and psychophysiological correlates of athletes' emotional stability.* Voprosy Psychologii, 1, 104–106.

Abolin, L.M. (1987). *Psychological mechanisms of human emotional stability.* Kazan: Kazan University Press.

Abramenkova, V.V. (2002). *Psychology of childhood in the context of child relations in the world.* Voprosy Psychologii, 1, 3–16.

Abramova, G. (2003). *The flow of life.* In: Psychology of maturity. Anthology. D.Ya. Raygorodsky (ed.). Samara: BAHRAKH-M, 244–314.

Abulkhanova-Slavskaya, K.A. (2003). *Life strategy: how to build it?* In: Psychology of maturity. Anthology. D.Ya. Raygorodsky (ed.). Samara: BAHRAKH-M, 527–566.

Al-Hadidi Saud, A.A. (2001). *Cross-cultural differences in the perception of emotions by Arab and Slovenian students (based on the study of perception of facial expression by Arabic and Slovenian students)*: Dissertation abstract. Kiev.

Alpatova O.V. (2002). *Psychological analysis of the regulatory function of teacher's empathy in the process of of junior pupils*: Dissertation abstract. Kiev, Institute of Psychology.

Aminov, N.A. (1988). *Psychophysiological and psychological prerequisites of pedagogical abilities.* Voprosy Psychologii, 5, 71–77.

Ananiev, A.M. (1996). *Visual psychodiagnostics of emotional manifestations in students*: Dissertation abstract. Odessa.

Andreeva, G.M. (2002). *Social psychology.* 5th edition. Moscow: Aspect Press.

Andreeva, G.M., Helkama, K., Dubovskaya, E.M., Stefanenko, T.G., Tikhomandritskaya, O.A. (1997). *The level of social stability and features of socialization in senior school age.* Vestnik Moskow University. Ser. 14. Psychology, 4, 31–41.

Andrienko, V.O. (1999). *Mathematical statistics for psychologists: Textbook.* Odessa: Astroprint.

Anokhin, P.K. (1964). *Emotions.* In: Big Medical Encyclopedia: Vol. 35. Moscow, 339–357.

Anziferova, L.I. (1980). *Psychological regularities of personality development of an adult and the problem of lifelong learning.* Psychological Journal, 2, 52–60.

Apetik, N.M. (2001). *Moral self-regulation as a condition to prevent deviant behavior in adolescents*: Dissertation abstract. Kiev: Publishing house Institute of Psychology of Kyiv.

Asmolov, A.G. (1984). *Personality as a subject of psychological research.* Moscow: Publishing House of Moscow State University.

Asmolov, A.G. (2001). *Psychology of the personality: principles of general psychological analysis.* Moscow: Smysl.

Avanesov, V.S. (1982). *Tests in sociological research.* Moscow: Nauka.

Bazhin, E.F., Korneva, T.V. (1981). *Mental pathology as a model for the study of impressive activity.* In: Psychology of interpersonal cognition. A.A. Bodalev (ed.). Moscow: Pedagogy, 196–211.

Bekh, I.D. (1986). *On mastering the personality's own emotional experiences.* In: Emotional regulation of educational and labor activity. Moscow. Odessa: Materials of the All-Union Conference Institute of Psychology, Society of Psychologists.

Bekhtereva, N.P., Smirnov, V.M. (1975). *Brain organization of human emotions.* Bulletin of the USSR Academy of Medical Sciences, 8, 8–12.

Belinskaya, E.P., Tikhomandritskaya O.A. (2001). *Social psychology of the personality.* Textbook for universities. Moscow: Aspect Press.

Bischof-Köhler, D. (1994). *Selbsobjektivierung und fremdbezogene Emotionen: identifikation des eigenen Spiegelbildes, Empathie und prosoziales verhalten im 2. Zeitschrift für Psychologie*, 4, 349–377

Boryshevsky, M.I. et al. (1995). *Self-regulation as the criterion and condition of socially relevant interaction of the person with other people.* In: Materials of the all- Ukrainian conference: problem and experience of artistic and general education. Odessa, Part 1, 17.

Bozhovich, L.I. (1977). *The concept of cultural and historical development of the psyche and its prospects.* Voprosy Psychologii, 2, 29–39.

Bozhovich, L.I. (1995). *Selected psychological works: problems of personality formation.* D.I. Feldstein (ed.). Moscow: International Academy of psychology.

Bratus, B.S. (1980). *To the problem of personality development in adulthood.* Bulletin of Moscow University, Series 14. Psychology, 2, 3–12.

Breslav, G.M. (1986). *Upbringing of moral norms of the child in the family.* Voprosy Psychologii, 1, 41–47.

Breslav, G.M. (1990). *Emotional characteristics of personality formation in childhood: the norm and deviations.* Moscow: Pedagogy.

Buchek, L.I. (1994). *Analysis of emotional stamina as a manifestation of the peculiarities of a person's self-regulation*: Dissertation abstract. Kiev.

Budnitska, O.A. (2001). *Individually specific determinants of emotional experiences in psychotraumatic situations*: Dissertation abstract. Kiev.

Burns, R. (1986). *The development of self-concept and education.* V.Ya. Pilipovsky (ed.). Moscow: Progress.

Bylkina, N.D., Lyusin, D.V. (2000). *The development of children's ideas about emotions in ontogenesis.* Voprosy Psychologii, 5, 38–48.

Cardwell, J.D., Dunn, T.P. (1986). *Self and self-concepts: a typology.* Journal of Human Behavior and Learning, 3, 1, 30–37.

Chebykin, O.Y. (1986). *Theoretical and methodological aspects of emotional regulation of educational and cognitive activity.* In: Emotional regulation of educational and labor activity. Moscow, Odessa: Materials of the All-Union Conference. Moscow Academy of Sciences of the USSR, 238–244.

Chebykin, O.Y. (1989a). *The problem of emotional stability.* In: Mental tension in labor activity. Moscow: IP AN SSSR, 197–217.

Chebykin, O.Y. (1989b). *Teacher and emotional regulation of educational activity of schoolchildren training.* Voprosy Psychologii, 6, 42–49.

Chebykin, O.Y. (1992). *Emotional regulation of educational and cognitive activity.* Odessa: Academy of Sciences, Society of Psychologists of the USSR.

Chebykin, O.Y. (1995). *The problem of emotional stability.* Odessa: South Ukrainian Pedagogical University. K. D. Ushinsky.

Chebykin, A.Y. (1989a). *Problems of emotional stability.* Materials of an All-Union Conference on Mental Tension of Labor Activity. Moscow, Institute of Psychology, 197–217.

Chebykin, A.Y. (1989b). *Teacher and emotional regulation of pupils' learning activity.* Voprosy psychologii, 6, 42–49.

Chebykin, O.Y., Abolin, L.M. (1984). *The study of emotional stability and psychological means of its formation.* Journal of Psychology, 4, 83–89.

Chebykin, O.Y., Pavlova, I.G. (2009). *Formation of emotional maturity of the personality.* Odessa: Southern Scientific Center of the Academy of Pedagogical Sciences of Ukraine.

Cherevko, V.P. (2001). *Formation of communicative competence of future managers in the process of professional training*: Dissertation abstract. Kiev.

Chernikova, O.A. (1962). *Emotions in sports (The nature of emotions and their significance in sports).* Moscow: Fizkultura i sport.

Chesnokova, O.B., Yaremchuk, M.V. (2002). *The phenomenon of "imaginary partner" in childhood.* Voprosy Psychologii, 2, 14–27.

Chirikova, A.E. (1976). *The application of the technique of visual representations method for diagnostics of affect in interpersonal relations.* Voprosy Psychologii, 5, 114–119.

Chomskaya, E.D. (2002). *Neuropsychology of emotions: hypotheses and facts.* Voprosy Psychologii, 4, 50–62.

Chomskaya, E.D., Batova, N.Y. (1992). *Brain and emotions: neuropsychological research.* Moscow: Publishing House of Moscow University.

Chudina, E.A. (2003). *Emotional maturity of a personality: concept definition and criteria selection.* In: Personality and development problems: Collection of works. E.A. Chudin (ed.). Moscow, 112–116.

Cohn, I.S. (1988). *Child and society: a historical and ethnographic perspective.* Moscow: Nauka.

Cohn, I.S. (1989). *The psychology of early adolescence: a book for the teacher.* Moscow: Prosveshcheniye.

Cole, M. (1997). *Cultural-historical psychology: the science of the future.* Moscow: Cogito-Centre.

Craig, G. (2000). *Psychology of development.* St. Petersburg: Peter.

Cunningham, M.R. (1977). *Personality and the structure of the nonverbal communication of emotion.* Journal Person, 45, 564–584.

Danilova, N.N., Krylova, A.L. (1997). *Physiology of higher nervous activity.* Moscow: Uchebnaya literatura.

Dashkevich, O.V. (1986). *Theoretical and methodological aspects of the psychological research of the problem of emotional regulation of activity.* In: Emotional regulation of educational and labor activity. Proceedings of the All-Union Conference of the Institute of Psychology, Society of Psychologists, Moscow, Odessa, 11.

Davydov, V.V. (1974). *The problem of periodization of mental development.* In: Age and pedagogical psychology. V.S. Merlin (ed.). Perm: Proceedings of the All-Union Workshop, 33–53.

Denisova, Z.V. (1978). *Mechanisms of emotional behavior of the child.* Leningrad: Nauka.

Diduk, I.A. (2001). *Relationships between children in family as a factor of their psychosocial development*: Dissertation abstract. Kiev.

Dodonov, B.I. (1972). *Types of general emotional orientation of people and tendencies in structuring the emotional sphere.* Voprosy Psychologii, 1, 45–55.

Donaldson, S.K., Westerman, N.A. (1986). *Development of children's understanding of ambivalence and causal theories of emotions.* Developmental Psychology, 26, 635–662.

Dorfman, L.Y. (1989). *Individual emotional style.* Voprosy Psychologii, 5, 88–95.

Dyachenko, M.I., Kandybovich, L.A. (2001). *Maturity.* In: Psychological dictionary. Minsk: Harvest, Moscow: AST, 90.

Dyachenko, M.I., Ponomarenko, V.A. (1990). *On approaches to the study of emotional stability.* Voprosy Psychologii, 1, 106–113.

Eidemiller, E.G., Yustitsky, V.V. (1989). *Family psychotherapy.* Leningrad: Medicine.

Elkonin, D.B. (1971). *On the problem of periodization of mental development in childhood.* Voprosy Psychologii, 4, 6–20.

Elkonin, D.B. (1989). *Selected psychological works.* V.V. Davidov, V.P. Zinchenko (ed.). Moscow: Pedagogica.

Fetisova, E.V. (1981). *To the question of perception and determination of the emotional state by expressive movements.* Journal of Psychology, 2, 142–146.

Field, T.M. et al. (1982). *Discrimination and imitation of facial expression by neonantes.* Science, 3, 179–181.

Fress, P. (1975). *Emotions.* In: Experimental psychology. P. Fress, J. Piaget (ed.). Moscow: Progress, Issue 5, 111–195.

Ganina, N.A., Korneva, T.V. (1984). *On the influence of an affective state on perception of facial expressions.* In: Socio-psychological problems of rehabilitation of neuropsychiatric patients: Collection of works. E.F. Bazhin (ed.). Leningrad: Medicine, 61–67.

Gavrilova, T.P. (1974). *Experimental study of empathy in children of primary and secondary school age.* Voprosy Psychologii, 5, 107–114.

Gavrilova, T.P. (1984). *On the education of moral feelings.* Moscow: Znaniye.

Geiko, Y.B. (2002). *Psychological features of manifestation of personality egocentrism in mental activity of teenagers*: Dissertation abstract. Kiev.

Gesell, A. (2002). *The cycle of mental development.* In: Psychology of abnormal child development. Anthology in 2 volumes. V.V. Lebedinsky, M.K. Bardyshevskaya (ed.). Vol. 1. Moscow: Moscow State University Publishing House, 488–496.

Gippenreiter, Y.B., Karyagina, T.D., Kozlova, E.N. (1993). *The phenomenon of congruent empathy.* Voprosy Psychologii, 4, 61–68.

Goleman, D. (1996). *Emotional intelligence.* London: Bloomsbury Publishing.

Goleman, D. (2000). *Working with emotional intelligence.* London: Bloomsburry Paperbacks.

Golovakha, E.I., Kronik A.A. (2003). *Psychological age of the personality.* In: Psychology of maturity. Anthology. D.Y. Raygorodsky (ed.). Samara: BAHRAKH-M, 119–144.

Gorbatkov, A.A. (2001). *Positive and negative emotions: interrelation and its dependence on the level of subjective development of the individual.* Psychological Magazine, 1, 61–71.

Goshovsky, Y.O. (1995). *The formation of self-image in the boarding school under conditions of deprivation of parential influence*: Dissertation abstract. Kiev.

Govorun, T.V. (2002). *Socialization of gender as a factor in the development of self-concept*: Dissertation abstract. Kiev.

Gozman, L.Y. (1987). *The psychology of emotional relations.* Moscow: Publishing House of Moscow State University.

Granovska, R.M. (1997). *Elements of practical psychology.* St. Petersburg: Peter.

Gray, D.A. (1968). *Nervous system strength, introversion - extraversion, conditioned reflexes and activation reaction.* Voprosy Psychologii, 3, 77–88.

Greene, A.L. (1990). *Great expectations: constructions of the life course during adolescence.* Journal of Youth and Adolescence, 19, 289–303.

Griffith, M.S. (1999). *Workplace bullying: responding with some emotional intelligence.* European Journal of Marketing. 20, 176.

Gurevich, K.M. (1970). *Professional suitability and basic properties of the nervous system.* Moscow: Nauka.

Horney, K. (2002). *Introspection. The psychology of a woman. New paths in psychoanalysis.* St. Petersburg: Peter, 252–259.

Ilyin, E.P. (2001a). *Differential psychophysiology.* St. Petersburg: Peter.

Ilyin, E.P. (2001b). *Emotions and feelings.* St. Petersburg: Peter.

Isaev, D.N. (1982). *Mental underdevelopment in children.* Lenungrad: Medicine.

Isaev, D.N. (2000). *Psychosomatic disorders in children: a guide for physicians.* St. Petersburg: Peter.

Izard, K.E. (1980). *Human emotions.* Moscow: Publishing House of Moscow State University.

Jakobson, P.M. (1977). *On expression in the actor's act.* Journal of Psychology Moscow, 1, 86–95.

Kagan, V.E. (2000). *Cognitive and emotional aspects of gender attitudes in children 3–7 years old.* Voprosy Psychologii, 2, 65–69.

Kairis, E.D. (2001). *Empathy as a factor of pedagogical competence.* Practical Psychology and Social Work, 8, 42–45.

Kirichenko, T.V. (2001). *Psychological mechanisms of self-regulation in the behavior of teenagers*: Dissertation abstract. Kiev.

Kirillova, M.G., Kurek, N.S. (2002). *Emotions and motivation of patients with schizophrenia in situations of cooperation and competition*. Psychological Journal, 5, 80–99.

Klee, M. (1991). *Psychology of a teenager: psychosexual development*. Moscow: Pedagogica.

Koblyanskaya, E.V. (1995). *Psychological aspects of social competence*: Dissertation abstract. St. Petersburg.

Kochnev, V.I. (1986). *The study of the dynamic characteristics of emotional reactivity in connection with the problem of acting abilities*. Voprosy Psychologii, 5, 153–159.

Kolot, S.A. (1999). *Psychological mechanisms and conditions of shaping the culture of emotions in students of higher technical educational institutions*: Dissertation abstract. Odessa.

Konopkin, O.A. (1980). *Psychological mechanisms of activity regulation*. Moscow: Nauka.

Konyukhov, N.I. (1996). *Dictionary of a practicing psychologist*. Voronezh: Voronezh University.

Kotirlo, V.K., Ladivir, S.O. (1985). *The influence of relations in family on the development of children's empathy*. Kiev: Radianska schkola, 24, 67–75.

Kotova, L.M. (2001). *Emotional stability as a factor of the formation of instrumental-effective reliability in students of musical and pedagogical departments*: Dissertation abstract. Kiev.

Kovalev, P.A. (1996). *Age-gender features of the reflection in the consciousness of the structure of own aggressiveness and aggressive behavior*: Dissertation abstract. St. Petersburg.

Kuznetsov, M.A. (2001). Types of emotionality and specificity of attitude to learning in students. *Bulletin of Kharkiv State Pedagogical University*. Psychology, Kharkiv State Pedagogical University Publishing, 8, 126–138.

Krauklis, A.A. (1963). *Self-regulation of higher nervous activity*. Riga: Publishing House of the Academy of Sciences of the Latvian SSR.

Krotenko, V.I. (2001). *Psychological peculiarities of empathy in adolescents*: Dissertation abstract. Kiev.

Krupnik, E.P., Lebedeva, E.N. (2000). *Psychological stability of life constructs in the period of maturity*. Psychological Journal, 6, 12–23.

Krysko, V.G. (2001). *Social psychology: dictionary*. Minsk: Harvest, Moscow: ACT.

Kulachkivska, S.E. (1986). *Understanding emotional manifestations of a teacher by children*. In: Psychology: Collection of works. Kiev: Radianska schkola, 27, 99–109.

Kulagina, I.Y., Kolyutsky, V.N. (2003). *Age psychology: the complete life cycle of human development*. Moscow: Yurayt.

Kulchitskaya, E.I. (2003). *Emotional and intellectual behavior*. Practical Psychology and Social Work, 1, 1–3.

Kulibaly, S. (1995). *Features of the emotional sphere in normal and pathological conditions (practice of cross-cultural and pathopsychological research)*: Dissertation abstract. Kiev.

Kulikov, L.V. (1995). *Psychological research*. St. Petersburg: Rech.

Kunitsyna, V.N., Kazarinova, N.V., Pogolsha, V.M. (2001). *Interpersonal communication*. Textbook for high schools. St. Petersburg: Peter.

Kurek, N.S. (1996). *Mental activity deficit: the passivity of personality and disease*. Moscow: Institute of Psychology of the Russian Academy of Sciences.

Labunskaya, V.A. (1987). *Peculiarities of the development of the ability to psychological interpretation of non-verbal behavior*. Voprosy Psychologii, 3, 70–77.

Lambert, C. (1998). *The emotional path to success*. Harvard Magazine.

Lebedinsky, V.V. (1985). *Disorders of the mental development of children*. Moscow: Publishing House of Moscow State University.

Lebedinsky, V.V., Bardyshevskaya M.K. (2002). Infective development in norm and in pathology. Vol. 2. Moscow State University Press, 1(2), 588–681.

Lebedinsky, V.V., Bardyshevskaya, M.K. (2002). *Affective development in norm and pathology.* In: Psychology of abnormal child development: Anthology in 2 volumes. V.V. Lebedinsky and M.K. Bardyshevskaya (ed.). Moscow: CheRo, Vyshaya Schkola, Publishing House of Moscow State University, Vol. 1, 588–681.

Leontiev, A.N. (1975a). *Activity. Consciousness. Personality.* Moscow: Politizdat.

Leontiev, A.N. (1975b). Preface. In: Experimental psychology. P. Fress, J. Piaget (ed.). Moscow: Progress Publishing House, Issue 5, 5–12.

Leontiev, A.N. (1984). *Needs, motives, emotions.* In: Psychology of emotions: Texts. V.K. Vilyunas, Y.B. Gippenreiter (ed.). Moscow: Publishing House of Moscow State University, 166–172.

Libin, A.V. (2000). *Differential psychology: at the intersection of European, Russian and American traditions.* Moscow: Smysl; Per Se.

Lichko, A.E. (1983). *Psychopathy and character accentuations in adolescents.* Leningrad: Medicine.

Ljutak, O.Z. (2001). *Psychological peculiarities of the socialization of senior school students*: Dissertation abstract. Ivano-Frankivsk.

Lomov, B.F. (1984). *Methodological and theoretical problems of psychology.* Moscow: Nauka.

Lopukhova, O.G. (2001). *The influence of ethno-cultural traditions on the formation of the psychological gender of a person.* Voprosy Psychologii, 5, 73–74.

Luk, A.N. (1982). *Emotions and personality.* Moscow: Znanie.

Makarenko, S.S. (2001). *Psychological conditions for the development of teacher's communicative competence*: Dissertation abstract. Kiev.

Maksimova, N.Y., Milyutina, K.L., Piskun, V.M. (1996). *Fundamentals of child pathopsychology: textbook.* Kiev: Perun.

Makushina, O.P. (2002). *Reasons of psychological dependence on parents in adolescence.* Voprosy Psychologii, 5, 135–143.

Malimon, L.Y. (2003). *Specificity of emotionality in persons with a different level of creativity*: Dissertation abstract. Kharkiv.

Manerov, V.K. (1990). *Successfulness of perception of the speaker depending on individual characteristics of the listeners.* Voprosy Psychologii, 1, 147–153.

Maslow, A.G. (1999). *Distant limits of the human psyche.* N.N. Akulina (ed.). St. Petersburg: Eurasia.

Maurer, A. (1990). *Emotional maturity as a criterion for readiness to study at school.* In: Diagnostics and regulation of emotional states. Part 2. Proceedings of the All-Union Conference of the Institute of Psychology, Society of Psychologists, Odessa, 67–74.

Mayer, J.D., Salovey, P. (1993). *The intelligence of emotional intelligence.* Intelligence, 17, 443–442.

Melnichuk, I.V. (2003). *The genesis of emotional peculiarities in children of different age and gender*: Dissertation abstract. Kharkiv.

Mendelevich, V.D. (1998). *Clinical and medical psychology.* Practical guide. Moscow: MEDpress.

Menninger, W.C. (1967). *A psychiatrist for a troubled world.* New York: Macmillan.

Miller, A. (1988). *Toward a theory of personality types.* Canadian Psychology, 29, 263–283.

Milrud, R.P. (1987). *Emotional regulation of teacher's behavior.* Voprosy Psychologii, 6, 46–55.

Mironenko, T.P. (2001). *Formation of public maturity in prospective teachers*: Dissertation abstract. Odessa.

Mitina, L.M., Asmakovets, E.S. (2001). *Emotional flexibility of the teacher: psychological content, diagnostics and correction*: Moscow: MPSI.

Morgun, V.F. (1977). *Psychologists are guided by practice.* Bulletin of Moscow University. Series 14. Psychology, 3, 90–93.

Morgun, V.F., Tkacheva, N.Y. (1981). *The problem of periodization of personality development in psychology.* Moscow: Publishing House of Moscow State University.

Morosanova, V.I. (2002). *Personal aspects of self-regulation of voluntary human activity.* Psychological Journal, 6, 5–17.

Moskvin, V.A. (1988). *Interhemispheric asymmetry and individual styles of emotional reactions.* Voprosy Psychologii, 6, 116–120.

Mukhina, V.S. (2000). *Age psychology: phenomenology of development, childhood, adolescence.* Moscow: Academy.

Myasishchev, V.N. (1960). *The basic problems and the current state of the psychology of human relations.* In: Psychological science in the USSR. (Ed.) B.G. Ananiev et al. Moscow: Publishing house of the Russian Academy of Pedagogical Sciences, Vol. 2 (2), 110–125.

Nebylitsyn, V.D. (1971). *Actual problems of differential psychophysiology.* Voprosy Psychologii, 6, 13–27.

Newcomb, N. (2002). *The development of the child's personality.* St. Petersburg: Peter.

Nosenko, E.L., Kovriga, N.V. (2003). *Emotional intelligence: conceptualization of the phenomenon, main functions.* Kiev: Vishcha schkola.

Obukhovsky, K. (1972). *Psychology of human drives.* Moscow: Progress.

Okano, K. (1994). *Shame and social phobia: a transcultural viewpoint.* Bulletin of the Menninger Clinic, 3, 323–338.

Okun, Y. (1974). *Factor analysis.* Moscow: Statistics.

Olshannikova, A.E. (1977). *The balance between some features of the adolescent' s emotional sphere and physiological indicators.* In: Problems of differential psychophysiology. Moscow: Institute of Psychology, Academy of Pedagogical Sciences, Moscow, Vol. IX, 128–140.

Olshannikova, A.E. (1983). *Emotions and education.* Moscow: Znanie.

Orban-Lembrik, L. (2003). *The influence of crisis and stable periods in person's life into the process of socialization.* Psychology and Society, 2, 55–65.

Oudshoorn, D.N. (2002). *Child and adolescent psychiatry.* In: Psychology of abnormal child development: Anthology in 2 volumes. V.V. Lebedinsky and M.K. Bardyshevskaya (ed.). Moscow: CheRo, Vyschaya shkola, Publishing House of Moscow State University. Vol. 1, 101–123.

Pasichniak, R.F. (1999). *Psychological peculiarities of personality self-determination in senior schoolchildren*: Dissertation abstract. Kiev.

Perepelitsa, A.D. (1990). *Musical culture and the crisis of emotions.* Voprosy Psychologii, 3, 121–125.

Pereverzeva, I.A. (1981). *The study of some features of color perception in relation with the tasks of studying emotionality.* In: Problems of differential psychophysiology. Moscow: Institute of Psychology, Academy of Pedagogical Sciences, 137–146.

Pereverzeva, I.A. (1989). *The manifestation of individual differences in emotionality in the function of controlling emotional expression.* Voprosy Psychologii, 1, 113–117.

Petrovsky, A.V. (1981). *Children and tactics of family upbringing.* Moscow: Znanije.

Petrovsky, A.V., Yaroshevsky, M.G. (1999). *Fundamentals of theoretical psychology.* Moscow: Infra-M.

Piaget, J. (1994). *Selected psychological works. Psychology of intelligence. The genesis of the number in a child. Logic and psychology.* Moscow; International Pedagogical Academy.

Pisarenko, V.M. (1986). *Instrumental feedback and improving the quality of emotional state governance.* Journal of Psychology, 5, 119–125.

Potapchuk, L.V. (2001). *Psychological peculiarities of the formation of personal maturity in senior schoolchildren*: Dissertation abstract. Kiev.

Psychology of personality: Dictionary. (2001). P.P. Ermine, T.M. Titarenko (ed.). Kiev: Ruta, 46, 67.

Rais, F. (2000). *Psychology of adolescence and youth.* St. Petersburg: Peter.

Ravich-Shcherbo, I.V. (1999). *Genotype-environmental relationships in individual development. Psychogenetics.* In: I.V. Ravich-Shcherbo, T.M. Maryutina, E.L. Grigorenko. Moscow: Aspect Press, 363–382.

Reber, A. (2000). *Big explanatory psychological dictionary in 2 vols.* - Moscow: Veche, AST, Vol.1, 287.

Reikovsky, Y. (1979). *Experimental psychology of emotions.* Moscow: Progress.

Remshmidt, H. (2002). *Psychology of growing up. Teenager and family. Anthology.* D.Y. Raygorodsky (ed.). Samara: BAHRAKH-M, 232–358.

Repnova, T.P. (2003). *Training of emotional maturity. Prevention of conflict behavior of young adolescents.* Odessa: Methodological Recommendations of the South Ukrainian Pedagogical University.

Rusalov, V.M. (1987). *A new version of the adaptation of the EPI personality test.* Journal of Psychology, 1, 113–126.

Rusalov, V.M. (1989). *Subjective and communicative aspects of human temperament.* Journal of Psychology, 1, 10–21.

Russell, J.A. (1991). *Culture and categorization of emotions.* Psychological Bulletin, 3, 426–450.

Rutter, M. (1966). *Children of sick parents: an environmental and psychiatric study.* Maudsley Monograph, 16. London: Oxford Univ. Press.

Sadokova, A.V. (2001). *The influence of individual characteristics of emotional and personal sphere onto the peculiarities of moral competence development in adolescence*: Dissertation abstract. Moscow.

Salovey, P., Mayer, J.D. (1990). *Emotional intelligence.* Imagination, Cognition and Personality, 9, 185–211.

Sannikova, O.P. (1984). *Emotionality and regulation of communication activity.* Voprosy Psychologii, 3, 123–128.

Sannikova, O.P. (2003). *Phenomenology of the personality: selected psychological works.* Odessa: SMIL, 102–108.

Satir, V. (1999). *Psychotherapy of the family.* St. Petersburg: Yuventa.

Sergeeva, I.V. (2001). *Coaching on development of adequate emotional reaction in teachers.* In: Problems of general and pedagogical psychology: collection of works. S.D. Maximenko (ed.) Kiev, Vol. 3, part 5, 199–204.

Shchetinina, A.M. (1984). *Perception and understanding by preschool children of the emotional state of a person.* Voprosy Psychologii, 3, 61–66.

Shmelev, A.G., Pokhilko, V.I. (1985). *Point analysis in the construction and implementation of test questionnaires: manual and computer algorithms.* Voprosy Psychologii, 4, 126–134.

Shtepa, O.S. (2004). *Proprium of a mature personality.* Practical Psychology and Social Work, 2, 26–35.

Simonov, P.V. (1981). *Emotional brain.* Moscow: Nauka.

Slutsky, V.M. (1996). *Social isolation and mental development in older preschoolers: an analysis of the cognitive, emotional and personal development.* Journal of psychology, 1, 86–96.

Smirnov, V.M., Trokhachev, A.I. (1974). *About psychology, psychopathology and physiology of emotions.* In: Feelings, drives, emotions. V.S. Deryabin (ed.). Leningrad: Leningrad University.

Solodukhova, O.G. (1996). *The formation of teacher's personality in the process of professional adaptation.* Donetsk: Lebid.

Spitz, R.A. (1946). *The smiling response.* Genetic Psychology Monographs, 57–125.
Starodubova, N.G. (2001). *Criteria for child's readiness to study at school.* In: The system of upbringing and additional education of children: from ideas to implementation (materials of the scientific-practical conference). Biysk, NRC BPGU, 76–78.
Strelkova, L.P. (1987). *Psychological features of empathy development in preschool children*: Dissertation abstract. Moscow.
Sukhanova, K.N. (2001). *Gender issues of emotions.* In: Psychology in the 21st century: theses of the International interuniversity scientific and practical Conference. St. Petersburg, 257–258.
Sukharev, A.V. (2001). *The ethnofunctional approach to self-knowledge of one's own mental life.* Journal of Applied Psychology, 5, 58–68.
Sukholenova, O.G. (2000). *Formation of an adequate image of self in girls from partial families*: Dissertation abstract. Lugansk.
Teplov, B.M. (2002). *Typological properties of the nervous system and their importance for psychology.* In: Psychology of individual differences. Y.B. Gippenreiter, V.Y. Romanova (ed.). 2nd ed. Moscow: CheRo, 172–178.
Thompson, R.A. (1994). *Emotion regulation: a them in search of definition.* Monographs of the Society for Research in Child Development, 59, 25–52.
Tolstykh, A.V. (2002). *Infantilism of an adolescent.* In: Adolescent and family: Anthology. D.Y. Raygorodsky (ed.). Samara: BAHRAKH-M, 388–407.
Tsagarelli, Y.A. (1981). *The study of dependence of abilities self-assessment on the properties of the nervous system.* In: Psychophysiological study of educational and sports activitiy: Collection of works. E.P. Ilyin (ed.). Leningrad: LGPI.
Umansky, L.I. (1980). *Psychology of organizational activity of schoolchildren.* Moscow: Prosveschenije.
Valion, N. (2000). *The phenomenon of psychological deprivation and its role in the development of personality.* Psychology and Society, 2, 124–133.
Vartanyan, G.A., Petrov, E.S. (1989). *Emotions and behavior.* Leningrad: Nauka.
Vasilishina, T.V. (1999). *Empathic skills of teachers.* Practical Psychology and Social Work, 4, 37–38.
Vasilishina, T.V. (2000). *Empathy as a factor in the effectiveness of pedagogical communication*: Dissertation abstract. Kiev.
Vecker, L.M. (2000). *Psyche and reality: a unified theory of mental processes.* Moscow: Smysl; Per Se.
Vershinin, S.I. (1986). *The place of emotional regulation in the general structure of activity regulation.* In: Emotional regulation of educational and labor activity. Moscow, Odessa: Proceedings of the All-Union Conference of the Institute of Psychology, Academy of Sciences, 5.
Vilyunas, V.K. (1976). *Psychology of emotional phenomena.* Moscow: Publishing House of Moscow State University.
Vilyunas, V.K. (1984). *The main problems of the psychological theory of emotion.* In: Psychology of emotions. Texts. Moscow: Publishing House of Moscow State University, 3–28.
Vitt, N.V. (1991). *Personal-situational mediation of expression and recognition of emotions in speech.* Voprosy Psychologii, 1, 95–107.
Vygotsky, L.S. (1984). *Collected works in 6 volumes.* A.V. Zaporozhets (ed.). Moscow: Pedagogy, Vol. 4.
Vysotskaya, N.E. (1979). *The conditionality of professionally important for the ballet dancer qualities properties of temperament and nervous system.* In: Psychophysiology: anthology. B.A. Ashmarina, E.P. Ilyin (ed.). Leningrad: LGPI, 20–31.

Winnicott, D.W. (1958). *The capacity to be alone.* The International Journal of Psychoanalysis. 39, 416–420.
Wundt, W. (1984). *Psychology of emotional unrest.* In: Psychology of emotions. Texts. V.K. Vilyunas, Y.B. Gippenreiter, (ed.). Moscow: Publishing House of Moscow State University, 47–64.
Yakobson, P.M. (1966). *Psychology of feelings.* Moscow: Publishing house of pedagogical sciences of the RSFSR. Part 2.
Yakobson, P.M. (1977). *About expressiveness in the actor's art.* Voprosy Psychologii, 1, 86–95.
Yakovleva, E.L. (1997). *Emotional mechanisms of personal and creative development.* Voprosy Psychologii, 4, 20–27.
Yurkevich, V.S. (1972). *Self-regulation as a factor of general giftedness.* In: Problems of differential psychology. Moscow: Institute of general and pedagogical psychology publishing house, Vol. 7, 233–249.
Zaika, E.V., Kartashov, O.G. (1993). *The method of research of individuality - the typicality of the emotional response.* Voprosy Psychologii, 4, 116–121.
Zakharov, A.I. (1988). *Neurosis in children and adolescents: anamnesis, etiology and pathogenesis.* Leningrad: Medicine.
Zaporozhets, A.V., Neverovich, Y.Z. (1974). *About genesis, function and structure of emotional processes in a child.* Voprosy Psychologii, 6, 59–73.
Zavalkevich, L.E. (2004). *Development of psychological flexibility as a factor of managerial activity efficiency.* Practical Psychology and Social Work, 1, 15–29.
Zavatska, N.E. (2002). *Peculiarities of personality differentiation of dependent behavior of adolescents and its correction*: Dissertation abstract. Kiev.
Zhorov, P.A., Ermolaeva-Tomina, L.B. (1971). *On physiological correlates of extraversion and neuroticism.* New Research in Psychology and Age Physiology. 2, 124–128.
Zhorov, P.A., Shulga, T.I. (1987). *Volitional qualities and emotional stability of schoolchildren.* New Studies in Psychology, 1, 36, 39–43.
Zhuravlova, L., Chebykin, O. (2021). *The development of empathy phenomenology, structure and human nature.* London, New York: Routledge Taylor and Francis.
Zueva, L.V. (1995). *Analysis of test results of boys and girls in terms of gender identity.* In: Formation of gender culture in students. Collection of articles and abstracts. Naberezhnye Chelny: Femina, 123–128.

4

CONCLUSIONS

In general, on the basis of the research findings, it is possible to make the following conclusions:

- The problem of developing the emotional sphere of children, adolescents and young adults is quite relevant to age psychology. This is due to the fact that emotions are closely intertwined with all mental properties, processes, qualities and conditions and can not only evaluate and reflect them but also influence them in different ways. In this case, the available data regarding the specificity of its manifestation at certain age periods of human life is not yet sufficiently disclosed.
- It is shown that the nature of the development of emotions in children can be determined by both internal factors of biological and psychophysiological order, and also by various socio-psychological conditions of their lives. Among the latter, the most widespread are those in which children stay in a full or incomplete family, kindergarten, childcare center, orphanage, house, school, college, or university. The given conditions and distinguished relevant groups of children, adolescents and young adults along with the living conditions are the subjects of the study of the development of their emotional sphere.
- It was established that regardless of the conditions of upbringing, age and gender characteristics of the children examined the dynamics of changes in the indicators that characterize the features of their emotional sphere (e.g. emotionality, anxiety, joy, emotional stability, fear, empathy and self-regulation) at the individual level have great variability in expressiveness from minimum to maximum values. This may indicate a high sensitivity of the emotional sphere of the personality which develops to different – both internal and external conditions of their vital activity.

DOI: 10.4324/9781003330943-4

- It has been revealed that in the process of growing up (from 4 to 23 years) and regarding changes in living conditions between the surveyed groups of subjects on average data in most indicators that characterize the specificity of the emotional sphere there is variability in the level of statistically reliable differences. Between groups of children 4–6 years old, the following is observed by the parameters of anxiety, emotionality, family comfort, resentment, anger, etc. It should be noted that the negative values of indicators that characterize features of the emotional sphere are more pronounced in the group of children deprived of parental care compared to others. Between the selected groups of adolescents 7–17 years, such differences are observed in the manifestation of aggression, emotional lability, emotional maturity, neuroticism and others. Accordingly, between groups of adolescents aged 18–23 such differences are observed by parameters of self-regulation, empathy, expressiveness and others. These and other intergroup differences that characterize the dynamics of the variability of different features of the emotional sphere at each age period indicate both the tendencies of their development as well as a certain dependence of this process on the living conditions of the persons examined.

An in-depth correlation and factor analysis has shown that peculiarities of the development of the emotional sphere in the selected groups surveyed concerning age, living conditions and gender data can be determined by a certain set of different emotional and personal characteristics among which exist the main ones – both alone or in a certain juxtaposition. Thus, for children 4–6 years, the latter may include anxiety, joy, emotionality, anger, confrontation and curiosity. For those 7–17 years old, the main characteristics are aggressiveness, anxiety, emotional lability, neuroticism, empathy, emotionality and others. Likewise for young adults aged 18–23, the main characteristics are self-regulation, empathy, expressiveness and others.

Expressed emotionality, aggression and anxiety that manifest themselves in all age groups may indicate the presence of significant stressors that children encounter when meeting their own needs in life. At the same time, as established in different age periods, these features are progressing at an increased rate, while at other ages they are reducing. Moreover, we can say that going through such stresses they not only adapt to them but also develop the necessary emotional resilience as a personal quality to overcome such obstacles in the future. The latter to some extent is confirmed by determination of different types of emotional maturity development by emotional stability in adolescents and young adults.

The following is also noteworthy: first of all, in each age period the selected components of emotional maturity have their own specifics of development (at the age of 11–13 years, there is expressiveness is progressing; at the age of 14–15 years, there is self-regulation; at 16–17 years, there is focus toward the convergence of the manifestation of all components; at 18–23, there is relative stability in the balanced manifestation of all components). Second, among the selected types of emotional maturity, (namely: expressive, empathic, self-regulatory, harmonious, expressive-self-regulatory, self-regulatory-empathic and expressive-empathic) the most common types are empathic and self-regulatory. Third, it is noted as a positive determination of the manifestation of these types of emotional maturity by such personal features as extroversion, sociability, self-esteem and also the negative manifestations, such as shyness, irritability and neuroticism. When it is necessary to choose the means for the prevention and psychotherapy of undesirable emotional manifestations the reliance on the characteristics of these and other data regarding their sensitivity in children may contribute to the adequate selection and efficient use. The proposed work system of prevention and reduction of undesirable emotional manifestations in children designed to prepare psychology students for their further professional activity may serve a certain confirmation in this aspect. This system is based upon scientific provisions of the theory and methodology of emotional regulation of educational and professional activities, as well as given in the research data on the study of the emotional sphere, and the characteristics of its peculiarities in the development of children. As evidenced by the results of the proposed system testing those students who have mastered it in practice have shown themselves to be very good at preventing and psychotherapeutizing the unwanted emotional manifestations in children. They also showed sufficient psychological competence in identifying the necessity of doing such work, adequacy of the choice of diagnostic tools for studying the emotional sphere of children, efficiency in advising educators and parents on the prevention of unwanted emotions, as well as the effectiveness of the selected techniques aimed at reducing unwanted emotional manifestations in children.

Further deepening of the study of the emotional sphere in youth actively continues through comprehensive research, aimed at understanding the manifestation of their emotional health (Chebykin, 2021–2022) under conditions of the COVID-19 epidemic as well as during the military situation in Ukraine. We expect to present these results in a future monograph.

APPENDIX 1 (CHAPTER 1)

According to the test "House. Tree. Man."

P1: Emotional insecurity:
Low: 0 points,
High: 18 points.
P2: Anxiety
Low: 0 points,
High: 13 points.
P3: Self-doubt
Low: 0 points,
High: 7 points.
P4: Feelings of inferiority:
Low: 0 points,
High: 7 points.
P5: Hostility:
Low: 0 points,
High: 14 points.
P6: Internal conflict (frustration):
Low: 0 points,
High:17 points.
P7: Communication difficulties:
Low: 0 points,
High: 17 points.
P8: Depressiveness:
Low: 0 points,
High: 11 points.

According to the test "Kinetic family drawing"

P9: Family comfort:
Low: 0 points,
High: 12 points.
P10: Anxiety:
Low: 0 points,
High: 17 points.
P11: Confrontation:
Low: 0 points,
High: 17 points.
P12: Feelings of inferiority:
Low: 0 points,
High: 12 points.
P13: Hostility
Low: 0 points,
High: 10 points.

According to the "Anxiety test"

P 14: Anxiety.
Low: (0–20%).
Average: (20–50%).
High: (50% above).

According to the method "Tapping test"

P15: Emotional stability:
Low: (0.3-0.6) conditional points.
Average (0.6-1.1) conditional points.
High: (1. 2- and higher) conditional points.

According to our modified method of Dembo scale, based on expert assessment.

P16: Joy, optimism:
Low: 0 points,
High: 10 points.
P17: Anger, rage.
Low: 0 points,
High: 10 points.
P18: Shyness
Low: 0 points,
High: 10 points.

P19: Interest, curiosity:
Low: 0 points,
High: 10 points.
P20: Offense:
Low: 0 points,
High: 10 points.
P21: Anxiety-fear:
Low: 0 points,
High: 10 points.
P22: Emotionality:
Low: 0 points,
High: 10 points.

According to the method of "The ratio of emotional and rational in behavior"

P23: Domination of emotional "+1"
Rational: "-1"
Balance: "0"

According to the Luscher color test

P24: Emotional stability
Positive index "+1"
Negative "-1"
Balance or absence of it "0"
P25: Self-regulation
Positive "+1"
Negative "-1"
Balance or absence of it "0"
P26: Emotional arousal
Positive "+1"
Negative "-1"
Balance or absence of it "0"
P27: Aggressiveness
Positive "+1"
Negative "-1"
Balance or absence of it "0",
P28: Confrontation
Positive "+1"
Negative "-1"
Balance or absence of it "0"
P29: Anxiety
Positive "+1"
Negative "-1"

Balance or absence of it "0"

P30: Frustration

Positive "+1"

Negative "-1"

Balance or absence of it "0"

According to self-assessment and expert assessment

P31; P32; P33; P34

Counted from min. "0" to max. "4" conditional points

APPENDIX 2 (CHAPTER 2)

CHARACTERISTICS OF THE EXPRESSIVENESS OF THE DIAGNOSED INDICATORS

Methodology of "Self-Assessment" (T.V. Dembo and others)

P1: personal self-esteem:
Low: 0 points;
High: 100 points.

Method "House-Tree-Man" (J. Buck)

P2: feeling of rejection:
Low: 0 points;
High: 10 points.
P3: hostility:
Low: 0 points;
High: 7 points;
P4: feeling of inferiority:
Low: 0 points;
High 11 points.

Methodology "Kinetic drawing of a family" (W. Wolf and others)

P5: anxiety in the family:
Low: 0 points;
High: 6 points.
P6: family aggressiveness:
Low: 0 points;
high: 10 points.

P7:-self-doubt:
Low: 0 points;
High: 6 points.

Method "Non-existent animal" (M. D. Drukorevich)

P8: personal anxiety:
Low: 0 points;
High: 12 points.
P9: personal aggression:
Low: 0 points
High: 7 points.
P10: personal self-esteem:
Low: 1 conditional point;
High: (-1) conditional points.

Personal questionnaire of G. Eysenck.

P11: neuroticism.
Concordat (C): (16–24) conditional points;
Normastenik (N): (9–15) conditional points;
Superdiscordat (S): (0; 8) conditional points;

"Anxiety Scales" (C.D. Spielberger and others)

P12: reactive anxiety:
Low: 30 conditional points;
High: 46 conditional points.
P13: personal anxiety:
Low: 30 conditional points;
High: 46 conditional points.
"Emotional Maturity Checklist"
P14: expressiveness:
Low: (9–12) points;
High: (0–4) points.
P15: self-regulation:
Low: (9–12) points;
High: (0–4) points.
P16: empathy:
Low: (9–12) conditional points;
High: (0–4) conditional points.

"Freiburg personality questionnaire"

P17: neuroticism:
Low: 1 point;
High: 9 points.
P18: spontaneous aggression of the "intratensive type":
Low: 1 point;
High: 9 points.
P19: depressiveness:
Low: 1 point;
High: 9 points.
P20: irritability:
Low: 1 point;
High: 9 points.
P21: balance:
Low: 1 point;
High: 9 points.
P22: reactive aggression of the "extratensive type":
Low: 1 point;
High 9 points.
P23: shyness:
Low: 1 point;
High: 9 points.
P24: emotional lability:
Low: 1 point;
High: 9 points.

APPENDIX 3 (CHAPTER 2)

TABLE 2.3.1 Levels of indicators that characterize the emotional characteristics of children of different age groups (%)*

Complex Age (years)	*Self-esteem*			*Anxiety*			*Aggression*			*Self-regulation*		
	l	*a*	*h*	*l*	*a*	*h*	*l*	*a*	*h*	*l*	*a*	*h*
7	32	4	64	23	34	43	80	–	20	–	–	–
8	36	–	64	30	18	52	36	30	34	–	–	–
9	20	–	80	34	33	33	-	36	64	–	–	–
11	20	–	80	21	45	34	15	34	51	7	72	21
12	13	9	78	-	66	34	28	12	60	18	58	24
13	30	–	70	13	37	50	52	22	26	15	64	21
14	19	11	70	17	40	43	31	28	41	18	61	23
15	24	25	51	22	42	36	28	41	31	16	58	26
16	30	54	16	10	44	46	16	37	47	23	43	34
17	55	10	35	16	38	46	35	29	36	13	61	26

*For all significance level (P(less) 0.05)

TABLE 2.4.1 Average values of indicators characterizing the features emotional sphere of children of different ages

Age	*P1*	*P3*	*P3*	*P4*	*P5*	*P6*	*P7*	*P8*	*P9*	*P10*	*P11*	*P12*
7 y.o.	71.20	2.47	2.14	1.58	2.53	1.15	1.90	1.41	1.33	0.16	–	–
8 y.o.	67.20	2.75	2.29	0.89	3.87	1.09	2.30	3.10	1.77	0.57	–	–
9 y.o.	69.98	2.41	1.64	1.14	1.95	1.42	1.44	2.17	1.24	1.01	–	–
11 y.o.	67.24	3.79	1.96	1.25	5.14	2.64	0.96	1.64	0.43	1.82	14.93	32.68
12 y.o.	70.46	4.00	2.52	1.48	1.30	1.65	0.74	–	–	–	–	27.17
13 y.o.	67.52	2.20	0.92	1.12	3.08	0.77	1.55	1.48	1.48	1.48	16.17	39.82
14 y.o.	61.79	2.71	1.52	1.24	1.53	1.11	1.13	2.38	1.99	1.76	14.83	41.89
15 y.o.	63.25	2.35	0.74	1.42	5.00	1.42	1.75	2.04	1.32	9.63	9.23	38.54
16 y.o.	76.53	–	–	–	–	–	–	–	–	–	12.79	18.00
17лет	63.58	5.32	1.71	1.10	2.51	1.07	1.95	2.37	1.43	1.63	14.69	41.33

Age	*P13*	*P14*	*P15*	*P16*	*P17*	*P18*	*P19*	*P20*	*P21*	*P22*	*P23*	*P24*
1	2	3	4	5	6	7	8	9	10	11	12	13
11 y.o.	41.50	6.50	7.07	7.25	5.89	6.86	7.11	7.68	6.82	7.75	7.14	6.39
12 y.o.	43.30	6.91	6.52	6.65	6.78	5.57	7.48	7.65	6.04	7.87	7.04	7.09
13 y.o.	45.73	6.59	6.27	6.51	6.58	6.22	7.35	7.31	5.57	7.64	7.06	7.15
14 y.o.	44.11	6.04	7.03	6.52	6.28	6.09	6.72	7.25	5.62	7.63	6.71	6.31
15 y.o.	42.46	6.67	7.18	7.21	6.32	6.50	7.02	7.33	5.58	7.75	6.63	6.67
16 y.o.	39.13	6.48	6.32	8.24	6.00	5.71	6.71	7.21	6.38	8.13	7.58	5.04
17 y.o.	42.31	6.63	6.47	7.37	6.09	7.10	6.61	7.38	5.91	7.82	7.05	6.87

TABLE 2.4.2 Features of statistically reliable differences on the indicators that characterize the genesis of the emotional sphere of children of different ages*

Age	*P1*	*P3*	*P3*	*P4*	*P5*	*P6*	*P7*	*P8*	*P9*
1	2	3	4	5	6	7	8	9	10
7–8 y.o.	n/s	n/s	n/s	0.72	−1.19	n/s	n/s	−1.51	n/s
t	n/s	n/s	n/s	3.21	2.16	n/s	n/s	4.08	n/s
8–9 y.o.	n/s	n/s	0.64	n/s	1.92	n/s	n/s	0.77	n/s
t	n/s	n/s	2.16	n/s	3.42	n/s	n/s	1.90	n/s
9–11 y.o.	n/s	−1.36	n/s	n/s	−3.19	−1.24	n/s	n/s	0.83
t	n/s	3.70	n/s	n/s	5.00	3.56	n/s	n/s	3.41
11–12 y.o.	n/s	n/s	n/s	n/s	3.84	0.99	n/s	n/s	n/s
12–13 y.o.	n/s	1.80	1.61	n/s	−1.81	0.88	−0.82	n/s	n/s
t	n/s	4.06	3.20	n/s	3.55	2.02	2.80	n/s	n/s
13–14 y.o.	n/s	n/s	−0.63	n/s	1.62	n/s	n/s	−0.92	−0.52
t	n/s	n/s	2.55	n/s	3.67	n/s	n/s	3.85	2.13
14–15 y.o.	n/s	n/s	0.75	n/s	−3.50	n/s	−0.74	0.64	n/s
t	n/s	n/s	3.12	n/s	5.00	n/s	2.68	2.44	n/s
15–16 y.o.	−13.34	n/s	n/s	n/s	n/s	n/s	n/s	n/s	n/s
t	3.34	n/s	n/s	n/s	n/s	n/s	n/s	n/s	n/s
16–17 y.o.	18.56	n/s	n/s	n/s	n/s	n/s	n/s	n/s	n/s
t	4.33	n/s	n/s	n/s	n/s	n/s	n/s	n/s	n/s

Age	*P10*	*P12*	*P15*	*P16*	*P17*	*P18*	*P19*	*P23*	*P24*
9–11y.o.	−0.82	n/s	n/s	n/s	n/s	n/s	n/s	n/s	n/s
t	1.91	n/s	n/s	n/s	n/s	n/s	n/s	n/s	n/s
11–12 y.o.	n/s	5.50	n/s	n/s	−0.89	1.29	n/s	n/s	n/s
t	n/s	3.26	n/s	n/s	2.22	2.53	n/s	n/s	n/s
12–13 y.o.	n/s	−12.64	n/s	n/s	n/s	n/s	n/s	n/s	n/s
t	n/s	4.58	n/s	n/s	n/s	n/s	n/s	n/s	n/s
13–14 y.o.	n/s	n/s	−0.80	n/s	n/s	n/s	0.65	n/s	0.85
t	n/s	n/s	2.30	n/s	n/s	n/s	2.39	n/s	2.67
14–15 y.o.	−0.80	12.99	n/s	n/s	n/s	n/s	n/s	n/s	n/s
t	2.19	5.07	n/s	n/s	n/s	n/s	n/s	n/s	n/s
15–16 y.o.	n/s	11.22	n/s	−1.02	n/s	n/s	n/s	−0.97	1.61

* For all significance level (P (less) 0.005)

TABLE 2.4.3 Statistically reliable differences in indicators characterizing self-esteem in boys and girls*

Age *Statistical values*	*Indicator*							
	P1		*P4*		*P7*		*P10*	
	B	*G*	*B*	*G*	*B*	*G*	*B*	*G*
1	*2*	*3*	*4*	*5*	*6*	*7*	*8*	*9*
7 y.o.								
x	71.3	69.3	1.7	1.4	2.0	1.8	0.3	0.0
t	= n/d		= n/d		= n/d		= n/d	
8 y.o.								
x	71.1	63	1.0	0.8	1.7	3.2	0.9	0.5
t	= 2.2		= n/d		= n/d		= n/d	
9 y.o.								
x	67.2	72.2	0.7	1.5	1.9	1.1	0.8	1.2
t	= n/d		= 2.6		= n/d		= n/d	
11 y.o.								
x	69.7	65.4	1.2	0.8	1.3	1.3	1.9	1.8
t	= n/d		= n/d		= n/d		= n/d	
12 y.o.							-	
x	75	61.9	1.1	0.1	1.6	1.3		
t	= n/d		= n/d		= 3.1			
13 y.o.								
x	63.3	77.1	1.9	1.2	0.8	1.6	1.4	1.6
t	= 2.0		= 2.7		= n/d		= n/d	
14 y.o.								
x	64.2	59.6	1.0	1.3	1.1	1.4	1.5	2.0
t	= n/d		= n/d		= n/d		= n/d	
15 y.o.								
x	65.2	62.5	1.3	1.5	2.2	1.8	1.8	2.8
t	= n/d		= n/d		= n/d		= n/d	
16 y.o.			-		-		-	
x	76.7	76.5						
t	= n/d							
17 y.o.								
x	59.6	56.6	2.1	2.1	1.0	1.1	0.8	3.0
t	= n/d		= n/d		= n/d		= 3.3	

**The differences shown in the table are significant at $p<0.05$;*

B - boys, G – girls. n/d – no data

TABLE 2.5.1 Features of correlational relationships of indicators that characterize emotional sphere of 7-year-old children*

Indicator	*P1*	*P2*	*P3*	*P4*	*P5*	*P6*	*P7*	*P8*	*P9*	*P10*
P1	1								0.2	
P2		1	0.2	0.4						
P3			1			0.2			0.3	
P4				1				−0.3		
P5					1	0.3	0.3	0.3	0.4	−0.5
P6						1			0.2	
P7							1		0.3	−0.3
P8								1	0.5	
P9									1	
P10										1

**Correlation level in all cases P<0.05.*

TABLE 2.5.2 Features of correlation relationships of indicators that characterize the emotional sphere of 8-year-old children*

Indicator	*P1*	*P2*	*P3*	*P4*	*P5*	*P6*	*P7*	*P8*	*P9*	*P10*
P1	1	0.2			0.3	−0.3	−0.4	0.3		
P2		1	0.5	0.3	0.4		−0.4	0.4	0.2	−0.6
P3			1			0.2	−0.2		0.2	−0.3
P4				1	−0.2		−0.3	0.4	0.3	
P5					1		0.3		−0.4	−0.2
P6						1				
P7							1	0.2	−0.3	
P8								1	0.5	−0.4
P9									1	−0.3
P10										1

**Correlation level in all cases P<0.05.*

TABLE 2.5.3 Features of correlation relationships of indicators that characterize the emotional sphere of 9-year-old children*

Indicator	*P2*	*P3*	*P5*	*P7*	*P8*	*P9*	*P10*
P2	1	0.2	0.2			0.4	
P 3		1	0.3				−0.3
P 5			1				
P 7				1			−0.3
P 8					1	0.4	
P 9						1	
P 10							1

**Correlation level in all cases* $P<0.05$.

TABLE 2.5.4 Features of correlation relationships of indicators, that characterize the emotional sphere of 11 years old*

Index	*P1*	*P2*	*P3*	*P5*	*P6*	*P9*	*P10*	*P11*	*P12*	*P13*	*P14*	*P16*	*P17*	*P18*	*P19*	*P20*	*P21*	*P22*	*P23*	*P24*
P1	1	−0.4																		
P2		1						0.5			0.4	0.4	0.5	0.5	0.6	0.4			0.4	0.7
P3			1					−0.3												−0.4
P5				1										0.4		0.5	0.4			
P6					1					0.5										
P9						1								−0.6	−0.4	−0.6		−0.6		
P10							1			−0.4					−0.4					
P11					-			1		−0.5			0.4	0.4	0.7					0.6
P12									1											
P13										1					0.5					0.5
P14											1									
P16												1								
P17													1		0.4					0.5
P18														1	0.6	0.7	0.4	0.4		0.6
P19															1	0.4			0.5	0.7
P20																1		0.6		
P21																	1			
P22																		1		
P23																			1	0.4
P24																				1

**Correlation level in all cases* $P<0.05$.

TABLE 2.5.5 Features of correlation relationships of indicators, that characterize the emotional sphere of 12-year-old children*

index	*P2*	*P3*	*P4*	*P5*	*P6*	*P7*	*P12*	*P13*	*P14*	*P15*	*P16*	*P17*	*P18*	*P19*	*P20*	*P21*	*P22*	*P24*
P2	1															0.5		
P3		1	0.6															
P4			1															
P5				1							−0.5							
P6					1		−0.5	−0.5				−0.6		−0.6				
P7						1												−0.5
P12							1	0.6				0.7						0.4
P13								1				0.4						
P14									1	0.4					0.5	0.4		
P15										1						0.5	0.5	
P16											1							
P17												1		0.6				0.5
P18													1		0.5	0.3	0.6	
P19														1				0.6
P20															1	0.4	0.4	0.5
P21																1	0.6	
P22																	1	
P24																		1

**Correlation level in all cases* $P<0.05$.

TABLE 2.5.6 Features of correlation relationships of indicators, that characterize the emotional sphere of 13-year-old children*

index	*P1*	*P2*	*P4*	*P6*	*P7*	*P8*	*P9*	*P10*	*P11*	*P12*	*P13*	*P14*	*P15*	*P16*	*P17*	*P18*	*P19*	*P20*	*P21*	*P23*	*P24*
P1	1		−0.3			−0.3									−0.4				−0.5		
P2		1												0.3							
P4			1			0.5	0.4														
P6				1		−0.3				0.3											
P7					1			0.4	0.3	0.3											
P8						1	0.4					0.4		0.4							
P9							1									0.4				−0.3	
P10								1	0.3								0.3				0.3
P11									1		0.5		−0.3		0.6	0.4	0.6	0.2	0.3	0.4	0.5
P12										1		0.4		0.3					0.4		
P13											1		−0.4		0.6	0.5	0.7	0.4		0.5	0.7
P14												1		0.6					0.3		
P15													1								
P16														1							
P17															1		0.7		0.4		0.5
P18																1	0.3	0.7			0.5
P19																	1		0.4		0.7
P20																		1			0.3
P21																			1		
P23																				1	0.4
P24																					1

**Correlation level in all cases* $P<0.05$.

TABLE 2.5.7 Features of correlation relationships of indicators, characterizing the emotional sphere of 16-year-old children*

index	*P11*	*P12*	*P13*	*P14*	*P15*	*P16*	*P19*	*P21*	*P24*
P11	1		0.6				0.5		
P12		1	0.7			0.4		−0.4	
P13			1		0.4		0.4		
P14				1	0.7				
P15					1		0.4		0.4
P16						1		−0.5	
P19							1		0.4
P21								1	
P24									1

**Correlation level in all cases P<0.05.*

TABLE 2.5.8 Features of correlation relationships of indicators, characterizing the emotional sphere of 17-year-old children*

index	*P3*	*P4*	*P5*	*P6*	*P7*	*P8*	*P9*	*P11*	*P12*	*P13*	*P14*	*P15*	*P16*	*P17*	*P18*	*P19*	*P20*	*P21*	P22	*P23*	*P24*
P3	1															−0.3					−0.3
P4		1							−0.3								−0.3				
P5			1					−0.3													
P6				1	0.3			−0.4						−0.3	−0.6	−0.4	−0.4				−0.4
P7					1																
P8						1	0.7				−0.4								0.4		−0.3
P9							1	−0.3			−0.3		−0.3						0.4		−0.3
P11								1	0.4	0.4			0.3	0.6		0.7	0.3			0.3	0.6
P12									1	0.5				0.3		0.4		−0.4		0.4	0.3
P13										1		−0.5		0.5		0.4		−0.3	−0.4	0.6	0.4
P14											1	0.3	0.7				0.3				
P15												1	0.5	−0.3							
P16													1								
P17														1		0.6	0.3			0.4	0.6
P18															1		0.4		0.3		0.3
P19																1	0.3			0.5	0.7
P20																	1				0.3
P21																		1			
P22																			1		
P23																				1	0.5
P24																					1

**Correlation level in all cases P<0.05.*

APPENDIX 4 (CHAPTER 3)

CONTENTS OF THE "DIAGNOSTICS OF EMOTIONAL MATURITY" QUESTIONNAIRE

Instructions:

The questionnaire contains 42 statements aimed at studying the characteristics of your emotional sphere. Your task is to answer all questions. Put "YES" (+) if you agree with the statement, and "NO" (-) if you disagree.

Do not waste time thinking, answer quickly, and give the first naturally occurring answer. Do not try to make a deliberately favorable or unfavorable impression. Freely express your opinion. Remember that there are no good or bad answers.

Questionnaire text

1 Is it possible to say that your face eloquently indicates your feelings?
2 Does your concern affect people you know?
3 Do you switch from one mood to another in communication? (For example, from funny to serious and vice versa.)
4 Would you say that as you communicate with people, you have learned to manage their emotions?
5 How often do you observe the interest of others in your actions?
6 Does your movement, and the movement of your hands always help you when you are telling a story?
7 Are you able to successfully copy (parody) faces and movements?
8 Do you always understand the humor of others?
9 Do you like being criticized?
10 Are you easily infected by the mood of others?
11 Do you often feel pity for people?
12 Can you force yourself to calm down quickly if you are very excited?

13 Does a change in your voice affect those around you?
14 Would you say that you have authority over your peers?
15 Do you enjoy being praised?
16 Do you always empathize with literary characters?
17 Do you experience lethargy or apathy before starting work or study?
18 Do people who know you empathize with you when you want them to?
19 Would you ask for a lower grade on an exam if you think it's too high?
20 Do your smile and laughter always enthrall those around you?
21 Do you prepare yourself with words of command or other techniques when you begin a responsible work?
22 Do you experience a change in heartbeat, breathing, tears, etc., when you observe acutely dramatic or positively resolving situations?
23 Can you keep your face expressionless when you are very excited?
24 Are there any among your acquaintances who you don't like?
25 Do you raise your voice when talking to someone who makes you angry?
26 Would you say that you are always trusted at work and school?
27 Can you attract the attention of others with your gaze?
28 Can people around you determine your mood by your face?
29 Do your stories often surprise and arouse the interest of others?
30 Do you hide your anxiety at work (school)?
31 Are you superstitious in any way (at least mentally)?
32 Could you communicate with gestures to a person who does not know your language?
33 Do you always tell the truth, regardless of the fact that sometimes it is not to your advantage?
34 Can you say that you feel and well understand the mood of the people around you when communicating?
35 Are your instructions carried out quickly?
36 Do people around you often show curiosity about what you are doing?
37 Do you have trouble getting attention when you need to?
38 Does your appearance have an effect on others?
39 Is it noticeable to others when an event throws you off balance?
40 Can you help someone calm down if they are in trouble?
41 When you change your personality in communication, is it noticeable to others?
42 Does your mood often affect others?

APPENDIX 5 (CHAPTER 3)

TABLE 3.5.6 Expressiveness of indicators of emotional maturity of a person in 11-year-old children

Level of expression	*Number of tested (%)*									
	Ex	*IEx*	*EEx*	*S*	*IS*	*ES*	*Em*	*IEm*	*EEm*	*EZ*
High	3.6	0	0.0	14.3	7.1	10.7	10.7	7.1	0	14.3
Medium	92.8	100	92.9	78.6	82.2	82.2	85.7	92.9	92.9	85.7
Low	3.6	0	7.1	7.1	10.7	7.1	3.6	0	7.1	0

TABLE 3.5.7 Expressiveness of indicators of emotional maturity of a person in 12-year-old children

Level of expression	*Number of tested (%)*									
	Ex	*IEx*	*EEx*	*S*	*IS*	*ES*	*Em*	*IEm*	*EEm*	*EZ*
High	17.4	8.7	13.0	13.0	4.3	8.7	13.0	4.3	4.4	17.4
Medium	69.6	78.3	82.6	65.2	78.3	78.3	60.9	87.0	82.6	65.2
Low	13.0	13.0	4.4	21.8	17.4	13.0	26.1	8.7	13.0	17.4

TABLE 3.5.8 Expressiveness of indicators of emotional maturity of a person in 13-year-old children

Level of expression	*Number of tested (%)*									
	Ex	*IEx*	*EEx*	*S*	*IS*	*ES*	*Em*	*IEm*	*EEm*	*EZ*
High	20.0	6.7	8.9	4.4	4.4	2.2	6.7	4.4	4.4	8.9
Medium	64.4	77.8	86.7	80.0	73.3	84.4	82.2	91.1	91.1	77.8
Low	15.6	15.6	4.4	15.6	22.2	13.3	11.1	4.4	4.4	13.3

TABLE 3.5.9 Expressiveness of indicators of emotional maturity of a person in 14-year-old children

Level of expression	*Number of tested (%)*									
	Ex	*IEx*	*EEx*	*S*	*IS*	*ES*	*Em*	*IEm*	*EEm*	*EZ*
High	10.3	11.5	7.7	12.8	12.8	10.3	12.8	5.1	7.7	11.5
Medium	76.9	84.7	71.8	78.2	83.3	73.1	79.5	93.6	79.5	73.1
Low	12.8	3.8	20.5	9.0	3.8	16.7	7.7	1.3	12.8	15.4

TABLE 3.5.10 Expressiveness of indicators of emotional maturity of a person in 15-year-old children

Level of expression	*Number of tested (%)*									
	Ex	*IEx*	*EEx*	*S*	*IS*	*ES*	*Em*	*IEm*	*EEm*	*EZ*
High	13.7	15.7	17.6	11.8	9.8	21.6	15.7	11.8	13.7	17.6
Medium	84.3	84.3	74.5	80.4	82.4	68.6	76.5	84.3	66.7	76.5
Low	2	0	7.8	7.8	7.8	9.8	7.8	3.9	19.6	5.9

TABLE 3.5.11 Expressiveness of indicators of emotional maturity of a person in 16-year-old children

Level of expression	*Number of tested (%)*									
	Ex	*IEx*	*EEx*	*S*	*IS*	*ES*	*Em*	*IEm*	*EEm*	*EZ*
High	9.8	2.4	12.2	2.4	4.9	7.3	9.8	14.7	4.9	4.9
Medium	73.1	78	78	75.6	85.1	73.2	82.9	78	82.9	82.9
Low	17.1	19.6	9.8	22.0	9.8	19.5	7.3	7.3	12.2	12.2

TABLE 3.5.12 Expressiveness of indicators of emotional maturity of a person in 17-year-old children

Level of expression	*Number of tested (%)*									
	Ex	*IEx*	*EEx*	*S*	*IS*	*ES*	*Em*	*IEm*	*EEm*	*EZ*
High	22.9	8.3	16.7	8.3	12.5	16.6	8.3	12.5	6.3	18.8
Medium	64.6	72.9	77.1	83.4	79.2	79.2	81.3	75.0	83.3	70.8
Low	12.5	18.8	6.3	8.3	8.3	4.2	10.4	12.5	10.4	10.4

TABLE 3.5.13 Expressiveness of indicators of emotional maturity of the individual in young people 18–23 years

Level of expression	*Number of tested (%)*									
	Ex	*IEx*	*EEx*	*S*	*IS*	*ES*	*Em*	*IEm*	*EEm*	*EZ*
High	22.9	8.3	16.7	8.3	12.5	16.6	8.3	12.5	6.3	18.8
Medium	64.6	72.9	77.1	83.4	79.2	79.2	81.3	75.0	83.3	70.8
Low	12.5	18.8	6.3	8.3	8.3	4.2	10.4	12.5	10.4	10.4

TABLE 3.5.14 Differences in the severity of indicators of emotional maturity of personality in representatives of different ages

Index	*Statistical index*	*Age*													
		11 y.o.	*12 y.o*	*12 y.o*	*13 y.o*	*13 y.o*	*14 y.o*	*14 y.o*	*15 y.o*	*15 y.o*	*16 y.o*	*16 y.o*	*17 y.o*	*17 y.o*	*18–23*
Expressiveness	X	6.50	6.91	6.91	6.60	6.60	6.05	6.05	6.67	6.67	6.51	6.51	6.69	6.69	7.91
	t	0.87		0.61		1.45		1.79		0.42		0.43		3.40★★	
Intro-expressiveness	X	3.79	3.70	3.70	3.60	3.60	3.31	3.31	3.24	3.24	3.44	3.44	3.52	3.52	3.62
	t	0.32		0.33		1.38		0.35		0.86		0.32		0.41	
Extra-expressiveness	X	2.71	3.30	3.30	3.00	3.00	2.73	2.73	3.43	3.43	3.07	3.07	3.17	3.17	4.29
	t	1.89		0.93		1.04		3.05★★		1.42		0.37		5.36★★	
Self-regulation	X	7.07	6.52	6.52	6.27	6.27	7.06	7.06	7.18	7.18	6.56	6.56	7.13	7.13	7.83
	t	1.05		0.51		2.30★		0.31		1.56		1.47		2.03★	
Intro-self-regulation	X	2.93	2.74	2.74	2.49	2.49	3.24	3.24	2.88	2.88	2.83	2.83	3.00	3.00	3.33
	t	0.54		0.76		3.47★★		1.76		0.24		0.77		1.56	
Extra-self-regulation	X	4.14	3.78	3.78	3.78	3.78	3.82	3.82	4.29	4.29	3.73	3.73	4.25	4.25	4.52
	t	1.15		0.02		0.20		1.96		2.10★		2.02★		1.26	
Empathy	X	7.25	6.65	6.65	6.51	6.51	6.58	6.58	7.22	7.22	7.90	7.90	7.71	7.71	8.69
	t	0.97		0.23		0.17		1.5		1.53		0.49		3.01★★	
Intraempathy	X	3.86	3.48	3.48	3.29	3.29	3.44	3.44	3.80	3.80	4.15	4.15	3.83	3.83	4.23
	t	1.09		0.58		0.66		1.60		1.34		1.24		1.73	
Extraempathy	X	3.25	3.17	3.17	3.20	3.20	3.14	3.14	3.41	3.41	3.83	3.83	3.88	3.88	4.45
	t	0.21		0.07		0.22		0.89		1.34		0.18		2.86★★	
Emotional maturity	X	20.8	20.1	20.1	19.4	19.4	19.7	19.7	21.1	21.1	21	21	21.5	21.5	24.4
	t	0.61		0.59		0.38		1.61		0.09		0.66		4.21★★	

Note. ★ - *significant differences at* $p < 0.05$; ★★ - *significant differences at* $p < 0.01$.

TABLE 3.5.15 Gender differences in the severity of indicators of emotional expressiveness

Age	*Statistical index*	*Index; gender*					
		Ex		*IEx*		*EEx*	
		male	*female*	*male*	*female*	*male*	*female*
11 y.o.	X	6.17	6.75	3.76	3.51	2.42	2.94
	t	1.39		0.91		1.49	
12 y.o.	X	6.60	7.5	3.60	3.88	3.13	3.63
	t	0.98		0.52		0.84	
13 y.o.	X	6.68	6.5	3.76	3.40	2.92	3.10
	t	0.31		1.06		0.42	
14 y.o.	X	5.94	6.14	3.28	3.33	2.64	2.81
	t	0.39		0.22		0.54	
15 y.o.	X	6.00	6.89	2.85	3.37	3.15	3.53
	t	1.36		1.46		0.80	
16 y.o.	X	6.47	6.55	3.37	3.50	3.11	3.05
	t	0.13		0.39		0.16	
17 y.o.	X	6.21	7.17	3.04	4.00	3.17	3.17
	t	1.68		2.75**		0.00	
18–23 y.o.	X	8.03	7.82	3.76	3.51	4.27	4.31
	t	0.52		0.91		0.15	

INDEX

For Product Safety Concerns and Information please contact our EU
representative GPSR@taylorandfrancis.com
Taylor & Francis Verlag GmbH, Kaufingerstraße 24, 80331 München, Germany

www.ingramcontent.com/pod-product-compliance
Ingram Content Group UK Ltd.
Pitfield, Milton Keynes, MK11 3LW, UK
UKHW020316270926
475702UK00050B/900
9781032362441